QUEEN'S OWN HIGHLANDERS
(Seaforth and Camerons)

AN ILLUSTRATED HISTORY

Field Marshal His Royal Highness The Prince Philip, Duke of Edinburgh,
KG, KT, OM, GBE,
Colonel in Chief Queen's Own Highlanders (Seaforth and Camerons)
1961 to 1994.

QUEEN'S OWN HIGHLANDERS
(Seaforth and Camerons)

AN ILLUSTRATED HISTORY

by
Angus Fairrie

Acknowledgements

This book has been published by Trustees of the Queen's Own Highlanders Amalgamation Trusts. The Trustees acknowledge with gratitude the generous financial contribution made by the Lovat Scouts Regimental Association.

The great majority of the prints and photographs reproduced in black and white are from the Regimental Museum Collection. The paintings reproduced as the colour plate, are all owned by the Queen's Own Highlanders Amalgamation Trusts.

The Trustees are grateful to the following for permission to reproduce illustrations:

> The Victoria and Albert Museum – Water colours by Eugene Lami on page 45
> Douglas N Anderson – Cover illustration, colour plate of uniforms, pages 35, 265
> Major D K Beaton MC – page 44

First published 1983 as *'Cuidich 'n Righ* – A History of the Queen's Own Highlanders'

2nd (revised) edition 1998

ISBN 0-9508986-2-7

Printed by The Northern Times Ltd., Main Street, Golspie, Sutherland KW10 6RA.

QUEEN'S OWN HIGHLANDERS
(Seaforth and Camerons)
AN ILLUSTRATED HISTORY
Introduction to the 2nd (revised) Edition

The book was first published in 1983 as *'Cuidich 'n Righ* – **a History of the Queen's Own Highlanders'**. This 2nd edition has been extensively revised and improved, but its purposes have not changed. It is intended to be a convenient reference book which can provide answers to many of the questions about the history of the Regiment received at the Regimental Museum each year.

At the Regimental Museum at Fort George the story of the Queen's Own Highlanders, and their antecedent regiments the Seaforth Highlanders and The Queen's Own Cameron Highlanders, is on permanent display. The arrangement of this book follows the sequence of displays in the museum, so that the visitor to the museum can also use it as a source of background information to each room.

Since the first edition was published, there has been astonishing progress in communications and computer technology, and genealogical study has developed into a major international interest. The descendants of those who served in the British and Commonwealth armies in World War I and II are rightly interested in what their forebears did, and in the regiments to which they belonged. A book this size cannot give the service records of individual officers and men. But it is hoped that it will allow researchers to identify the regiment or battalion, and the places in which their forebears served, and thus provide a start point for further research into personal records, regimental histories, and service in peacetime garrison, in battle, or on campaign. A list of further references and sources of information is included at the end of the book.

Another addition to the book is a short history of the Lovat Scouts. They shared a recruiting area with the Seaforth and Cameron Highlanders, and their museum collection is displayed in the Regimental Museum at Fort George, so it was logical to include their interesting history in the book.

In 1994 the Queen's Own Highlanders suffered amalgamation under government defence cuts, and the regiment was merged with The Gordon Highlanders to form The Highlanders (Seaforth, Gordons and Camerons). The revised edition brings the regimental history of the Queen's Own Highlanders up to the point of amalgamation in 1994.

AAF

Paintings of the Regiment

CHAPTER I

THE REGIMENTS BEFORE 1881

1. THE CLAN BACKGROUND OF THE REGIMENTS

THE MACKENZIES OF SEAFORTH

The Mackenzies, or Clan Kenneth, first held lands in Kintail in the early 14th Century. For the next 300 years their influence expanded until the clan territory extended across Ross-shire from coast to coast, and also included the island of Lewis. In 1609 Kenneth, 13th Chief of the clan, was created Lord Mackenzie of Kintail, and his son Colin became lst Earl of Seaforth in 1623. He took his title from Loch Seaforth on the Isle of Lewis.

The Clan Mackenzie were staunch supporters of the Stuart kings, and so became inextricably involved in the tragic politics and wars of the time. For his support of the Jacobite Rising of 1715, William 'Dubh', the 5th Earl, was attainted and his lands were forfeited. Thanks to the recommendation of General George Wade, the General Officer Commanding Scotland, William 'Dubh' was pardoned in 1726, and the family managed to recover its lands in 1741 on payment of a crippling sum of nearly £23,000. When the 1745 Jacobite Rising took place only

four years later, the 5th Earl's grandson, Lord Fortrose, had no alternative but to remain uncommitted, whatever the traditional loyalties of his house. This enforced change of heart had its reward in 1771 when his son Kenneth was created Earl of Seaforth in the Irish peerage.

Kenneth Mackenzie, Earl of Seaforth (1744-1781) Chief of Clan Mackenzie, who raised the 78th (later 72nd) Highlanders in 1778.

But the restoration of the Seaforth lands and title came at a bleak time in Highland history. The government, in its determination that there should never be another Jacobite Rising, had set about dismantling the clan system with uncompromising severity. While the disarming of the Highlanders removed the military threat, the deliberate repression also brought a time of misery for the whole country. Faced with economic ruin and the destruction of the traditional way of life in the Highlands, the clan chiefs realised that one way to provide employment and bring money to their tenants was by raising regiments of Highland infantry, and in 1771 Kenneth Earl of Seaforth offered to raise a regiment for the King. While he was certainly grateful for the restoration of his title, his motives were more than just patriotic. There were compelling social and economic reasons as well. A regiment would bring employment and income to his clansmen, and possibly even prize money too; and the authority to raise a regiment meant that he had the chance to recommend his kinsmen for commissions.

It was not until 1778, when three years of war in the American colonies had led to acute recruiting problems, that the government accepted with gratitude the Earl of Seaforth's offer to raise a regiment. Kenneth, Earl of Seaforth raised his 78th Highlanders and commanded the regiment for three years. When he died on the voyage out to India, he had no male heir, and his cousin Colonel Thomas Mackenzie-Humberston succeeded him as Chief of Clan Mackenzie and Colonel of the 78th. When Thomas Mackenzie-Humberston died in Bombay in 1783, from wounds received at sea in a fight against the Mahrattas, the link between the Seaforth family and the 78th Earl of Seaforth's Highland Regiment was to lapse.

Francis Humberston Mackenzie, who succeeded his brother Thomas as Chief of Clan Mackenzie, sat in Parliament as MP for Ross-shire from 1784-1790. Knowing that war with France was likely, and that the government would again require more infantry regiments, he offered to raise another Highland regiment from the Mackenzie lands. When war broke out in 1793, he received authority in a Letter of Service dated 7th March 1793 to raise the 78th Highlanders, and he himself received a commission as Lieutenant Colonel Commandant. The regiment was by coincidence designated the 78th, the same number as the Earl of Seaforth's Highland Regiment before it.

Francis Humberston Mackenzie was Colonel of the 78th for the first three years of its history. Then, having handed over the Colonelcy to his brother in law Colonel Alexander Mackenzie of Belmaduthy, he continued his military service by raising and commanding the Ross-shire Militia. In 1797 he was created Lord Seaforth and Baron Mackenzie of Kintail. He was appointed Governor of Barbados in 1801, and was promoted Lieutenant General in 1808. As Governor of Barbados he did much to improve the working conditions of the slaves on the sugar plantations. But the economic difficulties of his

Francis Humberston Mackenzie of Seaforth
(1754-1815)
Chief of Clan Mackenzie, who raised the
78th Highlanders (Ross-shire Buffs) in 1793.

own West Indian estates brought financial ruin, and he was obliged to sell most of the family estates in the Highlands, including Kintail.

Although he had four sons, they all pre-deceased him, and the male line of the family ended when he died in 1815. His great-grandson Colonel J A F H Stewart-Mackenzie, was created Baron Seaforth of Brahan in 1921. The last member of the family to hold the title of Lord Seaforth, he maintained a link with the regiment as Honorary Colonel of the 4th Battalion Seaforth Highlanders TA. He died without male heir in 1923.

In 1978 the Lord Lyon King of Arms recognised Major The Right Hon The Earl of Cromartie as 'Cabar Feidh', Chief of Clan Mackenzie. Lord Cromartie served as a regular officer in the Seaforth Highlanders and won the Military Cross serving with the 4th Territorial Battalion in France in 1940. Thus the connection between Clan Mackenzie and the Regiment has remained strong.

THE CAMERONS OF ERRACHT

Although the forebears of Clan Cameron lived in Lochaber from time immemorial, the first clan chief who can be established histo rically is Donald Dubh, by tradition the llth Chief. He came to power in the late 14th century, and unified the Lochaber tribes into a clan which earned an awesome reputation for its fighting qualities and for loyalty to the Sovereign. Ewen MacAllan of Lochiel, 13th Chief and grandson of Donald Dubh, married twice. The present Chiefs of Clan Cameron, the Camerons of Lochiel, are descended from him by his first wife; and the Camerons of Erracht were descended from him by the second. For generations the Camerons of Erracht held their lands on a wadset lease from Lochiel, and held the position of chieftains in the hierarchy of the clan.

The defeat of the Jacobites at Culloden in 1746 brought the traditional way of life in the Highlands to an end. The loyalty which Clan Cameron had shown to Bonnie Prince Charlie and the Stuart cause brought severe retribution from the Government. Highlanders were forbidden by Act of Parliament to carry arms or wear the Highland dress; the Episcopal Church was proscribed, Fort William was strongly garrisoned by regular troops; the leaders of Clan

Cameron were exiled or imprisoned; the Lochiel estate was forfeited to the Crown; and Achnacarry, and many of the houses in Lochaber were destroyed.

But despite this harsh repression after Culloden, life in Lochaber had to go on. One of the Cameron chieftains to escape exile or imprisonment was Ewen Cameron of Erracht. He was prevented by ill health from joining the Jacobite army, and so remained living at Erracht.

After the Rising, in the absence of the exiled Lochiel family, he was one of the few prominent members of Clan Cameron available to bring much needed leadership to the Lochaber community.

His eldest son Alan was born at Erracht in 1750 and grew up in Lochaber. After education in Inverness and at Aberdeen University, he returned to Erracht to run the farm and, like his father before him, became a prominent and popular figure in Lochaber. However in 1772 a serious dispute with a neighbour and kinsman, Alexander Cameron of Muirshearlich, led to a duel fought with broadswords in which Alan Cameron killed his adversary. Faced with a possible charge of murder, he was forced to go abroad, first to Jamaica and then to the North American colonies.

When the American War of Independence broke out, Alan Cameron was working with the Indian Department in South Carolina, and he soon had his first experience of military service. Turning down an offer of a commission with a rebel regiment of Rangers, he volunteered for service with the Crown instead. Commissioned in the Queen's Royal Regiment of Rangers he was employed on intelligence duties, and this valuable but dangerous work led to his capture by the American rebels. His two and a half years captivity as a prisoner of war were spent in constant attempts to escape but, although he got

Lieutenant General Sir Alan Cameron of Erracht (1750-1828) who raised the 79th Highlanders (Cameronian Volunteers) in 1793.

away three times, he was always recaptured. During one bid for freedom he fell from the roof of Philadelphia gaol, breaking both ankles. It was due to these crippling injuries that in 1778 he was eventually exchanged for an American rebel prisoner, and returned to Great Britain.

In 1779 his father, Ewen Cameron of Erracht, died and Alan succeeded to the wadset lease of Erracht. But his injuries, and the privations of life as a prisoner of the rebels, left him so badly crippled that he was unfit to return to farming in Lochaber, and he was obliged to remain in London for medical treatment. However his fortunes improved, and that same year he married Ann Phillips, 14 year old daughter of Nathaniel Phillips, a wealthy merchant and owner of estates in the West Indies. During fifteen years in London Alan Cameron of Erracht became a prominent figure in the Scottish community. Among his friends were William Pitt the Prime Minister, and Henry Dundas the Secretary for War. With other members of the Highland Society of London he fought the successful political campaign which led to the repeal the Act of Proscription, and to the restoration of the Highland dress.

His experience as an officer in America had made Alan Cameron of Erracht keen on the idea of raising a Highland regiment. He now had the financial backing of a wealthy father-in-law, and raising a regiment had acceptable prospects as a financial venture. As chieftain of Erracht he was a well respected figure in Lochaber, and he saw military service as the ideal form of employment for the young men of Clan Cameron, with their traditional fighting qualities, and thus being a most practical way to bring help to the devastated economy of the Highlands.

Anticipating war with France, he made repeated applications to the Government for permission to raise a regiment. In 1793, when the outbreak of war with France forced the government to increase the number of infantry regiments above the normal peacetime establishment of 77, his proposal was agreed. Alan Cameron of Erracht was authorised by Letter of Service dated the 17th August 1793 to raise the 79th Regiment of Foot, and was commissioned as its Major Commandant.

Alan Cameron of Erracht commanded the 79th in person from 1793 until 1808, when he handed over command to his eldest son Lieutenant Colonel Phillips Cameron. He remained as Colonel of the 79th until his death in 1828 as Lieutenant General Sir Alan Cameron of Erracht KCB. Nicknamed 'old *Cia mar tha*' from his habitual Gaelic greeting, he was very much the father figure of the Cameron Highlanders. His four sons all served in the 79th. His ambition that the 79th should be the regiment of Clan Cameron was fulfilled, and the Regiment today remains intensely proud of its Cameron and Lochaber origins. Many members of Clan Cameron have served as officers and soldiers in The Cameron Highlanders, their successors the Queen's Own Highlanders, and in The Highlanders today. Among prominent members of the regiment have been the Camerons of Lochiel, who have served with great distinction as Regular, Militia and Territorial officers of the regiment for many generations.

The Bicentenary of the 79th Cameron Highlanders was marked by an impressive ceremony at Erracht in 1993 when a memorial cairn was unveiled by Colonel Sir Donald Cameron of Lochiel KT, Chief of Clan Cameron, assisted by the direct descendants of Sir Alan Cameron of Erracht.

Colonel Sir Donald Cameron of Lochiel KT, Chief of Clan Cameron
with the Pipes and Drums of the 1st Battalion Queen's Own Highlanders
at the memorial cairn to Sir Alan Cameron of Erracht, 1993

2. THE 72nd HIGHLANDERS FROM 1778 TO 1881

The raising of the 78th (later 72nd) or Earl of Seaforth's Regiment – 1778

Kenneth, Earl of Seaforth received his commission as Lieutenant Colonel Commandant on 29th December 1777, and the Letter of Service which authorised him to raise his Highland regiment was signed on 8th January 1778. There followed four months of hectic recruiting to find the 47 officers and 1082 men required to fill the establishment.

Earlier Highland regiments had already tapped the manpower of the Highlands, but Lord Seaforth took every advantage of the traditional loyalty of his clan. The great majority of his men were recruited from Ross-shire and Lewis, while numbers were made up by about 300 men from the Lowlands, England and Ireland. Having concentrated his men at Elgin for the mandatory inspection by a General Officer, the regiment was reviewed by Major General Robert Skene on 15th May 1778 and passed as fit for service. It was designated the 78th Regiment of (Highland) Foot, and the regiment received its First Stand of Colours, provided by the Earl of Seaforth.

The dress of the 78th (later 72nd) Highlanders – 1778

The 78th wore the normal uniform of Highland infantry at the time, which was the kilt and belted plaid of Government (or Black Watch) tartan, with red jacket, red and white hose, and black buckled shoes. In the 18th Century each regiment was distinguished by its facing colour ('facing' was the material used to 'face' or partly line the jackets), by the style of lace on its jackets, and by the pattern of loops in which the lace was arranged. The 78th had yellow facings, and the lace loops were 'bastion' shaped. The regiment wore the 'hummel bonnet' embellished with ostrich feathers, a forerunner, although much smaller, of the feather bonnet of today. The Grenadier Company wore mitre caps of bearskin.

*Dress of the 78th (later 72nd) Highlanders in 1778
(From a painting by R Simkin)*

'The mutiny of the Macraes' – September 1778

A few days after its embodiment and inspection the Earl of Seaforth's regiment marched out of Elgin. At the time Great Britain was under threat of invasion by the French, and so the 78th was deployed first to Aberdeen, and then to Edinburgh and on the west coast, to counter any French attack. Before leaving Edinburgh there was the famous incident known as 'the affair of the wild Macraes'.

One of the characteristics of the Highland regiments when they were raised was that the soldiers were accustomed, under the clan system, to leadership that was traditionally open and above board. They expected that, having enlisted to fight for king and country, the government would abide by the terms of the Letters of Service, the contracts under which the regiments were raised. However the government, under pressure to find recruits from limited resources of manpower, was not always scrupulous in keeping to the Letters of Service. There were about seventeen instances of so called 'Mutiny' where Highland soldiers refused to carry out orders which seemed to them to be in breach of their contracts.

One of the most celebrated cases occurred in the Earl of Seaforth's regiment in September 1778. The 78th had been ordered to move to the Channel Islands but, when it paraded for embarkation, half the regiment refused to march to the ships at Leith. Led by a group of Kintail men, 'the Wild Macraes', most of the regiment marched instead to the summit of Arthur's seat where they entrenched themselves. The grievances of the soldiers concerned their pay and bounty money, the unfamiliar rigidity of military discipline, and a rumour that the regiment had been sold to the East India Company. It was to the credit of the Commander in Chief in Scotland, and to Lord Seaforth and his officers, that an honourable compromise was reached with the mutineers. A Court of Inquiry found that their complaints had no basis, but also showed clemency by granting them immunity from disciplinary action. The mutineers, having aired their grievances and demonstrated the traditional independence of the Highlander, agreed to soldier on.

The 78th (later 72nd) in the Channel Islands – 1778-1781

The 78th eventually sailed from Leith in October 1778, and on arrival in the Channel Islands was split between Guernsey and Jersey. The regiment's first experience of active service came in April 1779 when the French made an attempt to land in Jersey. The invaders were repulsed without difficulty by Major Thomas Mackenzie Humberston and five companies of the 78th which deployed on the cliffs at St Ouen's Bay, together with the Jersey Militia and Artillery.

The 78th (later 72nd) at the Battle of Jersey – 1781

In January 1781 the French force made a further more determined effort to capture Jersey. Led by Baron de Rullecourt, a force of 1,200 troops attempted a surprise landing during the night. About 700 French troops got ashore and succeeded in occupying the capital of Jersey, St Helier. But although the Lieutenant Governor of Jersey capitulated to the French, the British garrison and the Jersey Militia took the initiative. Five companies of the 78th Highlanders under the command of Major Francis Pierson of the 95th (Yorkshire) Regiment, the senior British officer present, advanced into St Helier and, after a brisk street fight, killed Baron de Rullecourt and released the Lieutenant Governor. The companies of the 78th earned much credit for their decisive and effective action in recapturing the capital of Jersey and in thwarting the French attempt to seize the island.

The 78th (later 72nd)'s voyage to India – 1781-1782

The 78th had expected to serve in the American war, but by 1781 hostilities were almost over. In May 1781 the regiment sailed from the Channel Islands to Portsmouth and embarked instead for India. The ten month voyage was one of the most melancholy episodes in the history of the regiment. On 27th August 1781, while the fleet was off West Africa, the Earl of Seaforth died at sea. By the time his regiment arrived in Madras on 31st March 1782, nearly 250 men had died of scurvy and tropical disease.

The 78th (later 72nd) on service with the East India Company – 1782-1798

At the time when the 78th arrived in India for service with the East India Company, only a small part of India was actually under British rule. This included Bengal, Madras and part of the east coast, and the object of the East India Company was trade rather than conquest. But, operating in direct competition with the French, the East India Company's treaties and trading agreements had to be backed by military strength. For the next fifteen and a half years the role of the regiment was to support the East India Company as it expanded its trade and influence among the independent Indian states.

The 78th landed at Madras in 1782 greatly weakened by disease. It was the start of the hot summer months, and at first the regiment was to suffer greatly from sickness and heat exhaustion. But comfort was improved by replacing the Highland dress with an issue of tropical uniform. The red jackets were worn with the linings removed, the kilt and belted plaid was superseded by white trousers and gaiters, and round hats with white linen covers replaced the feather bonnet. The 78th was to remain in this dress until its return to Great Britain in 1798.

An Officer of the 78th (later 72nd) Highlanders in India 1782

The 78th (later 72nd)'s first actions in India – 1782-1783

During its first year in India the 78th, having recovered from the voyage and become acclimatised to the heat, began its series of campaigns in support of the East India Company. Active service included a minor engagement at Arnee and a naval battle against the

French in which a detachment of Highlanders acted as Marines. The regiment's first major actions were the captures of the port of Cuddaldore from the French, and of the fort of Palghautcherry from Tippoo, Sultan of Mysore.

The 78th renumbered as the 72nd Highland Regiment – 1786

The soldiers of the 78th had been enlisted for 'three years or until the end of the Rebellion', and so when the war in America ended with the Treaty of Versailles in 1783, they were entitled to be discharged. An alternative was to serve on with the regiment in India for a bounty of 10 guineas, and 300 men of the 78th opted for this while the remainder returned home. The regiment was then brought up to strength by volunteers from other regiments returning home to Britain for disbandment.

In 1786, as the Infantry of the Line was reduced again to a peacetime total of 77 regiments, the 78th being on foreign service in India was retained on the establishment and renumbered as the 72nd. The following year it received its Second Stand of Colours provided by Major General James Murray, Colonel of the Regiment.

The 72nd in the Carnatic Campaign – 1789-1792

Among the most persistent threats to the East India Company's trading activities in South India was Tippoo, Sultan of Mysore. Having failed to stir up hostilities between France and Britain in 1789, he invaded the protected state of Travancore. For the next three years the Madras Army tried to bring Tippoo to battle. The 72nd formed part of the European Brigade, and this successfully captured a series of hill forts in preparation for an invasion of Mysore. For its part in the attack on Bangalore in 1791 the 72nd earned particular praise from Lord Cornwallis. In December 1791 the 72nd stormed the strongly-held hill fortresses of Savendroog and Outra Durgam, and then took part in the capture of Tippoo's capital Seringapatam, which brought the campaign to an end. A welcome outcome of the campaign was the payment of prize money by the East India Company to the troops which had taken part in the campaign. A private soldier's share of £14 amounted to more than a year's wages.

The 72nd in the campaigns against the French and Dutch – 1793-1796

As competition between the European nations for trade and colonial expansion increased, the East India Company's affairs increased in international significance. In 1793 the 72nd took part in the siege and capture of the fortified French settlement of Pondicherry. Following the French Revolution, France defeated the Dutch and forced them into an alliance. The Madras government was thus able to send an expedition which included the 72nd to seize the Dutch colony of Ceylon. The force landed at Trincomalee in 1795, and after a short campaign with no major engagements the Dutch capitulated. Ceylon (now Sri Lanka) was added to the East India Company's territory.

72nd BATTLE HONOURS

For its service in India and Ceylon from 1782 to 1798 the 72nd was awarded the Battle Honours:

$$\textbf{\textit{CARNATIC}}$$
$$\textbf{\textit{HINDOOSTAN}}$$
$$\textbf{\textit{MYSORE}}$$

The 72nd at Perth – 1798-1800

When the 72nd returned home in 1798 at the end of 17 years foreign service, the government faced a desperate shortage of men for its overseas military commitments in India and the colonies, and for the protection of Great Britain against French invasion. As was the normal custom, the 72nd was ordered to draft to other regiments in India the soldiers who still had foreign service commitments. The 72nd which returned to Great Britain consisted mainly of a cadre of officers, sergeants and drummers.

On its return to Great Britain the 72nd was re-issued with the Highland dress after 17 years in tropical uniform, and was allowed a couple of years in Scotland to recruit up to strength again. It received its Third Stand of Colours from Lieutenant General James Stuart at Perth in 1800.

Recruiting for the 72nd in 1800

The 72nd did not find recruiting easy in Scotland. The war with France had brought an unprecedented expansion in the army, and recruiting parties from newly raised regiments of the Line, the Fencibles, and the Militia had taken almost every available man. By 1800 the strength of the 72nd was still only 214, and so the regiment was ordered to move to Ireland, always a productive source of manpower. All Scottish Line regiments faced the same recruiting problem, and the government took the unusual step of authorising the Fencible regiments to allow volunteers to transfer to the Line regiments, and in this way the 72nd gained 13 officers and 589 men.

(Note. Fencible regiments were raised for the defence of Great Britain, and had no obligation to serve overseas. Their men were not normally allowed to transfer to the Regular regiments of the Line).

The 72nd in Ireland – 1800-1805

The 72nd spent five years in Ireland, combining recruiting with the maintenance of law and order. Its duties included riot control, guarding the mail coaches, seizing illicit whiskey stills, and other police work. The regiment was stationed first at Newry, and then marched south to Clonmel and Kilkenny, and later to Fermoy, Mallow, Rathkeale, Dublin and Cork.

The 72nd at the Capture of the Cape of Good Hope - 1805-1806

In 1794 France had defeated the Dutch, and forced Holland into an alliance. The harbours of the Dutch colony of the Cape of Good Hope were thus opened to French warships, which could threaten the sea route to India. This danger, and the need for a halfway port on the route to the East, prompted Britain to seize the Cape in 1795. After the Peace of Amiens in 1802 the Cape was returned to the Dutch, but when Napoleon prepared to invade Great Britain in 1805, a secret expedition was assembled to reoccupy the Cape. The force, led by Lieutenant General Sir David Baird, included three Highland regiments, the 71st, 72nd, and 93rd Highlanders, which together formed a Highland Brigade. On 6th January 1806 the expedition landed at Lospard's Bay under fire from Dutch skirmishers, pursued the defenders to the Blue Mountains, and then inflicted a quick and convincing defeat.

72nd BATTLE HONOUR

For its service at the Capture of the Cape of Good Hope, the 72nd was awarded the Battle Honour:

CAPE OF GOOD HOPE 1806

The 72nd in Cape Colony and Mauritius – 1805-1821

After the capture of the Cape of Good Hope the 72nd was to spend 16 years abroad on colonial garrison duty. It was stationed at Simonstown, Cape Town and Stellenbosch. In December 1810 the regiment took part in an expedition to capture the French island of Mauritius. The colony surrendered to the British without resistance, and the 72nd remained as garrison in Mauritius for three years until returning to Cape Town in 1814. There was a short excursion to India in 1815 when the regiment was sent to campaign against the Rajah of Nepal. But, on arrival at Calcutta, it found that the trouble was over, and the regiment returned to Cape Colony, where it remained until 1821.

2nd Battalion 72nd – 1804-1816

In 1804 the 72nd was authorised to raise a 2nd Battalion. The 2nd/72nd remained in Great Britain as the feeder battalion for the 1st/72nd in South Africa and Mauritius, and was stationed mainly in Ireland. When the Army was reduced in strength after the French Wars, the 2nd/72nd was disbanded at Londonderry in 1816.

The 72nd becomes Infantry of the Line – 1809

The extensive recruiting in the Highlands during the Napoleonic wars was to drain the Highlands of men. As the proportion of Highlanders in the Highland regiments fell, so that they were forced to rely on recruiting outside Scotland, the War Office decided to reduce the number of Highland regiments. On 11th April 1809 the 72nd, 73rd, 74th, 75th and 91st Highlanders were ordered to become ordinary Line infantry, and to discontinue wearing the much prized Highland dress. The 72nd, in South Africa at the time, therefore had to adopt the tropical uniform of a regiment of the Line, with red jacket, white trousers and round hat.

Despite the loss of the kilt and of the Highland name, the 72nd managed to preserve much of its Highland character. It maintained its pipers and continued to use the drum beatings and fife tunes of the Scotch Duty; it preserved minor distinctions in its uniform, such as the thistles engraved on the shoulder belt plates and embroidered on the coat tails of officers; and it still recruited in Scotland.

(Note: This most unpopular measure left only five kilted Highland Regiments on the Establishment, the 42nd, 78th, 79th, 92nd and 93rd Highlanders. The War Office order was bitterly resented by the regiments which lost the prestigious Highland status and distinctive Highland dress. Most regiments fought to regain them, and the 72nd was reinstated as a Highland regiment in 1823. Finally, under the Army Reforms of 1881, the 72nd, 73rd, 75th and 91st all regained the kilt).

The 72nd in the early Kaffir Wars – 1817-1821

When the British expedition captured the Cape of Good Hope from the Dutch in 1806, the government had not intended to extend the limits of Cape Colony. But, as the displaced Dutch settlers spread up the east coast of South Africa, they clashed continually with the Bantu tribes which had for two centuries been expanding their territory southwards. The 72nd spent four years patrolling, and manning the frontier posts in the east of Cape Colony to prevent the Kaffir tribes raiding the Boer settlements.

The 72nd returns to Great Britain – 1822

In December 1821, after fifteen years colonial service, the 72nd left South Africa and returned to Great Britain. The regiment remained in the south of England until 1823 when it moved to the Channel Islands for garrison duty.

The 72nd redesignated as a Highland regiment – 1823

In an order from the Horse Guards dated 19th December 1823, the 72nd Regiment received the welcome news that it was to be redesignated 'The 72nd or Duke of Albany's Own Highlanders', and that it was to resume the Highland dress. Thus, after 14 years as a Line regiment, the 72nd achieved its ambition of regaining its Highland status. On return to Edinburgh in September 1824 after 24 years away from Scotland, the regiment was quartered in Edinburgh Castle, and this allowed the 72nd to recruit in the Highlands and to restore its Highland character.

The 72nd did not resume its old Highland dress of the 42nd tartan kilt. Instead it adopted a unique new uniform which was to be among the most distinctive in the Army. The design, which comprised tartan trousers instead of the kilt, owed much to the enthusiasm for all things Highland generated by King George IV's visit to Edinburgh in 1822. The 72nd wore trews of Royal Stuart tartan in the Prince Charles Edward Stuart sett: the tartan which, by tradition, was worn by Bonnie Prince Charlie after the Jacobite army captured Edinburgh in 1745. The 72nd wore the normal red coatee and feather bonnet of a Highland regiment, and the pipers wore the kilt of Royal Stuart tartan. A radical change of dress such as this involved the design, approval and manufacture of a complete set of uniform, including buttons, badges, dirks, piper's sporrans and other accoutrements, and the process took a year and a half.

The 72nd Duke of Albany's Own Highlanders
(from a print published by W Spooner C 1840)

By August 1825 the 72nd was able to parade on Bruntsfield Links, Edinburgh for the presentation of new Colours. As a mark of respect for HRH The Duke of York and Albany, from whom the regiment derived its new title, the Colours bore the new regimental badge, the Cypher 'F' and Coronet of Prince Frederick, Duke of York and Albany. The Colours, which were the Fourth Stand to be carried by the regiment, were provided by the Colonel of the Regiment, General Sir John Hope, and presented by Lady Hope.

The 72nd in Ireland and London – 1825-1828

In 1825 the 72nd, a Highland regiment again in name, dress, and in the nationality of its men, was sent to Ireland in what has become a familiar peace-keeping role. Moving to London in 1827, it was quartered in the Tower of London, and shared ceremonial duties with the Household troops. In London its distinctive uniform of feather bonnets, red coatees and trews gave it such a sartorial advantage over the Foot Guards, that the Regiment became the centre of public attention, and even caught the eye of the Duke of Wellington.

The 72nd in Cape Colony – 1828-1840

In 1828 the 72nd left London for Canterbury, and then marched to Gravesend where it embarked for South Africa once more. It was to remain in Cape Colony for 12 years of garrison duty, interspersed by periods of active operations against the Kaffirs.

The 72nd in the Kaffir War – 1834-1835

In 1834 the Kaffirs, one of the main Bantu tribes which had for years harassed the European settlers in the east of Cape Colony, carried out a raid in considerable strength, removing a large proportion of the settlers' cattle. An expedition was mounted in reaction to the Kaffir attack, the 72nd taking a prominent part in the campaign in which the Kaffirs were firmly subdued, the cattle recovered, and Kaffir territory up to the Kei river annexed.

72nd BATTLE HONOUR

For its service in the campaign against the Kaffirs in 1835 the 72nd was awarded the Battle Honour:

SOUTH AFRICA 1835

The 72nd in England – 1840-1841

After its return to Great Britain in 1840, the Regiment received its Fifth Stand of Colours at Windsor Castle on 8th July 1841. The new Colours were presented on parade by Field Marshal the Duke of Wellington, and the ceremony was watched by HM Queen Victoria, Prince Albert, and the King of Prussia.

The 72nd in the industrial riots – 1842

In 1842, during a time of industrial unrest in Britain, the 72nd moved by railway train to Manchester, and was then deployed among the manufacturing towns of Lancashire. It had the difficult task of operating in support of the civil power, and on occasions was ordered by magistrates to open fire on rioters at Preston and Blackburn.

The 72nd in Ireland – 1843-1844

In 1843 the 72nd moved to Ireland where it spent over a year on internal security and garrison duties.

The 72nd Duke of Albany's Own Highlanders in 1854
(From a print published by R. Ackermann)

The 72nd in Gibraltar – 1844-1848

In November 1844 the 72nd embarked for Gibraltar. Its time there was spent on garrison duties and improving the defences of the fortress. Among the regiments of the Gibraltar garrison at the time was the 79th Cameron Highlanders. This was the first of many occasions when the two regiments served together, and was to be the foundation of a lasting friendship between them.

The 72nd in the West Indies – 1848-1851

In February 1848 the 72nd left Gibraltar for Barbados where, during its first year in the West Indies, a bad outbreak of yellow fever resulted in the deaths of 4 officers and 59 soldiers. The regiment spent from December 1849 to May 1851 in Trinidad, and then returned to Barbados. During the regiment's service in the West Indies detachments were also stationed in St Lucia, Demerara, Grenada, and Tobago.

The 72nd in Canada – 1851-1854

In July 1851 the 72nd moved from the West Indies to Halifax in Canada. In September it marched to New Brunswick, and returning to Halifax in 1853. International attention at the time was focused on the Russian threat to the Middle East and India, and war was expected. Many of the other Line regiments in Canada were being withdrawn to Europe, and the 72nd found it a particularly frustrating period as it awaited sailing orders with impatience. Meanwhile its Depot companies in Great Britain were required to send drafts to bring the 42nd and 79th Highlanders up to strength. When the 72nd eventually left Canada for Ireland in October 1854, the Crimean War had started and Sebastopol was already under siege.

The 72nd in Ireland – 1854

On the 72nd's return from Canada in October 1854, the Depot Companies rejoined the Service companies, and the regiment was reorganised on a war footing. But the Depot companies in Ireland, having been ordered to send every available man to bring the other Highland regiments up to strength, the 72nd found itself more than 300 men short of establishment. However, such was the demand for reinforcements to replace casualties from sickness in the Crimea, that the Service companies of the 72nd were ordered to sail for Malta in December 1854, leaving the Depot companies in Ireland to recruit.

The 72nd in Malta – 1855

In January 1855 the 72nd arrived in Malta, and there it remained until May, despite its impatience to reach the war in the Crimea.

The 72nd in the Crimea – 1855-1856

At last the 72nd received orders to sail for the Crimea, where it disembarked at Balaclava on 29th May 1855. On arrival the 72nd joined the 42nd, 79th and 93rd Highlanders in the Highland Brigade, commanded by General Sir Colin Campbell. The 72nd took its place in the trenches during the siege operations at Sevastopol until the Russian base was captured in September, and then served with the Highland Brigade and the Sardinians against an expected Russian attack on Kamara. From October 1855, until the withdrawal of the army from the Crimea in July 1856, the 72nd lived in the hutted camp established for the Highland Division at Kamara. The arrival of the 71st and 92nd Highlanders in the later stages of the war, as well as the 1st and 2nd Battalions of The Royal Scots, allowed the formation for the first time of a Highland Division.

72nd BATTLE HONOUR

For its service in the Crimea, the 72nd was awarded the Battle Honour:

SEVASTOPOL

Photographs taken in 1856 of soldiers of the 72nd on their return from the Crimea
Left - Pipe Major John MacDonald.
Centre - Colour Sergeant Andrew Taylor
Right - Drummer John Rennie.

The 72nd in Great Britain – 1856-1857

Having disembarked at Portsmouth on 31st July 1856, the 72nd was ordered to parade at Aldershot next day for inspection by HM Queen Victoria. The regiment was then sent to the Channel Islands until April 1857, when it joined the 79th in garrison at Shorncliffe. On 24th August 1857 the 72nd received its Sixth Stand of Colours from the Commander in Chief, HRH The Duke of Cambridge.

The 72nd moves to India for the Mutiny Campaign – 1857-1858

During August-September 1857 the 72nd sailed from Portsmouth to Bombay, where it was complete by early January 1858. The subsequent operations in which the 72nd took part were in a separate part of India from the better known events in the Ganges valley, but the regiment's campaign in Central India, where it contained the spread of the mutiny and hunted down bands of rebels, was a most successful chapter in its history.

The 72nd in the attack on Kotah – 1858

The first major engagement for the 72nd was the attack on Kotah, where the British resident and his sons had been murdered by mutineers, and the loyalty of the Rajah was suspect. The attack on the fortified town was carried out in three columns, the first of which included 260 men of the 72nd. They managed to storm through a gate blown in by the engineers. Then, having captured the bastion which was their objective, they exploited their success and seized another gate to the city. The other columns were equally successful and Kotah fell, the weapons captured including over 70 guns and a large ammunition magazine.

Lieutenant A S Cameron wins the Victoria Cross, 30th March 1858

During the attack on Kotah Lieutenant Aylmer Spicer Cameron was awarded the Victoria Cross, the first member of the 72nd Highlanders to win it. The citation read:

'For conspicuous bravery on the 30th March 1858, at Kotah, in having headed a small party of men, and attacked a body of armed fanatic rebels, strongly posted in a loopholed house, with one narrow entrance. Lieutenant Cameron stormed the house, and killed three rebels in single combat. He was severely wounded, having lost half of one hand by a stroke of a tulwar.
(London Gazette 11 November 1859)

Colonel A S Cameron, VC

The 72nd pursues the rebels

In June 1858, after a month in barracks at Neemuch, the companies of the 72nd were split up among the columns formed to pursue the rebels. In October a column which included the 72nd marched 110 miles in just over three days to prevent the city of Bhopal falling to the rebels. The 72nd remained on operations until January 1859, and detachments continued in the field until May. One detachment was estimated to have marched over 3,000 miles during the campaign.

72nd BATTLE HONOUR

For its service in the Indian Mutiny campaign the 72nd was awarded the Battle Honour:

CENTRAL INDIA

The 72nd in India after the Mutiny – 1859-1865

After the Mutiny campaign the 72nd remained in India until 1865, being stationed at Mhow, with detachments at Indore. During its last year in India the regiment moved to Poona for a few months, and then embarked for home in late 1865.

The 72nd in Great Britain – 1866-1871

On return to Great Britain the 72nd was stationed at first in Edinburgh Castle, where the Service companies and Depot companies joined up in March 1866. Then in May 1867 the regiment moved by sea and rail, complete with its families, to camp at Aldershot. In October it was sent to Manchester, and in February 1868 returned to Ireland. In 1871 it embarked once more for foreign service in India, leaving the Depot companies in Ireland.

The 72nd in India – 1871-1878

The 72nd arrived at Bombay in early 1871, and for the next seven years the regiment was stationed in the garrison towns of what is now Pakistan. Its stations included Umballa (1871), Peshawar (1873), Nowshera (1875), Cherat (1875), Sialkot (1876-78).

The shared Depot of the 72nd and 91st at Stirling – 1873-1881

Under the 'Localisation Scheme' of 1873 the 72nd was linked with the 91st Argyllshire Highlanders and allocated a joint recruiting area, designated No 58 Sub-District, consisting of the counties of Kinross, Clackmannan, Stirling, Dunbarton, Argyll, Bute and Renfrew. The two regiments shared No 58 Brigade Depot at Stirling, and the arrangement owed more to their common dress of trews than to the roots of the two regiments, for there was no connection with Ross-shire where the 72nd had originated. Under the new system the 72nd on Foreign Service in India now received drafts from the joint Depot at Stirling, as well as reinforcements from the Home Service battalion in Great Britain, the 91st Argyllshire Highlanders.

The Afghanistan Campaign – 1878

In 1878 the 72nd was ordered to march for Afghanistan to join the Kurrum Valley Field Force, and was to take part in one of the most distinguished campaigns of the regiment's history. The expedition into Afghanistan was intended to counter Russia's expansion to its south, which had for years been threatening India. Although Afghanistan, sandwiched between Russia and India, was traditionally neutral, the Afghans had alarmed the British Government by agreeing to accept a Russian embassy, while at the same time refusing to allow Great Britain to establish a Mission in Kabul. To restore the balance the British government decided to establish the Mission, by force if necessary, and despatched Major General Frederick Roberts VC with the Kurrum Valley Field Force to do so.

The 72nd at the Battle of Peiwar Kotal – 1878

In November 1878 General Roberts led his force into Afghanistan. At the Peiwar Kotal pass the Field Force encountered the Afghan army blocking the route from a strong stockaded hill-top position. Careful reconnaissance revealed a possible route by which the position could be outflanked, and so General Roberts sent part of his force, including the 72nd, to approach from the flank. On 2nd December 1878 the Right Wing of the 72nd Highlanders with the 5th Gurkhas, after a night approach march, scaled a precipitous ridge to storm the flank of the Afghan position, allowing the remainder of General Robert's force to attack from the front. The Afghan army was comprehensively defeated, and the British force captured 21 guns with large quantities of ammunition and food.

The 72nd Highlanders in Afghanistan 1878-79.

The Treaty of Gandamack – 1879

The 72nd remained in Afghanistan during the rest of the winter, in intensely cold conditions and under constant threat of further hostilities, until in May 1879 Yakoob Khan, Amir of Afghanistan, agreed at the Treaty of Gandamack to accept the British Mission. However the settlement was short lived. Only six weeks after the British Mission was established at Kabul its staff was massacred by an Afghan mob. General Roberts and his Field Force was again despatched, this time with instructions to occupy Kabul.

The 72nd at the Battle of Charasiah – 1879

In October 1879 General Roberts's force advanced into Afghanistan, and once again it found an Afghan army, some 12,000 strong, holding a strong hilltop position at Charasiah, and effectively blocking the route to Kabul. By careful reconnaissance General Roberts once more found a possible approach, and he gave the 72nd Highlanders and the 5th Gurkhas the task of attacking the flank. The two regiments succeeded in scaling and occupying a hill from which the enemy position could be enfiladed. The Afghan army was again defeated, and on 13th October 1879 General Roberts entered Kabul, capturing 200 guns and 7,000 rifles. To impress the Afghans with the scale of their defeat, the Field Force marched through Kabul with its bands playing. The Battle of Charasiah was the last occasion on which the 72nd carried its Colours in action.

The officers of the 72nd Highlanders in Kabul 1879

The 72nd in the occupation of Kabul – 1879-1880

During the winter of 1879-1880 General Robert's force occupied the Sherpore cantonment outside Kabul. Although the Afghans were at first subdued, their traditional belligerence soon resurfaced until by December they had declared a 'Jihad', or Holy War. The British Field Force in Kabul numbered only about 5,000, and it was forced to protect itself against a restless and hostile population by mounting aggressive local operations in the hills round Kabul. The 72nd fought a number of fierce actions against the Afghans between 11-23 December 1879.

Lance Corporal George Sellar wins the Victoria Cross, 14th December 1879

On 14th December 1879, during an attack by the Field Force and its artillery on a large Afghan position on the Asmai Heights outside Kabul, the 72nd Highlanders reached the highest peak and attacked it at the point of the bayonet. The attack, in which 600 Afghans were killed, was witnessed by General Roberts through his glass, and Lance Corporal George Sellar was awarded the Victoria Cross for his gallantry. The citation read:

'For conspicuous gallantry displayed by him at the assault on the Asmai Heights, round Kabul, on the 14th December 1879, in having in a marked manner led the attack, under a heavy fire, and, dashing on in front of the party up a slope, engaged in a desperate conflict with an Afghan who sprang out to meet him. In this encounter Lance Corporal Sellar was severely wounded.'
(London Gazette 18 October 1881)

*Sergeant
George Sellar, VC*

The 72nd on the march from Kabul to Kandahar 1880

While the Field Force maintained ascendancy on the area round Kabul, it could not prevent the Afghans elsewhere massing an army of over 100,000. The 72nd remained in Kabul until the summer of 1880, when in late July came news of the disaster at Maiwand near Kandahar. A British column had been attacked, losing over 1,100 men, and General Roberts was ordered to move to the relief of Kandahar without delay.

The famous march was never intended to break any speed records, but it was by any standards a remarkable feat of organisation. After only three days preparation General Roberts set out to march a force of 10,000 troops, with 11,000 animals and 8,000 camp followers, through more than 300 miles of hostile, trackless country. The temperature varied as much as 80 degrees daily, from 110 degrees at midday to freezing point at night. This famous march was accomplished in 22 days without any losses from enemy action.

The 72nd at Kandahar – 1880

When General Roberts's reached Kandahar with the Field Force he found the Afghan army, under Ayub Khan, holding strong hill top positions to the north west of the town and making preparations to attack. General Roberts waste no time, and he attacked the Afghan army next day, 1st September 1880. The 72nd were part of the flanking attack which advanced through Kandahar and routed the Afghans. The cost to the 72nd was 2 officers and 11 men killed, including the Commanding Officer Lieutenant Colonel Francis Brownlow CB.

72nd BATTLE HONOURS

For its service in the Afghanistan campaign of 1878-1880 the 72nd was awarded the Battle Honours:

PEIWAR KOTAL
CHARASIAH
KABUL 1879
KANDAHAR 1880
AFGHANISTAN 1878-1880

72nd in India – 1880-1881

Two weeks after the battle of Kandahar the 72nd marched out of Afghanistan and then travelled by train to rejoin the families and rear details at Mean Meer. The regiment had been on campaign for nearly two years. In November 1880 it moved to Lucknow.

The 72nd becomes the 1st Battalion Seaforth Highlanders – 1881

Under the Army Reforms of 1881 the 72nd Duke of Albany's Own Highlanders were amalgamated with the 78th Highlanders (Ross-shire Buffs). The 72nd became the 1st Battalion Seaforth Highlanders and the 78th became the 2nd Battalion.

Of particular significance to the 72nd, 73rd, 75th and 91st, four of the regiments which had lost the Highland dress in 1809, was the restoration of the kilt. For the 72nd the change meant a radical difference in both the uniform and character of the regiment. Instead of being linked with the 91st Argyllshire Highlanders with a strong Campbell background, the 72nd was now amalgamated with the 78th, a regiment which shared the distinction of having been raised by the Mackenzie of Seaforth family. Instead of a Depot at Stirling, and a territorial area in Argyll and the Central Lowlands, the regiment now had its Depot at Fort George, and a territorial area which included the old Mackenzie lands of Ross-shire and Lewis. The trews of Prince Charles Edward Stuart tartan were replaced by the kilt of Mackenzie tartan. To the general satisfaction of the regiment, the clock had been put back 72 years.

The designation of the new regiment was at first described as 'Seaforth Highlanders (Ross-shire Buffs)', but this was amended in November 1881 to include the old title of the 72nd, so that the full name was:

SEAFORTH HIGHLANDERS
(ROSS-SHIRE BUFFS, THE DUKE OF ALBANY'S)

3. THE 78th HIGHLANDERS FROM 1793 TO 1881

The raising of the 78th Highlanders – 1793

On 7th March 1793 Francis Humberston Mackenzie of Seaforth was granted the Letter of Service authorising him to raise a Highland regiment, and he was commissioned as its Lieutenant Colonel Commandant. The regiment was assembled at Fort George, Inverness, and was inspected by Lieutenant General Sir Hector Munro on 10th July 1793. Designated the 78th (Highland) Regiment of Foot, it was the first new regiment to be raised after the government was forced to increase the strength of the army when war broke out with France after the French Revolution.

The First Stand of Colours of the 78th Highlanders, which were provided by Lieutenant Colonel Francis Humberston Mackenzie of Seaforth, were taken into service at Fort George.

The dress of the 78th Highlanders – 1793

The uniform of the 78th comprised red coatee, kilt and belted plaid, sporran, red and white hose, and feather bonnet: the normal uniform of the Highland regiments at the time. The main distinctions of the uniform were the buff facings on the coats, the Bastion shaped loops of the lace, and the addition of red and white overstripes to the 42nd Government (or Black Watch) tartan. It is likely that the 78th were the first regiment to wear this tartan, which later became known as the Mackenzie tartan, and is now widely used as the tartan of Clan Mackenzie.

Other unique features in the dress of the 78th included the dress of the pipers who wore a buff jacket with green wings, and a green hackle in the feather bonnet. The bandsmen of the Band of Music were dressed in the kilt of Royal Stuart tartan, with white jackets.

Dress of the 78th Highlanders in 1793
(From a painting by R Simkin)

The tartan of the 78th was later worn as the kilt by the Seaforth Highlanders and their successors the Queen's Own Highlanders. Since the formation of The Highlanders in 1994 the 78th tartan has been worn as trews by the present regiment. The buff facings of the 78th still survive today in the pipe banners and mess uniform facings of The Highlanders.

(Note. The 71st Regiment, also a Mackenzie regiment, seem to have adopted the 78th tartan in 1797. Their descendants the Royal Highland Fusiliers still wear trews of the tartan to the present day).

The 78th in Guernsey and Newport – 1793-1794

During August and October 1793 the 78th left Scotland in two contingents for service in the Channel Islands. Their roles were to garrison the coast against invasion by the French, and to support the French Royalists in Brittany in resisting the French Revolution. In January 1794 the 78th left Guernsey for Newport, returning to Guernsey in March.

2nd Battalion 78th raised – 1794

On 8th February 1794 Colonel Mackenzie of Seaforth was authorised to raise a further battalion. The 2nd Battalion 78th was inspected and passed as fit for service in June 1794 at Fort George, Inverness, and received its Colours, provided by Seaforth. In July the 2nd/78th was designated the 'Ross-shire Buffs', the name being derived from the buff facings of the regiment, and this was to become part of the official title of the regiment.

The 1st/78th in the Netherlands – 1794-1795

In September 1794 the 78th went on active service for the first time. The campaign in the Netherlands was one of the less successful ventures in which the British Army has taken part. The purpose of the British and Hanoverian expeditionary force commanded by Prince Frederick, Duke of York and Albany, in co-operation with Austrian and Dutch allies, was to check the advance of the armies of Revolutionary France. After a modestly successful start to the campaign, the Austrians were heavily defeated by the French, leaving the British force isolated in the Netherlands and in danger of being overrun.

Among the reinforcements sent out to join the Duke of York's army were the 1st Battalion 78th Highlanders and also the newly raised 79th Cameron Highlanders. The 78th's first encounter with the enemy was at the defence of Nimjegen on 4th November 1794, when the regiment made a gallant sortie against a besieging battery of French artillery. In late December the 78th made a successful counter-attack against an enemy force which had crossed the frozen River Waal. On 5th January 1795, by good discipline and fire control, it repelled a charge by French cavalry. During the intense cold of early 1795 the British force withdrew through Germany, and by the time it eventually embarked at Bremerhaven in April the 78th had lost over 350 men, mainly through the severe winter weather.

The 1st/78th on the expedition to L'Isle Dieu – 1795-1796

On return from this disastrous campaign in the Netherlands, the 1st Battalion 78th Highlanders was stationed for short periods at Chelmsford, Harwich, and Southampton. In August 1795 it joined an expedition to Brittany intended to give military support to French Royalists who were still opposing the Revolution in France. The 1st/78th landed on the island of L'Isle Dieu off the coast of Brittany, but by then French Royalist resistance had collapsed, and the force was withdrawn. On its return to England in January 1796, the 1st/78th was quartered at Poole.

The 2nd/78th at the capture of the Cape of Good Hope – 1795

After the defeat of the Netherlands by the French in 1795, and the formation of the Batavian Republic, Great Britain found herself at war with the Dutch. With the Cape of Good Hope and the port of Cape Town in hostile hands, the security of the sea route to India was threatened. An expedition was despatched to seize the Cape of Good Hope from the Dutch. In July 1795 the 2nd/78th and a party of marines landed and captured Simonstown. In subsequent operations the Dutch settlers were defeated at Wynberg, Cape Town surrendered, and after two months resistance the colony capitulated.

The 1st and 2nd Battalions 78th amalgamated – 1796

In November 1795, as part of the reduction of the army, the 1st and 2nd Battalions of the 78th were ordered to amalgamate. The 1st/78th sailed from England in March 1796, and the amalgamation of the battalions to form the 78th Highlanders (Ross-shire Buffs) took place at Cape Town in June 1796.

The 78th arrives in India – 1797

In November 1796 the 78th left South Africa for its first period of service in India, arriving at Calcutta in February 1797, just a month before the 72nd were to leave India for home. By 1797 the East India Company had expanded the territory under its control into the Presidencies of Bengal, Madras and Bombay. Within these territories trade prospered, much to Great Britain's advantage, but outside the Presidencies anarchy prevailed. In the south Tippoo, Sultan of Mysore, with his French-trained army, and further north the Mahrattas, kept India in a state of permanent turmoil.

The 78th spent the next six years in this unstable political situation, on garrison duty in Bengal, Oudh, and on the east coast of India. In about 1801 the regiment received its Second Stand of Colours, provided by Major General Alexander Mackenzie-Fraser.

The 78th in the 2nd Mahratta War – 1803

The 78th was not involved in the conquest of Mysore and the defeat of the southern Mahrattas, but its turn came in 1803 when the Governor General of India, the Marquess of Wellesley, launched a military campaign against the northern Mahrattas, whose French-trained army was continually raiding British territory. The force was led by his younger brother, Major General the Hon Arthur Wellesley (later to become the Duke of Wellington). The 78th moved by sea to Bombay, and then marched to Poona. Wellesley's first step was to secure a firm base for his operations, and he besieged the Mahratta fortress of Ahmednuggar. The attack was headed by the European infantry of the army, the 74th and 78th Highlanders, and to the astonishment of the Mahrattas the fortress was taken in only four days. Wellesley now had the base and communications centre which he needed for the campaign.

The 78th at the Battle of Assaye – 23rd September 1803

On 23rd September 1803 Wellesley with his army of 7,000 British and Indian troops encountered the main Mahratta force estimated at over 40,000 men. The enemy were apparently starting to retreat and so Wellesley, intending to catch them strung out on the line of march, decided to attack immediately. But he had been badly misinformed. The Mahratta army, with over 100 cannon to Wellesley's 22, and with a 20 to one superiority in cavalry, was drawn up in a strong position in the angle formed by the junction of two rivers, beside the village of Assaye.

Wellesley however, with characteristic tactical genius, saw that it was possible to take the unwieldy Mahratta army from the flank, where its overwhelming fire power could not be brought to bear. By personal reconnaissance he found a ford over the Kaitna river by which his army could cross and then deploy across the narrow neck of land between the two rivers. The rivers would both deny the enemy room to manoeuvre and protect his own flanks. As Wellesley's army advanced, the Mahratta line wheeled to face it.

The attack was launched in three echelons, with the 78th in the all-important position on the left flank of the leading echelon. The 78th was the first of Wellesley's troops to reach the Mahrattas as they realigned their front line, and the regiment's determined attack played a critical part in the capture of the Mahratta guns and the subsequent rout of their infantry. In later years the great Duke of Wellington was to rate the tactical handling of his army at the battle of Assaye as the best thing he had ever done on the battlefield.

78th BATTLE HONOUR
For its part in the Battle of Assaye in 1803 the 78th was awarded the Battle Honour:

ASSAYE

The 78th was also granted the badge of the **'Elephant superscribed Assaye'**, which is one of the collar badges of the Highlanders, and is borne as a device on the Regimental Colour today.

The Assaye Colour of the 78th

The three British regiments in Wellesley's force at Assaye, the 74th and 78th Highlanders and the 19th Light Dragoons, were each permitted to carry an Honorary third Colour presented by the East India Company.

(Note. It is not known what happened to the original 'Assaye' Colour of the 78th. It probably disintegrated as a result of the climate during the years of service in the East Indies. A replica was made in 1889 and is now in the regimental chapel at Fort George).

The 78th at the Battle of Argaum – 1803

After Assaye, Wellesley's army was joined by a further column, giving him a total of 11,000 men. He wasted no time in following up the defeated Mahrattas. On 29th September 1803 his force caught up with the Mahratta army, still 30,000 strong. By advancing through shoulder high corn the army was able to approach the enemy unobserved, and it attacked at last light. The 78th was on the right of the assaulting line, and the attack took its direction from the regiment. By 11 pm Wellesley's army had won a further devastating victory, capturing the remaining Mahratta guns and ammunition, their Colours, elephants, camels and baggage train.

The 78th at the capture of Gawilghur – 1803

The final battle of the Mahratta war was the attack on the supposedly impregnable hill fortress of Gawilghur. After a week of siege operations, the defences were successfully breached.

The military superiority which Wellesley established during the campaign brought the collapse of Mahratta morale and resistance, and the campaign was won before a general assault was necessary. After the fall of Gawilghur a peace treaty was arranged with the Rajah of Berar, which left the British government and the East India Company in control of the major part of central India. All troops who had taken part in the campaign were rewarded with prize money, a private soldier's share being 13 rupees.

The 78th in Bombay and Goa – 1804-1811

The colonial empire of Great Britain's ally Portugal was also under constant threat of French attack, and a British garrison was maintained in the Portugese colony of Goa. After the Mahratta war the 78th remained in and around Bombay for three years, and then spent a period of uneventful garrison duty in Goa from 1807 to 1811.

2nd Battalion 78th raised again – 1804

In 1804, when a French invasion of Great Britain seemed imminent and Britain's land forces were dangerously over-stretched, the Government authorised the raising of a number of 2nd battalions. Most of these were intended to be 'feeder' battalions, with the task of recruiting and training reinforcements for their lst Battalions overseas, but the 2nd Battalion 78th Highlanders had an unusually interesting record of service. During its 13 years existence it experienced extremes of triumph and disaster.

The new 2nd/78th was raised by Major General Alexander Mackenzie-Fraser, who had succeeded his brother-in-law Major General Francis Humberston Mackenzie, Lord Seaforth, as Colonel of the Regiment. The 2nd/78th Highlanders was inspected at Fort George, Inverness on 6th December 1804, and received Colours from General Mackenzie-Fraser.

The 2nd/78th under training with Sir John Moore – 1805

With the serious threat of French invasion, large bodies of troops were concentrated for training in the South of England. The 2nd/78th embarked at Fort George in early 1805, and spent six months at Hythe in Kent. The battalion joined Major General Sir John Moore's troops as he developed his ideas on discipline and tactics, and on the training of light infantry: measures which were to prove so effective in the Peninsular War. By the time the 2nd/78th was ordered abroad, it had achieved a notably high standard of discipline, morale and training.

The 2nd/78th in Gibraltar – 1805-1806

The 2nd/78th sailed for Gibraltar in September 1805, and its journey coincided with momentous naval events. As the British transports sailed south along the coast of Portugal they encountered a large French and Spanish fleet, and were forced to seek refuge in the mouth of the River Tagus off Lisbon. Their plight was dramatically relieved by the historic British naval victory at the Battle of Trafalgar, and the 70th sailed on to reach Gibraltar safely.

The 2nd/78th in Sicily – 1806

The new 2nd/78th was to see its first active service in Italy. The Kingdom of the Two Sicilies, comprising the south of Italy and the island of Sicily itself, had joined the alliance against Napoleon. The French, under Napoleon's elder brother Joseph Bonaparte, invaded the Kingdom in 1806 and deposed King Ferdinand. A British force was sent to support the King, and in May 1806 the 2nd/78th sailed from Gibraltar to join it in Sicily.

The 2nd/78th at the Battle of Maida – 1806

When the 2nd/78th reached Sicily, the French in Italy appeared to be about to invade the island itself. The British troops in Sicily were ordered to pre-empt the invasion by attacking the French on the mainland of Italy. The British force of 4,800, under General Sir John Stuart, landed in Calabria, the 'toe' of Italy. On 4th July 1806 it attacked the French force of roughly 6,400 troops commanded by General Regnier.

*Dress of the 2nd Battalion 78th Highlanders
(Ross-shire Buffs) in 1806.
(From a painting by R. Simkin)*

The British used new tactics. Deploying in two ranks against the French who were formed in three, the British engaged the enemy with brisk musketry fire, then charged with the bayonet. The French, met by musketry of an accuracy and intensity which they had not experienced before, broke and fled. The battle was won by British linear tactics, combined with the notable improvements that had been achieved in discipline, musketry and training, and was an impressive demonstration that the formidable French columns were not invincible.

2nd/78th BATTLE HONOUR

For its part in the campaign of 1806 the 2nd/78th was awarded the Battle Honour:

MAIDA

The 2nd/78th in the expedition to Egypt – 1807

In 1806 Turkey entered the war as allies of the French, and closed the Dardanelles to Russian shipping. A British fleet was sent to bombard Constantinople on behalf of the Russian allies, but was forced to withdraw ignominiously in the face of the Turkish defences. Great Britain therefore decided to attack Turkey at a vulnerable point of the Ottoman Empire, and British troops landed again in Egypt. As a result of this chain of international events, the 2nd/78th in Sicily was ordered to join the expeditionary force of 5,000 troops which landed at Alexandria in March 1807. It was hoped that by occupying the city the Egyptian Mamelukes would rebel against their Turkish rulers and join forces with the British expedition.

The disaster at El Hamet – 1807

In the event the Mameluke rising never materialised. As the British force attempted to capture the town of Rosetta, it was itself attacked by the Turks and caught with its troops vulnerably dispersed. On 21st April 1807 three companies of the 2nd/78th were surrounded by an overwhelming force of Turkish cavalry at El Hamet. Despite heroic resistance, in which 163 of the unfortunate 2nd/78th including their Commanding Officer Lieutenant Colonel Patrick MacLeod of Geanies were killed, the three companies were forced to surrender.

The 2nd/78th returns to England – 1807-1808

The British force, with the remainder of the 2nd/78th, withdrew to Alexandria and held the city until September. Then, because there seemed to be no intention of reinforcing or evacuating the force, the commander negotiated a truce with the Turks and the prisoners were released. The 2nd/78th returned to Sicily and thence to England, arriving in early January 1808.

The legend of Drummer MacLeod and Private Thomas Keith

One of the most intriguing stories of this sad episode concerned the fate of two Highlanders of the 2nd/78th taken prisoner at El Hamet. After the battle they became the property of a Turkish officer, and so were not repatriated with the other prisoners. Both men turned Mohammedan, gained their freedom, and had successful careers in the Ottoman Empire. Drummer MacLeod, from Lewis, took the name Osman, and as 'Osman Effendi' became a well known doctor in Cairo. Private Thomas Keith, an apprentice gun maker from Leith, had been the regimental armourer of the 2nd/78th. He took the name of Ibrahim, and his skill with weapons earned him military promotion as a cavalry officer. He rose to be Ibrahim Aga, Governor of Medina, and was killed in a cavalry charge in 1815.

The 2nd/78th in Great Britain – 1809-1814

On its return to Great Britain the 2nd/78th was quartered in the south of England where it was supplied drafts for the 1st/78th in Goa. The battalion moved to Fort George in early 1809, leaving a draft of 370 men under orders for India. In 1811 the headquarters moved from Fort George to Aberdeen, where it remained until 1814.

The draft of the 2nd/78th at Walcheren – 1809

The draft for India got no further than Cowes before it was diverted to join the Earl of Chatham's expedition to Walcheren in Holland. The operation was intended to be a strong raid on the French-occupied port of Antwerp, with its dockyards and arsenals. However the British force was not only led by a wholly incompetent commander, but was so badly affected by malaria that 11,000 men out of a total of 40,000 were unfit for operations. The expedition had to be withdrawn in disarray.

The 1st/78th in the capture of Java – 1811

When the French defeated the Dutch and established the Batavian Republic in 1795, the colony of Java fell under French control. The Dutch had established Java in 1596, and considered it their most valuable Colony. In 1811 the British government of India decided to eject the French occupation force, and the 78th formed part of the expeditionary force which sailed from Bombay in March 1811.

As the force landed in Java, the French garrison abandoned the capital Batavia to the invaders, and withdrew to a defensive position at Weltervreeden. On 10th August 1811 the British force attacked the French, forcing them to retreat to a strong position at Fort Cornelis. On 25th August the British attacked, and in a fiercely fought three hour assault against well-prepared defences, routed the French again. Among the 154 British and Indian troops killed, was Brevet Lieutenant Colonel William Campbell, acting Commanding Officer of the 78th. The French lost the disastrous figures of over 1,000 killed, 3,000 wounded, and 6,000 taken prisoner, and 430 French guns were captured. The French commander General Jansens managed to avoid capture, but he was caught on 18th September by a pursuing force which included the 78th, and compelled to sign an unconditional surrender of the colony. Stamford Raffles (later the founder of the Colony of Singapore) was appointed Governor of Java.

The 1st/78th in Java – 1811-1816

The 78th remained in Java for five years. During the first few months spent in the port of Sourabaya, the regiment's families arrived from Goa to join them. In 1812 the Sultan of Djocjocarta, who strongly resented the European settlement of his island, rebelled against the rule of the East India Company. A force of about 1000 troops, including the 78th, was sent to check the revolt. It successfully stormed the Sultan's fortified krattan (palace), deposed the Sultan, and took possession of his treasure.

The 78th remained in Java for five years. While regularly involved in minor expeditions and incidents with rebellious local tribes, its most persistent enemies were the climate and tropical disease, which caused over 600 casualties.

lst/78th BATTLE HONOUR

For its service in Java between 1811-1816 the 1st/78th was awarded the Battle Honour:

JAVA

The shipwreck of the 1st/78th – 1816

In September 1816 the 78th left Java for Bengal. The Headquarters of the regiment had an uneventful journey, but the ship 'Frances Charlotte', with six of the companies aboard, struck a reef and sank off Preparis, a small uninhabited island north of the Andamans. Most of the 78th Highlanders and their families managed to get ashore where they survived precariously until rescued five weeks late, but a number died of starvation, drowning and exposure. The 78th lost its baggage, records and £2,000 of regimental funds in the shipwreck, but one interesting item that was saved was the pair of silver tureens bought by the officers of the 78th with their prize money after the capture of the Sultan of Djocjocarta's treasury. The tureens, of Goanese silver, had been presented by the Emperor Napoleon to the Sultan when the French took control of Java. The survivors of the shipwreck were eventually rescued and taken to Calcutta, where they arrived in December 1816.

The 1st/78th returns to Great Britain – 1817

The 1st/78th sailed for home in March 1817 on the 'Prince Blucher', the ship which had rescued the shipwrecked companies from the island of Preparis. The regiment arrived at Portsmouth, and then sailed on to Aberdeen, arriving in July. The 78th had been abroad for 21 years.

The 2nd/78th at Merxem

The main role of the 2nd/78th, like other 'feeder' battalions, was to recruit and to keep its 1st Battalion up to strength for active service. But as the British, Russian, Prussian and Austrian allies brought France to defeat in early 1814, the 2nd/78th was ordered to join the British army in Holland. Although less than 300 strong, the battalion took part in the advance on Antwerp, and particularly distinguished itself at the village of Merxem, on the outskirts of Antwerp, when it routed a force of four French battalions.

The 2nd/78th in Holland and Belgium – 1814-1816

After the abdication of Napoleon Bonaparte in March 1814, the 2nd/78th remained on garrison duty in Holland and Belgium. When Bonaparte escaped from Elba and returned to France for his final campaign, the 2nd/78th were still at low strength and further reduced in numbers by sickness. In June 1815 they formed part of the Allied reserve at Nieuport, and did not take part in the final defeat of the French at the Battle of Waterloo. The battalion eventually returned to Great Britain in February 1816, and remained at home until amalgamated with the 1st/78th.

The 1st and 2nd Battalions of the 78th amalgamate - 1817

In 1817 the 1st and 2nd Battalions of the 78th amalgamated at Aberdeen to form a single regiment once again.

The 78th in Scotland – 1817

After the amalgamation of its two battalions the 78th's tour of duty in Scotland was short. The Headquarters remained in Aberdeen, with detachments at Perth, Fort George, Fort William, and Fort Augustus. When rioting broke out at

Dress of the 78th Highlanders
(Ross-shire Buffs) in 1822
(from a painting by R Simkin)

Calton in Glasgow in August 1817, the 78th was ordered to send companies to act in aid of the civil power. They were so fiercely attacked while escorting prisoners to gaol that they were obliged to open fire on the Glasgow mob.

The 78th in Ireland – 1817-1826

In November 1817 the 78th moved to Belfast. The regiment was to remain in Ireland for nine relatively uneventful years, receiving its Third Stand of Colours, provided by Major General Sir Samuel Auchmuchty, in 1818. During the visit of King George IV to Dublin in 1821 the 78th was brigaded on parade with the 42nd, 79th, and 93rd Highlanders, and the only kilted regiment absent from the Highland Brigade was the 92nd, which was in Jamaica at the time.

The 78th in Ceylon – 1826-1837

In 1826 the 78th sailed for Ceylon, and remained on garrison duty on the island for 11 years. The main enemy was disease, and the regiment lost 299 officers and men from cholera and other tropical sickness.

The 78th in Great Britain – 1838-1841

The 78th left Ceylon in 1837 and arrived in Ireland in February 1838. Later that year, when serious unrest broke out in Canada, the 78th was ordered to supply volunteers to reinforce the regiments sent to support the Canadian garrisons and Militia regiments. Being thus reduced to well below strength, the 78th returned to Scotland in 1839 to recruit.

Dress of the 78th Highlanders
(Ross-shire Buffs) in 1834
(From a painting by R. Simkin)

Stationed in Glasgow and then Edinburgh, the regiment was soon recruited up to strength again, and its Fourth Stand of Colours was presented by Lieutenant General Paul Anderson. During the industrial riots of 1840 the 78th was sent to Liverpool and Manchester for duties in aid of the civil power, and companies were detached to many of the manufacturing towns of Lancashire and Yorkshire. the 78th returned to Ireland in November 1841.

Among the regiment's more unusual acquisitions during its time in Ceylon was a young elephant, presented to the regiment as a mascot because the regimental badge incorporated the 'Elephant superscribed Assaye'. The elephant was trained to march in front of the Regimental Band. When the 78th left Ireland for India again in 1842, the elephant was presented to the Edinburgh Zoological Society.

The 78th returns to India – 1842

In early 1842 news reached Britain of one of the greatest military disasters of the 19th Century, the massacre by the Afghans of 4,500 British and Indian troops, with 12,000 camp followers, while withdrawing from Kabul to India. The sole survivor of the disaster to reach India was Dr William Brydon. A punitive expedition had been assembled from forces in India, and the 78th was hurriedly despatched to take the place of the troops required for service in Afghanistan. The regiment arrived in Bombay in July 1842, over 1,000 strong, and spent the next three years in Poona and Karachi.

The 78th Highlanders (Ross-shire Buffs)
(From a print published by W. Spooner C 1840)

Cholera strikes the 78th – 1844-1845

The years 1844-1845 were the most melancholy period in the history of the 78th, for cholera struck the regiment, bringing losses on a scale which it never encountered in battle. Tropical illness had to be accepted as a recurrent hazard of service in India, and during the regiment's time in Bombay and Poona there had been occasional outbreaks of disease. But in 1844, when the 78th was moved to Karachi and marched to Sukkur, in Sind, cholera broke out on a devastating scale. In eight months the regiment lost 535 officers and men, and 202 of its wives and children. In early 1845 the survivors of the regiment returned to Bombay, just over 300 strong. A monument in St Giles Cathedral, Edinburgh is a moving memorial to this miserable episode.

The 78th restored to strength – 1845

Happily the 78th made a quick and total recovery from this disaster. The Depot companies were allowed to recruit generally throughout Great Britain and Ireland, and volunteers were permitted to transfer from other regiments in India due to return home on completion of their foreign service. This included a draft of 100 from the 2nd Foot, The Queen's Royal Regiment. By the end of the year the 78th was restored to strength, and remained based in the Bombay Presidency, in Poona, Kirkee and Belgaum for four years.

What did change was the nationality of the men who composed the regiment. Before the cholera epidemic the 78th had been 91% Scottish, but the influx of 732 new men, few of whom were Scots, inevitably changed this. The 78th, which was to fight with such distinction in the campaigns in Persia and the Indian Mutiny, was composed of 47% Scotsmen, 30% English and 23% Irish. As is so often the case the customs, character, and morale of the regiment survived, and the men, whatever their origins, were proud to be 78th Highlanders (Ross-shire Buffs) and to wear the kilt of 78th tartan.

The 78th Highlanders (Ross-shire Buffs)
(From a print published by R. Ackermann in 1846)

78th Highlanders (Ross-shire Buffs) 1852
(From a painting by R. Simkin)

The 78th in Aden – 1849-1853

After its capture by an expedition from Bombay in 1839, the garrison of Aden was provided by detachments from regiments stationed in Bombay. Life in this inhospitable station was occasionally interrupted by minor friction with the Sultan of Lahej, from whom Aden had been captured. The 78th took its turn at this hot and unrewarding garrison duty for over three years from late 1849 to early 1853. The monotony of military garrison life is well commemorated by the famous pipe tune 'The Barren Rocks of Aden', composed by Piper James Mauchline of the 78th during the 78th's time there. (The tune is said to have been 'improved' by Pipe Major Alexander MacKellar of the 78th, who is sometimes credited with its composition).

The 78th in Poona – 1853-1857

In 1853 the 78th moved to Poona, half the regiment returning to India from Aden and half travelling from Bombay. There in 1854 the regiment received its Fifth Stand of Colours, provided from the estate of the late General Paul Anderson, and these Colours were to see much action during the campaigns in Persia and India which ensued.

The 78th in the expedition to Persia – 1857

As Great Britain developed its trade and extended its control over India, there were inevitably clashes with Russia which was expanding to its south. Afghanistan, on the north west frontier of India, became the buffer state whose neutrality had to be preserved at all costs as a barrier to further Russian expansion. Persia too was a 'no-man's land' between the rival powers. When the Shah of Persia, prompted by the Russians, besieged the Afghan town of Herat, Britain had to intervene with armed force, and an expedition was sent from India to the Persian Gulf. The expedition successfully captured the port of Bushire to use as a base, and then waited until further reinforcements arrived from India. The 78th was sent from Poona as part of these reinforcements.

The 78th at the Battle of Koosh-Ab – 1857

As the Persians were assembling a large army to recover Bushire, the commander of the expedition to Persia, Lieutenant General Sir James Outram, decided to preempt them by taking the offensive. He quickly located and captured the enemy camp, the Persians having fled as the force approached. However the Persian cavalry rallied and made an attempt to threaten the British force as it withdrew during the night. Outram took up a defensive position near the village of Koosh-Ab then, having waited until daylight on 8th February 1857 his force deployed into line and attacked the Persians. In a rather one-sided engagement the Persians were routed with the loss of 700 troops, while the British and Indian force lost only 10. The 78th, on the right of the first line of the attack, had no casualties at all.

The 78th at Mohomrah – 1857

Over the next few weeks the Persians managed to concentrate their army again, and fortified a camp at Mohomrah beside the Shat-el-Arab waterway. General Outram employed a system of combined operations, using the guns of his fleet to bombard the Persians while his transport steamers landed the army. The 78th again led the advance on the Persian position, but the prospect of another attack was too much for the enemy who abandoned their position and fled.

78th BATTLE HONOURS
For its service in the Persian campaign the 78th was awarded the Battle Honours:

KOOSH-AB
PERSIA

The 78th and the start of the Indian Mutiny – 1857

The 78th arrived back in India in May 1857 to find the country in a state of emergency. In April 1857 Sepoy troops (Indian troops trained by Europeans) had started to mutiny against British rule. Within a few weeks the discontent had spread through the Sepoy regiments in Bengal, which represented four fifths of the East India Company's army. On its arrival in Bombay the 78th was ordered to continue by sea to Calcutta, where it arrived in June 1857. After the regiment had disarmed the mutinous Sepoy troops at Barrackpore, four companies moved to Allahadad where they joined Major General Sir Henry Havelock's column as it prepared to march to relieve the besieged garrison of Cawnpore.

The 78th at the recapture of Cawnpore – 1857

On 12th July 1857 the 78th had its first encounter with the enemy in the field when Havelock's column routed a small force of mutineers at Futtehpore. It was the enemy's first defeat of the campaign, and three days later Havelock won another minor action at Aong. But when Havelock's column arrived at Cawnpore it was to find one of the most horrifying scenes of the Indian Mutiny. Cawnpore had been besieged by a force of about 3,000 mutineers under Dandhu Panth, known as 'the Nana Sahib', a rebel Mahratta Rajah. The European garrison of about 300 soldiers, with roughly 600 civilians, women and children, had held out for three weeks. Then, with the assurance of safe conduct, the majority of the garrison had been allowed to leave the city and to embark in boats on the River Ganges. As they went on board they were brutally shot down by the mutineers, only four men of the garrison surviving the massacre.

As Havelock's column reached Cawnpore it launched a series of quick attacks on the rebels, in which the 78th played the key role, and the Nana Sahib's army was briskly routed. But unknown to the relieving force 206 women and children of the Cawnpore and Futteghur garrisons were still alive in the town. As the British force approached these were brutally butchered and thrown down a dry well. The column entered Cawnpore on 17th July, the day after the massacre, to make their grisly discovery. The brutal excesses of the Nana Sahib were an incident which the British army did not forget or forgive during the campaign.

Lieutenant Andrew C Bogle wins the Victoria Cross at Oonao – 29th July 1857

Lieutenant Andrew Cathcart Bogle of the 78th Highlanders was recommended for the award of the Victoria Cross for gallantry during the advance to Cawnpore. The citation read:

'For conspicuous gallantry on 29 July 1857, in the attack on Oonao, in leading the way into a loopholed house, strongly occupied by the enemy, from which a heavy fire harassed the advance of his regiment. Captain Bogle was severely wounded in this important service.'
(London Gazette 2 September 1859)

The 78th in the advance to Lucknow – 1857

General Havelock's next task was to reach Lucknow where the garrison of 1,700 British and loyal Indian troops was besieged by about 60,000 mutineers. Havelock's column was itself only 1,500 strong, but even that would almost double the garrison, and so he crossed the river Ganges and marched for Lucknow. Six miles further on General Havelock was again forced to clear a rebel position by a frontal attack

Major Andrew Cathcart Bogle, VC

on the village of Bashiratganj. Although these two attacks were successful, they cost nearly 100 casualties. To add to the difficulties, cholera had broken out, reducing the strength of the column to about 850 fit men, and so Havelock was forced to wait for reinforcements. Taking advantage of this halt the mutineers reoccupied a position at Boorbia-ki-Chauki just beyond Bashiratganj. On 11th August, despite his shortage of men General Havelock attacked again. Next day his four companies of 78th Highlanders led the attack with a spirited bayonet charge.

Lieutenant Joseph P H Crowe wins the Victoria Cross at Boorbia-ki-Chauki – 12th August 1857

When complementing the 78th for the regiment's spirited attack on the rebel positions in the village of Boorbia-ki-Chauki, Brigadier General Havelock undertook that if it could be ascertained which officer or soldier first entered the enemy position, he would recommend him for the Victoria Cross. The Commanding Officer reported that two officers, Lieutenants Crowe and Campbell, had entered the enemy position together. The matter was resolved by the sad death of Lieutenant Campbell from cholera a few days later, and the award went to Lieutenant Joseph Crowe, who became the second member of the 78th to win the Victoria Cross. The citation read:

'For being the first to enter the redoubt at Boorzeke Chowkee, the entrenched village in front of the Busherutgunge on 12th August. (Telegram from the late Major General Havelock to the Commander-in-Chief in India dated 18 August 1857).'
(London Gazette 15 January 1858)

Lieutenant Colonel Joseph P H Crowe, VC

The 78th at the Relief of Lucknow – September 1857

These actions against the mutineers had reduced General Havelock's column to below viable fighting strength, and so once again he withdrew to Cawnpore. Here the remainder of the 78th joined the force, followed by another column of about 1500 men under General Sir James Outram. The relief column could now muster a division of over 3,000 men, and in late September it marched on Lucknow. It reached the Alam Bagh, a royal palace in a walled garden outside Lucknow, on 23rd September 1857.

The hardest part of the operation was still to come. The British garrison at Lucknow still held out in the Residency, two miles away on the far side of the rebel held town. On 25th September Havelock's column left its sick and wounded, its 5,000 native camp followers, its ordnance stores and its commissariat at the Alam Bagh, and fought its way across the Char Bagh canal bridge. Skirting round the town of Lucknow to avoid getting involved in street battles, it reached the Residency in the evening after a long hot day of continuous fighting. There was an emotional welcome from the defenders, but it had been a costly fight which cost the 78th 41 killed and 81 wounded.

At the relief of the garrison at Lucknow six Victoria Crosses were awarded to the 78th Highlanders.

Lieutenant Herbert T Macpherson wins the Victoria Cross at Lucknow – 25th September 1857

During the advance through Lucknow Lieutenant Herbert Taylor Macpherson, the Adjutant of the 78th Highlanders, was awarded the Victoria Cross. The citation read:

'For distinguished conduct at Lucknow on the 25th September 1857, in setting an example of heroic gallantry to the men of the regiment at the period of the action in which they captured two brass 9-pounders at the point of the bayonet'. (London Gazette 18th June 1858)

Brigadier General Sir Herbert T. Macpherson, VC
awarded the Victoria Cross as
Lieutenant and Adjutant of the 78th in 1857

Surgeon Joseph Jee wins the Victoria Cross at Lucknow – 25th/26th September 1857

Surgeon Joseph Jee was awarded the Victoria Cross during the advance on Lucknow. The citation read:

'For most conspicuous gallantry and important services on the entry of the late Major General Havelock's relieving force into Lucknow on 25th September 1857, in having, during action (when the 78th Highlanders, then in possession of the Char Bagh, captured two 9-pounders at the point of the bayonet), by great exertion and devoted exposure, attended to the large number of men wounded in the charge, whom he succeeded in getting removed on cots and the backs of their comrades, until he had collected the dhooly bearers, who had fled. Subsequently on the same day, in endeavouring to reach the Residency with the wounded men, Surgeon Jee became besieged by an overwhelming force in the Mote Mehal, where he remained during the whole night and the following morning, voluntarily and repeatedly exposing himself to a heavy fire in proceeding to dress the wounded men who fell while serving a 24-pounder in a most exposed position. He eventually succeeded in taking many of the wounded through a cross-fire of ordnance and musketry safely into the Residency, by the river bank, although repeatedly warned not to make the perilous attempt.' (London Gazette 9 November 1860)

Surgeon Joseph Jee, VC

Assistant Surgeon Valentine M McMaster wins the Victoria Cross at Lucknow – 25th September 1857

For its gallant advance to the Residency at Lucknow on 25th September 1857, the 78th Highlanders was awarded the Victoria Cross as a regiment. The 78th was instructed to vote on who should wear the award, and it was unanimously agreed that it should go to Assistant Surgeon Valentine Munbee McMaster who also carried the Queen's Colour during the final stages of the advance to the Residency. The citation read:

'For the intrepidity with which he exposed himself to the fire of the enemy, in bringing in and attending to the wounded on the 25th September 1857 at Lucknow'.
(London Gazette 18 June 1858)

Colour Sergeant Stewart McPherson, VC

Surgeon Valentine M McMaster, VC

Colour Sergeant Stewart McPherson wins the Victoria Cross at Lucknow – 26th September 1857

Colour Sergeant Stewart McPherson was awarded the Victoria Cross. The citation read:

'For daring gallantry in the Lucknow Residency on 26th September 1857, in having rescued at great personal risk, a wounded private of his company, who was lying in a most exposed situation under very heavy fire. Colour Sergeant McPherson was also distinguished on many occasions by his coolness and gallantry in action'.
(London Gazette 12 April 1859)

Private Henry Ward wins the Victoria Cross at Lucknow – 25th/26th September 1857

Private Henry Ward was awarded the Victoria Cross.

'For his gallant and devoted conduct in having, on the night of the 25th and morning of the 26th September 1857, remained with the dooly of Captain Havelock, 10th Foot, DAAG Field Force, who was severely wounded, and on the morning of 26th September escorted that officer and Private Thomas Pilkington, 78th Highlanders, who was also wounded, and had taken refuge in the same dooly, through a very heavy cross fire of ordnance and musketry. This soldier remained by the side of the dooly, and by his example and exertions kept the dooly bearers from dropping their double load through the heavy fire with the same steadiness as if on parade, thus saving the lives of both, and bringing them in safety to the Baillie Guard'.
(London Gazette 18 June 1858)

Private Henry Ward, VC

Private James Hollowell wins the Victoria Cross at Lucknow – 26th September 1857

Private James Hollowell was awarded the Victoria Cross. The citation read:

'A party on 26 September was shut up besieged in a house in the city of Lucknow by the rebels. Private James Hollowell, one of the party, behaved throughout the day in a most admirable manner: he directed, encouraged and led the others, exposing himself fearlessly, and by his talent in persuading and cheering, prevailed on nine dispirited men to make a successful defence in a burning house, with the enemy firing through four windows.' (London Gazette 18 June 1858)

The 78th in the Defence of Lucknow – September-November 1857

Although the arrival of Havelock's column at the Residency brought relief for the besieged garrison of Lucknow, the siege by the mutineers continued. The relieving column had doubled the strength of the garrison, and given it new heart, but it had not raised the siege. For the next seven weeks the 78th became part of the besieged garrison defending the Residency.

Private James Hollowell, VC

The 2nd Relief of Lucknow – 17th November 1857

In November 1857 a column commanded by General Sir Colin Campbell, the Commander in Chief in India, reached the Alam Bagh. It then fought its way round Lucknow to reach the beleaguered Residency on 17th November. After the Residency had been relieved for the second time, it was clear that it was untenable without a much stronger garrison. With understandable regret Sir Colin Campbell decided to abandon it. The 78th, having led the original relief force, was selected to form the rearguard as the garrison withdrew. A sad epilogue to the withdrawal from the Residency was the death from dysentery a week later of Major General Sir Henry Havelock, under whom the 78th had served in Persia, Cawnpore, and at the Relief and Defence of Lucknow.

The 78th in the Recapture of Lucknow – 1857-1858

After abandoning the Residency, Sir Colin Campbell set up a new defensive position outside Lucknow beside the Alam Bagh, and here General Outram's force, including the 78th, held their ground from November 1857. By March 1858 Sir Colin Campbell had mustered a force of over 25,000 troops, comprising four infantry divisions, and was strong enough to retake Lucknow from the rebels. During the recapture of Lucknow, which took 19 days fighting, the role of the 78th was to hold the firm base at the Alam Bagh.

78th BATTLE HONOUR

For its part in the Relief and Defence of Lucknow the 78th was awarded the Battle Honour:

LUCKNOW

The 78th at the capture of Bareilly – 1858

In March 1858 the 78th joined the Rohilkand Field Force in what, for the regiment, was to be the last phase of the campaign. The force, which also included the Highland Brigade (the 42nd, 79th and 93rd Highlanders), marched north west out of Oudh, attacked the rebels at Bareilly and captured the town. The 78th remained in garrison at Bareilly until January 1859 when it received welcome orders to return to Great Britain.

The 78th leaves India – 1859

The 78th returned to Bombay, where it was reunited with its families after an absence of over two years. After a rapturous welcome and an official banquet, the regiment embarked for home 532 strong. Of the regiment which had arrived in India 17 years earlier, only 59 were still serving with it. In September 1859 the 78th arrived at Fort George where the Depot companies rejoined the Service companies.

Great Britain welcomes 'The Saviours of India – 1859-61

When the Indian Mutiny broke out, the 78th had been nearly at the end of its tour of Foreign service, and so at the end of the campaign it was among the first regiments to return home. The 78th's part in the First Relief of the garrison of the Residency at Lucknow had caught the public's imagination, and on the regiment's arrival in Scotland it was hailed as the 'Saviours of India'. The 78th was feted in Nairn and Inverness, and there were celebrations at Rosehaugh, Brahan and throughout the north.

When the 78th moved to Edinburgh in February 1860, the welcome continued. There were banquets in Edinburgh and Hamilton, and Lady Havelock, widow of Major General Sir Henry Havelock, presented the regiment with its campaign medals. The campaign is worthily commemorated by the fine monument in the form of a runic cross erected by the regiment in 1861 on Edinburgh Castle esplanade.

*The 78th Highlanders (Ross-shire Buffs) 1859
(From a painting by R. Simkin)*

The 78th in Great Britain – 1861-1865

In 1861 the 78th moved to Aldershot where it was inspected by the Duke of Cambridge, and received the welcome news that all those who had served in General Havelock's First Relief of Lucknow were to receive an additional year's service. Moving on to Shorncliffe in 1862, the 78th was presented with a magnificent silver centre piece and cup by the counties of Ross and Cromarty, and Keith Stewart-Mackenzie of Seaforth gave a Pipe Major's pipe banner. After a final year of home service spent in Dublin, the 78th sailed for Gibraltar in August 1865.

The 78th in Gibraltar – 1865-1867

The two regiment's two year period of garrison duty in Gibraltar was uneventful, and marred only by occasional outbreaks of cholera.

The 78th in Canada – 1867-1871

In July 1867 the 78th sailed for Canada and landed at Montreal. Next year, on 30th May 1868, the Sixth Stand of Colours was presented on the Champs de Mars at Montreal by Lady Windham, wife of General Sir Charles Windham the Commander of the British Forces in North America. In 1869 the regiment moved to Halifax where it spent two years, with a detachment at St John's, New Brunswick.

(Note. The 78th's period in garrison at Halifax is commemorated today by a museum and an interpretative display at the Citadel, Halifax).

The 78th Highlanders (Ross-shire Buffs) in Canada 1869

The 78th in Ireland – 1871-1873

In late 1871 the 78th left Canada for what was to be a turbulent tour in Northern Ireland. The regiment was stationed in Belfast, with four companies in Londonderry. In August 1872 there were particularly vicious disorders between Roman Catholics and Protestants in Belfast and then Lisburn. Further outbreaks followed in early 1873 in Monaghan, Downpatrick and Ballymena. The 78th earned particular commendation for its steadiness and patient impartiality in these sectarian squabbles.

The shared Depot of the 71st and 78th at Fort George – 1873-1881

Under the experimental Localisation Scheme of 1873, the 78th was linked with the 71st Highland Light Infantry. The two regiments had much in common, for both originated from Ross-shire, the 71st having been raised by John Mackenzie, Lord MacLeod. There were notable similarities of dress, including the Mackenzie tartan which the 78th wore as the kilt and the 71st as trews, and the buff facings used by both regiments.

The joint recruiting area, designated No 55 Sub-District, consisted of the Shetland and Orkney Islands, and the counties of Caithness, Sutherland, Ross and Cromarty, Inverness, Nairn and Moray The two regiments shared No 55 Brigade Depot at Fort George.

The 78th at Fort George – 1873-1874

In May 1873 the 78th left Belfast and returned to Fort George where it joined the newly established joint Depot of the 71st and 78th.   But Fort George was so overcrowded that two companies had to be accommodated at Aberdeen, and these provided the Queen's Guard at Ballater in 1873.

The 78th Highlanders (Ross-shire Buffs) 1877
(From a painting by R. Simkin)

The 78th in Great Britain – 1874-1879

In 1874 the 78th moved to Aldershot where it was brigaded with the 42nd, 79th and 93rd Highlanders in a Highland Brigade commanded by Major General W. Parke, late of the 72nd. The brigade was inspected by the Czar of Russia. It was a memorable reunion for the few veterans of the Indian Mutiny who were still serving, as the four regiments had served together at the final capture of Lucknow in 1858. The 78th moved to Dover in 1875, to Edinburgh in 1876, and back to Ireland in 1878. The main task during this series of peacetime garrison postings was to supply regular drafts to the linked regiment the 71st, then stationed in Malta. In 1879 the 78th left Ireland for foreign service once again in India.

The 78th returns to India – 1879

On the arrival of the 78th in Bombay in March 1879 the regiment travelled by train to Poona. It was the fifth time it had been stationed there.

The 78th in Afghanistan – 1879-1881

When the 78th arrived in India the campaign in Afghanistan, in which the 72nd was serving, was in progress. When the news arrived of the attack on a British column at Maiwand, the 78th was also ordered to move to Afghanistan. The regiment was at first employed on protection of the lines of communications. After the Battle of Kandahar the 78th moved into Afghanistan, spending an extremely cold winter in tents at Kandahar, before returning to Sitapur in India in May 1881.

78th CAMPAIGN HONOUR

For its work in guarding the lines of communication, and in the occupation of Kandahar, the 78th was awarded the Campaign Honour:

AFGHANISTAN 1879-1880

The 78th becomes the 2nd Battalion Seaforth Highlanders – 1881

Under the Army Reforms of 1881 the 78th Highlanders (Ross-shire Buffs) was amalgamated with the 72nd Duke of Albany's Own Highlanders. The 78th became the 2nd Battalion Seaforth Highlanders and the 72nd became the 1st Battalion.

It was a friendly amalgamation, because the 72nd and the 78th shared the origins of being raised by the Mackenzie of Seaforth family. For the 78th there was little change to the arrangements under the Localisation Scheme of 1873. The Depot remained at Fort George, and the territorial area was unchanged, except for the loss of Inverness-shire and Nairn which became the territorial area of The Queen's Own Cameron Highlanders, and the Shetland Islands which went to the Gordon Highlanders. The uniform of the 78th was little affected by the amalgamation, for the Seaforth Highlanders adopted the Mackenzie kilt of the 78th. The 72nd was glad to return to the kilt, which it had lost in 1809. The main concession by the 78th was to change to the yellow facings of the 72nd; but even this was altered in 1899 when the Seaforth Highlanders were allowed to adopt the buff facings of the old 78th.

The name of the new regiment, at first designated 'The Seaforth Highlanders (Ross-shire Buffs), was amended in November 1881 to include the old title of the 72nd, so that the full name became:

SEAFORTH HIGHLANDERS
(ROSS-SHIRE BUFFS, THE DUKE OF ALBANY'S)

4. THE 79th CAMERON HIGHLANDERS FROM 1793 TO 1881

The raising of the 79th (or Cameronian Volunteers) - 1793

On 17th August 1793, Alan Cameron of Erracht was granted the Letter of Service which authorised him to raise the 79th Regiment of Foot, or Cameronian Volunteers. On the same date he was commissioned as Major Commandant of the new regiment.

The barracks of Fort William, where the Lochaber recruits for the 79th mustered in November 1793

After the outbreak of war with the French Republic, Great Britain was expecting an invasion daily, and so the coastal towns of Scotland were garrisoned by Fencible regiments. Fort George, the largest barracks in Scotland, was already occupied by the newly formed 78th Highlanders. As a base for his Headquarters and accommodation for nearly 700 men Erracht chose Stirling. There was a small military barracks in the castle, inns to accommodate the recruits, and it was a conveniently central point at the gateway to the Highlands. It became the first Headquarters of the 79th.

Alan Cameron of Erracht had always intended that his regiment should be the regiment of Clan Cameron, and the main source of recruits was Lochaber, Appin, Mull and North Argyll. Competition for recruits was fierce, because at the time many new Fencible regiments were being raised, but the Recruiting Officer in Lochaber was Erracht's brother Captain Ewen Cameron, and by November 1793 he had assembled at Erracht a complete company of Lochaber men. They were first mustered at the old barracks at Fort William, and marched by the military road to Stirling. As they left Fort William the company piper played the historic tune *'Gabhaidh sinn an rathad mor'* ('We will take the good old way'). As well as the core of Lochaber men, Erracht's recruiting parties gathered recruits from all over the Highlands, from the main cities such as Edinburgh and Glasgow, and the industrial towns where many Highlanders sought work.

By the end of the year Erracht had recruited his full establishment of 654 men, and on 4th January 1794 the 79th paraded in the King's Park at Stirling for inspection by General Leslie, and was passed fit for service. The 79th was the second regiment to be added to the Army's establishment after the outbreak of the French Revolutionary wars, a matter of months after Mackenzie of Seaforth's 78th Highlanders

A sergeant of the 79th in 1794
(From a painting by Douglas N Anderson)

The uniform of the 79th – 1794

The 79th wore the normal uniform of the Highland regiments at the time, with red coatee, white waistcoat, kilt and belted plaid, sporran, red and white hose, and feather bonnets. The facings of the 79th were green.

The most distinctive feature of the 79th was its tartan. By tradition the 79th tartan was designed by Alan Cameron's mother, a Maclean of Drimnin and, although the story of its origin has been lost in time, the tartan is thought to be a variation of a sett which was popular in Lochaber at the time. It has the distinction of being the only military tartan of the time which was not based on the 42nd or Government tartan. The 79th, or Cameron of Erracht tartan, has always been a matter of particular pride to the regiment, and was one of the two tartans used by the Queen's Own Highlanders, the successor regiment to the 79th. Today it is still used by The Highlanders, being worn as the kilt by the pipers and drummers, and as the patch in the Balmoral bonnet by the remainder of the regiment.

The First Stand of Colours, provided by Major Alan Cameron of Erracht, was taken into use at Stirling in January 1794.

The 79th in Ireland – 1794

As soon as the 79th was passed as fit for service, the regiment received marching orders for service in Ireland. Leaving Stirling on 11th January 1794 it marched to Portpatrick and embarked for Belfast. During its five months in Ireland, the issue of uniform and equipment was completed. Service in Ireland had its advantages, for it allowed the regiment to be put on the Irish establishment. This meant an increase in strength to 1000 rank and file, and Major Cameron of Erracht to be promoted to Lieutenant Colonel Commandant.

The 79th in the Netherlands – 1794-1795

In June 1794 the 79th received orders to join the Duke of York's expedition to the Netherlands. Leaving Ireland it moved to Southampton and embarked with other reinforcements. The regiment's first taste of active service was in one of the Britain's less distinguished campaigns. The British and Hanoverian expeditionary force, in coalition with Austrian and Dutch allies, were attempting to contain the expansion of Revolutionary France. But the French defeated the Austrians, and the British force, finding itself isolated in the Netherlands, had to withdraw across Germany and embark at the port of Bremerhaven. It was one of the hardest winters on record, when the cold was so intense that brandy froze in the bottle. The bitter winter weather cost the 79th nearly 200 men.

The threat to draft the 79th – 1795

Having returned from this ordeal in April 1795, the 79th was stationed at Newport, Isle of Wight. The regiment's stay there was short, but memorable for the celebrated contretemps between Colonel Alan Cameron of Erracht and the Commander in Chief, Prince Frederick, Duke of York. On its return from Holland the 79th was under orders to embark for India, when Erracht learned of proposals to draft the 79th to other regiments. Knowing that his Letter of Service gave a specific undertaking that the 79th, if disembodied, should 'not be drafted into any other regiment', he sought an interview with the Commander in Chief. The celebrated exchange went:

Cameron of Erracht: *'To draft the 79th is more than you or your Royal father dare do'.*
Duke of York: *'The King, my father, will certainly send the regiment to the West Indies'.*
Cameron of Erracht: *'You may tell the King, your father, from me, that he may send us to hell if he likes, and I'll go at the head of them, but he daurna' draft us'.*

And so the 79th survived its first brush with Whitehall.

The 79th in the West Indies – 1795-1797

On 10th July 1795 the 79th sailed for Martinique. During the next two years in the West Indies the 79th, like nearly every regiment which served there, was decimated by yellow fever and malaria. Having lost 267 officers and men to tropical disease the regiment fell below effective strength and, despite Erracht's vigorous objections, the General Officer Commanding in the West Indies ordered the 79th to be drafted. Erracht had no option but to send 229 of his men to the 42nd Highlanders and other regiments, while he returned to Great Britain with a cadre of officers, NCOs and drummers to recruit the 79th up to establishment once again.

The 79th in Great Britain – 1797-1798

On his arrival back in London Colonel Cameron of Erracht wasted no time in complaining forcibly to the Commander in Chief about the drafting of his regiment, and demanding that he should be allowed to recruit it up to strength again. On this occasion he had a more sympathetic hearing, for there was pressing need for more regiments to fight the French war. Erracht established his headquarters at Inverness, and was authorised to recruit throughout Britain. Despite intense competition from other Line, Fencible and Militia regiments, he succeeded against all the odds in parading his regiment 780 strong in June 1798. Erracht had lost none of his unrivalled skill as a recruiter. In September 1798 the 79th sailed for garrison duty in Guernsey.

The 79th in the Helder campaign – 1799

In August 1799 the 79th embarked again for active service, joining the Duke of York's Anglo-Russian expeditionary force to attack the French in the Netherlands. The 79th served in Sir John Moore's Brigade. After a hazardous landing on a lee shore, the expedition captured the Dutch fleet and the fortress of Den Helder, but it then ran into difficulty operating over countryside criss-crossed with canals and ditches.

The 79th at the Battle of Egmont op Zee – 1799

The main tactical success of the Helder campaign was a flanking attack by Sir John Moore's brigade along the coastal dune land, which drove the French from a strong position at Egmont op Zee. In this, the 79th's first major engagement, the regiment lost 2 officers and 13 men of the regiment killed, while Erracht himself was badly wounded. But its reputation with the Commander in Chief was fully restored, and the 79th earned particular praise from the Duke of York for its gallant conduct.

A soldier of the 79th Highlanders
in Holland, 1799
(From a painting by Major J. W. Van Oorschot)

79th BATTLE HONOUR

For its part in the Helder campaign and the Battle of Egmont op Zee the 79th was awarded the battle honour:
EGMONT OP ZEE

The 79th in the raids against the Spanish ports – 1800

On its return to England in late October the 79th was quartered at Chelmsford, and from April 1800 on the Isle of Wight. The regiment's next active service was in August 1800, when it joined an expedition to attack the Spanish arsenals at Ferrol and Cadiz. In the event the attack on Ferrol was abandoned, and Cadiz surrendered before the force could attack, and the 79th were eventually landed in Malta.

The 79th in the campaign in Egypt – 1801

In 1798 Napoleon had landed a French force in Egypt with the object of establishing a base for the conquest of India. But his fleet was located by the British fleet under Admiral Nelson and destroyed at Aboukir Bay. Napoleon returned to France, abandoning his army in Egypt. In 1801 an expedition commanded by Sir Ralph Abercromby was sent to attack the marooned French army. After the confusion which had occurred during the landing in Holland in 1799, the operation was prepared with great thoroughness, and the fleet and the troops trained and rehearsed the beach landing at Marmorice Bay in Turkey. The practice paid off for, despite heavy French fire, the brigades and regiments were landed in the correct order. During the advance on Alexandria the 79th fought a successful engagement with the French near Aboukir. The regiment took part in the battle of Alexandria, which led to the fall of Cairo and the surrender of the French army

79th BATTLE HONOUR

For its part in the Campaign in Egypt in 1801 the 79th was awarded the Battle Honour:

EGYPT

The 79th was also granted the **'Sphinx superscribed Egypt'** as a device to be borne on the Colours.

The 79th in Minorca and the United Kingdom – 1801-1807

After leaving Egypt, the 79th spent six months in Minorca, which was at the time a British possession. In 1802 it returned to Scotland, and spent six months recruiting in Dundee before moving to Ireland in early 1803. After nearly two years of peace keeping operations and the unpopular duty of confiscating illicit whiskey stills, the 79th moved to Kent in December 1805. While there the 79th paraded on 9th January 1806 at St Paul's Cathedral, London, for the funeral of Admiral Lord Nelson, who had been killed at the battle of Trafalgar.

During 1806-1807 the regiment was stationed in Essex at Colchester, Weeley and Harwich. A sad accident occurred on 18th April 1807 when a sailing ship carrying a company of the regiment capsized at Harwich with the loss of 60 officers and men, and their families which were travelling with them.

The 79th redesignated – 1804 and 1806

The original designation of the regiment, the '79th or Cameronian Volunteers', was certainly not Alan Cameron of Erracht's choice of name. It was probably a clerical mistake made at the War Office. In 1804 the name of the regiment was changed to the '79th Cameronian Highlanders', and two years later, apparently at the request of both the 79th and the 26th Foot (The Cameronians), the 79th was redesignated 'The 79th Cameron Highlanders'.

2nd Battalion 79th – 1804-18

In 1804, when a French invasion of Great Britain seemed imminent, and the Line regiments were stretched to their limits in India and the colonies, the government authorised a number of regiments to raise 2nd battalions. These had the dual commitments of home defence against invasion, and of acting as 'feeder' battalions for their regiments overseas. The 2nd Battalion 79th was raised at Stirling during 1804 – 1805, and its first Commanding Officer was Lieutenant Colonel Phillips Cameron, 22 years old and the eldest son of Colonel Alan Cameron of Erracht. The 2nd/79th served in Great Britain, supplying drafts to the 1st Battalion abroad on active service in the Peninsular War and in Belgium. When the Napoleonic wars ended after the Battle of Waterloo, the 2nd/79th was disbanded in August 1815. Its last Commanding Officer was Lieutenant Colonel Nathaniel Cameron, Sir Alan Cameron of Erracht's second son.

The 1st/79th at the Siege of Copenhagen – 1807

In 1807 Napoleon and Czar Alexander of Russia met at Tilsit and agreed that France and Russia, with the involuntary alliance of Austria, Denmark and Portugal, would impose a trade embargo against Britain. The Danish fleet was to be used by the French to enforce the blockade. The British government reacted quickly and, before the French could seize the Danish fleet, an expedition was sent to secure it and occupy Zealand. The 1st/79th embarked at Harwich in July to join Lord Cathcart's expedition. After a three day siege Copenhagen surrendered and the Danish fleet was taken. The 79th was billeted in the citadel at Copenhagen, sailing back to Great Britain in November 1807 on board the commandeered Danish ships.

The 1st/79th in the expedition to Sweden – 1808

The 1st/79th took part in a brief expedition to Sweden in May 1808, but the army was not ordered to land, and the battalion returned to Portsmouth.

The 1st/79th in Portugal – 1808

The 79th's first long campaign was the Peninsular War, where it established its lasting reputation as a reliable and courageous fighting regiment. The French had invaded Portugal in 1807, and occupied Lisbon. Next year Napoleon deposed the King of Spain and gave the throne to his own brother Joseph Bonaparte. Lieutenant General Sir Arthur Wellesley (later the Duke of Wellington) was sent to Portugal with a British force in 1808. Landing north of Lisbon, he fought the skilful defensive battle of Vimiero which forced the French to withdraw from Lisbon. The 1st/79th, which was still embarked en route for Portugal at the time of the battle of Vimiero, joined Wellesley's army in Lisbon.

On arriving in Lisbon Colonel Alan Cameron of Erracht was appointed to command a brigade, and after 15 years in command he handed over the 1st Battalion to his eldest son Lieutenant Colonel Phillips Cameron.

The 1st/79th at the Battle of Corunna – 1809

After the Convention of Cintra, the peace agreement which followed Wellesley's victory at Vimiero, General Sir John Moore was appointed Commander in Chief of the British forces in the Peninsula. In 1809 he advanced from Lisbon into Spain with 20,000 troops, including the 1st/79th. His plan was to cooperate with the Spanish armies in attacking the long lines of communication of the French armies in the Peninsula. But the Spanish troops were no match for the French, and Moore his force, surrounded and outnumbered, were forced to withdraw. Having retreated through the Galicia mountains in bitter December weather, the British force was evacuated by the fleet at Corunna, although Sir John Moore himself was killed during the rearguard action. The 79th earned particular praise for having maintained its discipline and efficiency throughout the operation.

79th BATTLE HONOUR

For its part in the Battle of Corunna the 79th was awarded the Battle Honour:

CORUNNA

The 1st/79th in the Walcheren Expedition – 1809

The 1st/79th returned from Corunna in February 1809. Stationed at Weeley in Essex, the battalion suffered much from fever and sickness. In July it was sent to Holland to join the Earl of Chatham's army which was to attack Antwerp. But after two months in Walcheren, the British Force was so badly affected by Walcheren fever (a form of malaria) that, with its strength reduced by over a quarter, it had to be withdrawn. The 79th were fortunate enough to avoid the sickness which affected most of the rest of the army.

The Detachment of the 79th at the Battle of Talavera – 1809

On his return to Portugal in April 1809 to resume command of the British and Portuguese army, Sir Arthur Wellesley took the offensive against the three French armies in the Peninsula. First he advanced north, crossed the River Douro, and drove Marshal Soult's army out of Oporto. He then moved south, joined up with the allied Spanish army, and defeated Marshal Victor and the French at Talavera. Wellesley's army included a 'Battalion of Detachments' comprising the sick who had been left in Lisbon by their regiments when Moore had advanced into Spain in 1808. It included 5 officers and 49 men of the 79th, and this detachment fought under Sir Arthur Wellesley at the battle of Talavera on 28th July 1809. Brigadier General Alan Cameron of Erracht was also present at Talavera, commanding a brigade in the 1st Division. (Note. Sir Arthur Wellesley was created Viscount Wellington after the victory of Talavera).

The 1st/79th in the defence of Cadiz – 1810

In January 1810 the 1st/79th returned to Portugal. Having disembarked at Lisbon it was quickly reembarked with Sir Thomas Graham's force, and sent to the relief of Cadiz, under siege by the French army of Marshal Victor. The 79th took part in the defensive operations which saved Cadiz from capture.

The 1st/79th at the Battle of Busaco – 1810

When the 1st/79th returned from Cadiz to Lisbon, Wellington was planning the remarkable operations of the Defence of Portugal. The battalion rejoined the army blocking the French advance by the northern route through Ciudad Rodrigo. Wellington had selected several possible defensive positions on the routes back to Lisbon, and the one he chose to hold was the steep 1,800 foot ridge at Busaco.

The 79th formed part of Sir Brent Spencer's 1st Division which held the centre of the British line. Drawn up on the reverse of the ridge, with picquets posted on the forward slope, it awaited the French advance. The French advance on 27th September came in two columns which assaulted the left and right of Wellington's position on the ridge. The 1st Division in the centre of the ridge escaped the main impact of the French attack. The 79th had one picquet overrun but held its ground without difficulty.

By his tactical skill in choosing to defend the Busaco ridge, described as 'one of the best defensive positions in Europe', Wellington brought the French offensive to a halt. His troops were then able to retire to the security of the prepared defensive positions, the Lines of Torres Vedras

79th BATTLE HONOUR

For its part at the Battle of Busaco in 1810 the 79th was granted the Battle Honour:

BUSACO

The 1st/79th in the Lines of Torres Vedras – 1810-1811

Wellington's army now withdrew to the security of the the Lines of Torres Vedras, the three lines of defences protecting the port of Lisbon, which had been constructed in great secrecy during the previous year. The 79th reached the Lines by 8th October 1810. The 50 miles of fortifications, with 50 forts, 152 redoubts and 600 guns, proved impregnable to the French. After a month of frustration they withdrew 25 miles north, the 79th taking part in a follow-up operation to Cartaxo. The battalion then remained in the Lines for the winter.

After a miserable winter of starvation outside the Lines of Torres Vedras, the French withdrew from Portugal in March 1811. Wellington's army followed up the retreat, and the Light Company of the 79th had a sharp engagement with Ney's rearguard at Foz d'Aronce.

The 1st/79th at the Battle of Fuentes d'Onor – 1811

In April 1811 the British re-entered Spain, but further progress was impossible while the French still held the frontier fortresses of Almeida, Ciudad Rodrigo, and Badajoz. Wellington had started investing Almeida, when Marshal Massena's army marched from Ciudad Rodrigo to relieve the garrison.

Abandoning the siege Wellington deployed his army to block the route of the French advance into Portugal. He selected a position on the reverse slope of a ridge overlooking, and protected by, the River Dos Casas. At the centre of the position was the village of Fuentes D'Onor. It lay on the forward slope, astride the main road from Ciudad Rodrigo which formed the French axis. Wellington correctly anticipated that the French would launch a frontal attack against the village, and made it the strong point of his defence. It was a maze of low, stone houses with walled yards and gardens, ideal for defence by sharpshooters, and Wellington held it with 2,260 men from the 28 Light companies of his infantry regiments.

An officer of the 79th Cameron Highlanders
(From a print published by W. Heath)

On 3rd May the French launched a massive frontal attack up the main road, with eight divisions As the Light companies were pushed back through the village by overwhelming numbers, Wellington sent in his reserve, the 79th and 71st Highlanders, who recaptured the village by nightfall.

After a day of reconnaissance, the French advanced again on 5th May, attempting to outflank the Allied line. Wellington had to deploy much of his reserve to secure the rear of his position, leaving the village of Fuentes d'Onor held by the 79th and 71st. In the afternoon the French switched their main attack back to the village, and 18 French battalions attempted to force the position. But in what was some of the heaviest fighting the regiment experienced in the Peninsular war, the 79th and 71st, supported by the 74th Highlanders and the 88th Connaught Rangers, charged and counter attacked repeatedly, and the village remained in Allied hands. Fuentes D'Onor cost the 79th 287 casualties, including its Commanding Officer Lieutenant Colonel Phillips Cameron, Erracht's eldest son. But it was certainly its most distinguished action of the long campaign, and where the 79th made its mark as a great regiment.

79th BATTLE HONOUR

For its part in the Battle of Fuentes d'Onor the 79th was awarded the Battle Honour:

FUENTES D'ONOR

The 1st/79th at the Battle of Salamanca – 1812

The casualties at Fuentes d'Onor, followed by several bad outbreaks of dysentery and fever, reduced the 1st/79th to such low strength that it did not take part in further operations until reinforced by drafts from the 2nd Battalion. By June 1812 the three frontier fortresses had fallen, and the 1st/79th marched with Wellington's army into Northern Spain. On 22 July 1812, after weeks of manoeuvring, Wellington succeeded in catching Marshal Marmont's French army deployed on the march near Salamanca. In one of the most brilliant opportunist attacks ever made, he inflicted a most decisive defeat. The 1st Division, which included the 79th, were deployed on a flank, and only lightly engaged. In August 1812 Wellington's army entered Madrid and were welcomed as heroes by the Spanish, the 79th being billeted in the Escurial palace

79th BATTLE HONOUR

For its part in the Battle of Salamanca the 79th was awarded the Battle Honour:

SALAMANCA

The 1st/79th at the Siege of Burgos – 1812

The next French stronghold to block the Allied advance was the fortress of Burgos. It comprised a strongly prepared hill-top keep, with two lines of defences, occupied by a garrison of 2,000, with adequate weapons and lavish reserves of ammunition and supplies. On an adjacent hill 200 yards away was a strong hornwork which covered the approach to the fortress. Although critically short of siege artillery and ammunition, Wellington invested Burgos on 19th September.

There was an early success when a Light battalion made up from the Light companies of five regiments including the 79th, and commanded by Major the Hon Charles Cocks of the 79th, managed to seize the hornwork by escalade. But although three breaches were made in the outer defences of the main stronghold, the lack of siege artillery, and of trained sappers and miners prevented further progress. Wellington finally abandoned the siege on 21st October. The fighting at Burgos cost the 79th 125 casualties, including the gallant Major Cocks who was killed on 8th October.

The 1st/79th at the Battles of the Pyrenees – 1813

After spending the winter of 1812-1813 in the security of Portugal, the Allied army advanced into Spain again. On 21st June 1813 Wellington inflicted an overwhelming defeat on the French at Vitoria (where the 6th Division, including the 79th, were not engaged, being detached to protect the newly established supply route through the ports on the north coast of Spain). Marshal Soult then withdrew the survivors of the French armies over the Pyrenees into France. On 28th July 1813, as Wellington tackled the two remaining French strongholds in Spain at San Sebastian and Pamplona, Marshal Soult's combined French army counter-attacked across the Pyrenees in a desperate attempt to relieve the garrison at San Sebastian.

The 79th Cameron Highlanders in 1813
(A print by W. Heath, from a sketch by Captain Unett RA, published by T. McLean)

The 79th was at Lanz with the 6th Division, having marched to intercept the French General Clausel's Corps. The division was hastily redeployed by Wellington, and sent to reinforce General Cole's 4th Division at the village of Sorauren. After a forced march through the mountains it took up a blocking position at Oricain on 28th July, arriving just in time to check the French attack. On 30th July Wellington counter attacked, and the 79th took part in clearing the enemy out of Sorauren. The French attacks had failed, and they withdrew into France.

79th BATTLE HONOUR

For its part at the Battle of Sorauren, in the Battles of the Pyrenees, the 79th was awarded the Battle Honour:

PYRENEES

The 1st/79th at the Battle of the Nivelle – 1813

Having defeated Soult's counter attack and captured San Sebastian, Wellington was ready to enter France. By September 1813 the political circumstances were favourable, and Napoleon faced the alliance of the three main continental powers, Russia, Prussia and Austria, on his eastern frontiers. Wellington's plan was to cross the River Bidassoa near the coast, to capture the French positions on the Greater Rhune, and to open up the French port of St Jean de Luz for resupply.

During the crossing of the Bidassoa on 7th October 1813 the role of the 6th Division, including the 79th, was to keep the French occupied at the passes over the Pyrenees. In the attack on the French lines on 10th November 1813 the 79th crossed the frontier over the pass of Maya, and took part in the assault on the French lines on the River Nivelle, earning praise from General Sir Rowland Hill for its steady advance under fire.

79th BATTLE HONOUR

For its part in the Battle of the River Nivelle the 79th was awarded the Battle Honour:

NIVELLE

The 1st/79th at the Battle of the River Nive – 1813

Having been driven out of the Peninsula, Marshal Soult concentrated his armies in the strong fortress of Bayonne and along the River Nive. Wellington planned to close on Bayonne from the east and south, forcing the French to evacuate the city. The eastern advance was to be astride the River Nive. On 9th December 1813 the 6th Division, including the 79th, crossed the Nive on a pontoon bridge near Ustarits, and advanced on Bayonne. During the three days of fighting the 79th took part in clearing the French positions south east of Bayonne, and in checking Marshal Soult's counter attack at St Pierre.

79th BATTLE HONOUR

For its part in the Battle of the River Nive the 79th was awarded the Battle Honour:

NIVE

The 1st/79th at the Battle of Toulouse – 1814

The 1st/79th spent two months outside Bayonne, and received much needed supplies of clothing and equipment which arrived at St Jean de Luz. The regiment rejoined the 6th Division as Wellington advanced from his victory at Orthes and closed in on Marshal Soult at Toulouse. In the final battle of the Peninsular War Wellington's army had to cross the River Garonne and attack a town which was well fortified, but had a tactical weakness in the long 600 foot high Calvinet ridge which dominated the town. The 6th Division was given the task of attacking this key part of the defences.

The 79th with the 42nd and 91st Highlanders formed Sir Denis Pack's Highland Brigade which assaulted the flank of the French positions on the Calvinet ridge on 10th April 1814. In what was one of the most distinguished actions of the campaign the Highland Brigade charged and captured the French redoubts of 'La Colombette' and 'Le Tour des Augustins', and then held them against determined counter attacks. The 79th lost 233 casualties and it was particularly commended in Wellington's despatch.

Next day, as Wellington entered Toulouse, news arrived from Paris of Napoleon's abdication two weeks earlier on 30th March 1814. The battle had been fought after peace had been declared.

79th BATTLE HONOURS

For its part in the capture of Toulouse, and for its service in the Peninsular campaign, the 79th was awarded the Battle Honours:

TOULOUSE
PENINSULA

The 1st/79th in Ireland – 1814-1815

In July 1814, after five years of active service in the Peninsula, the 79th sailed for Ireland. It was stationed at Cork until it embarked for North America in January 1815. However fate intervened when the transport ships were driven back by gales, and the 79th returned to Belfast. Before the fleet was ready to sail again the move, was overtaken by the news that Napoleon Bonaparte had escaped from exile in Elba on 26th February, and was already in Paris. Instead of moving to America, the 79th left Ireland for the Netherlands in May 1815.

Napoleon's last campaign – 1815

The first two Allied armies in the field against Napoleon were the Duke of Wellington's British, Dutch, Belgian and German force, which he assembled in the Netherlands, and Marshal Blucher's Prussians. Further afield, Russian, Austrian and Spanish armies were also on the march. Napoleon took the offensive without delay, advancing north east from Paris with the aim of engaging and defeating Wellington's and Blucher's armies in turn. When news of Napoleon's advance reached Wellington in Brussels, his army was still widely dispersed in the garrison towns of the Netherlands. There followed a rapid concentration of the army to meet the French as they crossed the frontier south of Charleroi and advanced up the axis of the Brussels road.

The 1st/79th at Quatre Bras – 1815

The 1st/79th, in quarters at Brussels, formed part of Sir James Kempt's Brigade in Sir Thomas Picton's 5th Division, and was among the first British troops in action. At 10 pm on 15th June the 79th was put at immediate notice to march, and the regiment assembled on the Place Royale at midnight. By daybreak on 16th June it was on the march, and at 3 pm reached the cross-roads of Quatre Bras, 22 miles south of Brussels, where Picton's Division had been ordered to take up a blocking position astride the Brussels to Charleroi road. Meanwhile, five miles to the east at Ligny, Napoleon's main force was already attacking the Prussians.

On reaching Quatre Bras the 79th with Sir James Kempt's brigade deployed immediately, occupying a position in the fields south of the Namur road and extending the left of the Allied line. The attack by the French left wing under Marshal Ney had already begun, and for the next six hours the 79th was under continuous fire from skirmishers and charges by French cavalry. In this critical preliminary to the Battle of Waterloo the regiment suffered 27 killed and 277 wounded, being reduced to almost half its effective fighting strength. But the success of the British and Dutch troops in halting Ney's advance gained time for Wellington to concentrate his army at the ridge nine miles further north where he intended to stop the French.

The 1st/79th at Waterloo – 1815

Next day Wellington broke contact with the French at Quatre Bras and withdrew to his chosen position on the ridge of Mont St Jean, two miles south of the village of Waterloo. Here the survivors of Quatre Bras were joined by the rest of the Allied army. The 79th, in Kempt's Brigade of Sir Thomas Picton's Division, was sited on the east side of the main Brussels-Charleroi road, in the centre of the Allied line. The army had withdrawn from Quatre Bras in heavy rain, and spent the night of 17th-18th June in miserable bivouac on the ridge at Mont St Jean. The French opened the battle of Waterloo shortly before noon on 18th June 1815 with an attack on Hougoumont farm, the strongpoint securing the right of the Allied line. They followed this at 1 pm with a heavy artillery bombardment by a Grand Battery of 80 guns. The 79th, lying down on the reverse slope, allowed the cannon balls to pass harmlessly overhead.

The 79th were first involved at about 2 pm when the French infantry attacked the centre and left of the Allied position in Columns of Battalions. When Picton ordered his Division up to the crest of the hill to meet them, the 79th waited behind the hedge along the lateral road on the ridge line of Mont St Jean. As the massed columns approached, the 79th pushed through the hedge in line. Having engaged the French with a devastating volley at close range, it followed up with a bayonet charge which sent the column reeling back down the hill in disorder. The routed French infantry were then charged by the Union Brigade, the British heavy cavalry, which pushed through the gaps in Picton's Division and ploughed downhill over the heavy clay into the bewildered French battalions.

Piper Kenneth Mackay at the Battle of Waterloo
(From the painting by Lockhart Bogle)

But General Picton had been killed by a musket shot during this action, and his Division was now heavily attacked by the French cuirassiers. The 79th, having formed square, succeeded in regaining its position on the ridge under fierce cavalry attack. At this moment of intense enemy pressure occurred one of the best known incidents of individual heroism at Waterloo when Piper Kenneth Mackay, of the Grenadier company of the 79th, stepped outside the security of the regimental square playing the ancient rallying tune *'Cogadh no Sith'* ('War or Peace-the Gathering of the Clans'), to encourage the hard-pressed 79th.

The Allied line held against successive assaults by the French cavalry and finally the Imperial Guard, until in the late afternoon the Prussian army reached the field from Ligny. The French, having narrowly failed to break through Wellington's line, were now attacked in the flank by the Prussians. At about 8.15 pm Wellington was able to give the order for the Allied line to advance, and the French retreated before it.

The 79th, in the centre of the Allied line, had held their ground throughout the day, but at heavy cost. The regiment was reduced to just over 200 strong, and the senior unwounded officer was Lieutenant Alexander Cameron, a nephew of Sir Alan Cameron of Erracht.

He led the 79th off the field of Waterloo, and that night it bivouacked at the farm of La Belle Alliance, where Wellington and Blucher met after the battle. Out of the 675 officers and men of the 79th who had left Brussels two days earlier, 456 were casualties, of whom 103 were killed. But there was particular praise for the 79th from the Duke of Wellington. Together with the 42nd and 92nd Highlanders and the 28th Foot, it shared the distinction of being one of the four infantry regiments mentioned specifically in his Waterloo despatch.

79th BATTLE HONOUR

For its part in the Battles of Quatre Bras and Waterloo, on 16 and 18th June 1815, the 79th was awarded the Battle Honour:

WATERLOO

The 1st79th in France – 1815-1818

After the Battle of Waterloo the 1st/79th marched to Paris where it formed part of the Allied Army of Occupation. It was brought up to strength with drafts from the 2nd Battalion, before the 2nd/79th was disbanded in December 1815.

On the 79th's return from the Peninsula War in 1814 its First Stand of Colours was in such bad condition after the rigours of the campaign that a new set was ordered. When the 79th was sent to Brussels, the new Colours were not ready, and so the 1st Battalion carried the Colours of the 2nd/79th at Waterloo. The 1st/79th received its Second Stand of Colours in Paris in 1815. The 79th was among the regiments on parade for a series of Reviews by the Emperor of Austria, the Emperor of Russia, the King of Prussia, and the Dukes of Kent, Cambridge and Wellington.

The 79th in England and the Channel Islands – 1818-1820

The 79th remained in France for three years until October 1818, when it returned to England and was stationed in Chichester. In March 1819 it moved to the Channel Islands, the companies being split up between Jersey, Guernsey and Alderney.

The 79th in Ireland – 1820-1825

The 79th moved to Ireland in May 1820 and spent five years of duties in aid of the civil power, including two turbulent years in Limerick. During the visit of King George IV to Dublin in 1821 the 79th was brigaded with the 42nd, 78th and 93rd to form a Highland Brigade. (The only other kilted regiment in the army, the 92nd, was abroad in Jamaica).

The 79th in Canada – 1825-1836

In 1825 the 79th sailed for Canada , arriving at Quebec in October. Moving to Montreal in 1828, it received its Third Stand of Colours on the Champs de Mars on 18th June -Waterloo Day- 1828. Next year it moved to Kingston, providing detachments for the garrison of Fort Henry. In 1831 it moved again to Toronto, and finally returned to Quebec in 1833, where it remained until returning to Scotland in 1836.

The 79th in Great Britain – 1836-1840

In October 1836 the 79th landed in Glasgow, moving to Edinburgh in 1837 and to Dublin in 1838. During the period of industrial unrest caused by the Chartist rioters in 1839-1840, the regiment was sent for duty in aid of the civil power in the manufacturing towns of the north of England .

An officer of the 79th Cameron Highlanders with his family, C 1835.
(From a painting by William Kidd RSA)

The 79th in Gibraltar – 1841-1848

The 79th left Great Britain for Gibraltar in December 1840 under the acting command of Major the Hon Lauderdale Maule, who succeeded to command of the regiment in 1842. The 79th was to spend six-and-a-half years in garrison at Gibraltar, an uneventful era of peace among the European powers, and a period of unprecedented regimental stability and prestige. Colonel Maule was a powerful and respected commanding officer whose absorbing interest was the quality and appearance of his regiment. He had a deserved reputation as a man of influence in the Army, and his brother Captain the Hon Fox Maule (later 11th Earl of Dalhousie) was a prominent politician and became Secretary at War in 1846.

During his 10 years in command, Colonel the Hon Lauderdale Maule made many improvements to the uniform of the 79th. New bonnet badges, accoutrements, sporrans, sgian dubhs, and dirks were introduced. Many of his innovations were followed by other regiments, including the Glengarry bonnet, the green tunics of the pipers, and the red and green hose which replaced the universal red and white.

The 79th in Canada – 1848-1851

In 1848 the 79th sailed for Canada, its departure being commemorated by Pipe Major John Macdonald's famous pipe tune, 'The 79th's Farewell to Gibraltar'. The regiment's arrival in Canada was less auspicious, for the transport ship Lady Cremorne, carrying most of the mess plate, was wrecked in the St Lawrence river. The 79th spent three years in Quebec, returning to Scotland in 1851.

A Piper of the 79th Cameron Highlanders, 1853
(From a painting by Eugene Lami,
in the Victoria and Albert Museum)

An Ensign, 79th Cameron Highlanders, 1853   *A Corporal, 79th Cameron Highlanders, 1853*
(From paintings by Eugene Lami, in the Victoria and Albert Museum)

The 79th in Great Britain – 1851-1854

The 79th returned to Stirling in September 1851, and early the following year moved to Edinburgh Castle. On 18th November 1852 a representative party attended the funeral of the Duke of Wellington in London. The regiment took part in the Camp of Exercise at Chobham of 1853, the first major peacetime manoeuvres held by the army in Great Britain.

The 79th moves to the Crimea – 1854

When war with Russia broke out in 1854, the 79th was at Portsmouth. The Fourth Stand of Colours was taken into use at Portsmouth shortly before embarking for Turkey. In June 1854 the regiment joined Sir Colin Campbell's Highland Brigade at Varna in Bulgaria, together with the 42nd and 93rd Highlanders. After a couple of months at Varna the British and French allied army embarked for the Crimea, landing at Kalamita Bay on 14th September 1854.

The 79th at the Battle of the Alma – 1854

After landing in the Crimea the army marched on the city and port of Sevastopol. The first Russian troops encountered in any strength were holding strong hill top positions behind the River Alma. On 20th September 1854 the Allied army carried out a frontal assault on the heights of Alma. There was little attempt at tactical manoeuvre. On the left of the line the Highland Brigade, having waded the River Alma under heavy artillery fire, fought its way up to the crest of the hill where it charged the Russian in their redoubts with the bayonet. The Russians retreated in confusion, and the steadiness of the British regiments won the day.

79th BATTLE HONOUR

For its part in the Battle of the Alma the 79th was awarded the Battle Honour:

ALMA

The 79th in the Crimea – 1854-1856

Having by-passed Sevastopol, the Allied army occupied the port of Balaclava as a base for its operations. The main aim of the British, French, Turkish and Sardinian Allies was to capture the strongly fortified Russian port of Sevastopol, and for a year they conducted a costly and often disheartening siege. The 79th took its turn in the trenches and held positions round Balaclava, until Sevastopol eventually fell on 8th September 1855. In May 1855 the regiment took part in the expedition to capture the towns of Kertch and Yenikale.

Like every regiment in the campaign the 79th suffered from outbreaks of cholera while at Varna and in the Crimea, and from the hardships of the Russian winter during 1854-55. The extent of the epidemics and the harsh conditions is highlighted by the fact that, of 367 Cameron Highlanders who died in the war, only nine died as a result of enemy action.

79th BATTLE HONOUR

For its part in the Siege of Sevastopol the 79th was awarded the Battle Honour:

SEVASTOPOL

The 79th returns to Great Britain – 1856

On its return from the Crimea in June 1856, the 79th was reviewed by Queen Victoria at Aldershot. The regiment was then stationed at Dover with its former comrades of the Highland Brigade, the 42nd and the 93rd, and in June 1857 moved to Dublin.

The 79th moves to India – 1857

When the Indian Mutiny broke out, the 79th was quickly brought up to strength with drafts from other regiments, and sailed for India with 1000 rank and file. Arriving at Calcutta in November 1857 the 79th marched to Allahabad in December. Its first brush with the mutineers was in January 1858 when it attacked their position at

Secundragunge, killing or capturing 600 rebels without loss. Next month the regiment moved to Cawnpore, and then joined Sir James Outram's force at the Alam Bagh position outside Lucknow.

The 79th in the final capture of Lucknow – 1858

The operations to recapture Lucknow began on 4th March 1858, under General Sir Colin Campbell, the Commander in Chief. The 79th, in the 3rd Division with Sir John Outram's Force, carried out a flanking attack, crossing the river Gumti and advancing up the north bank, while the main force advanced through the outskirts of Lucknow itself. The 79th attacked a series of rebel-held positions, and finally crossed over the river on a bridge of casks and recaptured the abandoned Residency. It took nearly two weeks of continuous fighting to clear the enemy positions and, in the attack on the last rebel stronghold in the outlying Musa Bagh, the 79th captured the Colours of the 7th Oude Irregular Infantry.

79th BATTLE HONOUR

For its part in the Recapture of Lucknow the 79th was awarded the Battle Honour:

LUCKNOW

The 79th at the capture of Bareilly – 1858

After the fall of Lucknow, the 79th joined the Rohilkand Field Force under Sir Colin Campbell which advanced up the River Ganges in pursuit of the Sepoy mutineers. In the capture of Bareilly in May 1858 the Highland Brigade, consisting of the 42nd, 79th and 93rd Highlanders formed the first line of the attack.

The 79th in the later stages of the Indian Mutiny Campaign – 1858-1859

The 79th fought several further engagements, including the relief of Shahjahanpore, before spending the hottest part of the summer at Cawnpore. In the final stages of the campaign the 79th's actions included the storming of Rampore Kussia, the crossing of the River Gogra, the capture of Baubasia and Bundwa Kote.

The 79th in India after the Indian Mutiny – 1859-1871

The Indian Mutiny campaign ended in January 1859, but the 79th continued on foreign service, remaining on garrison duty in India until 1871. The subsequent stations of the regiment included Mean Meer (1859), Ferozepore (1861), Nowshera (1862), Peshawar (1862), Rawalpindi (1864), Roorkee (1866), Delhi (1869), Kamptee (1869-1871). The 79th sent four companies to operate on the North West Frontier during disturbances in 1863-64. The main enemy of garrison life in India was fever, from which the 79th lost 336 officers and men during their 13 years in India.

The 79th returns to Great Britain – 1871

On its return to Great Britain in 1871, the 79th was stationed for two years at Parkhurst, Isle of Wight. During this period Queen Victoria was in residence at Osborne nearby, and the 79th frequently provided Guards of Honour and ceremonial duties for the Royal Household. Her

The officers of the 79th Cameron Highlanders at Rawalpindi in India, 1864.

Majesty held the 79th in particular affection, and on 17th April 1873 she presented the 79th with its Fifth Stand of Colours at Parkhurst.

The 79th redesignated The 79th Queen's Own Cameron Highlanders – 1873

In July 1873 Queen Victoria commanded that the regiment should be designated 'The 79th Queen's Own Cameron Highlanders'. The green facings of the 79th, as a Royal regiment, were changed to blue, and it was permitted to bear in the centre of the Regimental Colour the 'Thistle ensigned with the Imperial Crown'; being the Royal Badge of Scotland as sanctioned by Queen Anne in 1707. The badge formed the central part of the badge of the Queen's Own Highlanders, which remains the badge of The Highlanders today.

The 42nd and 79th Depot at Perth – 1873-1881

Under the Localisation Scheme of 1873, the 79th was linked with the 42nd Royal Highlanders. The joint recruiting area, designated No 57 Sub-District, consisted of the counties of Perthshire, Kincardine and Forfarshire, and the two regiments shared No 57 Brigade Depot at Perth. The role of the home service battalion was to keep the foreign service battalion up to strength by providing drafts of reinforcements as necessary. When the 42nd was sent at short notice to join General Wolseley's operations on the Gold Coast in 1873, the 79th supplied a draft of 132 volunteers to bring it up to strength during the Ashanti Campaign.

The 79th in Great Britain – 1871-1879

After two years at Parkhurst, the 79th moved to Aldershot in 1873. During the summer manoeuvres of 1874 the regiment was brigaded with the 42nd, 78th and 93rd Highlanders, and there was a friendly reunion for the veterans of the Indian Mutiny campaign who were still serving. The 79th moved to Edinburgh Castle in 1875, to Fort George in 1876 , and to Glasgow in 1878. During this period the regiment provided the Royal Guard at Ballater in 1876, 1877 and 1878.

The 79th in Gibraltar – 1879-82

On returning to foreign service the 79th sailed for Gibraltar in 1879, where it relieved its linked regiment, the 42nd Royal Highlanders. The regiment was stationed there when the proposals for reorganising the infantry were announced, and took effect from 1st July 1881.

The Army Reforms of 1881

Under the Army Reforms of 1881 the infantry of the Line was reorganised into two battalion regiments. The regiments numbered from the 1st to the 25th Foot already had two battalions, and those from the 26th onward were amalgamated in pairs. It was proposed that the 79th, being designated the 'Queen's Own', should become Household troops by amalgamating the regiment with the Scots Guards. But thanks to the personal intervention of Queen Victoria, her Cameron Highlanders were spared this fate, and the 79th remained a single battalion infantry regiment. (A second battalion was subsequently raised in 1897).

Under the Reforms of 1881 the Cameron Highlanders were allocated a territorial area comprising the counties of Inverness and Nairn, with a Depot at Inverness. The construction of this Depot had started in 1876 when it was planned to form the Inverness and Ross Regiment from the 71st and 78th Highlanders. The buildings now became Cameron Barracks, the Depot of The Queen's Own Cameron Highlanders. From 1881, until the completion of Cameron Barracks in 1886, the Regimental Depot of The Cameron Highlanders was accommodated at Fort George with the Depot Seaforth Highlanders.

Under the 1881 Reforms the old regimental numbers were discontinued, and so the 79th became:

THE QUEEN'S OWN CAMERON HIGHLANDERS

5. THE DEPOTS BEFORE 1881

The Depot companies and battalions 1854-1870

Until the Crimean War of 1854-1856, an infantry regiment did not have a permanent base or depot in Great Britain, and there were no permanent territorial links with districts or counties. When a regiment was sent on foreign service it divided into two parts. The Service companies went abroad, and the Depot companies remained in Great Britain or Ireland to recruit and to train reinforcements for the Service companies. The Depot companies at home were given normal military roles, such as garrison duty or aid to the civil power. In 1854, to improve the system of training and recruiting during the Crimean War, the Depot companies of regiments were grouped together, several to each industrial town. After the war ended this centralisation was taken a stage further by the formation of Depot battalions. For example the Depot battalion at Aberdeen in 1863 comprised the Depot companies of the 42nd, 71st, 72nd, 78th, 79th, 92nd, and 93rd Highlanders: all the Highland regiments which existed at the time.

Depots attached to Home Service battalions – 1870-1873

In 1870 the Depot battalions were replaced by a system of pairing, under which the Depot companies of regiments overseas were attached to regiments at home. The 72nd stationed at Cork, had the Depot companies of the 71st attached; the 78th stationed in Canada left its Depot companies with the 93rd in Aberdeen; and the 79th stationed in India left its Depot companies with the 42nd in Aldershot.

The Localisation Scheme of 1873-1881

Under the Localisation Scheme of 1873, 70 infantry regimental Sub-Districts were formed. Each Sub-District comprised a county or group of counties, worked out on county population figures, and it was required to recruit enough men to sustain two linked line regiments. The military establishment of each Sub-District included a permanent Brigade Depot, with two skeleton companies from each of its two line regiments. The Brigade Depot also included the Headquarters and permanent staff of the local Militia regiments, and the Rifle Volunteer battalions came under its command. The three Sub-Districts which included antecedent regiments of the Queen's Own Highlanders were No 55, 57, and 58.

55 SUB-DISTRICT at Fort George, Inverness

No 55 Brigade Depot was at Fort George, and the two linked regiments were the 71st Highland Light Infantry and the 78th Highlanders (Ross-shire Buffs). Both regiments had buff facings, and both wore the Mackenzie tartan, the 71st as trews and the 78th as the kilt.

Infantry Sub-District No 55 comprised the counties of Inverness, Elgin, Nairn, Ross and Cromarty, Sutherland, Caithness, the Orkney and the Shetland Islands. The Sub-District included the 76th Highland Light Infantry Militia (the Inverness Militia), the 96th Highland Rifle Militia (the Ross-shire Militia), and four battalions of Rifle Volunteers.

For all the spacious buildings and ranges at Fort George, the accommodation was considered to be sub-standard and the barracks too isolated, and so in 1876 work began on the building of a new Brigade Depot on the hill of Knockintinnel at Inverness.

Officers and NCOs of the 71st and 78th Highlanders and the Highland Rifle Militia at No 55 Brigade Depot, Fort George, in 1877.

57 SUB-DISTRICT at Perth

No 57 Sub-District was at Perth, and the two linked regiments were the 42nd Royal Highlanders (Black Watch) and the 79th Queen's Own Cameron Highlanders. Both regiments were kilted, and they shared the blue facings of Royal regiments.

Infantry Sub-District No 57 comprised the counties of Perth, Fife and Forfar. The Sub-District included the Royal Perth Militia and seven battalions of Rifle Volunteers.

Officers of the 79th Cameron Highlanders and the 42nd Royal Highlanders on the formation of No 57 Brigade Depot at Perth in 1873.

58 SUB DISTRICT at Stirling

No 58 Sub-District was at Stirling, and the two linked regiments were the 72nd Duke of Albany's Own Highlanders and the 91st Argyllshire Highlanders. Both regiments, although Highland, wore trews.

Infantry Sub-District No 58 comprised the counties of Renfrew, Bute, Stirling, Dumbarton, Argyll, Kinross, and Clackmannan. The Sub-District included the Highland Borderers Light Infantry Militia and the Royal Renfrew Militia, and also six battalions of Rifle Volunteers.

Permanent Regimental Depots established in 1881

Under the Army Reforms of 1881, after extended lobbying by all the Scottish regiments, a very different pattern of Regimental Districts and pairings emerged. the 72nd and 78th were amalgamated to form the Seaforth Highlanders, and were given a permanent Depot at Fort George. The 79th became The Queen's Own Cameron Highlanders, remaining a single battalion regiment with its Depot at Inverness.

The Inverness Barracks had been begun in 1886 as the Depot for the 71st and 78th, a pairing which never materialised. In 1881, when the barracks were re-allocated to the Queen's Own Cameron Highlanders as the regimental depot, the construction was only half finished, and so the Depot of the Cameron Highlanders was accommodated temporarily at Fort George with the Depot of the Seaforth Highlanders, until the Cameron Barracks were completed in 1886.

6. THE MILITIA BEFORE 1881

The Scottish Militia Force in the French wars

The Scottish Militia battalions originated in the Napoleonic Wars. The Regular army, stretched by commitments in India and the colonies, and required to furnish expeditionary forces for service on the continent of Europe, could not provide adequate troops for the defence of Great Britain and Ireland against invasion by the French. The Militia regiments were intended mainly for home defence, and they supplemented the regular army garrisons. In the days before the establishment of a full time Police force, the Militia had a secondary role of acting in support of magistrates in controlling riots and disturbances, particularly in the manufacturing towns during the turbulent times of the Industrial Revolution.

Under the 'Scotch Militia Act' of 1802 the country was divided up into Militia districts. These territorial areas were based on population figures, and each comprised one or more counties. The responsibility for providing officers and raising men for the Militia was delegated to the Lord Lieutenants of counties, each being allocated a share of commissions, and a statutory number of men to be raised from the county. Selection was made by ballot in every parish, and those picked were enlisted for a 3 year period of part time service. During the Napoleonic Wars the Militia regiments were all embodied for full time service from time to time. After the war the Militia was seldom called out for training, and even the annual ballots lapsed. In 1852 the ballot system was superseded by voluntary service.

The Militia during the Crimean War

The Militia proved its value again during the Crimean War. The problem of an acute shortage of recruits for the Regular army was largely overcome by allowing Militia soldiers to volunteer for service with the Line regiments. The success of this prompted a reorganisation of the Militia, and each regiment was given a permanent training staff of regular officers and NCOS, with a small barracks and stores in its main county town.

The Militia in the Localisation Scheme of 1873

The Infantry Sub-Districts introduced under the Localisation Scheme of 1873, were based on the existing Militia Districts. Each Sub-District comprised its Brigade Depot, its two linked Line regiments, the Militia regiments and Rifle Volunteers within its counties. The staffs of the Brigade Depot trained men for both its Line and Militia regiments.

THE ROSS-SHIRE MILITIA 1798-1881

2nd NORTH BRITISH (or ROSS-SHIRE) REGIMENT OF MILITIA – 1798-1802

The 2nd or Ross-shire Militia was raised in 1798 by Colonel Francis Humberston Mackenzie of Seaforth, who also raised the 78th Highlanders (Ross-shire Buffs). The Ross-shire Militia drew its men from the counties of Ross, Elgin, Nairn, Cromarty and Sutherland. It was embodied at Fortrose and Dingwall, and served on garrison duty in Scotland until 1802, when all but the permanent staff were disbanded. The regiment wore the normal uniform of a Line regiment.

5th ROSS, SUTHERLAND, SHETLAND AND CROMARTY MILITIA – 1803-1831

The Ross-shire Militia was embodied again in 1803, under a slightly changed designation. The counties were reallocated, so that Elgin and Nairn became part of the Inverness-shire Militia district. The Ross-shire Militia served for 11 years on garrison duty throughout Great Britain until disbanded in 1814. Re-embodied in 1815, it served in Northern Ireland for a year before being disbanded again at the end of the Napoleonic wars. Thereafter it was called out for training periodically, but was not required to leave the north of Scotland.

96th ROSS, CAITHNESS, SUTHERLAND AND CROMARTY MILITIA – 1831-1854

In 1831 the regiment was renumbered the 96th Militia. During this long period of peace little, if any, formal training was carried out. The ballots were not held and the permanent staff was not kept up to strength.

The 96th Ross-shire, Caithness, Sutherland and Cromarty Rifles, at Fort George C 1855.

The 96th Highland Rifle Militia C 1860

96th ROSS-SHIRE, CAITHNESS, SUTHERLAND AND CROMARTY RIFLES – 1854-1860

During the Crimean War the Ross-shire Militia was embodied at Dingwall in 1855. Redesignated as Rifles, and given the role of a Rifle corps, it was dressed in green uniform similar to the Rifle Brigade. After the Crimean war a Militia barracks was built in Dingwall to house the permanent staff and stores of the regiment.

96th HIGHLAND RIFLE MILITIA – 1860-1881

In 1860 the regiment was redesignated the Highland Rifle Militia, and its uniform was changed to Highland dress. The new uniform was designed in 1855 by the artist R. R. Mclan, well known for his sketches of the 'Clans of the Scottish Highlands'. It included a rifle green doublet, kilt of Mackenzie tartan, and flat blue bonnets. In 1866 the uniform was further embellished with belted plaid, diced hose and brown spats, and a 'set up' bonnet with a grouse wing. In 1870 this rather elaborate kilted uniform was changed to Mackenzie tartan trews, green tunic, and green shako.

The officers of the 96th Highland Rifle Militia, Fort George 1869

Pipe Major Ronald Mackenzie and the pipers of the 96th Highland Rifle Militia, at Fort George 1880.

In 1867 the stores and arms were moved from Dingwall to Fort George, where the regiment normally carried out training, and the Militia barracks in Dingwall were converted to quarters for the permanent staff.

THE INVERNESS-SHIRE MILITIA 1798-1881

1st NORTH BRITISH (or ARGYLL) REGIMENT OF MILITIA – 1798-1802

When the Militia was first raised in Scotland during the Napoleonic wars, Inverness provided its quota of men to the Argyll Militia, which was drawn from the counties of Argyll, Dumbarton, Bute, and Inverness.

THE INVERNESS, BANFF, ELGIN AND NAIRN MILITIA – 1802-1804

The Inverness Militia was formed in 1802, the counties being redistributed so that its men were drawn from the counties of Inverness, Banff, Elgin and Nairn. The regiment was commanded by Sir James Grant of Grant, Bart, Lord Lieutenant of Inverness-shire, and first embodied in February 1803. It wore the normal uniform of a Line regiment. The regiment received its Colours in 1803.

10th INVERNESS, BANFF, ELGIN AND NAIRN MILITIA – 1804-1833

In March 1804 the Inverness Militia was designated the 10th Militia. During the Napoleonic wars the regiment served on garrison duty throughout Great Britain, returning from Portsmouth to Inverness in 1814 to be disembodied. Thereafter it was called out periodically for training.

The Band of the 76th
Highland Light Infantry Militia C 1870.

Pipe Major Alexander MacLennan and pipers of the 76th
Highland Light Infantry Militia C 1868.

76th INVERNESS, BANFF, ELGIN AND NAIRN MILITIA – 1833-1855

In 1833 the Inverness Militia was redesignated the 76th. During the Crimean War the regiment was embodied at Inverness.

76th HIGHLAND LIGHT INFANTRY MILITIA – 1855-1881

The Crimean War gave the Inverness Militia new impetus. Commanded by the Master of Lovat, it was redesignated the 76th Highland Light Infantry Militia (there was no connection with the Line regiment, the 71st Highland Light Infantry), and the uniform was changed to Highland dress, with the kilt of Hunting Fraser tartan. In 1856 the Militia barracks were built in Telford Street, Inverness, to house the permanent staff and stores. From 1858 to 1871 the regiment carried out its annual training period at Fort George, and after 1872 in a tented camp at Muir of Ord.

The Permanent Staff of the Highland Light Infantry Militia at Telford Street Barracks, Inverness in 1877.

7. THE VOLUNTEERS BEFORE 1881

The 1st Inverness-shire Rifle Volunteers at Inverness C1880.

A large number of Volunteer regiments were raised during the Napoleonic Wars, but they were disbanded after 1815, and have no direct connection with the Rifle Volunteers from which the Territorial Army of today is descended. In 1859-1860 the belligerence of the French under the Emperor Napoleon III prompted a wave of patriotism in Great Britain, and many new Volunteer corps were formed. They were first formed as independent companies, but a set of 'Regulations for the Volunteer Force' was published in 1861, giving instructions for the administration, discipline and training of the Volunteers. The uniform was largely at the discretion of the volunteers themselves. For convenience, the companies were grouped into Administrative battalions, but they retained a high degree of autonomy.

Constitutionally the Volunteers came under the jurisdiction of the Lord Lieutenants of the counties. Under the 'Regulation of the Forces Act' of 1871 the Volunteers were transferred to the Secretary of State for War, so that they became subject to the Articles of War and the Mutiny Act.

There was little formal association with the Regular Army until 1873 when, under the Localisation Act, the Volunteer battalions were put under command of the Brigade Depots. Under the Army Reforms of 1881 the Volunteer battalions became an integral part of the territorial regiments

THE ROSS-SHIRE RIFLE VOLUNTEERS

The companies of ROSS-SHIRE RIFLE VOLUNTEERS – 1860-61

The Ross-shire Rifle Volunteers were formed in 1860-61. The uniforms of the six original companies of the were:

1860	1st Invergordon Company	Grey tunic and trousers.
1860	2nd Dingwall Company	Grey tunic and trousers.
1860	3rd Avoch Company	Grey tweed jacket and knickerbockers.
1860	4th Knockbain Company	Light grey tunic and trousers.
1861	5th Alness Company	Grey tunic and trousers.
1861	6th Alness Company	Grey tunic and trousers.

The Ross-shire Rifle Volunteers and 1st Volunteer Battalion Seaforth Highlanders (From 'Records of the Scottish Volunteer Force' by Major General J. M. Grierson)

1st ADMINISTRATIVE BATTALION ROSS-SHIRE RIFLE VOLUNTEERS – 1861-1880

In 1861 the six original companies were incorporated in the 1st Administrative Battalion, Ross-shire Rifle Volunteers with its Headquarters at Dingwall. In 1864 the whole battalion adopted the same uniform of red tunics and blue trousers, except No 3 Company which chose to wear the Mackenzie kilt.

Three more companies were added in 1866-67. Their uniforms were:

1866	7th Evanton Company	Red tunic and Mackenzie kilt.
1866	8th Moy Company	Red tunic and Mackenzie kilt.
1867	9th Gairloch Company	Red tunic and Mackenzie kilt.

Under the Localisation Scheme of 1873 the 1st Administrative Battalion came under command of 55 Brigade Depot at Fort George. In 1875 the battalion adopted a new uniform of red doublet and Mackenzie tartan trews, except for 3, 7, 8, 9 Companies which retained the kilt.

1st ROSS-SHIRE (ROSS HIGHLAND) RIFLE VOLUNTEERS – 1880-1881

In 1880 the battalion was consolidated as the 1st Ross-shire (Ross Highland) Rifle Volunteers with its headquarters at Dingwall. After the Army Reforms of 1881, the battalion became an integral part of the Seaforth Highlanders (Ross-shire Buffs, The Duke of Albany's).

THE SUTHERLAND RIFLE VOLUNTEERS

The companies of SUTHERLAND RIFLE VOLUNTEERS – 1859-64

The Sutherland Rifle Volunteers were formed in Sutherland, Caithness, Orkney and Shetland in 1859-1860. The uniforms of the eight original companies were:

The Sutherland Rifle Volunteers
(From 'Records of the Scottish Volunteer Force'
by Major General J. M. Grierson)

Sutherland

1859	1st Golspie Company	Grey tunic and trousers.
1859	2nd Dornoch Company	Grey tunic and trousers.
1860	3rd Brora Company	Grey tunic and trousers.
1861	4th Rogart Company	Red doublet and Sutherland kilt

The Rogart Company, known as 'Duchess Harriet's', was the first Volunteer company in Scotland to adopt the red tunic.

Caithness

1860	1st Thurso Company	Grey tunic and trousers.
1861	2nd Wick Company	Grey tunic and trousers.
1861	3rd Halkirk Company	Grey tunic and trousers

Orkney and Shetland

1860	1st Lerwick Company	Grey tunic and trousers.

1st ADMINISTRATIVE BATTALION, SUTHERLAND RIFLE VOLUNTEERS – 1864-1880

In 1864 these eight companies were incorporated in the 1st Administrative Battalion Sutherland Rifle Volunteers, with its Headquarters at Golspie. In 1864 the Orkney and Caithness Companies changed their uniform to red tunic with dark grey trousers, and in 1867 all the Sutherland companies adopted the Sutherland tartan kilt and belted plaid. Two more companies were added in 1867:

Caithness
1867   4th Watten Company

Sutherland
1868   5th Bonar Bridge Company

In 1866 HRH The Prince of Wales (later King Edward VII) became Honorary Colonel of the battalion. Under the Localisation Scheme of 1873 the battalion came under command of 55 Brigade Depot at Fort George.

1st SUTHERLAND (SUTHERLAND HIGHLAND) RIFLE VOLUNTEERS – 1880-1881

In 1880 the battalion was consolidated as the 1st Sutherland Highland Rifle Volunteers with its Headquarters at Golspie. After the Army Reforms of 1881 the battalion became an integral part of the Seaforth Highlanders, (Ross-shire Buffs, The Duke of Albany's), although it retained its distinctive uniform of the Sutherland tartan kilt and the Sutherland badge.

ELGIN RIFLE VOLUNTEERS

The companies of *ELGIN RIFLE VOLUNTEERS* – 1860

The Elgin Rifle Volunteers were formed in 1860.   The uniforms of the four original companies were:

1860	1st Forres Company	Dark grey tunic and trousers.
1860	2nd Elgin Citizens Company	Elcho grey tunic and trousers.
1860	3rd Elgin Artisans Company	Elcho grey tunic and trousers.
1860	4th Rothes Company	Elcho grey tunic and trousers.

The Elgin Rifle Volunteers and 3rd Volunteer Battalion Seaforth Highlanders (From 'Records of the Scottish Volunteer Force' by Major General J M Grierson)

1st ADMINISTRATIVE BATTALION, ELGIN RIFLE VOLUNTEERS – 1860-1880

In 1860 the companies were incorporated as the 1st Administrative Battalion, Elgin Rifle Volunteers with its Headquarters at Elgin. In 1862 the battalion changed its uniform to red tunics and blue trousers, except for the 6th Company which adopted red doublets and the kilt of Grant tartan. Five companies were added between 1861-1871:

1861   5th Fochabers Company
1861   6th Carr Bridge Company
1863   7th Lhanbryde Company
1867   8th Garmouth Company
1871   9th Grantown Company

Under the Localisation Scheme of 1873 the battalion came under command of No 55 Brigade Depot at Fort George.

1st ELGIN RIFLE VOLUNTEERS – 1880-1881

In 1880 the battalion was consolidated as the 1st Elgin Rifle Volunteers with its Headquarters at Elgin. Under the Army Reforms of 1881 the battalion became an integral part of the Seaforth Highlanders (Ross-shire Buffs, The Duke of Albany's).

THE INVERNESS-SHIRE RIFLE VOLUNTEERS

The companies of INVERNESS-SHIRE RIFLE VOLUNTEERS – 1859-61

The Inverness-shire Rifle Volunteers were formed in 1859-1861. The uniforms of the original four companies were:

1859	lst Inverness Provost's Company	Dark grey tunic and trousers.
1860	2nd Lochaber Company	Dark grey tunic and trousers.
1860	3rd Inverness Merchants Company	Slate grey tunic and trousers.
1860	4th Clachnacuddin Company	Elcho grey tunic and trousers

The Inverness-shire Rifle Volunteers and 1st Volunteer Battalion The Queen's Own Cameron Highlanders. (From 'Records of the Scottish Volunteer Force' by Major General J. M. Grierson)

1st ADMINISTRATIVE BATTALION, INVERNESS-SHIRE RIFLE VOLUNTEERS – 1860-1880

In 1860 these companies were incorporated in the 1st Administrative Battalion Inverness-shire Rifle Volunteers with its Headquarters at Inverness. Three more companies were added in 1860-1861.

1860	5th Inverness Celtic Company	Grey doublet, Celtic tartan kilt.
1861	6th Badenoch Company	Elcho grey tunic and trousers.
1861	7th Beauly Company	Elcho grey tunic, Fraser tartan trews.

In 1863 all companies adopted the Elcho grey doublet, but the remainder of the dress varied widely.

1st Company	42nd tartan trews
2nd Company	79th or Cameron of Erracht tartan kilt
3rd, 4th,5th Companies	42nd tartan kilt
6th Company	MacPherson tartan kilt
7th Company	Fraser tartan kilt.

Three more companies were raised in 1867-1869 and wore the kilt:

1867	8th Portree Company	MacDonald of the Isles tartan kilt
1867	9th Ardersier Company	42nd tartan kilt
1869	10th Roy Bridge Company	Mackintosh tartan. kilt

1st INVERNESS-SHIRE (INVERNESS HIGHLAND) RIFLE VOLUNTEERS – 1880-1881

Under the Localisation Scheme of 1873 the battalion came under the command of 55 Brigade Depot at Fort George. In 1880 it was consolidated as the 1st Inverness-shire (Inverness Highland) Rifle Volunteers, with headquarters at Inverness, and its uniform was changed to red doublets, buff facings and 42nd tartan kilt for all companies.

Under the Army Reforms of 1881 the battalion was at first attached to No 72 Regimental District, but when No 79 Regimental District was established in 1883, the battalion became an integral part of The Queen's Own Cameron Highlanders.

The Band of the Inverness-shire Rifle Volunteers C. 1870.

CHAPTER II – THE REGIMENTS 1881-1914

1. THE REGULAR ARMY

1st BATTALION SEAFORTH HIGHLANDERS

lst Seaforth in Aden – 1882

In the final year of its tour of foreign service the lst Battalion Seaforth Highlanders (as the old 72nd Highlanders had been redesignated in 1881) left India for Aden, where the garrison was provided by the British regiments serving in India. The 1st Seaforth reached Aden in February 1882, but only four months later it was warned for active service in Egypt. Having left behind a large number of men in order to keep the 2nd Battalion (the former 78th) up to strength for foreign service in India, the 1st Seaforth was low in numbers, and so in early August it was reinforced by two companies of the 2nd Seaforth sent from Lucknow.

lst Seaforth move to Egypt – 1882

Insurrection had broken out in Egypt in 1882 when the Egyptian Army, led by Colonel Arabi Pasha the Egyptian Minister of War, revolted against the Khedive (the Turkish viceroy) in protest against government corruption and foreign interference in the country's affairs. At the Khedive's invitation Great Britain sent an expeditionary force to restore order. Led by General Sir Garnet Wolseley, the force was comprised mainly of troops from Great Britain and the Mediterranean garrisons, but was augmented by a Contingent of troops serving in India, which included the lst Seaforth from Aden.

lst Seaforth at Tel-el-Kebir – 1882

General Wolseley's force landed at Ismailia with the intention of marching on Cairo, following the line of the Sweetwater Canal (a cutting which took fresh water from the Nile to Ismailia). The Egyptian Army prepared a strong defensive position in the desert at Tel-el-Kebir to block the British advance. General Wolseley's force faced a well-entrenched position, held by an army of about double its own strength. To achieve surprise it was decided to make a silent night approach march, and then to attack at dawn on 13th September 1882.

The roles of the Indian Contingent, commanded by Major General Sir Herbert Macpherson VC (late 78th Highlanders), were to protect the flank of the main attack and to prevent the Egyptians escaping. Led by the 1st Seaforth, the Indian contingent advanced along the side of the Sweetwater Canal in the darkness. As the main attack went in, the lst Seaforth charged and captured a battery of four guns, then cleared a series of infantry and artillery positions. The plan to take the enemy by surprise was successful and, despite stiff resistance, the Egyptian base was captured in less than 30 minutes. While the British force consolidated on the captured stronghold and collected its casualties, the Indian Contingent followed up the Egyptian retreat. By the time that it reached Zag-a-Zig in the evening it had covered 33 miles in the day, a remarkable feat of endurance by well-acclimatised troops in the intense heat of the Egyptian summer.

1st SEAFORTH BATTLE HONOURS
For its part in the campaign in Egypt, the 1st Seaforth was awarded the Battle Honours:
TEL-EL-KEBIR
EGYPT 1882

1st Seaforth returns to Great Britain – 1882

Having taken part in the grand review before the Khedive in Cairo, the lst Seaforth embarked for England, while the reinforcements from the 2nd Battalion returned to Lucknow. There was a heroes welcome for the 1st Seaforth on the battalion's arrival in England, and at its new station at Parkhurst, Isle of Wight. It took part in the great review by Queen Victoria on Horse Guards parade, and was inspected by the Queen at Parkhurst. In 1884 the battalion had the sad duty of parading at the funeral of HRH Prince Leopold, Duke of Albany, Queen Victoria's fourth son, who had been appointed Honorary Colonel of the 3rd Militia Battalion Seaforth Highlanders in 1882. On 16th August 1884 the lst Seaforth received new Colours from Queen Victoria at Osborne House. They were the Seventh Stand of Colours to be carried by the battalion and its predecessor the 72nd Highlanders.

During the 1st Seaforth's time at Parkhurst the new uniform of the Seaforth Highlanders was introduced, and the battalion changed its dress from the trews of Royal Stuart tartan to the kilt of the 78th or Mackenzie of Seaforth tartan.

1st Seaforth at Windsor and Aldershot – 1885

The Dervish revolt in the Sudan, and the murder of General Charles Gordon in Khartoum, required the despatch of a further expeditionary force to Egypt, and the lst Seaforth therefore took over public duties from the Foot Guards at Windsor from February to September 1885 to release them for active service. During this period the Sixth Stand of Colours, which had been retired in 1884, was presented to Queen Victoria and hung in Windsor Castle. On the return of the Guards from the Sudan, the 1st Seaforth marched to Aldershot and remained there for the rest of the year.

The tailors of 1st Battalion Seaforth Highlanders making kilts of Mackenzie tartan to replace the trews of Prince Charles Edward Stuart tartan at Parkhurst, Isle of Wight, 1883.

1st Battalion Seaforth Highlanders, Edinburgh Castle 1887.

1st Seaforth in Edinburgh – 1886-1888

In January 1886 the 1st Seaforth moved by sea from Portsmouth to Edinburgh, where the battalion was to spend two years in Edinburgh Castle. It made the most of its return to Scotland after 19 years abroad by sending recruiting tours into the territorial area which had been allocated to the Seaforth Highlanders in the Army Reforms of 1881. Parties visited the Orkney Islands, Caithness, Sutherland, Ross-shire, Skye, and Lewis. The Highland counties took a keen interest in their territorial regiment, and the recruiting tours of the Highlands attracted many high calibre recruits to the Seaforth Highlanders. Between 1882-1888 the 1st Seaforth, as the home service battalion, despatched over 1000 men to the 2nd Battalion in India. Among ceremonial and public duties the 1st Seaforth provided the Royal Guard at Ballater in 1886 and 1887, and ceremonial troops for the General Assembly of the Church of Scotland.

lst Seaforth in Glasgow – 1888-1889

The lst Seaforth moved from Edinburgh to Glasgow in March 1888. The battalion was quartered in Maryhill Barracks for a year, during which it provided guards and duties for the great International Exhibition which was visited by Queen Victoria.

lst Seaforth in Ireland – 1889-1895

In 1889 the 1st Seaforth moved to Ireland where it spent six mainly uneventful years in Dublin, Fermoy and Tipperary. The responsibility of the 1st Battalion, as the home service battalion of the regiment, was to maintain the 2nd Battalion in India up to strength. Despite the success of the recruiting tours round the

1st Battalion Seaforth Highlanders provide the Royal Guard at Ballater in 1886.

regiment's territorial area in the Highlands, the limited manpower resources of the sparsely populated north of Scotland made recruiting a persistent problem, and so from time to time the Seaforth Highlanders were opened to General enlistment. This accounted for the significant number of Englishmen and Irishmen who served in the regiment before World War I.

1st Seaforth in Aldershot – 1895-1897

In early 1895 the 1st Seaforth moved to Aldershot. The main event of the annual routine of an infantry battalion on home service with the Aldershot garrison was the Autumn Manoeuvres, carried out in full dress uniform, and conducted under the personal supervision of the Commander in Chief, Field Marshal HRH the Duke of Cambridge.

1st Seaforth in Malta – 1897-1898

In early 1897 the 1st and 2nd Battalions exchanged roles as the home and foreign service battalions. The 1st Seaforth sailed to the Mediterranean, reaching Malta in February 1897. Having come from home service the battalion was less than 500 strong. But returning from India with the 2nd Battalion were over 500 men who had not completed their overseas service engagements, and these were transferred to the 1st Battalion in Malta to bring it up to strength.

1st Seaforth in the Occupation of Crete – 1897

During 1897 the 1st Seaforth took part in the International Occupation of Crete. The island, under Turkish military rule, had a mixed population of Turks and Greeks, and there was constant agitation from the Greeks for union between Crete and Greece. Guerilla warfare between Greeks and the Turkish soldiers led to the declaration of war between Greece and Turkey. An International Occupation Force was formed from contingents supplied by Great Britain, France, Russia, Italy and Austria. In what was a forerunner of a United Nations peace-keeping operation, the 1st Seaforth spent from March to September in Crete. The only occasion on which force used was when the Allied fleets carried out a naval bombardment of the insurgent positions.

The Reconquest of the Sudan – 1898

After the Mahdi's revolt in 1884 against Turkish rule of the Sudan, the British Government, at the invitation of the Khedive (the Turkish viceroy of Egypt), sent General Charles Gordon to command the garrison holding the Sudanese capital Khartoum. But the Mahdi and his Dervish troops murdered Gordon and established a Mahdist state independent of Egypt. After the Mahdi died in 1885, his successor the Khalifa allowed Sudan to slide into anarchy. In 1897 the British and Egyptian governments agreed to send an Egyptian Army expedition under Major General Sir Herbert Kitchener to recover the Sudan. The Dervish army, though poorly armed, proved to be of formidable size, and Kitchener requested a brigade of British troops as reinforcements. In early 1898 a British Brigade comprising the 1st Warwicks, 1st Lincolns, 1st Seaforth, and 1st Camerons was assembled in Egypt.

1st Seaforth move to Egypt and Sudan – 1898

In March 1898 the 1st Seaforth moved from Malta to Egypt, and on arrival in Cairo it was sent south to join Kitchener's army in the north of Sudan. The battalion's journey included travel by train, by Nile river boat, by Kitchener's desert railway, by sailing boat, and a final stage by camel.

1st Seaforth at the Battle of the Atbara – 8th April 1898

The first major action of the campaign was an attack on a Dervish army holding a well-prepared dem (defensive position) beside the dried up Atbara River. Kitchener's force comprised the British Brigade and two Egyptian Army brigades. In the plan of attack for the British Brigade the 1st Camerons had the task of breaching the zariba (thorn fence) surrounding the Dervish position, while the 1st Seaforth and the two other British battalions passed through the breaches and fought through the dem. In a short fierce fight the 1st Seaforth, as the centre battalion of the brigade, cleared the position, with the loss of two officers and six soldiers killed.

1st SEAFORTH BATTLE HONOUR
For its part in the Battle of the Atbara River the 1st Seaforth was awarded the Battle Honour:

ATBARA

1st Seaforth at the Battle of Khartoum (or Omdurman) – 2nd September 1898

After the successful attack on the Dervishes at the Atbara River, General Kitchener's expeditionary force was reinforced by a second British Brigade, and then continued south up the Nile towards Omdurman and Khartoum. Five miles north of the Dervish capital at Omdurman the force encountered a huge Dervish army of about 60,000 troops.

The Dervish army was roughly twice the strength of Kitchener's force, but it lacked effective rifles, machine guns and artillery, and its standards of training and organisation were primitive compared with those of a European power. Kitchener established his force in a carefully sited defensive position beside the Nile, protected by a thorn zariba, with a fleet of gunboats in immediate support. There on 2nd September 1898 the expedition awaited the Dervish attack.

The Dervish advance was awesome in size, and in the centre of the 1st British Brigade the companies of the 1st Seaforth, with the rising sun behind them, were able to engage the enemy with section volleys at 1,800 yards range. Despite the firepower of Kitchener's force, some of the Dervish attackers managed to establish fire positions within 800 yards of the 1st British Brigade. But the battle was a one-sided affair. 11,000 Dervishes were killed by the overwhelming fire power of well-trained British and Egyptian troops, armed with modern rifles, with the fire support of Maxim machine guns, artillery, and the gunboats. Kitchener's force lost 48 killed.

As the attack petered out Kitchener resumed the advance, and the 1st Seaforth reached Omdurman that evening. During the next few days the old Sudanese capital at Khartoum was reoccupied, and the battalion attended a memorial service for General Gordon, where its pipers played the lament. With Anglo-Egyptian rule of the Sudan re-established, the 1st Seaforth embarked for the return journey to Cairo.

1st SEAFORTH BATTLE HONOUR

For its part in the Battle of Khartoum (or Omdurman) the 1st Seaforth was awarded the Battle Honour:

KHARTOUM

After the Battle of the Atbara, the 1st Battalion Seaforth Highlanders and 1st Battalion The Queen's Own Cameron Highlanders bury their dead.

1st Seaforth in Egypt – 1898-1903

The 1st Seaforth was to remain in Cairo until 1903, and this included the period of the South African War when, to the chagrin of the 1st Battalion, it was the 2nd Battalion at Fort George which went on active service. The 1st Seaforth in Cairo provided the 2nd Seaforth in South Africa with strong drafts of reinforcements and two companies of Mounted Infantry. There was a rare opportunity for the Regular and the Militia battalions to serve together when the 3rd (Militia) Battalion Seaforth Highlanders was sent on voluntary overseas service to reinforce the Mediterranean garrison, and served with the 1st Battalion in Cairo for nearly 18 months.

1st Seaforth return to India – 1903

The 1st Seaforth sailed from Egypt to Bombay in February 1903 and was stationed at Nasirabad. Much of its training was carried out in the same area where the 72nd had fought in the Indian Mutiny campaigns of 1858. In late 1905 the battalion moved to Nowshera. It spent the summer of 1907 at Ghora Dhaka in the Murree Hills.

1st Seaforth in the Zakka Khel expedition – 1908

In February 1908 the 1st Seaforth formed part of a punitive expedition against the Zakka Khel tribe on the North West frontier. The two brigades of the Bazar Valley Field Force were involved in some hard fighting as they destroyed the villages of the rebel tribesmen. Among the casualties suffered by the 1st Seaforth was the acting Commanding Officer Major Hon. Douglas Forbes-Sempill who was killed.

1st Seaforth in the Mohmand expedition – 1908

Two months later the 1st Seaforth took part in a further expedition against the turbulent Mohmand tribe on the North West frontier. Between 30,000 and 40,000 Mohmands and Afghans were threatening to cross the frontier, and a force of three brigades was sent to oppose them. In a tough six week campaign of mountain warfare the incursion was suppressed with some severity, and 170 fortified towers destroyed.

1st Seaforth in India – 1905-1914

The 1st Seaforth remained in India until 1914, being stationed at Nowshera (1905-1909), Peshawar (1909), Shahjahanpur (1909), Chaubattia and Bareilly (1910-1912), Agra (1912-1914). The battalion took part in King George V's visit to Delhi for his Coronation Durbar in 1911, and on 11th December the King presented the 1st Seaforth with its Eight Stand of Colours.

On the outbreak of World War I in 1914 the 1st Seaforth left India for France with the Indian Expeditionary Force.

2nd BATTALION SEAFORTH HIGHLANDERS

2nd Seaforth at Lucknow and Bareilly – 1882-1889

In early 1882 the 2nd Battalion Seaforth Highlanders (as the old 78th had been redesignated in 1881) moved from Sitapur to Lucknow. When the 1st Seaforth moved to Aden to complete its Indian tour, it left behind with the 2nd Battalion a large number of men who volunteered to remain in India.

In 1882, when the 1st Battalion in Aden was ordered to join the Indian contingent in the British expeditionary force to Egypt, it was below strength for active service, and so the 2nd Seaforth supplied two companies of reinforcements. They joined the 1st Battalion in Aden, taking part in the campaign in Egypt and in the battle of Tel-el-Kebir, before returning to the 2nd Seaforth in Lucknow. In 1885 the 2nd Seaforth moved from Lucknow to Bareilly, where the battalion remained until 1889.

2nd Seaforth in the Hazara (or Black Mountain) expeditions – 1888 and 1891

During 1888 the 2nd Seaforth joined a punitive expedition on the North West Frontier of India against the Asakis and Hassanzais, two tribes which had murdered a Gurkha officer and caused much local trouble. The 2nd Seaforth were split between two columns which operated for two months in extremely rough, mountainous country. Frequently attacked, and operating under very arduous conditions, the expedition succeeded in forcing the tribesmen to submit to the authority of the British Government of India. In March 1891 the battalion again took part in a punitive expedition in Hazara, and spent three months operating in the mountains of the North West Frontier until the tribesmen again submitted to the Government's terms.

2nd Seaforth at Rawalpindi and Ferozepore 1889-1897

In 1889 the 2nd Seaforth moved to Rawalpindi and, while stationed there, took part in the second Black Mountain expedition of 1891. In 1893 the battalion left Rawalpindi for Ferozepore, its last garrison station before returning to Great Britain.

2nd Battalion Seaforth Highlanders on active service in Chitral 1895

2nd Seaforth at Chitral – 1895

In March 1895 the British agent and a small British garrison were besieged by hostile tribesmen in Chitral. A relief expedition of 15,000 men was assembled at Nowshera, and the 2nd Seaforth joined the 3rd Brigade of the Field Force. The battalion took part in the advance to clear the Malakand Pass, and then marched into Swat, Beiaur and Dir, until the garrison at Chitral was successfully relieved.

2nd SEAFORTH BATTLE HONOUR

For its service in the expedition to relieve the garrison at Chitral, the 2nd Seaforth was awarded the Battle Honour:

CHITRAL

2nd Seaforth at Dover and Fort George – 1897-1899

In February 1897, after 18 years in India, the 2nd Seaforth returned home to be stationed at Dover. In June the battalion was on parade in London, lining the streets for Queen Victoria's Diamond Jubilee. In January 1899 it moved north to Fort George, with the prospect of a peaceful tour of duty in the regimental area. The battalion furnished the Royal Guard for the Queen at Balmoral, marched through Easter Ross on a recruiting tour, and received its Seventh Stand of Colours from Queen Victoria at Balmoral on 29th September.

2nd Seaforth moves to South Africa – 1899

In South Africa, the long standing hostility between the Boers (the settlers of Dutch descent) and the British led to the declaration of war on 11th October 1899 between the British government and the South African Republic. The peaceful tenor of garrison life at Fort George was suddenly broken when the 2nd Seaforth was hastily ordered to mobilise, call up reservists, and issue kit before sailing from Glasgow on 20th October 1899. On arrival at Cape Town the battalion joined the Highland Brigade, commanded by Major General Andrew Wauchope, and comprising the 2nd Battalion The Black Watch, 1st Battalion The Highland Light Infantry, 2nd Battalion Seaforth Highlanders, and 1st Battalion The Argyll and Sutherland Highlanders.

Faced with a resourceful enemy, skilled in fieldcraft and marksmanship, the battalion quickly reverted to campaign uniform similar to that used in India. It wore khaki drill jackets, and sun helmets with khaki covers. A khaki kilt apron covered the kilt, spats were left unwhitened and buttons unpolished, sporran badges and medal ribbons discarded, and officers gave up carrying swords.

2nd Seaforth at Magersfontein – 11th December 1899

The 2nd Seaforth joined Lord Methuen's force which had crossed the Modder River and was advancing to relieve the besieged town of Kimberley. About six miles beyond the Modder River the Boers held a well prepared defensive position based on the hill of Magersfontein Kop, which the Highland Brigade and Guards Brigade were ordered to attack. Lord Methuen's plan was based on his experience at Tel-el-Kebir, when a silent night approach followed by an attack at dawn had caught the Egyptians by surprise. But he underestimated the standard of the Boer tactics. The Boers, instead of siting their trenches in the traditional way on the top of the range of hills, had dug them 150 yards forward of the kopjes (hills). Here the trajectory of their rifle fire could be used to the greatest advantage in covering the ground where they foresaw that Methuen's force would form up for its attack.

The Highland Brigade moved forward after midnight, and because of the intense darkness of cold rainy conditions, used the closest possible formation, moving in brigade mass of quarter companies. At 3.20am the battalions began to deploy for the attack, unaware that they were already within 300-400 yards of the Boer trenches. As dawn broke the Boers opened fire at close range. General Wauchope was killed and the Highland Brigade was pinned down by the Boer fire for the rest of the day. Despite many acts of great bravery, including two gallant flanking attacks by small parties of Seaforth Highlanders, it was a disastrous day. The battalions of the Highland Brigade were the unfortunate victims of a defective plan and lack of proper reconnaissance. The 2nd Seaforth had 69 killed and 143 wounded out of over 900 casualties suffered by The Highland Brigade. There was deep gloom in Scotland where the Highland regiments had known nothing but victory for nearly a century, and that sad day was commemorated in pipe music by the expressive retreat march 'The Highland Brigade at Magersfontein'.

The reorganisation of the British forces and a fresh start

The disastrous start to the South African war, in which the Boers were successful against British forces at Colenso, Stormberg and Magersfontein, was to be known in Great Britain as 'Black Week'. But the three separate setbacks brought a wave of popular sympathy for the British troops in the field, and the government's took effective action to put things right.

In early 1900 Britain's most experienced campaign soldier, Field Marshal Lord Roberts VC, arrived in South Africa as Commander in Chief of the British forces, with General Lord Kitchener as his Chief of Staff. They brought clear and decisive direction to the war, and events soon took a turn for the better. Lord Methuen's division was broken up and the Highland Brigade transferred to the 9th Division. The Highland Brigade also received a new commander, Major General Hector MacDonald, the popular hero 'Fighting Mac', a Ross-shire soldier who had risen from the ranks to distinguish himself as a brigade commander with the Egyptian Army at the battle of Omdurman.

The 2nd Seaforth were reinforced by drafts from the 1st Battalion in Cairo, and from the Militia and Volunteer battalions. A mass of letters, messages and gifts from home did much to restore morale in the Highland Brigade.

2nd Seaforth at Paardeberg – 1900

Lord Roberts renewed the offensive to relieve Kimberley. On 7th February 1900 the 2nd Seaforth, in the Highland Brigade, took part in the action at Koodoosberg which drew the Boer defenders away from Kimberley and allowed the cavalry to break through to relieve the garrison. By late February the British advance had cornered the Boer commander General Cronje, with over 4,000 Boers at Paardeberg. The opening stage of the battle was a hard fought attack on well prepared Boer positions in which the 2nd Seaforth lost 53 killed and 100 wounded. But after Lord Roberts switched to siege tactics, Cronje and his Boers were shelled into surrender. It was the first major British military success of the war and did much to restore the self esteem of the British army.

2nd Seaforth in the march to Heilbron – 1900

2nd Battalion Seaforth Highlanders on the march in South Africa

The Highland Brigade continued its advance, occupying Bloemfontein on 14th March 1900, and halting there for six weeks to refit and reorganise. In late April it resumed the advance to Pretoria, but was then sent to occupy Heilbron. The eight day march covering 120 miles was against constant minor opposition, and included a fierce action against a Boer attack at Roodeport, before the 2nd Seaforth reached Heilbron.

2nd Seaforth in the attack on Retief's Nek – 1900

On 24th July, in the depth of the South African winter, the 2nd Seaforth took part in the attack on General Prinsloo's force of 4,000 occupying hill top positions on either side of the pass at Retief's Nek. During the British advance, made in a blizzard, the 2nd Seaforth carried out a successful flanking attack. The operation resulted in the second major surrender of Boer troops during the war.

2nd Seaforth in the later stages of the Boer War – 1900-1902

During the second half of 1900, the 2nd Seaforth took part in a series of smaller operations, including actions further south at Fauresmith, Jagersfontein and Phillippolis. The campaign developed into guerilla warfare against small Boer forces, involving long marches and the destruction of Boer farms. During 1901 and 1902 the 2nd Seaforth were engaged in building and manning the lines of strategic blockhouses by which Kitchener aimed to divide up the country into districts, and then to clear each area methodically. After peace was signed at Pretoria on 31st May 1902, the battalion remained in the Transvaal until its return to Great Britain in 1903.

Reinforcements for the 2nd Seaforth in South Africa – 1899-1902

During the South African War the demand for reinforcements to keep the Regular army battalions up to strength was so great that officers and men of the Militia and Volunteer battalions were allowed to volunteer for service overseas. The 2nd Seaforth received over 2,000 reinforcements, and these included drafts from the Depot at Fort George, the 1st Battalion in Cairo, the 3rd Militia Battalion, and three companies of volunteers from the 1st Ross-shire, the Sutherland and Caithness, and the 3rd Morayshire Volunteer Battalions. The South African War was the first real test of the Territorial system introduced in 1881, and proved it effective.

Sergeant John Mackenzie, VC

Sergeant John Mackenzie wins the Victoria Cross in Ashanti – 1900

While serving on attachment to the West African Frontier Force in Ashanti, Sergeant John Mackenzie DCM of the 2nd Seaforth was awarded the Victoria Cross for gallantry.

'On 6th June 1900 at Doompassi, in Ashanti, Sergeant Mackenzie, after working two Maxim guns under a hot fire and being wounded while doing so, volunteered to clear the stockades of the enemy, which he did in the most gallant manner, leading the charge himself and driving the enemy headlong into the bush'. (London Gazette, 15th January 1901)

2nd SEAFORTH BATTLE HONOURS

For its service in the South African War, the 2nd Seaforth was awarded the Battle Honours:

PAARDEBERG
SOUTH AFRICA 1899-1902

2nd Seaforth in Ireland – 1903-1904

On its return from South Africa in February 1903 the 2nd Seaforth was sent to Dublin. The battalion took part in the Royal Review in the Phoenix Park in July and furnished Guards of Honour for the King's Levee.

2nd Seaforth in Aldershot and Edinburgh – 1904-1909

In 1904 the 2nd Seaforth returned from Ireland to Aldershot. Later the same year it moved to Edinburgh, where it was to spend five years from 1904 to 1909 quartered in the Castle. In 1905 HRH Prince Leopold, Duke of Albany and Saxe Coburg, was appointed Colonel in Chief of the Seaforth Highlanders, and he paid his first visit to the regiment when he inspected the 2nd Seaforth at Edinburgh in 1907.

The Colours and Assaye Colour of 2nd Battalion Seaforth Highlanders C 1903.

The battalion's ceremonial duties in Scotland included Guards of Honour for the General Assembly of the Church of Scotland, the Royal Guard at Balmoral, and the opening of the Queen Victoria School, Dunblane.

2nd Seaforth at Fort George – 1909-1912

In 1909 the 2nd Seaforth moved to Fort George, where it was able to take full advantage of its return to the regimental area. The battalion trained with the Seaforth and Cameron Brigade of the Territorial Force, paraded with the 3rd (Special Reserve) Battalion, and sent companies to camp and train at Strathpeffer, Loch Broom, Lossiemouth and Grantown-on-Spey. The battalion travelled by railway to Thurso and then marched back to Fortrose, crossing the Moray Firth from Chanonry point to Fort George in small boats. Next year a similar march was carried out through Morayshire, and in 1911 through Easter Ross.

2nd Seaforth at Shorncliffe – 1912-1914

In 1912 the 2nd Seaforth moved to Shorncliffe, and the battalion was stationed there when war broke out on 4th August 1914.

1st BATTALION THE QUEEN'S OWN CAMERON HIGHLANDERS

1st Camerons in Gibraltar

The orders for the Army Reforms of 1881 for reached the 79th Queen's Own Cameron Highlanders while the regiment was stationed in Gibraltar. Under the new arrangements the 79th was redesignated the 1st Battalion The Queen's Own Cameron Highlanders, with a Depot at Inverness, and with a 2nd (Militia) Battalion formed from the Inverness Militia.

1st Camerons move to Egypt – 1882

The 1st Camerons saw active service the following year. In 1882 the Egyptian Army, led by its Minister of War Colonel Arabi Pasha, revolted against the Khedive (or Turkish viceroy) in protest against the corruption of the Turkish government of Egypt, and foreign interference in Egypt's affairs. At the Khedive's invitation, Great Britain sent to Egypt an expeditionary force commanded by General Sir Garnet Wolseley. The 1st Camerons embarked at Gibraltar, and on the battalion's arrival in Egypt it joined the Highland Brigade which formed at Alexandria under the command of Major General Sir Archibald Alison. The Highland Brigade comprised the 1st Battalion The Black Watch, 2nd Battalion The Highland Light Infantry, 1st Battalion The Gordon Highlanders and 1st Battalion The Queen's Own Cameron Highlanders.

1st Camerons at the Battle of Tel-el-Kebir – 1882

The Egyptian Army, with about double the strength of General Wolseley's force, had taken up a strongly entrenched position in the open desert at Tel-el-Kebir. General Wolseley decided to land his troops from the Suez Canal, and then advance towards Tel-el-Kebir up the axis of the Sweetwater Canal (the cutting which carried fresh water from the Nile to Ismailia). He planned to gain surprise by a silent night approach march, followed by an attack at dawn. The Highland Brigade were to be the left forward brigade of the attack.

The force assembled at last light, and waited until 1.30am before beginning its six mile advance. So silent was advance that the Highland Brigade reached within 200 yards of the enemy before the Egyptians realised that they were there. As the defenders opened fire the Highlanders assaulted the position. The 1st Camerons charged with pipers playing, scrambled over the ditch and parapet, and fought through the Egyptian position. Despite some desperate resistance the enemy were routed in 30 minutes, and the Egyptian army destroyed.

1st Battalion The Queen's Own Cameron Highlanders in the desert 1885

1st CAMERONS BATTLE HONOURS
For its part in the Battle of Tel el Kebir the 1st Camerons was granted the Battle Honours:

TEL-EL-KEBIR
EGYPT 1882

1st Camerons in the Expedition to Khartoum – 1884

Having taken part in the grand review by the Khedive in Cairo, the 1st Camerons in the Highland Brigade remained in Egypt with the Army of Occupation. Meanwhile there was fresh trouble to the south where a Sudanese religious leader, the 'Mahdi' Mohammed Ahmed, had declared a holy war against the Turkish Government in Egypt which ruled the Sudan. As the Mahdi's Dervish army overthrew the Egyptian garrisons, the British Government sent General Charles Gordon to evacuate the Khedive's troops and government officials from Sudan. But Gordon was then besieged in the Sudanese capital Khartoum, and an expeditionary force was sent up the Nile to rescue him. In November 1884 the 1st Camerons embarked on steamers and barges and moved up the Nile with Wolseley's relief expedition.

1st Camerons with the Sudan Frontier Field Force – 1884-1886

The 1st Camerons reached Korosko when news arrived that the Dervishes had captured Khartoum and murdered General Gordon. The battalion was then to remain for one and a half years on the Sudanese border, operating with the Frontier Field Force. Together with 250 men of the 9th Sudanese Battalion of the Egyptian Army, the 1st Camerons held the fort of Kosheh against a Dervish force of 7,000, and routed the Dervishes at the battle of Giniss. In April 1886 the battalion returned to Cairo.

(Note. The 1st Camerons marked the association with the 9th Sudanese Battalion during the defence of Kosheh and the battle of Giniss, by presenting it with a regimental Colour. This was carried by the 9th Sudanese Battalion until it was disbanded in 1930, and the Colour was then handed back to The Queen's Own Cameron Highlanders. It is now in the regimental museum),

1st CAMERONS BATTLE HONOUR
For its part in the expedition up the Nile and operations on the Sudanese border, the 1st Camerons was awarded the Battle Honour:

NILE 1884-85

1st Camerons in Great Britain – 1887-1892

The 1st Camerons returned to Great Britain in 1887 to find the future of the regiment in doubt. As the only single battalion infantry regiment in the army, the lack of a home service battalion made it particularly difficulty to keep the 1st Battalion up to strength when serving abroad. It was therefore proposed once again to convert the Cameron Highlanders into a 3rd Battalion of the Scots Guards. But, thanks to vociferous protest from a wide range of influential opinion throughout Great Britain, and the intervention of the Queen, the idea was shelved for the time being.

The 1st Camerons was stationed at Devonport until 1888 when it relieved the 1st Seaforth at Edinburgh Castle. The battalion then spent four years in Scotland, providing the Royal Guard at Balmoral from 1888-1891. Among its many ceremonial commitments was the Guard of Honour for the opening of the Forth Bridge by the Prince of Wales in 1890.

1st Camerons in Malta and Gibraltar – 1892-1897

The 1st Camerons spent six uneventful years in the Mediterranean garrisons, stationed in Malta from 1892 to 1895, and Gibraltar from 1895 to 1897, with a company in Cyprus in 1897.

The centenary of the raising of the 79th was marked by the erection of the Regimental Memorial, in the form of a statue of a Cameron Highlander, in the Station Square at Inverness. It was unveiled on 14 July 1893 by Donald Cameron of Lochiel, Lord Lieutenant of Inverness-shire.

A most welcome piece of news in early 1897 was the announcement that the government was to increase the number of regular battalions in the army, and among the new battalions raised was to be a 2nd Battalion of The Cameron Highlanders. The recurrent threat of amalgamation with the Scots Guards was ended.

lst Camerons in the later stages of the Boer War – 1900-1902

The lst Camerons spent the rest of 1900 in the Orange River Colony on operations round Kroonstad. The battalion's operations included treks to Ladybrand and to the north west of the colony. In 1901 it moved north to the Transvaal, and took part in the work of building and manning the lines of strategic blockhouses by which General Kitchener divided up the country and cleared each area. During two-and-a-half years in South Africa, the 1st Camerons covered nearly 3,000 miles of marching on operational duty. The battalion lost 24 officers and soldiers from enemy action during the campaign.

Reinforcements for the lst Camerons in South Africa – 1900-1902

During the South African war the 1st Camerons received reinforcements of a Volunteer Service Company from the lst Volunteer Battalion The Queen's Own Cameron Highlanders, eight drafts from the 2nd Battalion in Gibraltar, and volunteers from the 3rd (Militia) Battalion which was embodied during 1900.

1st CAMERONS BATTLE HONOUR

For its service in the South African War, the 1st Camerons was awarded the Battle Honour:

SOUTH AFRICA 1900-1902

1st Camerons at Inverness – 1902-1904

On the return of the lst Camerons from South Africa, the battalion was stationed at Fort George. The 1st Camerons received a most enthusiastic reception throughout the Highlands and was accorded a formal welcome and banquet in Inverness. There was a memorable parade at Fort George on 17th August 1903 when Field Marshal Lord Roberts VC presented Queen's South African War medals to the battalion. In 1904 the 1st Camerons provided the Royal Guard at Balmoral.

lst Camerons in Ireland – 1904-1907

In 1904, after a farewell banquet at Nairn, the 1st Camerons left Fort George for Ireland. For three years the battalion took part in the largely ceremonial life of Dublin, parading for the visits of King Edward VII, the Duke of Connaught, and the Prince of Wales who was appointed Colonel in Chief of the Cameron Highlanders in 1902. During serious rioting in Ulster in 1907, the 1st Camerons was sent to reinforce the Belfast garrison. The battalion spent a month on duty in the docks, and was called out for a major riot in the Falls Road.

1st Battalion The Queen's Own Cameron Highlanders in Dublin 1907.

1st Camerons in Tidworth and Aldershot – 1907-1913

In 1907 the 1st Camerons moved to Tidworth, and in 1909 to Aldershot. The battalion paraded in London for the funeral of King Edward VII in 1910. The Coronation ceremonies of King George V in June 1911 were attended by a detachment of the Cameron Highlanders of Canada. The newly formed allied regiment, raised at Winnipeg in February 1910, was billeted with the 1st Camerons at Aldershot, and a strong association was established.

1st Camerons in Edinburgh – 1913-1914

In 1913 the 1st Camerons returned to Edinburgh. After war with Germany broke out in August 1914, the battalion marched out of the Castle for France, the last battalion to occupy Edinburgh Castle as a peacetime garrison.

2nd BATTALION THE QUEEN'S OWN HIGHLANDERS 1897-1914

The formation of the 2nd Camerons – 1897

Under the Army Reforms of 1881 The Queen's Own Cameron Highlanders remained the only regiment in the Army with a single regular battalion, and this led to difficulties in manning the 1st Battalion when it went overseas. During the operations up the Nile in 1884-85 the lack of a home service battalion had left the 1st Camerons short of men. There was recurrent speculation that the 1st Camerons was to be converted into a 3rd Battalion of the Scots Guards, and in 1887 and 1893 proposals for this were only defeated by intense pressure from influential Highlanders, and eventually by the intervention of Queen Victoria herself.

The logical solution was to raise a second regular battalion, and the opportunity arose in 1897 when the government authorised an expansion of the infantry to meet the growing colonial commitments. In March 1897 authority was given to raise a 2nd Battalion of The Cameron Highlanders. At the same time the 2nd (Militia) Battalion was redesignated as the 3rd (Militia) Battalion.

HM Queen Victoria presents Colours to the newly raised 2nd Battalion The Queen's Own Cameron Highlanders at Balmoral 1898.

The 2nd Camerons was formed at Fort George on 1st April 1897. A nucleus from the 1st Battalion returned from Gibraltar and the new battalion was allowed to recruit throughout Scotland. The plan was to raise three companies in 1897, three more in 1898, and two in 1899. The 2nd Battalion furnished the Royal Guard at Balmoral in 1898, and on 29th October that year Queen Victoria presented the 2nd Camerons with Colours at Balmoral Castle. In December 1898 the 2nd Camerons moved to Aldershot 618 strong, and the final two companies were raised by May 1899.

2nd Camerons in the Mediterranean – 1899-1903

In October 1899 the 2nd Camerons sailed for Gibraltar to relieve a Guards battalion for the South African war. There the 2nd Battalion provided the Gibraltar garrison while carrying out its main role of supplying drafts of reinforcements for the 1st Battalion on active service in South Africa. The 2nd Camerons left Gibraltar in 1902 for service in the other Mediterranean garrisons, with Battalion Headquarters and four companies in Crete, three companies in Malta, and one company in Cyprus. In 1903 the whole battalion was concentrated in Malta.

2nd Camerons in South Africa – 1904-1907

In April 1904 the 2nd Camerons left Malta for South Africa where the battalion was stationed in Pretoria. During disturbances among the Zulus and the African population of Natal the battalion spent from February to August 1906 in Pietermaritzburg, but it was not required to go on active service. In 1907 a contingent was sent to Johannesburg for duty in aid of the civil power during strikes in the goldfields.

2nd Camerons in China – 1908-1909

The 2nd Camerons left Pretoria in December 1907 for China. To overcome the extreme change of climate from the South African summer to the North China winter, the battalion spent two months acclimatising in Hong Kong before moving to Tientsin. It was a period of much instability in China, and the battalion served with the international force made up of contingents from Great Britain, France, Germany, Japan, Russia and the USA. The European powers had to maintain strong guards at their legations in Peking, and the 2nd Camerons furnished the two company guard at the British Legation.

2nd Camerons in India – 1909-1914

The 2nd Camerons left China in November 1909, arriving in Bangalore in December, and remaining there for four years. In 1911 a representative detachment attended King George V's Coronation Durbar at Delhi. In the Highland Brigade Gathering held at Agra in 1913, the 2nd Camerons won the Championship Cup. The battalion moved to Poona in 1913 , and was stationed there when war with Germany broke out in August 1914.

2. THE DEPOTS AND MILITIA BATTALIONS

The Regimental Districts and Depots – 1881

Under the Army reforms of 1881 the country was divided into Regimental Districts, each comprising a regiment of the Regular army, the Militia battalions as a First Line reserve, the Volunteer battalions as a Second Line reserve, and the Regimental Depot as the Headquarters of the regiment. The Depot was a regiment's permanent home, serving the Regular and Militia battalions, and where recruiting and training were centralised. The Depot of each infantry regiment soon became the established military focal point of the counties comprising the Regimental District.

The Army Reforms of 1908

In the early years of the 20th century, as the threat of war with Germany grew, the main role of the Regular army battalions on home service was to provide a British Expeditionary Force for service on the continent of Europe. It was realised that warfare with modern artillery and machine guns would inevitably incur heavy losses of troops, and that there had to be an effective system of reinforcement.

In the Army Reforms of 1908 Lord Haldane, the Secretary of State for War, introduced radical changes to the Regimental Districts in order to provide adequate reserves. The Militia battalions were integrated with the Depots to become Special Reserve battalions, with the roles of recalling and equipping reservists, and forming drafts of reinforcements for the battalions of the Regular army. The Volunteer battalions were redesignated as Territorial Force battalions, and became the First Line reserve. The Territorial Force was reorganised and re-equipped on the same lines as the British Expeditionary Force of the Regular army, and it formed a duplicate Expeditionary Force for service on the continent of Europe.

DEPOT, SEAFORTH HIGHLANDERS, *Fort George*

The choice of Fort George as the Depot of the Seaforth Highlanders was unusual, for it was sited in Inverness-shire, which was not a county allocated to the Regimental District of the Seaforth Highlanders. The long term intention was to build the Depot Seaforth at Dingwall, a plan which never materialised. But Fort George had well-established links with the Seaforth Highlanders. The Ross-shire Militia, which became the 3rd (Militia) Battalion Seaforth Highlanders in 1881, had used the Fort since 1867; the Depot of the 78th Highlanders had shared the Fort with the 71st since 1873; and the Fort was conveniently situated between Ross-shire and Moray, the two parts of the Regimental District. Fort George also accommodated the headquarters of the 72nd and 79th Regimental District.

Fort George in the 1890s

The Depot of the Seaforth Highlanders was therefore established at Fort George in 1881, and there the recruits were trained for the Regular and Militia battalions of the Seaforth Highlanders. Fort George became the headquarters of the 3rd (Militia) Battalion Seaforth Highlanders, and the three Volunteer battalions used it regularly for annual camps.

Fort George remained the Depot of the Seaforth Highlanders from 1881 until the amalgamation of the Seaforth and Cameron Highlanders in 1961. The Regimental Museum of the Queen's Own Highlanders, and of their successors The Highlanders, perpetuates the long standing association of the Seaforth Highlanders with Fort George.

SEAFORTH HIGHLANDERS MILITIA

3rd (MILITIA) BATTALION SEAFORTH HIGHLANDERS – 1881-1908

In the Army Reforms of 1881 the 3rd (Militia) Battalion Seaforth Highlanders was formed by redesignation of the 96th Highland Rifle Militia (the old Ross-shire Militia). Its uniform conformed with the Regular battalions of the regiment, except that it continued to wear trews of Mackenzie tartan instead of the kilt. The headquarters of the battalion was at Fort George, where mess accommodation was shared with the Depot Seaforth Highlanders, and annual training normally took place at the Fort.

In 1882 HRH Prince Leopold, Duke of Albany, was appointed Honorary Colonel of the 3rd Seaforth. Sadly his Colonelcy was short-lived, for he died in 1884.

3rd (Militia) Battalion Seaforth Highlanders in camp at Fort George 1896.

During the South African War the 3rd Seaforth, as the First Line Reserve for the Seaforth Highlanders, was embodied. The battalion volunteered to a man for active service abroad, and was sent to Egypt in May 1900. Although it never saw active service as a battalion, it served in Cairo Egypt for 18 months as part of the Mediterranean garrison, and was quartered with the 1st Seaforth.

3rd SEAFORTH HONOUR
For its service abroad during the South African War the 3rd Seaforth was granted the Honour:
MEDITERRANEAN 1900-01

3rd (SPECIAL RESERVE) BATTALION SEAFORTH HIGHLANDERS - 1908-1914

In 1908, under the Haldane reforms of the Army, the 3rd (Militia) Battalion was merged with the Depot establishment and became the 3rd (Special Reserve) Battalion of the Seaforth Highlanders. Its role was altered to the provision of reinforcements for the Regular battalions in wartime. The headquarters of the battalion remained at Fort George, with a contingency plan to move to Cromarty on the outbreak of war to form part of the defences of the naval base in the Cromarty Firth. Annual training for reservists continued at Fort George.

DEPOT THE QUEEN'S OWN CAMERON HIGHLANDERS
Cameron Barracks, Inverness.

The construction of a regimental Depot on Cnoc-an-tionnail, the 'Hill of the Gathering', on the east side of Inverness, started in 1886 when it had been intended to form the 'Inverness and Ross Regiment' from the 71st and 78th Highlanders; an amalgamation which did not materialise. In 1881, when The Queen's Own Cameron Highlanders were allocated a Depot at Inverness, the Inverness barracks were still under construction, and so the

Depot Cameron Highlanders was accommodated at Fort George for the first five years of its existence. On the completion of Cameron Barracks, the Depot Camerons occupied its new home on 11th June 1886. Until 1897 the Camerons were a single Regular battalion regiment, and so were allowed an enlarged Depot establishment to compensate for the lack of a home service battalion.

The Depot Cameron Highlanders remained at Cameron Barracks until the Depots of the Seaforth and Camerons were combined at Fort George in September 1960, shortly before the amalgamation of the two regiments in 1961. Since then the Regimental Headquarters of the Queen's Own Highlanders and their successors The Highlanders, situated at Cameron Barracks, perpetuate the association with The Queen's Own Cameron Highlanders.

The quarter guard mounts at Cameron Barracks in 1901

THE QUEEN'S OWN CAMERON HIGHLANDERS MILITIA

2nd (MILITIA) BATTALION
THE QUEEN'S OWN CAMERON HIGHLANDERS – 1881-1897

In the Army Reforms of 1881 the 2nd (Militia) Battalion The Queen's Own Cameron Highlanders was formed by redesignation of the 76th Highland Light Infantry Militia (the old Inverness Militia). Its uniform conformed with the Regular battalion of the regiment. The headquarters of the battalion was at the Telford Street Barracks, Inverness, and annual camp was normally held at Muir of Ord. After the battalion was issued with the more powerful Lee-Metford rifles in 1893, its annual camp was held at Fort George where the ranges were safer.

3rd (MILITIA) BATTALION
THE QUEEN'S OWN CAMERON HIGHLANDERS – 1897-1908

In 1897, on the formation of a 2nd Regular battalion of The Queen's Own Cameron Highlanders, the 2nd (Militia) Battalion was renumbered as the 3rd (Militia) Battalion. During the South African war, while the lst Camerons was on active service in South Africa and the 2nd Camerons in garrison at Gibraltar, the 3rd (Militia) Battalion was embodied. It served in Aldershot, and then moved to Ireland, where it was stationed at Mullingar.

Recruits of the 3rd (Militia) Battalion The Queen's Own Cameron Highlanders in camp at Cameron Barracks C 1906

3rd (SPECIAL RESERVE) BATTALION
THE QUEEN'S OWN CAMERON HIGHLANDERS – 1908-1914

Under the Haldane reforms of the Army in 1908, the 3rd (Militia) Battalion became the 3rd (Special Reserve) Battalion of The Queen's Own Cameron Highlanders. At the same time the permanent staff of the 3rd Camerons and the Depot were merged into one establishment with the role of providing reinforcements for the Regular battalions in wartime. The headquarters of the battalion moved from the Telford Street Barracks in Inverness to Cameron Barracks, with a contingency plan to move to Invergordon on the outbreak of war to form part of the defences of the naval base in the Cromarty Firth.

On 28th June 1909 the 3rd Battalion was presented with new Colours by Colonel The Mackintosh of Mackintosh while at camp at Fort George.

3. RIFLE VOLUNTEERS AND TERRITORIAL FORCE

The Rifle Volunteers – 1881-1908

Under the Army Reforms of 1881 the Rifle Volunteers became an integral part of the local regiments, with a role of providing a Third Line reserve force for home defence, and no liability to serve overseas. The independent spirit of the Scottish Volunteer Movement was deeply ingrained, and the Volunteer battalions had their own perception of military service and discipline. There was little urgency to conform with the identity and dress of the parent regiments. In 1887-1888 the Rifle Volunteers were redesignated as Volunteer battalions of their parent regiments, and their uniform was gradually brought into line with that of the Regular and Militia battalions.

The Territorial Force – 1908-1914

It was the threat of war with Germany which brought the most significant change in the role of the Volunteers when, under Lord Haldane's Army Reforms of 1908, the Rifle Volunteers became the Territorial Force (TF). Instead of the traditional role of providing a Third Line Reserve for home defence, the Territorial Force was organised and equipped on the same lines as the Regular army, and given the role of providing a reserve Expeditionary Force for service on the continent of Europe.

Under the Reforms of 1908 the Territorial Force battalions of the Seaforth and Cameron Highlanders formed the Seaforth and Cameron Brigade in the Highland Territorial Division. The brigade trained together each year at annual camp, and the battalions were embodied on the outbreak of war in August 1914.

ROSS-SHIRE VOLUNTEERS and TERRITORIALS

1st ROSS-SHIRE (ROSS HIGHLAND) RIFLE VOLUNTEERS – 1881-1887

Under the Army Reforms of 1881 the 1st Ross-shire Rifle Volunteers became part of the Seaforth Highlanders.

1st (ROSS HIGHLAND) VOLUNTEER BATTALION, SEAFORTH HIGHLANDERS – 1887-1908

In 1887 the battalion was redesignated as the 1st (Ross-Highland) Volunteer Battalion Seaforth Highlanders to conform with the title of its parent regiment. The battalion adopted the full dress uniform of the Seaforth Highlanders, except that the Glengarry was worn instead of the feather bonnet, and the headquarters of the battalion were at Dingwall.

During the South African war the 1st Volunteer Battalion Seaforth Highlanders sent 110 volunteers for service with the 2nd Seaforth and other regiments in South Africa.

CAMPAIGN HONOUR
For the service of its volunteers in the South African war the battalion was granted the Campaign Honour:

SOUTH AFRICA 1900-02

4th (ROSS HIGHLAND) BATTALION SEAFORTH HIGHLANDERS TF– 1908-1914

Under the Haldane reforms of 1908, the battalion became the 4th (Ross Highland) Battalion Seaforth Highlanders in the Territorial Force. The 4th Seaforth received its Colours from King Edward VII at Windsor in 1909. It was brigaded in the Seaforth and Cameron Brigade of the Highland Territorial Division.

*Officer and Colour Sergeant
1st (Ross Highland) Volunteer
Battalion Seaforth Highlanders at
Dingwall 1887*

SUTHERLAND VOLUNTEERS and TERRITORIALS

1st SUTHERLAND (SUTHERLAND HIGHLAND) VOLUNTEER RIFLE CORPS – 1881-1908

Under the Army Reforms of 1881 the 1st Sutherland Highland Rifle Volunteers became part of the Regimental District of the Seaforth Highlanders but, unlike the Ross-shire and Morayshire Volunteers, the battalion did not adopt the name or uniform of the Regular army regiment. It remained as the lst Sutherland (Sutherland Highland) Volunteer Rifle Corps. The headquarters were at Golspie.

In 1884 the Lerwick Company was disbanded and was replaced by a new company at Lairg, and in 1890 the addition of new companies at Wick and Reay brought the battalion up to a total of twelve companies. The battalion replaced its brass band in 1883 with a band of thirty pipers dressed in the Sutherland kilt with plaids of Royal Stuart, evidently in honour of the Honorary Colonel, the Prince of Wales.

During the South African war the battalion sent 87 volunteers to serve with the 2nd Seaforth and other regiments in South Africa.

*Officers and the Sergeant Major
1st Sutherland Volunteer Rifle Corps 1895.*

CAMPAIGN HONOUR
For the service of its volunteers in the South African war the battalion was granted the Campaign Honour:

SOUTH AFRICA 1900-02

5th (SUTHERLAND AND CAITHNESS) BATTALION SEAFORTH HIGHLANDERS TF – 1908-1914

Under the Haldane reforms of 1908 the battalion became the 5th (Sutherland and Caithness) Battalion Seaforth Highlanders in the Territorial Force. Although it conformed to its parent regiment in name, it was allowed to retain its own uniform, with the clan badge of Sutherland and the kilt of the 42nd or Government tartan (Sutherland sett). The battalion was brigaded in the Seaforth and Cameron Brigade of the Highland Territorial Division.

MORAYSHIRE VOLUNTEERS and TERRITORIALS

1st ELGIN RIFLE VOLUNTEERS – 1881-1887
Under the Army Reforms of 1881 the 1st Elgin Rifle Volunteers became part of the Seaforth Highlanders. In 1886 the battalion adopted the red doublet and Mackenzie tartan trews of the Seaforth Highlanders.

3rd (MORAYSHIRE) VOLUNTEER BATTALION SEAFORTH HIGHLANDERS – 1887-1908

In 1887 the battalion was redesignated as the 3rd (Morayshire) Battalion Seaforth Highlanders. Its headquarters were at Elgin. In 1898 the battalion changed to the kilt of Mackenzie tartan.
During the South African war the battalion sent 193 volunteers for service with the 2nd Seaforth and other regiments in South Africa.

CAMPAIGN HONOUR
For the service of its volunteers in the South African war the battalion was granted the Campaign Honour:
SOUTH AFRICA 1900-02

6th (MORAYSHIRE) BATTALION SEAFORTH HIGHLANDERS TF – 1908-1914

Under the Haldane reforms of 1908 the battalion became the 6th (Morayshire) Battalion Seaforth Highlanders in the Territorial Force. The 6th Seaforth received its Colours from the Duke of Richmond and Gordon at Elgin in 1909, the Colours having been gifted by Sir George Cooper. The battalion was brigaded in the Seaforth and Cameron Brigade of the Highland Territorial Division.

Officers 3rd (Morayshire) Volunteer Battalion Seaforth Highlanders, 1892.

INVERNESS-SHIRE VOLUNTEERS and TERRITORIALS

1st INVERNESS-SHIRE (INVERNESS HIGHLAND) RIFLE VOLUNTEERS – 1881-1887

Shortly after the Army Reforms of 1881 the 1st Inverness-shire (Inverness Highland) Rifle Volunteers became part of The Queen's Own Cameron Highlanders.

The Band of 1st Volunteer Battalion The Queen's Own Cameron Highlanders in 1899

1st (INVERNESS HIGHLAND) VOLUNTEER BATTALION THE QUEEN'S OWN CAMERON HIGHLANDERS – 1887-1908

In 1887 the battalion was redesignated as the 1st (Inverness Highland) Volunteer Battalion The Queen's Own Cameron Highlanders to conform with the parent regiment. The headquarters of the battalion was at Inverness. In 1893 it was authorised to change its uniform to that of The Queen's Own Cameron Highlanders, except the Glengarry was worn instead of the feather bonnet.

During the South African war 245 volunteers from the battalion served in South Africa, the highest proportion of its strength of any battalion in Scotland. The main contingents served with the 1st Camerons and the Lovat Scouts.
CAMPAIGN HONOUR
For the service of its volunteers in the South African war the battalion was granted the Campaign Honour:

SOUTH AFRICA 1900-02

4th BATTALION THE QUEEN'S OWN CAMERON HIGHLANDERS TF – 1908-1914

Under the Haldane reforms of 1908, the battalion became the 4th Battalion The Queen's Own Cameron Highlanders in the Territorial Force. The 4th Camerons received its Colours from King Edward VII at Windsor in 1909, the Colours having been gifted by Major General Spencer Ewart CB. The battalion was brigaded in the Seaforth and Cameron Brigade of the Highland Territorial Division.

THE LOVAT SCOUTS

THE LOVAT SCOUTS (IMPERIAL YEOMANRY) – 1900-1902

One of the main weaknesses of the British army in the early stages of the South African War was its inability to gain accurate information about the Boers, whose fieldcraft made them an elusive and often invisible enemy. After the three disasters of 'Black Week' in December 1899 Lord Lovat was allowed to raise from the stalkers, ghillies and shepherds of the northern Highlands two companies of scouts for service in South Africa. The First Contingent of Lovat Scouts, comprising one company mounted on garrons (Highland ponies) and one company on foot, assembled and trained at Beaufort Castle in early 1900. Dressed in khaki tunics and breeches, with slouch hats bearing a patch of red Fraser tartan, they were armed with Lee Metford rifles and equipped with stalking glasses.

The Lovat Scouts on active service in South Africa 1900

The Lovat Scouts left for South Africa in March 1900, and 1st Company joined the Highland Brigade commanded by Major General Hector Macdonald, who used them in their proper role as scouts The 2nd Company, after a period as Mounted Infantry, also joined the Highland Brigade as scouts. Operating with spyglass and rifle, moving on their ponies, and communicating by heliograph and semaphore, the Lovat Scouts transformed the standard of intelligence gathering, and fully justified Lord Lovat's faith in the value of Highland stalking skills on the battlefield.

The Scouts had enlisted for one year's service, and so Lord Lovat returned to Inverness from South Africa in early 1901 to raise a Second Contingent. It served in South Africa as the 99th and 100th Companies Imperial Yeomanry. After the tragic loss of 54 casualties in a Boer night attack on the camp of 100th Company, a Third Contingent of company strength was formed in October 1901 and joined the Second Contingent in South Africa as reinforcements until the end of the war in May 1902.

BATTLE HONOUR
For their service in the South African War the Lovat Scouts were awarded the Battle Honour:

SOUTH AFRICA 1900-02

1st & 2nd REGIMENTS LOVAT SCOUTS (YEOMANRY) – 1903-1908

Pipers of the Lovat Scouts at camp in 1906

After the South African War Lord Lovat was allowed to raise the Lovat Scouts again as Yeomanry. The Scouts were recruited from the counties of Caithness, Sutherland, Ross and Cromarty, Inverness, Nairn and the Outer Hebrides. An allowance of £5 was made for each suitable pony brought to camp. Two regiments were raised, each 500 strong, with Lord Lovat in command, and the training was similar to the role of the Mounted Infantry in South Africa.

The Lovat Scouts wore Yeomanry uniform, of khaki tunic and breeches, with bandolier, and a dark blue diced bonnet with the badge of the Frasers of Lovat, a Royal stag and the motto 'Je Suis Prest' (I am ready). The pipers wore the kilt of Hunting Fraser tartan.

1st & 2nd REGIMENTS LOVAT SCOUTS, YEOMANRY, TF – 1908-1914

Under the Haldane reforms of 1908 the 1st and 2nd Lovat Scouts, together with the Fife and Forfar Yeomanry and the Inverness Battery Royal Horse Artillery, were formed into the Highland Mounted Brigade, under Lord Lovat's command.

THE LIVERPOOL SCOTTISH

8th (SCOTTISH) VOLUNTEER BATTALION, THE KING'S LIVERPOOL REGIMENT – 1900-1908

On 30th April 1900, at the time of the South African War, the War Office authorised the formation of the 8th (Scottish) Volunteer Battalion, The King's Liverpool Regiment. The battalion was raised from the Scottish community of Liverpool, and in 1901 was authorised to wear Highland dress. The Liverpool Scottish chose to wear the kilt of Forbes tartan as a compliment to their first Commanding Officer, Colonel Christopher Forbes Bell. The headquarters of the Liverpool Scottish were built in Fraser Street, Liverpool in 1904.

During the South African war the Liverpool Scottish sent a volunteer detachment for service in South Africa where it served with the 1st Battalion Gordon Highlanders.

CAMPAIGN HONOUR

For the service of its volunteers in the South African war the battalion was granted the Campaign Honour:

SOUTH AFRICA 1902

10th (SCOTTISH) BATTALION THE KING'S (LIVERPOOL) REGIMENT TF – 1908-1914

Under the Haldane reforms of 1908 the Liverpool Scottish became the 10th (Scottish) Battalionn The King's (Liverpool) Regiment in the Territorial Force. The battalion's First Stand of Colours were gifted by Lord Strathcona, and presented by King Edward VII at Knowsley in 1909.

The affiliation between the Liverpool Scottish and The Queen's Own Cameron Highlanders originated shortly before World War I, and the Liverpool Scottish became part of The Queen's Own Cameron Highlanders in June 1922.

10th Scottish Battalion The King's Liverpool Regiment, 1911
(From the painting by R. Caton Woodville)

CHAPTER III
THE REGIMENTS IN WORLD WAR I
1. BATTALIONS IN WORLD WAR I

6th Battalion Seaforth Highlanders at Greenland Hill, Arras, 29th August 1918.

Introduction

During the First World War the regiments were greatly expanded, and between the Seaforth, Camerons, Lovat Scouts and Liverpool Scottish there were over forty battalions. Each battalion has its own separate story, and these vary from the bloodiest battles of the Western Front, to the unspectacular, but nevertheless indispensable roles of home defence and training reinforcements.

In a book such as this it is impossible to tell in full the history of each battalion, or to list the innumerable periods spent in trenches or in billets out of the line; and so only the main battles are given, with a few of the subsidiary actions or smaller operations, in order to give an element of continuity. This inevitably results in some duplication where several battalions of the same regiment served in the same operation, but it does make it possible to give a continuous, though sketchy, narrative for each battalion.

To find out details of battles, operations, or individual actions, and to identify dates and places for periods spent in the trenches or in billets behind the lines, it is necessary to refer to sources such as the battalion war diaries, individual accounts, and published histories of battalions and formations.

The casualty figures quoted are taken from the war diaries, and for simplicity the figures given are normally the totals of those killed, wounded and missing. This may tend to exaggerate the scale of losses, for the numbers killed were sometimes only a small proportion of the total, but it serves to illustrate the resilience with which battalions continued to fight, even when they were only able to muster a fraction of their original strength. For example, when the 8th Seaforth lost 718 casualties at Loos, the total was made up of 49 killed, 371 wounded, and 290 missing. Many of those listed as missing were in fact prisoners of war or wounded.

BATTALIONS AND DEPOTS OF THE REGIMENTS IN WORLD WAR I

	Seaforth Highlanders	The Queen's Own Cameron Highlanders	Lovat Scouts and Liverpool Scottish
REGULAR ARMY			
Line Battalions	1st Seaforth 2nd Seaforth	1st Camerons 2nd Camerons	
Special Reserve Battalions	3rd Seaforth	3rd Camerons	
Depots	Depot Seaforth	Depot Camerons	
TERRITORIAL FORCE			
Field units	1/4th Seaforth 1/5th Seaforth 1/6th Seaforth	1/4th Camerons 10th (Lovat Scouts) Bn (from 1916)	1/1st Lovat Scouts (to 1916) 1/2nd Lovat Scouts (to 1916) Lovat Scouts Sharpshooters 1/10th Liverpool Scottish 2/10th Liverpool Scottish (from 1917)
2nd Line Home Defence Battalions	2/4th Seaforth 2/5th Seaforth 2/6th Seaforth	2/4th Camerons	2/1st Lovat Scouts 2/2nd Lovat Scouts 2/10th Liverpool Scottish (to 1917)
Third Line Reserve Battalions	3/4th Seaforth 3/5th Seaforth 3/6th Seaforth 4th Reserve Training Bn	3/4th Camerons	3/1st Lovat Scouts 3/2nd Lovat Scouts 3/10th Liverpool Scottish
Volunteer Battalion		1st Volunteer Bn Camerons	
NEW ARMY			
Service Battalions	7th Seaforth 8th Seaforth 9th Seaforth (Pioneers)	5th Camerons 6th Camerons 7th Camerons 11th Camerons	
Reserve Battalions	10th Seaforth	8th Camerons	
Garrison Battalion	1st Garrison Bn		
Labour Battalion		9th Camerons	

2. BRIGADES AND DIVISIONS OF WORLD WAR I

With the 51st (Highland) Division in Flanders

During the Great War, to encourage morale, much emphasis was given to cultivating the identity of brigades and divisions in the fighting areas. The published histories of these formations are useful sources of information on the battalions which served in them. The system of numbering, as far as it affected the regiment, was as follows.

Regular Army

The Regular Army divisions which existed before the outbreak of war in 1914 were numbered 1, 2, 3, 4, 5, 6. The Indian Army had its own similar system.

Further Regular Army divisions formed after 1914 included the 7th and 8th Divisions formed from battalions on home service, and the 27th, 28th, 29th Divisions, from battalions such as the 2nd Camerons returning from India and the overseas garrisons.

Territorial Force

The Territorial Force divisions which existed before the war had territorial names, such as The Highland Territorial Division. The divisions were numbered in the order in which they went overseas, being given numbers from 42 to 56. They also retained their territorial titles, becoming the 51st Highland Division and the 52nd Lowland Division.

Each division was composed of three brigades, also numbered. Within the 51st Highland Division the brigades were numbered 152, 153, and 154. The pre-war Seaforth and Cameron Brigade thus became the 152nd Highland Brigade.

New Army

The New Army divisions formed in 1914 were numbered from 9 to 26, and those formed in 1915 from 30 to 41.

There were two Scottish divisions in the New Army. The 9th (Scottish) Division comprised 26 (Highland) Brigade, 27 (Lowland) Brigade, and 28 Brigade. The 15th (Scottish) Division included 44 (Highland) Brigade, 45 Brigade, and 46 Brigade.

FORMATIONS IN WHICH BATTALIONS OF THE REGIMENT SERVED

The battalions of the regiment which took part in active service operations were grouped as follows.

Battalion	Dates	Brigade	Division

REGULAR ARMY

Battalion	Dates	Brigade	Division
1st Seaforth	Aug 14-Nov 18	19 Indian (Dehra Dun) Brigade	7th Indian (Meerut) Division
2nd Seaforth	Aug 14-Nov 18	10 Brigade	4th Division
1st Camerons	Aug-Sep 14	——	Army Troops
	Sep 14-Nov 18	1 Brigade	1st Division
2nd Camerons	Nov 14-Nov 18	81 Brigade	27th Division

TERRITORIAL FORCE

Battalion	Dates	Brigade	Division
1/4 Seaforth	Aug-Nov 14	Seaforth and Cameron Brigade	Highland Division
	Nov 14-Nov 15	19 Indian (Dehra Dun) Brigade	7th Indian (Meerut) Division
	Jan 16-Nov 18	154 Highland Brigade	51st Highland Division
1/5th Seaforth	Aug 14-May 15	Seaforth & Cameron Brigade	Highland Division
	May 15-Nov 18	152 Highland Brigade	51st Highland Division
1/6th Seaforth	Aug 14-May 15	Seaforth & Cameron Brigade	Highland Division
	May 15-Nov 18	152 Highland Brigade	51st Highland Division
1/4th Camerons	Aug 14-Feb 15	Seaforth & Cameron Brigade	Highland Division
	Feb-Apr 15	24 Brigade	8th Division
	Apr-Dec 15	21 Brigade	7th Division
	Dec 15-Jan 16	91 Brigade	7th Division
	Jan-Feb 16	154 Highland Brigade	51st Highland Division
1/1st Lovat Scouts	Aug 14-Sep 16	Highland Mounted Brigade	Highland Mounted Division
1/2nd Lovat Scouts	Aug 14-Sep 16	Highland Mounted Brigade	Highland Mounted Division
10th Camerons (Lovat Scouts)	Oct 16-Jun 18	82 Brigade	27th Division
	Jul-Nov 18	——	Lines of Communication troops
Lovat Scouts Sharpshooters	Nov 16-Nov 18	——	1 Corps
1/10th Liverpool Scottish	Aug-Nov 14	South Lancashire Brigade	West Lancashire Division
	Nov 14-Jan 16	9 Brigade	3rd Division
	Jan 16-Nov 18	166 Brigade	55th Division
2/10th Liverpool Scottish	Feb 15-Apr 18	172 Brigade	57th Division

NEW ARMY

Battalion	Dates	Brigade	Division
7th Seaforth	Aug 14-Nov 18	26 (Highland) Brigade	9th Scottish Division
8th Seaforth	Sep 14-Nov 18	44 (Highland) Brigade	15th Scottish Division
9th Seaforth	Dec 14-Nov 18	Divisional Pioneers	9th Scottish Division
1st Garrison Battalion Seaforth	Mar 17-Sep 18	228 Brigade	28th Division
5th Camerons	Aug 14-Nov 18	26 (Highland) Brigade	9th Scottish Division
6th Camerons	Sep 14-Nov 18	45 (Highland) Brigade	15th Scottish Division
7th Camerons	Jan 15-Jun 18	44 (Highland) Brigade	15th Scottish Division
9th Camerons	Sep 16-Apr 17	——	Lines of Communication troops
11th Camerons	Jun-Nov 18	120 Brigade	40th Division

3. THE REGULAR ARMY BATTALIONS

1st BATTALION SEAFORTH HIGHLANDERS

1st Seaforth moves to France – 1914

At the outbreak of war the 1st Seaforth was stationed at Agra in India, and embarked for France as the British battalion with 19 Indian (Dehra Dun) Brigade in the 7th Indian (Meerut) Division of the Indian Expeditionary Force. The 1st Seaforth arrived in France in October 1914.

La Bassée – Winter 1914-15

During the winter of 1914-15 the 1st Seaforth held positions in the line north of La Bassée, at Richebourg-St Vaast, Neuve Chapelle, and Festubert. The battalion was heavily attacked at Givenchy in December 1914, and fought alongside the 4th Seaforth which had been grouped in the same brigade.

Neuve Chapelle – March 1915

On 10th March 1915 the 1st Seaforth took part in the attack by the Indian Corps on the German lines at Neuve Chapelle. The attack started with an intense artillery bombardment by 480 guns, followed by an infantry assault which was expected to sweep the stunned German defenders out of their positions. This pattern of attack, in which 19th (Dehra Dun) Brigade made some gains, was to be followed by many subsequent offensive operations.

Aubers Ridge – May 1915

On 9th May 1915 the 1st Seaforth took part in the attack on Aubers Ridge. The advance lacked adequate fire support, and the attacking infantry were decimated by machine gun fire. The following week 19 Indian Brigade, having suffered such heavy casualties in the attack on Aubers Ridge, was held in reserve for the attack on Festubert.

Loos – September 1915

The Indian Corps was allocated a diversionary role on the flank for the attack at Loos. The 1st Seaforth did not leave its positions, but suffered over 100 casualties.

1st Seaforth moves to Mesopotamia – November 1915

In November 1915 the 7th Indian (Meerut) Division, including the 1st Seaforth, moved to Mesopotamia with the task of relieving the garrison of Kut-el-Amara, which was besieged by the Turks. The battalion landed at Basra in the Persian Gulf.

Sheikh Saad, Wadi, and Umm-el-Hannah – January 1916

The force, which included the 7th Indian (Meerut) Division, started its advance up the River Tigris in January 1916. The 1st Seaforth took part in three costly attacks on the Turkish positions at Sheikh Saad on 7th January, Wadi on 13th January, and Umm-el-Hannah on 21st-22nd January. These attacks across flat, featureless country without cover, reduced the strength of the 1st Seaforth to just over 100 men.

The 'Highland Battalion' – 1916

The 1st Seaforth and the 2nd Black Watch both suffered casualties on a similar scale, and so on 4th February 1916 the two battalions were temporarily amalgamated to form the 'Highland Battalion'. They fought under this designation until reinforcements allowed the two battalions to resume their normal identities on 12th July 1916.

Sanniyat – April 1916

In early April the force advanced again, by-passing the Turkish position at Sanniyat. The Highland Battalion managed to penetrate the Turkish positions, but the ground was so water-logged that it was forced to withdraw. The combined battalion lost 921 officers and men in three weeks of bitter fighting.

Corporal Sydney Ware,VC

Corporal Sydney Ware wins the Victoria Cross, 6th April 1916

During the operations at Sanniyat No 920 Corporal Sydney Ware, from Whatcombe in Dorset, was awarded the Victoria Cross. The citation read:

'For most conspicuous bravery at Sanniyat, Mesopotamia, on 6th April 1916. An order was given to withdraw to the cover of a communication trench. Corporal Ware, whose cool gallantry had been very marked during the advance, was one of the few men remaining unwounded. He picked up a wounded man and carried him some 200 yards to cover and then returned for others, moving to and fro under very heavy fire for more than two hours, until he had brought in all his wounded and was completely exhausted.'
(London Gazette 29 September 1916)

Sanniyat – February 1917

On 22nd February 1917 the 1st Seaforth took part in a further attack on the Turkish positions at Sanniyat. This time, with much improved fire support, three lines of enemy trenches were captured.

Sergeant Thomas Steele wins the Victoria Cross, 22nd February 1917

During the attack on Sanniyat No 811 Sergeant Thomas Steele, from Oldham in Lancashire, was awarded the Victoria Cross. The citation read:

'For most conspicuous bravery and devotion to duty near Sanniyat, Mesopotamia, on 22nd February 1917. At a critical moment, when a strong enemy counter-attack had temporarily regained some of the captured trenches, Sergeant Steele rushed forward and assisted a comrade to carry a machine gun into position. He kept the gun in action till relieved, being mainly instrumental in keeping the remainder of the line intact.

Sergeant Thomas Steele, VC

Some hours later, a strong attack enabled the enemy to re-occupy a portion of the captured trenches. Again Sergeant Steele showed the greatest bravery, and by personal valour and example was able to rally troops who were wavering. He encouraged them to remain in the trenches and led a number forward, thus greatly helping to establish our line. On this occasion he was severely wounded. These acts of valour were performed under very heavy artillery and rifle fire.'
(London Gazette 8 June 1917)

The occupation of Baghdad – March 1917

The 1st Seaforth were present on 11th March 1917 when the force, after two weeks hard marching, captured Baghdad.

1st Battalion Seaforth Highlanders passing the arch of Ctesiphon in Iraq 1917

Moushahdieh, Beled, and Istabulat – March – April 1917

The advance was continued beyond Baghdad, and in March-April 1917 the 1st Seaforth fought three actions at Moushahdieh, Beled, and Istabulat during which the railway system was secured.

1st Seaforth moves to Egypt – January 1918

At the end of 1917 the 1st Seaforth moved back to Basra where the battalion embarked for Egypt on 1st January 1918. After two months spent resting and re-fitting at Ismailia, the 1st Seaforth joined General Allenby's XXIst Corps in Palestine.

Beit Lid – September 1918

The 1st Seaforth took part with General Allenby's force in the pursuit of the retreating Turks. The battalion's final action of the war was the attack on Beit Lid on 20th September 1918. After a 34 mile approach march over rough country, the Turkish position was assaulted and taken.

1st Seaforth at the end of the War – 1918-1919

From Beit Lid the 1st Seaforth marched north to Beirut and Tripoli. The battalion was in Beirut at the time of the Armistice, returning to Alexandria in March 1919, and embarking for home in June 1919.

2nd BATTALION SEAFORTH HIGHLANDERS

2nd Seaforth move to France – August 1914

When war broke out on 4th August 1914, the 2nd Seaforth was stationed at Shorncliffe in Kent. The battalion was brought up to strength with Regular Army Reservists and landed in France on 23rd August. It belonged to 10 Brigade, in the 4th Division of the British Expeditionary Force.

Le Cateau, the Retreat from Mons, and the Marne – September 1914

The 2nd Seaforth first went into action at Le Cateau. The battalion then fought back with 10 Brigade during the retreat from Mons, until the German advance was halted at the River Marne in early September 1914.

The capture of Meteren – October 1914

On 10th October 1914 the 2nd Seaforth took part in the capture of the German-held village of Meteren. It was one of the last actions to be fought in open countryside before the miserable trench warfare which developed by the end of 1914.

The 2nd Battle of Ypres – April-May 1915

During April-May 1915 the 2nd Seaforth was heavily engaged in the defence of the Ypres salient against the German advance. The counter attack on St Julien on 25th April was the battalion's most costly action since the outbreak of war, and the loss to the 2nd Seaforth was 348 officers and men.

On 2nd May the battalion had its first experience of poison gas. At the time there was little protection against gas except for an ineffective respirator of impregnated cloth, or even a handkerchief, and the 2nd Seaforth lost 24 dead from gas, with 324 sick. The German attacks between 25th April-24th May 1915 cost the battalion over a thousand casualties.

Albert and Arras – 1915-1916

After the crippling casualties suffered at Ypres, the 2nd Seaforth was transferred to the quieter sector of the 3rd Army front between Albert and Arras. Here the battalion had a chance to absorb and train reinforcements, between minor operations and periods in the trenches.

The Battle of the Somme – July 1916

On 1st July 1916 the British offensive on the River Somme opened with an unprecedented artillery bombardment lasting seven days. The objective of the 2nd Seaforth was the village of Beaumont Hamel. By the end of the first day of the battle the British army had lost 57,470 casualties, of whom over 20,000 were killed. The 2nd Seaforth alone lost over 500 casualties.

The Battle of the Somme lasted for four months, during which the 2nd Seaforth remained in and out of the front line. The total gain was three or four miles of enemy-held ground.

Drum Major Walter Ritchie, VC

Drummer Walter Ritchie wins the Victoria Cross, 1st July 1916

During the 2nd Seaforth attack on the first day of the Somme No 68 Drummer Walter Ritchie, from Glasgow, was awarded the Victoria Cross. The citation read:

'For most conspicuous bravery and resource North of Beaumont Hamel, France, on 1st July 1916, when, on his own initiative, he stood on the parapet of the enemy trench, and, under heavy machine gun fire and bomb attacks, repeatedly sounded the "Charge", thereby rallying many men of various units who, having lost their leaders, were wavering and beginning to retire. This action showed the highest type of courage and personal initiative. Throughout the day Drummer Ritchie carried messages over fire-swept ground, showing the greatest devotion to duty.'
(London Gazette 9 September 1916)

Arras – April-May 1917

After a winter in the trenches the 2nd Seaforth took part in the attacks at Arras in April-May 1917. In the attack by the 4th Division on 9th April the battalion advanced successfully to their objective 4$\frac{1}{2}$ miles inside the German lines. But by 11th April the attacks degenerated to the deadly stalemate of trench warfare. In the attack on the factory at Fampoux, the 2nd Seaforth suffered 526 casualties, amounting to 93% of the battalion strength. Three of the companies lost all their officers.

Lieutenant Donald Mackintosh wins the Victoria Cross, 11th April 1917

During the attack at Arras Lieutenant Donald Mackintosh was awarded the Victoria Cross. The citation read:

'For most conspicuous bravery and resolution north of Fampoux, France, on 11th April 1917, in the face of intense rifle fire. During the initial advance he was shot through the right leg, but though crippled, he continued to lead his men and captured an enemy trench. In the trench Lieutenant Mackintosh collected men of another company who had lost their leader and drove back a counter-attack. He was again wounded and, although unable to stand, he continued nevertheless to control the situation. With only fifteen men he ordered his party to be ready to advance to the final objective, and with great difficulty got out of the trench and encouraged his men to advance. He was again wounded and fell. The gallantry and devotion to duty of this officer were beyond all praise.'
(London Gazette 8 June 1917)

Lieutenant Donald Mackintosh, VC

Pipes and drums of 2nd Battalion Seaforth Highlanders on the eve of the Battle of the Somme, 1916.
Drummer Walter Ritchie, who was to win the Victoria Cross, is second from the left.

The 3rd Battle of Ypres – October 1917

In the further attempts to break the grim stalemate at Ypres, the 2nd Seaforth took part in the attack in October 1917 which aimed to drive the Germans off the Passchendaele ridge overlooking Ypres. The battalion suffered 457 casualties in the month.

The final German offensive – 1918

After another winter in the trenches the 2nd Seaforth was holding a sector of the line at Arras when the Germans launched their final major offensive on 21st March 1918. Arras lay between the two main German thrusts, and as the allies fell back on either side, it became a salient. When the German advance was eventually halted, the 2nd Seaforth was moved to reinforce the front at La Bassée.

The Allied counter-offensive – 1918

In the Allied counter-offensive which began in early August 1918 the 2nd Seaforth advanced again, with relatively few casualties. The battalion ended the war near Valenciennes.

1st BATTALION
THE QUEEN'S OWN CAMERON HIGHLANDERS

1st Battalion The Queen's Own Cameron Highlanders march out of Edinburgh Castle for France, 12th August 1914.

1st Camerons move to France – August 1914

When war broke out on 4th August 1914 the 1st Camerons was stationed in Edinburgh Castle. Within a week the battalion had been reinforced by 700 Army Reservists, and it left for France on 12th August 1914.

Mons and the Marne – September 1914

During the Retreat from Mons, the 1st Camerons was tasked as Army troops for the defence of the British Expeditionary Force Headquarters. Then it joined the 1st Division and remained in this formation for the rest of the war. The 1st Camerons formed part of the 1st Brigade which, until the 2nd Guards Brigade was formed in 1915, also included 1st Battalion Coldstream Guards, 1st Battalion Scots Guards, and 1st Battalion The Black Watch. In early September the 1st Camerons took part in the successful counter offensive on the River Marne.

The Aisne – September 1914

The first major engagement for the 1st Camerons was the battle of the Aisne, fought before the war had developed into the static operations of trench warfare. On 14th September 1914 the 1st Camerons attacked the German lines, but came up against strongly prepared positions and lost 151 casualties. On 25th September the 1st Camerons had a particular stroke of ill luck when battalion headquarters, which was sited in a cave in a chalk quarry, was hit by a shell. The acting Commanding Officer Captain D N C C Miers and almost the entire battalion HQ staff were killed.

**Private Ross Tollerton wins the Victoria Cross
– 14th September 1914**

During the 1st Camerons attack at the Aisne No 7281 Pte Ross Tollerton was awarded the VC for saving the life of Lieutenant J S M Matheson. The citation read:

'For most conspicuous bravery and devotion to duty on the 14th September at the battle of the Aisne. He carried a wounded officer under heavy fire as far as he was able to a place of safety, then, although himself wounded in the head and hand, he struggled back to the firing line, where he remained till his battalion retired, when he returned to the wounded officer and lay beside him for three days until they were both rescued.'
(London Gazette 19 April 1915)

Private Ross Tollerton, VC

The 1st `Battle of Ypres – October 1914

During October 1914 the 1st Camerons fought dogged defensive actions at Langemarck, Gheluvelt, Nonne Bosschen and Givenchy, which eventually brought the German advance to a halt outside Ypres.

Givenchy – December 1914

In December 1914 the 1st Division was sent to the Bethune area to strengthen the line. On 21st/22nd December the 1st Camerons took part in the attack by the 1st Division which made gains at Givenchy.

Aubers Ridge – May 1915

On 9th May 1915 the 1st Camerons took part in the unsuccessful attack on Aubers Ridge, suffering 104 casualties from enemy machine guns which artillery bombardment had failed to neutralise.

Loos – 1915

In the opening attack at the battle of Loos on 25th September 1915, the 1st Brigade was one of the few formations to break through the German lines. The 1st Camerons penetrated as far as the town of Hulloch, but the loss of 364 casualties reduced the battalion to a strength of only 4 officers and 200 soldiers. Later in the battle of Loos the 1st Camerons took part in the attack on the Hohenzollern Redoubt at Hulloch on 13th October 1915.

The Battle of the Somme – 1916

Three weeks after the opening of the Battle of the Somme, the 1st Camerons took part in the 1st Brigade's attack on Bazentin Ridge on 21st-23rd July 1916. By this stage of the conflict the development of trench warfare had reduced the fighting to a stalemate, and the attack could make little progress against the elaborate German defences.

High Wood – September 1916

During September 1916 the 1st Camerons and the 1st Black Watch attacked the German positions in High Wood and, although they took their objective, they suffered so many casualties that they could not hold them against subsequent German counter attacks. One company of the 1st Camerons was reduced to a strength of 12 men.

(Note The two regiments afterwards erected a memorial at High Wood, in the form of St Andrew's Cross, to this gallant but costly attack).

Passchendaele – 1917

In November 1917 the 1st Camerons returned to Ypres, and on 15th November the battalion carried out a successful attack on Vocation Farm at Passchendaele, north east of Ypres.

The German final offensive of 1918

When the Germans launched their final offensive in March 1918 the 1st Camerons were in the Bethune area which was not at first heavily attacked. On 18th April the battalion fought a tough defensive battle at Givenchy where, despite over 100 casualties, the British line remained intact.

Epéhy – September 1918

In September 1918 the 1st Camerons returned to the Somme. Between 18-24th September 1918 the battalion attacked successfully at Epéhy, capturing its objective and a large quantity of German weapons. The 1st Division took 1100 prisoners.

The Selle – October – November 1918

On 17-18th October 1918 the 1st Division attacked through the mist, with enemy smoke and gas shells falling. The 1st Camerons captured its objective of La Vallée Mulatre ridge. In the 1st Camerons final operation of the war it attacked across the Sambre and L'Oise Canal, capturing 500 prisoners and a large number of German machine guns and field artillery.

2nd BATTALION
THE QUEEN'S OWN CAMERON HIGHLANDERS

2nd Camerons move to France – 1914

When war broke out in August 1914, the 2nd Camerons was stationed at Poona in India. In October 1914 the battalion sailed for Great Britain, joining 81st Brigade in the 27th Division, which was formed from battalions returning from overseas. The 2nd Camerons arrived in France on 19th December 1914.

The 2nd Battle of Ypres – 1915

After the 2nd Camerons took over in the trenches south of Ypres in January 1915, the 27th Division was to bear the brunt of the German efforts to take Ypres. But resolute defence brought the enemy advance to a halt. Holding positions in the Ypres Salient from 21-29 April 1915, the 2nd Camerons took part in the gallant defence of Hill 60 against determined German attacks. At the end of April 1915 the 27th Division redeployed to new positions centred on Frezenberg village, a semi-circular defensive line about 2½ miles east of Ypres, with the 2nd Camerons holding positions astride the Menin road and in Sanctuary Wood. The Second battle of Ypres prevented the Germans capturing the town, but the cost to the 2nd Camerons was 673 casualties during the month of fighting. After Ypres, the 2nd Camerons held positions on the Somme during the summer of 1915.

2nd Camerons move to Macedonia – 1915

In September 1915 Bulgaria entered the war as an ally of Austria-Hungary and Germany, and the Bulgarians invaded Serbia, reaching as far as Macedonia. A French and British force was sent to protect Greece, but was forced back by the Bulgarians.

In November 1915 the 27th Division, with the 2nd Camerons, was sent from France to Macedonia to reinforce the Allied army which was now holding positions known as the 'Birdcage' round the port of Salonika.

Bala and Zir – 1916

In May 1916 the Bulgarians advanced into Greece, and the 27th Division left its positions to reinforce the line in the Struma Valley. From 30th September-3rd October the 2nd Camerons led the successful attack on the Bulgarians which captured the villages of Bala and Zir.

The Struma Valley – 1916-1918

After this defeat of the Bulgarians the 2nd Camerons held positions in the trenches in the Struma Valley for two years. Compared with the Western front, it was a low key campaign, most casualties being caused by malaria, against which no effective preventive medicine had yet been developed.

2nd Battalion The Queen's Own Cameron Highlanders, dress worn in Salonika

Homondos – 1917

On 13th/14th October 1917 the 2nd Camerons and the Scottish Horse carried out a successful night attack on the Bulgarians at Homondos. Achieving surprise by a night march round the enemy position, they attacked from the flank, and the 2nd Camerons killed 120 and took 152 prisoners for the loss of 39 casualties.

Armistice with Bulgaria – 1918

In September 1918 the Bulgarians were abandoned by their German allies, and the British advanced forward into Serbia and Bulgaria. An Armistice was agreed on 30th September 1918.

2nd Camerons in Trans-Caucasia – 1918

The final phase of the war for the 27th Division was to move by sea to Batum in Georgia, at the east end of the Black Sea, to expel the Germans from Trans-Caucasia. The 2nd Camerons returned to Great Britain from Georgia in May 1919.

4. SPECIAL RESERVE BATTALIONS AND DEPOTS

3rd (SPECIAL RESERVE) BATTALION SEAFORTH HIGHLANDERS

On the outbreak of war on 4th August 1914, the 3rd (Special Reserve) Battalion Seaforth Highlanders mobilised at Fort George. The battalion moved by sea to Cromarty on 12th August 1914, and remained as the garrison in Cromarty until the end of the war, forming part of the coastal defences around the naval base in the Cromarty Firth.

The wartime role of the 3rd Seaforth was to provide drafts of reinforcements for the Regular and Service battalions in the front line. The men passed through the Depot at Fort George, and included new enlistments from the recruiting offices, and men who had been evacuated to Great Britain as casualties from the front, and were once again passed as fit for service. The strength of the battalion varied from between 1150 to 2600.

At the end of the war the 3rd Seaforth moved from Cromarty to Glencorse. On the disbandment of the battalion in 1919, it provided a nucleus for the 1st Battalion which returned from Egypt to Edinburgh at cadre strength. Having re-formed at Glencorse, the 1st Seaforth became the home service battalion of the Seaforth Highlanders.

DEPOT SEAFORTH HIGHLANDERS, Fort George

The immediate task of the Depot Seaforth at the start of World War I was to recall the Regular Army Reservists, and to despatch them to Shorncliffe to bring the 2nd Seaforth up to strength for service with the British Expeditionary Force in France. The joint establishment of the Depot and the 3rd (Special Reserve) Battalion then separated, the 3rd Seaforth mobilising and moving off to Cromarty, while the Depot Seaforth staff remained at Fort George as a holding unit.

The next main task was the formation of the New Army battalions, and from August 1914 onwards the 7th, 8th, and 9th Seaforth were formed at Fort George, and despatched south to join the newly forming divisions of the New Army. For the remainder of the war the Depot received all recruits for the Regular and Service battalions, carrying out medical checks and issuing clothing, before sending them to the 3rd Seaforth at Cromarty for training and to be formed into drafts for the front.

3rd (SPECIAL RESERVE) BATTALION THE QUEEN'S OWN CAMERON HIGHLANDERS

When war broke out on 4th August 1914 the 3rd (Special Reserve) Battalion The Queen's Own Cameron Highlanders, under the command of Lieutenant Colonel Donald W Cameron of Lochiel, mobilised at Cameron Barracks. It then moved by train to Invergordon. The battalion formed part of the defences for the naval base in the Cromarty Firth, being responsible for the protection of the oil tanks at Invergordon.

The wartime role of the 3rd Camerons was to provide drafts of reinforcements for the Regular and Service battalions at the front. The men, who were normally first processed and kitted out at the Depot in Cameron Barracks, included new enlistments from the recruiting offices, and casualties who had been evacuated from France for treatment in Great Britain, and who were once again passed as fit for service. During the war the 3rd Camerons despatched 15,583 officers men to the battalions at the front.

In August 1914 Lochiel was commissioned to raise a Service Battalion, and he was succeeded in command by Colonel the Mackintosh of Mackintosh commanded the 3rd Camerons until 1917. In November 1917 the 3rd Camerons moved from Invergordon to Ireland where the battalion was stationed at Birr and Ballyvonare. The 3rd Camerons returned from Ireland in 1919, being billeted at Redford Barracks and Dreghorn Camp in Edinburgh, until the battalion was put into 'suspended animation'. The 3rd (Special Reserve) Battalion was eventually disbanded in 1953.

DEPOT THE QUEEN'S OWN CAMERON HIGHLANDERS,
Cameron Barracks, Inverness

The immediate task of the Depot Camerons at the start of World War 1 was to recall of the Regular Army Reservists, and to despatch them to Edinburgh to bring the 1st Camerons up to strength for service with the British Expeditionary Force in France. The joint establishment of the Depot and the 3rd (Special Reserve Battalion then separated, the 3rd Camerons mobilising and moving to Invergordon, leaving the Depot at Cameron Barracks as a holding unit.

The next priority was the formation of the New Army battalions, which owed the remarkable success of their recruiting to the work of Lieutenant Colonel Donald W Cameron of Lochiel. From August 1914 onwards the 5th, 6th, 7th, and 8th Camerons were formed at the Depot and despatched south to join the newly forming divisions of the New Army. For the remainder of the war the Depot received all recruits for the Regular and Service battalions, carrying out medical checks and issuing clothing, before passing them on to the 3rd Camerons for training and to be formed into drafts for the front. An example of the volume of work carried out by the Depot staff was the total of over 11,000 kilts turned out by the tailors at Cameron Barracks during the war.

5. THE TERRITORIAL FORCE BATTALIONS
1/4th (ROSS-HIGHLAND) BATTALION SEAFORTH HIGHLANDERS

Mobilisation, and training at Bedford – August 1914

When war broke out on 4th August 1914 the 4th Seaforth mobilised at Dingwall. The battalion's first task was to prepare defences at Nigg for the protection of the naval base in the Cromarty Firth. On 15th August the 4th Seaforth, which formed part of the Seaforth and Cameron Brigade of the Highland Territorial Division, moved to Bedford, where the battalion was brought up to strength by new recruits. In September 1914 the 2/4th Battalion was formed at Dingwall to provide reinforcements for the 1/4th Battalion.

1/4th Seaforth moves to France – 1914

The 1/4th Seaforth was one of the first Territorial Force battalions to go to France, and it arrived there on 6th November 1914. For several weeks an epidemic of scarlet fever kept the battalion in the rear areas, but on 20th December it joined the 1st Seaforth in 19 Indian (Dehra Dun) Brigade of the 7th Indian (Meerut) Division.

Neuve Chapelle – March 1915

The first major action for the 1/4th Seaforth was the attack on Neuve Chapelle on 10th March 1915, an operation that achieved limited success. The 1/4th Seaforth attack was delayed until the evening, and during the night's fighting the battalion lost 168 casualties, but it acquitted itself well beside the Regular troops of the brigade.

Aubers Ridge – May 1915

In May 1915 the 1/4th Seaforth, alongside the 1st Seaforth in 19 Indian (Dehra Dun) Brigade, suffered over 200 casualties in the unsuccessful attack on Aubers Ridge.

Loos – September 1915

At the Battle of Loos which began on 25th September 1915 the 1/4th Seaforth provided a party of 100 men to protect the cylinders of poison gas, which was used by the British for the first time. The battalion, by now reduced to low strength by casualties, did not take part in the main attack on Loos.

1/4th Seaforth returns to the Highland Division

In November 1915 the 7th Indian (Meerut) Division left France for the Persian Gulf, and so the 1/4th Seaforth returned to the 51st Highland Division, joining 154 Highland Brigade in January 1916.

The Battle of the Somme – 1916

During the Battle of the Somme the 1/4th Seaforth had five hard days hard fighting from 22nd-26th July 1916 in the attempts to capture High Wood, where the German and British lines nearly met. The thick trees and undergrowth made effective artillery support impossible, and the actions were mainly infantry attacks.

The Ancre – 1916

The 1/4th Seaforth returned to the Somme on 3rd October, and the battalion took part in the fourth phase of the Somme offensive, known as the Battle of the Ancre. The attack by the 51st Highland Division on Beaumont Hamel began on 13th November, and the 1/4th Seaforth was committed to this highly successful operation from the 14th-19th November.

Arras and the Scarpe – 1917

On 9th April 1917 the 1/4th Seaforth was in the first line of the 51st Highland Division attack at Arras. Despite suffering over 200 casualties, the battalion took its final objective successfully, capturing 167 prisoners. On 23rd April the 1/4th Seaforth succeeded in capturing the German positions in the Chemical Works at Roeux, beside the River Scarpe Canal, which had caused severe casualties in early attempts to take them. Although hit by heavy artillery fire, including a misdirected British bombardment, the battalion successfully resisted fierce German counter-attacks.

The 3rd Battle of Ypres – 1917

On 31st July 1917 began the major Allied attack on the German positions overlooking Ypres. In the advance by the 51st Highland Division, which was the only division to achieve its objectives on the first day, the 1/4th Seaforth had its first encounter with enemy gas. The 1/4th Seaforth in 154 Brigade took part in the 51st Highland Division's attack on 20th September and, despite over 200 casualties, gained another 1000 yards.

Cambrai – November 1917

On 20th November 1917 the 1/4th Seaforth took part in the first massed tank attack in history. The attack at Cambrai by seven divisions, including 324 tanks, achieved a major breakthrough, but cost the battalion over 300 casualties.

The German offensive – 1918

When the Germans launched their last major offensive on 21st March 1918 the 1/4th Seaforth was holding positions on the Beaumetz-Morchies line. The battalion's stand, together with the 7th Argyll and Sutherland Highlanders, was considered to be one of the finest, though costliest, actions fought by battalions of the 51st Highland Division.

The counter-attack in Champagne – 1918

In July the 51st Highland Division was withdrawn from the line and moved South to Epernay to support the French Army. It attacked in the close country of the River Ardre, but ran into strong German opposition and suffered some of the worst fighting of the war.

Sergeant John Meikle wins the Victoria Cross, 20th July 1918

During the fighting in the Ardre Valley No 200854 Sergeant John Meikle MM, from Nitshill, Renfrew, was awarded the Victoria Cross. The citation read:

'For most conspicuous bravery and initiative near Marfaux, France, on 20th July 1918, when, his company having been held up by machine gun fire, he rushed single handed a machine gun nest. He emptied his revolver into the crews of the two guns and put the remainder out of action with a heavy stick. Then standing up he waved his comrades on. Very shortly afterwards, another hostile machine gun checked progress and threatened also the success of the company on the right. Most of his platoon having become casualties, Sergeant Meikle seized the rifle and bayonet of a fallen comrade and again rushed forward against the gun crew, and was killed almost on the gun position. His bravery allowed two other men, who had followed him, to put the gun out of action. This gallant Non-commissioned Officer's valour, devotion to duty, and utter disregard for his personal safety, were an inspiring example to all.' (London Gazette 14/16 September 1918)

The final Allied offensive – 1918

The 1/4th Seaforth returned to Cambrai in October 1918, and took part in the 51st Highland Division's final operation of the war, the advance towards Valenciennes. In a series of attacks the 1/4th Seaforth encountered fierce German resistance, and lost over 300 casualties. But when the Division was relieved in the line on 28th October, it had made substantial gains of ground.

Sergeant John Meikle, VC

1/5th (SUTHERLAND & CAITHNESS) BATTALION SEAFORTH HIGHLANDERS

Mobilisation, and training at Bedford August 1914

When war broke out on 4th August 1914, the 5th Seaforth mobilised at Golspie. The battalion's first task was to construct defences on the North Sutor at the entrance to the Cromarty Firth naval base. The 5th Seaforth was a battalion of the Seaforth and Cameron Brigade in the Highland Territorial Division. It moved south with the division and spent eight months training at Bedford. In September 1914 the 2/5th Battalion was formed at Golspie to provide reinforcements for the 1/5th Battalion.

The 1/5th Seaforth moves to France – May 1915

The 1/5th Seaforth moved to France on 1st May 1915. On arrival at the front the battalion relieved the 1/6th Seaforth in the trenches at Richebourg-St Vaast, near La Bassée, on 22nd May 1915.

Festubert – June 1915

On 15th June 1915 the 1/5th Seaforth saw its first major offensive action of the war, taking part in the attack by 153 and 154 Brigades on the German line at Festubert.

Laventie, Albert, Arras, – 1915-1916

During June-July 1915 the 1/5th Seaforth held sections of the line around Laventie, and from August to December in the Albert Sector. In March 1916 the 51st Highland Division took over the 'Labyrinth' North of Arras.

The Somme – 1916

During the early stages of the Battle of the Somme the 51st Highland Division held positions in the line on Vimy Ridge . In late July 1916, after the first phase of the Somme offensive was over, the 1/5th Seaforth moved to the Somme, holding the line at High Wood and Mametz Wood.

The Ancre – 1916

In October 1916 the 1/5th Seaforth took over in the line opposite the ruined village of Beaumont Hamel. When the 51st Highland Division launched its attack on the village on 13th November, the 1/5th Seaforth led the 152 Brigade advance. In this celebrated capture of the key German defensive position, the battalion took its objective despite suffering over 300 casualties, and it captured over 600 prisoners.

Arras and the Scarpe – 1917

On 9th April 1917 the three Scottish divisions, the 9th, 15th and 51st Highland Divisions, attacked at Arras. The 1/5th Seaforth advancing on the left front with 152 Brigade, took its objective at a cost of over 300 casualties. During the German counter-attacks on Roeux which followed, the battalion held Roeux and the Chemical works, resisting a particularly strong German attack on 15-16th May.

The 3rd Battle of Ypres – 1917

The 51st Highland Division took part in the major offensive on 31st July 1917 against the German positions overlooking Ypres, the 1/5th Seaforth successfully capturing its objectives and taking 700 prisoners. The battalion remained in the Ypres salient until 24th September 1917.

Cambrai – November 1917

On 20th November 1917 the 1/5th Seaforth took part in the first attack ever carried out with massed tanks. The battalion quickly broke through the German lines and captured the village of Ribecourt, with 300 prisoners. Next day the 1/5th Seaforth captured its objective of Flesquières, and was relieved on 24th November.

Lance Corporal Robert McBeath wins the Victoria Cross, 20th November 1917

During the advance of the 1/5th Seaforth at Cambrai No 240171 Lance Corporal Robert McBeath, from Kinlochbervie, Sutherland was awarded the Victoria Cross. The citation read:

'For most conspicuous bravery west of Cambrai, France, on 20th November 1917, when, with his company in attack and approaching the final objective, a nest of enemy machine guns in the western outskirts of a village opened fire both on his own unit and on the unit on his right. The advance was checked and heavy casualties resulted. When a Lewis gun was called for to deal with these machine guns, Lance Corporal McBeath volunteered for the duty and immediately moved off alone with a Lewis gun and revolver. He found, however, several other hostile machine guns in action and, with the assistance of a tank, attacked them and drove the gunners to ground in a deep dug-out. Lance Corporal McBeath, regardless of danger, rushed in after them, shot an enemy who opposed him on the steps, and drove the remainder of the garrison out of the dug-out, capturing 3 officers and 30 men. There were in all five machine guns mounted round the dug-out and, by putting them out of action, he cleared the way for the advance of both units. 'The conduct of Lance Corporal McBeath throughout three days of severe fighting was beyond all praise.'

(London Gazette 11th January 1918)

Lance Corporal Robert McBeath, VC

The German offensive – 1918

When the Germans launched their last major offensive on 21st March 1918, the 1/5th Seaforth was in the line astride the Bapaume-Cambrai road. The German attack started with an intense bombardment of gas and shells, but the battalion held its ground for six days until relieved, sustaining 377 casualties in the fighting. On 4th April 1918 the 1/5th Seaforth returned to the line on the River Lawe sector north of Bethune, and again held off heavy attacks on 11-12 April at a further cost of over 200 casualties.

The counter-attack in Champagne – 1918

In July 1918 the 51st Highland Division was moved south to support the French Army in the Epernay area. The 1/5th Seaforth was to experience some of its heaviest fighting in stopping the German break through on the Marne. From 21st-28th July, in the Valley of the River Arde, the battalion lost 369 casualties, but the offensive action turned the tide of the German advance.

The Scarpe – 1918

In August 1918 the 1/5th Seaforth returned to the area of Rouex on the River Scarpe, and took part in the recapture of the infamous chemical works and the town of Rouex itself.

The final Allied offensive – 1918

After the 51st Highland Division returned to the Cambrai area the 1/5th Seaforth took part in the attack on 12-13th October, the division's final major operation before the Armistice. The last battle of the war for the 1/5th Seaforth was the attack at Thun St Martin. The final 16 days fighting had cost the battalion over 400 casualties.

1/6th (MORAYSHIRE) BATTALION SEAFORTH HIGHLANDERS

Mobilisation, and training at Bedford – August 1914

When war broke out on 4th August 1914 the 6th Seaforth mobilised at Elgin. The 6th Seaforth was a battalion in the Seaforth and Cameron Brigade in the Highland Territorial Division. The 6th Seaforth moved south with the division and spent eight months training at Bedford. In September 1914 the 2/6th Battalion was formed at Elgin to provide reinforcements for the 1/6th Battalion.

The 1/6th Seaforth moves to France – May 1915

The 1/6th Seaforth left for France on 1st May 1915, and moved into the trenches at Richebourg-St Vaast, north of La Bassée, on 19th May. The battalion was relieved by the 1/5th Seaforth three days later.

Festubert – June 1915

On 15th June 153 and 154 Brigades attacked at Festubert, and the task of the 1/6th Seaforth was to give covering small arms fire. The attack provoked a heavy counter bombardment, and in the packed trenches the battalion suffered 140 casualties from shell fire.

Laventie, Albert, Arras – 1915-1916

In late June 1915 the 1/6th Seaforth took over in the trenches at Laventie, and from August to December in the Albert sector. In March 1916 the Highland Division took over 'the Labyrinth' sector from the French. The routine was that each battalion did six days in the line, then six days in the support trenches, a further six days in the line, and then six days rest in billets. On 28th April the Germans exploded seven large mines simultaneously under the forward company positions, and followed this with heavy artillery fire. The battalion lost 67 casualties, but its dogged resistance prevented a German breakthrough.

The Battle of the Somme – 1916

During the preparations for the offensive on the Somme, the 51st Highland Division took over positions on Vimy Ridge. In mid July, after the first phase of the Somme offensive was over, the 1/6th Seaforth took over the line at Mametz Wood and High Wood.

The Ancre – 1916

On 13th November the 51st Highland Division attacked the key German positions in the ruined village of Beaumont Hamel, which had for long resisted capture, and which the Germans considered impregnable. The German ruse was to shelter in deep bunkers during the British advance, and then to emerge and attack the assaulting troops from the rear. A complete company of the 1/6th Seaforth was allotted to the task of countering this. The battalion took its objectives at the cost of 277 casualties.

Arras and the Scarpe – 1917

On 9th April 1917 the 1/6th Seaforth took part in one of the most successful actions of the war when the 51st Highland Division, together with the 9th and 15th Scottish Divisions, attacked the German positions at Arras. The attack achieved notable success and drove the enemy back between four and five miles in places. In late April and May the 1/6th Seaforth held the line against strong German counter attacks in the area of the Roeux chemical works.

1/6th Battalion Seaforth Highlanders in the trenches 1916.

The 3rd Battle of Ypres – 1917

On 31st July 1917 the 1/6th Seaforth took part in the 51st Highland Division's advance at Ypres which achieved its objectives with considerable success.

Sergeant Alexander Edwards wins the Victoria Cross, 31st July-1st August 1917

During the advance of the 1st/6th Seaforth at Ypres Sergeant Alexander Edwards, from Lossiemouth, Moray, was awarded the Victoria Cross. The citation read:

'For most conspicuous bravery in action north of Ypres, Belgium, on 31st July/1st August 1917, when, having located a machine gun in a wood, he with great dash and courage led some men against it; killed the team, and captured the gun. Later, when a sniper was causing casualties he crawled out to stalk him, and although badly wounded in the arm, went on and killed him. One officer only was now left with the company and, realising that the success of the operation depended on the capture of the further objective, Sergeant Edwards, regardless of his wound, led his men on till the objective was captured. He subsequently showed great skill in consolidating his position and very great daring in personal reconnaissance. Although twice wounded on the following day, this very gallant Non-commissioned Officer maintained throughout a complete disregard for personal safety, and his high example of coolness and determination engendered a fine fighting spirit among his men.' (London Gazette 13/14 September 1917)

Sergeant Alexander Edwards, VC

Cambrai – November 1917

On 20th November 1917 the 1/6th Seaforth took part in the first attack ever made with massed tanks. 152 Brigade was allocated 36 of the 324 tanks in the attack. Because breakdowns were frequent, the 1/6th Seaforth at battalion level had the support of only seven tanks. The battalion broke through the Hindenburg line and captured its objective, part of the village of Flesquières. The attack achieved a major breakthrough and, for the loss of 69 casualties, the battalion took 300 prisoners.

The German offensive – 1918

When the Germans launched their last major offensive on 21st March 1918, the 1/6th Seaforth was holding the line between Beaumetz and Morchies. For five days the battalion came under intense artillery bombardment and infantry attack, but despite nearly 400 casualties, it held its ground. Among those killed was the gallant Sergeant Alexander Edwards, VC.

On the withdrawal of flanking units to stabilise the line, the 1/6th Seaforth carried out an orderly withdrawal to a new positions. On 9th April 1918 the battalion returned to the line on the River Lawe north of Bethune, where it held off heavy German attacks on 11-12 April 1918.

The counter-attack in Champagne – 1918

In July 1918 the 51st Highland Division moved south to support the French Army in the Epernay area. In the operations which halted the German advance on the Marne, the 1/6th Seaforth suffered some of the heaviest casualties of the war, losing over 400 killed, wounded and missing. In the counter-attack in the valley of the River Ardre, which turned the tide of the German advance, the battalion took part, although reduced to the strength of a composite company.

The Scarpe – 1918

The 1/6th Seaforth returned in August 1918 to the Arras area, and took part in the attacks on Greenland Hill near Roeux, a feature which was vital for the final British offensive.

The final Allied offensive – 1918

The 1/6th Seaforth moved back to the Cambrai area in October 1918 where, in its final operation of the war, the 51st Highland Division advanced towards Valenciennes. The 1/6th Seaforth took part in a series of attacks by 152 Brigade. By the stage when it reached its final objectives before being relieved in the line on 28th October, the battalion had lost over 300 casualties.

1/4th BATTALION
THE QUEEN'S OWN CAMERON HIGHLANDERS

Mobilisation, and training at Bedford – 1914

When war broke out on 4th August 1914 the 4th Camerons mobilised at Inverness. The battalion's first task was to prepare defences at Cromarty for the protection of the naval base in the Cromarty Firth. The 4th Camerons formed part of the Seaforth and Cameron Brigade of the Highland Territorial Division. The battalion moved to Bedford with the division, and was brought up to strength with extra recruits, many coming from the London Scottish. In September 1914 the 2/4th Battalion was formed at Inverness to provide reinforcements for the 1/4th Battalion.

The 1/4th Camerons moves to France – 1915

Because the 1/4th Camerons was up to strength, the battalion was warned for an early move to France, but its departure was delayed by an outbreak of measles in which 28 men died. By February 1915 the epidemic had passed, and the battalion arrived in France on 20th February 1915, 960 strong. The 1/4th Camerons joined 24 Brigade in the 8th Division, and the battalion took over in the line on the Estaires-La Bassée road on 28th February 1915.

Neuve Chapelle – March 1915

The first major action of the war for the 1/4th Camerons was the attack on Neuve Chapelle, north of La Bassée, during 10th-17th March 1915. 24 Brigade's task was to secure the flank of the advance against enemy counter attack. The 1/4th Camerons repulsed a strong counter attack on 12th March, capturing 300 Germans. The seven days fighting cost the battalion 140 casualties.

Festubert – May 1915

In April 1915 the 1/4th Camerons was transferred to 21 Brigade in the 7th Division. The battalion played a gallant part in the attack at Festubert on 17th May. The attack was at night, and took place in heavy rain. The 1/4th Camerons had to advance over 800 yards of ground, intersected by deep, wide ditches of water, but nevertheless it succeeded in taking its objective. However the battalion on its flank failed to make progress, and the 1/4th Camerons was left unsupported and had to withdraw, with the loss of over 250 casualties.

Givenchy – 1915

The Pipes and Drums of 1/4th Battalion The Queen's Own Cameron Highlanders, TF in France 1915.

On 15th-16th June 1915 the 1/4th Camerons took part in the attack by the 7th Division and 51st Highland Division at Givenchy, intended as a preliminary to the attack at Loos.

Loos – September 1915

On 25th September 1915 the 1/4th Camerons attacked with the 7th Division at St Elie, on the left of the main advance. Seven days of bitter and continuous fighting cost the battalion nearly 200 casualties, but brought the 7th Division some gains.

The 1st/4th Camerons drafted – 1917

After Loos, the 7th Division was reorganized and reinforced with New Army battalions, and in January 1916 the 1/4th Camerons returned to the 51st Highland Division as a battalion in 154 Brigade. But the casualties at Festubert and Loos had reduced the 1/4th Camerons to below an effective strength of 500. The reinforcement system at home was concentrating on the New Army Service battalions of the Camerons, and as there seemed to be no immediate prospect of bringing the battalion up to strength, it was broken up and drafted, the majority of men being drafted to the lst Camerons, and 12 of the officers to the 1/10th Liverpool Scottish. The final nucleus of the battalion was dissolved in February 1917.

1/1st REGIMENT THE LOVAT SCOUTS
1/2nd REGIMENT THE LOVAT SCOUTS

Mobilisation – August 1914

The records of the two regiments of Lovat Scouts from 1914 – 1916 are very similar, and so they are combined in this account. When war broke out on 4th August 1914 the 1st and 2nd Regiments of the Lovat Scouts, with a total strength of about 1,200 men and their ponies, mobilised at Beaufort.

Training and home defence in England – 1914-1915

The 1st and 2nd Regiments Lovat Scouts joined the Highland Mounted Brigade at Huntingdon. The brigade, commanded by Lord Lovat, included the Fife and Forfar Yeomanry and the Inverness Battery, Royal Horse Artillery. In mid November 1914 the brigade moved to Grimsby to take over the defence of the coastline between Sutton-on-sea and Skegness. The brigade was relieved in April 1915, and rode south to billets in and around Hunstanton, on the Wash. In August 1915 it received orders to hand over the ponies to the Second Line and to prepare for service in the Mediterranean. The 2/1st and 2/2nd Lovat Scouts were formed in 1914 to provide reinforcements for the First Line regiments.

Gallipoli – September-December 1915

In September 1915 the 1/1st and 1/2nd Regiments Lovat Scouts, equipped as dismounted yeomanry, embarked at Devonport and landed with the 2nd Mounted Division (dismounted) at Suvla Bay on 27th September 1915. After a short time in the reserve trenches at Salt Lake, the Lovat Scouts took over a section of the front line trenches. The Scouts, although trained as mounted yeomanry, proved to be highly effective in the infantry role, their sniping and observation skills being particularly effective. But, like other regiments in the Dardanelles, they suffered many cases of dysentery. When the decision was taken to evacuate Gallipoli in December 1915, the Lovat Scouts and the Gurkhas were selected to provide the rearguard to cover the final withdrawal from Suvla Bay. Thanks to their scouting skills, the withdrawal was one of the most successful phases of an otherwise infamous campaign.

Egypt – 1915-1916

The Lovat Scouts after the evacuation of Gallipoli.

On their withdrawal from Gallipoli the 1/1st and 1/2nd Regiments Lovat Scouts reorganised in Cairo. In February 1916 they deployed into the Western Desert to operate against the Senussi, a Bedouin tribe paid by the Germans to conduct a guerrilla campaign. The tasks included the extension of the railway beyond the Kharga terminus.

The formation of the 10th Cameron Highlanders – September 1916.

In September 1916 the 1/1st and 1/2nd Regiments Lovat Scouts, by now low in strength, were amalgamated to form one infantry battalion, The battalion was made up to strength by the 3rd Scottish Horse which provided D Company, and designated the 10th (Lovat Scouts) Battalion The Queen's Own Cameron Highlanders.

10th (LOVAT SCOUTS) BATTALION
THE QUEEN'S OWN CAMERON HIGHLANDERS

Formation of the 10th (Lovat Scouts) Battalion – September 1916

After withdrawing from Gallipoli in December 1915, and while serving as dismounted yeomanry in Egypt, the 1/1st and 1/2nd Regiments of the Lovat Scouts fell to very low strength. The two regiments, together with a company formed from the 3rd Scottish Horse, were amalgamated on 27th September 1916 to form one infantry battalion designated the 10th (Lovat Scouts) Battalion, The Queen's Own Cameron Highlanders. The battalion was still referred to as The Lovat Scouts, and continued to wear its blue diced bonnets, badges, and Fraser tartan shoulder patches.

Macedonia – 1916-1918

The 10th (Lovat Scouts) Battalion landed at Salonika on 20th October 1916 and joined 82 Brigade in the 27th Division. The battalion's skill at sniping, observation and fieldcraft, and its aptitude for patrolling, made it most valuable in the operations in the Struma Valley. In October 1917 the Lovat Scouts carried out a particularly successful attack on the enemy held village of Salmah, where the battalion surprised the Bulgarians, killing 70 and capturing over 100.

France – 1918

In June 1918 the 10th (Lovat's Scouts) Battalion left Macedonia and moved to France. For the last few months of the war the Lovat Scouts retrained in observation and signalling, and were sent to join the Observer Groups of the Lovat Scouts (Sharpshooters) which Lord Lovat had formed in 1916 for service on the Western front. The battalion was disbanded in April 1919.

THE LOVAT SCOUTS (SHARPSHOOTERS)

Formation in 1916

The Lovat Scouts (Sharpshooters) were formed by Lord Lovat in October 1916 with the intention of providing skilled observation on the battlefield, in the same way that the Lovat Scouts had been used in the South African war. The Sharpshooters, picked stalkers and expert with the spyglass, were selected from the reserve regiments, and from Scouts who had returned wounded from the Middle East.

France – 1916-1918

After training in Scotland a force of nine observer groups, each consisting of an officer and twenty men, started operating in France in late 1916. The groups were commanded at first by Colonel Lord Lovat, and controlled from Corps Headquarters from where they were deployed for specific tasks, such as close observation of enemy activity, or providing detailed intelligence on a section of the enemy lines before an attack.

Such was the value of the particular skills of spying and reconnaissance patrolling, in which the Lovat Scouts had no equals on either the allied or the enemy side, that when the war ended in 1918 there were plans to allocate Lovat Scouts observer groups to every British division.

1/10th (SCOTTISH) BATTALION THE KING'S (LIVERPOOL) REGIMENT

Mobilisation – August 1914

When war broke out in August 1914 the Liverpool Scottish mobilised at Liverpool and moved to Edinburgh. The battalion formed part of the Forth defences. In September 1914 a 2nd Battalion was formed.

The 1st Liverpool Scottish moves to France – November 1914

On 10th October the lst Liverpool Scottish moved south to Tunbridge Wells, and on 1st November 1914 embarked at Southampton for France on SS Maidan. The battalion landed at Le Havre on 3rd November.

Ypres – 1914-1915

The 1st Liverpool Scottish joined 9 Brigade in the 3rd Division of the British Expeditionary Force. The battalion saw its first service in the front line at Kemmel on 27th November 1914. During the winter of 1914-1915 it held the line in the Ypres salient.

1st Battalion Liverpool Scottish reinforcements advancing at Hooge, 16th June 1915.
A photograph taken by Pte F A Fyfe as he lay wounded.

Hooge – June 1915

The 1st Liverpool Scottish took part in its first major offensive operation at Hooge (officially termed the First Action at Bellewaarde) on 16th June 1915. The attack by 9 Brigade was intended to capture the German trenches north of the Menin road at Hooge, which overlooked Ypres. The attack succeeded, but at the cost for the lst Liverpool Scottish of 402 casualties, or 74% of the battalion's strength. It was over a year before the battalion had been rebuilt and retrained.

The Somme – 1916

In early 1916, on the formation of the 55th (West Lancashire) Division, the 1st Liverpool Scottish was transferred to 166 Infantry Brigade. The Battle of the Somme started on 1st July 1916, and from 9th-14th August the lst Liverpool Scottish was engaged in the attempt to take the village of Guillemont, losing 280 casualties. In September the battalion held the line at Delville Wood, extending the trenches in preparation for an attack.

Captain Noel G Chavasse, MC wins the Victoria Cross, 9th August 1916

During the attack on Guillemont Captain Noel Chavasse, the Medical Officer of the 1st Liverpool Scottish was awarded the Victoria Cross. The citation read:

'For the most conspicuous bravery and devotion to duty. During the attack on Guillemont, on 9th August 1916, this officer continued to tend the wounded in the open all day under a heavy fire, frequently exposing himself to view of the enemy. He organised parties to get the wounded away most successfully. That night he spent four hours searching the ground in front of the enemy's lines for wounded lying out. On the following day he proceeded with one stretcher-bearer to the advanced trenches and carried an urgent case for 500 yards under a very heavy shell fire. During this performance he was wounded in the side by a shell splinter. The same night he took up a party of 20 volunteers, and succeeded in recovering three more of the wounded from a shell hole 25 yards from the German trench, buried the bodies of two officers, and collected a number of identity discs, although fired on by bombs and machine guns. Altogether this officer was the means of saving the lives of 20 seriously wounded men under the most trying circumstances, besides the ordinary cases which passed through his hands. At one time, when all the officers were shot down, he helped to rally the firing line.'
(London Gazette 26th October 1916)

Captain Noel G Chavasse, VC and Bar, MC

Reinforcements from the Cameron Highlanders – 1916

Although the affiliation between the Liverpool Scottish and The Queen's Own Cameron Highlanders was still unofficial at that stage, among welcome reinforcements after the Somme were twelve officers from the 1st/4th Camerons, when that battalion had to be drafted due to the heavy casualties sustained at Loos. This tangible assistance did much to strengthen the link.

The 3rd Battle of Ypres – July 1917

On 31st July 1917 the 1st Liverpool Scottish took part in the successful attack by the 55th Division which broke through the German lines, capturing 630 prisoners and taking all its objectives. Although the battalion lost 240 casualties, it achieved conspicuous success which did much to restore confidence after the costly and frustrating operations in the Battle of the Somme.

Captain Noel G Chavasse, VC, MC wins a Bar to the Victoria Cross

During the attack at Ypres on 31st July 1917 Captain Noel Chavasse, VC, MC, the Medical Officer of the 1st Liverpool Scottish, was posthumously awarded a Bar to the Victoria Cross. The citation, dated 14th September 1917, read:

'Though severely wounded early in the action whilst carrying a wounded soldier to the dressing-station, he refused to leave his post, and for two days not only continued to perform his duties, but in addition went out repeatedly under heavy fire to search for and attend to the wounded who were lying out. During these searches, although practically without food during this period, worn with fatigue and faint with his wound, he assisted to carry in a number of badly wounded men over heavy and difficult ground. By his extraordinary energy and inspiring example he was instrumental in rescuing many wounded who would have otherwise undoubtedly succumbed under the bad weather conditions. This devoted and gallant officer subsequently died of his wounds.'
(London Gazette 14th September 1917)

Epéhy – 1917

In September 1917 the 1st Liverpool Scottish moved from Ypres to a lightly defended sector of the line at Epéhy near Cambrai. On 20th November the enemy attacked the 55th Division in great strength, and almost overran it. The 1st/5th South Lancashire Regiment, on the left of the division, lost every single man as a casualty or prisoner. In the centre the 1st Liverpool Scottish fought a most determined defence, but lost two complete companies. Of their 622 casualties, over half were taken prisoner.

Givenchy – 1918

After the Germans started their final offensive in March 1918, the 55th Division moved into the line at Givenchy. On 9th April 1918 the enemy attacked the division in great strength, and the 1st Liverpool Scottish fought another determined defensive battle. The 55th Division succeeded in holding its line intact and saving Bethune from capture.

The final Allied offensive – 1918

On 3rd October 1918 the 1st Liverpool Scottish started its final operation of the war when the 55th Division advanced from La Bassée. By the Armistice on 9th November the division had advanced nearly 50 miles, and the 1st Liverpool Scottish finished the war at Ath.

2/10th (SCOTTISH) BATTALION
THE KING'S (LIVERPOOL) REGIMENT

2nd Liverpool Scottish formed – 1914

The 2nd Liverpool Scottish was formed at Liverpool as the second line battalion in September 1914. The battalion was stationed at Blackpool, and formed part of the South Lancashire Brigade. In February 1915 the 2nd Liverpool Scottish moved to Tunbridge Wells, and it was subsequently stationed in Kent, Surrey and Hampshire with the 57th Division, with the roles of home defence and of supplying reinforcements for the 1st Liverpool Scottish in France.

2nd Liverpool Scottish move to France – February 1917

In early 1917 the Second Line role of the 57th Division was changed, and the division was ordered to move to France. The 2nd Liverpool Scottish embarked at Southampton, and arrived at Le Havre on 22nd February 1917. The battalion took over a section of the trenches at Armentières on 26th February, and remained in the sector until October 1917.

Ypres – 1917-1918

Having moved to Ypres with the 57th Division in October 1917, the 2nd Liverpool Scottish held the line at Langemarck during the 3rd Battle of Ypres. The neighbouring battalion over the New Year was its affiliated regiment the 1st Camerons.

Amalgamation with 1st Liverpool Scottish – April 1918

The losses sustained by the 1st Liverpool Scottish during the fighting at Epéhy and Givenchy had reduced it to below effective fighting strength, and so on 30th April 1918 the 1st and 2nd Battalions Liverpool Scottish were amalgamated.

After the war the 2nd Liverpool Scottish received a King's Colour in 1919.

2nd LINE RESERVE BATTALIONS of the TERRITORIAL FORCE

Soon after the outbreak of war in 1914, each TF battalion was ordered to establish a 2nd and 3rd Line reserve. When the 1st Line battalion was sent overseas with the British Expeditionary Force, the 2nd Line battalion provided reinforcements, and took its place in the home defence of Great Britain. In March 1915 the TF battalions formed 3rd Line battalions to supply drafts for the other two.

2/4th (ROSS HIGHLAND) BATTALION SEAFORTH HIGHLANDERS

The 2/4th Seaforth was formed at Dingwall in September 1914. It formed part of the 191st Brigade in the 64th Division. The 2/4th Seaforth served at Fort George, Blair Atholl, Pitlochry and Stirling until 1916. It then moved to Norfolk, and was absorbed into the 4th Reserve Battalion Seaforth Highlanders formed in April 1918.

2/5th (SUTHERLAND AND CAITHNESS) BATTALION SEAFORTH HIGHLANDERS

The 2/5th Seaforth was formed at Golspie in September 1914. It formed part of the 191st Brigade in the 64th Division. The 2/5th Seaforth served at Fort George and Blair Atholl. In 1915 it was combined with the 2/6th Seaforth.

2/6th (MORAYSHIRE) BATTALION SEAFORTH HIGHLANDERS

The 2/6th Seaforth was formed at Elgin in September 1914. It formed part of the 191st Brigade in the 64th Division. The 2/6th Seaforth served at Fort George, Blair Atholl and Crieff, and in November 1915 was combined with the 2/5th Seaforth. The combined battalion served in Norfolk from 1916 until disbanded in September 1917.

2/4th BATTALION THE QUEEN'S OWN CAMERON HIGHLANDERS

Formed at Inverness in September 1914, the 2/4th Camerons formed part of the 191st Brigade in the 64th Division. The 2/4th Camerons served at Fort George, Blair Atholl, and Aberfeldy, until it moved to Norfolk in 1916. It was disbanded in 1918. The battalion supplied 2,077 men in drafts to the BEF.

2/1st REGIMENT LOVAT SCOUTS

Formed in 1914, the 2/1st Regiments Lovat Scouts belonged to the 2/1st Highland Mounted Brigade. The regiment became cyclists in the 1st Cyclist Brigade in the 1st Cyclist Division in Norfolk. The regiment merged with the 2/2nd Lovat Scouts in November 1916 to form the 1st (Lovat Scouts) Yeomanry Cyclist Regiment.

2/2nd REGIMENT LOVAT SCOUTS

Formed in 1914, the 2/2nd Regiment Lovat Scouts belonged to the 2/1st Highland Mounted Brigade. The regiment became cyclists in the 1st Cyclist Brigade in the 1st Cyclist Division in Norfolk. The regiments merged with the 2/1st Lovat Scouts in November 1916 to form the 1st (Lovat Scouts) Yeomanry Cyclist Regiment.

2/10th (SCOTTISH) BATTALION THE KING'S (LIVERPOOL) REGIMENT

Formed in Liverpool in September 1914, the 2nd Liverpool Scottish served in Great Britain with the South Lancashire Brigade until February 1917. The 2nd Line role was then changed and the battalion moved to France, where it took part in operations until amalgamated with the 1st Liverpool Scottish in April 1918.

3rd LINE RESERVE BATTALIONS of the TERRITORIAL FORCE

The 3rd Line battalions of the Territorial Force were formed in early 1915. They acted as depots for officers and men who were convalescent, and waiting to return to their fighting units in France.

3/4th (ROSS HIGHLAND) BATTALION SEAFORTH HIGHLANDERS

The 3/4th Seaforth was formed at Dingwall in April 1915, and was stationed at Ardersier Camp. In November 1915 it moved to Ripon where in August 1916 it became the 4th Reserve Training Battalion Seaforth Highlanders.

3/5th (SUTHERLAND AND CAITHNESS) BATTALION
SEAFORTH HIGHLANDERS

The 3/5th Seaforth was formed at Golspie in April 1915, and was stationed at Ardersier Camp. In November 1915 it moved to Ripon where in August 1916 it was absorbed into the 4th Reserve Training Battalion Seaforth Highlanders.

3/6th (MORAYSHIRE) BATTALION SEAFORTH HIGHLANDERS

The 3/6th Seaforth was formed at Elgin in April 1915, and was stationed at Ardersier Camp. In November 1915 it moved to Ripon where in August 1916 it was absorbed into the 4th Reserve Training Battalion Seaforth Highlanders.

4th RESERVE TRAINING BATTALION SEAFORTH HIGHLANDERS

The 4th Reserve Training Battalion Seaforth Highlanders was formed on 1st August 1916 at the 3rd Line Training Centre of the Highland Division at Ripon. The battalion was made up of the 3/4th, 3/5th and 3/6th Battalions Seaforth Highlanders, TF. In May 1918 the battalion moved to Glencorse, and was disbanded in 1919.

3/4th BATTALION THE QUEEN'S OWN CAMERON HIGHLANDERS

The 3/4th Camerons was formed at Inverness in April 1915 and accommodated in the town of Inverness, mainly in church halls. It moved to Ripon in November 1915. In September 1916 the battalion was absorbed into the 3rd (Special Reserve) Battalion Cameron Highlanders at Invergordon.

3/1st REGIMENT LOVAT SCOUTS

The 3/1st Regiment of the Lovat Scouts was formed at Beauly in July 1915, and affiliated to a reserve cavalry regiment at Aldershot. In June 1916 the regiment moved to Perth. It was disbanded in January 1917, and absorbed by the 2nd Line and the 3rd (Special Reserve) Battalion Cameron Highlanders.

3/2nd REGIMENT LOVAT SCOUTS

The 3/2nd Regiment of the Lovat Scouts was formed at Beauly in July 1915, and affiliated to a reserve cavalry regiment at Aldershot. In June 1916 the regiment moved to Perth. It was disbanded in January 1917, and absorbed by the 2nd Line and the 3rd (Special Reserve) Battalion Cameron Highlanders.

3/10th (SCOTTISH) BATTALION THE KING'S (LIVERPOOL) REGIMENT

The 3rd Liverpool Scottish was formed at Liverpool in May 1915 as the draft-finding battalion for the 1st and 2nd Battalions. The 3rd Battalion served at Blackpool and Oswestry. The battalion was disbanded in early 1919.

HOME DEFENCE VOLUNTEER BATTALION

1st VOLUNTEER BATTALION
THE QUEEN'S OWN CAMERON HIGHLANDERS

In 1917 a battalion of part time volunteers was raised as the 1/1st Battalion Northern Counties Highland Volunteer Regiment, and in 1918 it became the 1st Volunteer Battalion Cameron Highlanders. It was raised from the counties of Inverness and Nairn, under arrangements of the Territorial Force Association. Based in Inverness, its four companies recruited from Inverness and Beauly, Nairn-shire, Badenoch, and Lochaber. Its role was home defence, and it was similar to the Home Guard of World War II. The battalion was composed of men whose age, fitness or employment made them ineligible for normal military service except in an emergency. The battalion held a camp at Fort George in 1918, and was disbanded in February 1920.

6. THE 'NEW ARMY' BATTALIONS

Seaforth Highlanders in the line during World War I

At the outbreak of war in 1914, Field Marshal Lord Kitchener was appointed Secretary of State for War. Convinced that the war would last for at least three years, he set about organising a massive expansion of the Army. Instead of using the framework of the Territorial Force, as had been intended in Haldane's reorganisation of the Army in 1908, Kitchener decided to raise separate New Armies for service in the field.

The first Service Battalions were raised in August - September 1914 and were grouped into three new armies, K1, K2 and K3, each of six infantry divisions. In October 1914 a fourth Army, K4, was formed, but was subsequently broken up to reinforce the first three Armies.

7th (SERVICE) BATTALION SEAFORTH HIGHLANDERS

Formation of the 7th Seaforth – August 1914

The 7th Seaforth was formed at Fort George in August 1914 as part of Kitchener's First New Army, K1. The battalion joined 26 (Highland) Brigade of the 9th (Scottish) Division at Aldershot, together with the 8th Black Watch, 8th Gordons, and 5th Camerons. During the winter of 1914-1915 the battalion trained in the South of England and on Salisbury Plain.

Move to France – May 1915

The 9th Division was the first of the new Army Divisions to reach France. In May 1915 the 7th Seaforth landed at Boulogne, and on 1/2 July 1915 the 9th Division took over in the trenches near Festubert.

Loos – September 1915

The first major battle for the 7th Seaforth was the attack at Loos which started on 25th September 1915. It was the first occasion on which the British used poison gas. The 7th Seaforth and the 5th Camerons together attacked the strong German position on the Hohenzollern Redoubt. In a series of attacks over three days, the battalion took its objective at a cost of over 500 casualties.

The Ypres Salient – 1915-1916

The 7th Seaforth spent October-December 1915 in the Salient at Ypres, in the particularly bleak period of cold, muddy trench warfare when the British Corps clung grimly to the gains it had made in the battle of Ypres. From January-May 1916 the 9th Division held the Ploegsteert ('Plugstreet') area where the trenches and billets were better, and morale improved greatly.

The Battle of the Somme – 1916

The Battle of the Somme started on 1st July 1916. The 9th Division began its attack on the German positions at Longueval and Delville Wood on 14th July, and in a week of most severe fighting the 7th Seaforth achieved some notable success, but at the cost of over 450 casualties.

The Butte de Warlencourt – 1916

The 9th Division battalions, including the 7th Seaforth, were now badly under strength, and so the division was withdrawn from the line on 23rd

7th (Service) Battalion Seaforth Highlanders comes out of action on 19th July 1916 at the Somme, led by Piper 'Scott' MacKay.

July 1916. The 7th Seaforth held positions on Vimy Ridge during August-September. In October 1916 the battalion returned to the Somme, and took part in the attacks in the area of the Butte de Warlencourt, made in the most unpleasant and difficult muddy conditions.

Arras – 1916-1917

In December 1916 the 9th Division moved to a sector of the line near Arras. On 9th April 1917 the 7th Seaforth, as the right leading battalion of 26 Brigade, took part in the attack at Arras. The only serious resistance met was on the battalion's flank at the 'Island' near Blangy, which was stormed and captured. The six days fighting achieved considerable gains. The battalion's losses were 181 casualties.

Passchendaele – 1917

The 7th Seaforth held positions at Cambrai in July 1917, and then in September moved to Ypres. On 12th October the battalion took part in the attack on Passchendaele Ridge. In wet miserable conditions, and operating in deep mud, the battalion suffered over 230 casualties in some of the grimmest and most unpleasant fighting of the war.

The German offensive – 1918

When the Germans launched their last major offensive on 21st March 1918, the 7th Seaforth was holding positions on the Somme. This sector bore the full brunt of the German attack, and in a hard fought withdrawal operation the 7th Seaforth suffered over 300 casualties.

The final Allied offensive – 1918

In April 1918 the 7th Seaforth was moved north to Flanders, and on 16th April the battalion carried out a most successful attack which recovered the village of Wytschoete from the Germans. In September 1918 the 7th Seaforth was in the line at Ypres. Between 28th September and 25th October the 9th Division advanced from its positions on the Frezenberg Ridge outside Ypres, and the 7th Seaforth took part in the series of attacks which carried the line forward over 20 miles to near Harlebecke. The final operation cost the 7th Seaforth 331 casualties.

The 7th Seaforth was presented with a King's Colour by General Sir Henry Plumer at Solingen, Germany, on 19th February 1919.

8th (SERVICE) BATTALION SEAFORTH HIGHLANDERS

Formation of the 8th Seaforth – September 1914

The 8th Seaforth was formed at Fort George in September 1914 as part of Kitchener's Second New Army, K2. The battalion joined 44 Brigade of the 15th (Scottish) Division at Aldershot in September 1914, together with the 9th Black Watch, 10th Gordons, and 7th Camerons.

Move to France – July 1915

The 8th Seaforth left for France in July 1915, landed at Boulogne, and concentrated at St Omer. The battalion took over a sector in the line at Loos on 6th August 1915.

Loos – September 1915

The first major battle for the 8th Seaforth was the attack at Loos on 25th September 1915, which was preceded by the first British gas attack of the war. The 8th Seaforth, in the right hand brigade, had a hard fight through Loos village, and after house to house fighting the battalion broke through to attack Hill 70 beyond. The 44th Brigade took Hill 70, but the casualties were so high that it had only a tenuous hold on its objective. When the 8th Seaforth was relieved that night, the battalion had lost 718 out of the 776 who had started the day.

During the winter of 1915-1916 the 15th (Scottish) Division was given a chance to recover its strength, but it took almost a year before the losses at Loos were made good. The 8th Seaforth was reinforced with drafts, and the battalion retrained and reorganised, taking its turn in the trenches in the Loos Sector and the Hohenzollern Redoubt.

The Battle of the Somme – 1916

The Battle of the Somme started on 1st July 1916, and the 15th (Scottish) Division was committed during the third phase in August. The 8th Seaforth took part in raids on the enemy lines, and held the captured Switch Line against heavy counter attacks on 17th-19th August 1916.

Arras – 1917

In the attack on the German positions east of Arras, which started on 9th April 1917, the 8th Seaforth was in reserve, providing men for working parties and carrying ammunition. On 23rd April 1917 the battalion attacked the German line at Guemappe with some success, but with a loss of over 300 casualties.

The Third Battle of Ypres – 1917

In July 1917 the 8th Seaforth took part in the attack on the German positions on Passchendaele Ridge, overlooking Ypres. The attack by the 15th Division gained 2000 yards and did much to improve the security of the British lines round Ypres, but cost the 8th Seaforth 203 casualties.

In early August the battalion was reinforced again, but there was little opportunity to absorb and train the new drafts before the battalion was back in the line. On 22nd August 1917 the 8th Seaforth attacked again and gained ground, but a further 393 casualties reduced the battalion to just over 200 strong.

RSM Mackenzie (right), Sergeant J B McClurg (centre), and a CSM of 8th (Service) Battalion Seaforth Highlanders in France.

The German offensive – 1918

During the winter of 1917-1918 the 8th Seaforth held the line in the Arras and Cambrai area, while new drafts arrived and the battalion was retrained. When the final German offensive started on 21st March 1918, the 8th Seaforth was at Monchy, West of Arras. After giving some ground the 15th (Scottish) Division succeeded in saving Arras from being overrun.

The Marne – 1918

In July 1918 the 15th (Scottish) Division was moved south to support the French in the Epernay sector on the River Marne. On 28th July the 8th Seaforth took part in the 44 Brigade attack which captured the village of Buzancy.

The final Allied offensive – 1918

In its last operation of the war, the 8th Seaforth returned to Loos. The battalion held almost the same ground where it had first gone into battle in 1915. In October, as the Germans withdrew, the 15th (Scottish) Division advanced, and the 8th Seaforth ended the war at Huissignies.

The 8th Seaforth was presented with a King's Colour by Lieutenant General Sir Richard Butler at Nivelles, Belgium, on 10th February 1919.

9th (SERVICE) BATTALION
SEAFORTH HIGHLANDERS (PIONEERS)

Formation of the 9th Seaforth – October 1914

The 9th Seaforth was formed at Fort George on 8th October 1914. The battalion joined the 9th (Scottish) Division at Aldershot in December 1914 and in early 1915 became the Pioneers of the 9th Division. The 9th Seaforth was the first Pioneer unit formed and the first to land in France. Many of its officers were qualified engineers, and the soldiers were mainly bricklayers, miners and labourers. They were trained in both infantry skills and simple engineering work. The tasks of the battalion included building roads, communication trenches, strong points, trench mortar emplacements, drainage, and field tramways.

Move to France – May 1915

The 9th Seaforth moved to France in May 1915 and first went into the trenches at Bailleul.

Loos – September 1915

The first major operation for the 9th Seaforth was the battle of Loos which started on 25th September 1915. The battalion's task was to link up the captured trenches, and it dug two major communication trenches from the front line to the Hoherzollern Redoubt. The 9th Seaforth earned commendation for its excellent work under heavy fire, and the battalion was often required to fight as infantrymen and pioneers.

The Battle of the Somme – 1916

During the Battle of the Somme the 9th Seaforth was split up in support of the Brigades of the 9th Scottish Division. The battalion took part in the difficult fighting at Longueval and Delville Wood, and in the attacks on Butte de Warlencourt. The tasks of the 9th Seaforth included keeping the roads in repair, often in the muddiest and most difficult conditions, consolidating captured positions, and constructing strongpoints. The battalion often worked under heavy fire.

Arras – 1917

The 9th Seaforth took part in the 9th Division's attack at Arras in April 1917 when the battalion had to cease pioneer work and repel a German counter attack with rifle and bayonet. On 5th June the 9th Seaforth carried out a particularly fine piece of pioneering work when it entrenched a newly captured piece of ground in the dark, under heavy fire, despite heavy casualties.

The final German offensive – 1918

When the Germans launched their last major offensive on 21st March 1918, the 9th Seaforth was supporting the 9th Scottish Division in positions on the Somme. The battalion fought in an infantry role, and distinguished itself by its determined defensive action at St Pierre Vaast Wood, followed by acting as rearguard through Rancourt and Combles. Two platoons protected a battery of Divisional Field Artillery as it withdrew, firing over open sights. The battalion held a further position on the railway embankment between Albert and Dernancourt, despite being shelled by allied artillery.

The final Allied offensive – 1918

In the final offensive in September-October 1918, the 9th Seaforth took part in the 9th Division's advance from Ypres to its final engagement of the war near Harlebecke. The 9th Seaforth (Pioneers) was presented with a King's Colour by Brigadier General A. H. Marindin at Malmedy, Belgium on 10th June 1919.

10th (RESERVE) BATTALION SEAFORTH HIGHLANDERS

Formation of the 10th Seaforth – October 1914

The 10th Seaforth was formed at Cromarty on 28th October 1914 as part of Kitchener's Fourth New Army, K4. The battalion was started with a nucleus of officers and men from the 3rd (Special Reserve) Battalion, and many of the NCOs were in their 60s and even 70s. The battalion formed part of 101st Brigade in the 34th Division.

Fort George and Tain – 1915

In March 1915 the 10th Seaforth moved to Fort George and became a Reserve Battalion, instead of a Service Battalion. It moved to Tain in May 1915 forming part of the 9th Reserve Brigade. The role of the battalion was to train new recruits and despatch drafts for the front. After the Battle of Loos the 10th Seaforth was able to send large numbers of reinforcements to the 8th Seaforth to make up the casualties suffered at Loos.

Catterick and Dunfermline – 1915-1916

The 10th Seaforth moved to Catterick in October 1915 and to Dunfermline in April 1916. In September 1916 the battalion was redesignated No 39 Training Reserve Battalion in the 9th Training Reserve Brigade, but carried on wearing the uniform of the Seaforth Highlanders until it was disbanded in 1919. It supplied a total of 59 drafts to other Seaforth battalions.

After the war a King's Colour was issued for the 10th Seaforth.

1st GARRISON BATTALION SEAFORTH HIGHLANDERS

Formation of the lst Garrison Battalion – 1916

The 1st Garrison Battalion Seaforth Highlanders was formed at Tillicoultry in July 1916. It was made up of men who were below the normal standard of fitness for fighting, including those who had been wounded or who were too old. The battalion wore the uniform of the Seaforth Highlanders, and its head dress included a white hackle in the Balmoral bonnet.

Salonika – 1916-1918

In August 1916 the 1st Garrison Battalion moved to Salonika. Although intended for duty in the city, it was sent up to the Struma front and spent 18 months of duty in the trenches facing the Bulgarians.

Rumania, Turkey – 1918-1919

After the Armistice with Bulgaria in October 1918, the battalion served in Constanza, in other towns in Rumania, and finally in Constantinople. It was disbanded in June 1919.

5th 'Lochiel's' (SERVICE) BATTALION,
THE QUEEN'S OWN CAMERON HIGHLANDERS

Formation of the 5th Camerons – September 1914

When Field Marshal Lord Kitchener appealed for 100,000 volunteers for his New Armies, he asked Lieutenant Colonel Donald W Cameron of Lochiel to raise a Service battalion by direct appeal. Lochiel, who was commanding the 3rd (Special Reserve) Battalion at Invergordon, set about recruiting with the greatest energy. His appeal brought such an overwhelming response from all over Scotland, that the Cameron Highlanders had enough recruits to form four Service battalions.

The 5th 'Lochiels' Camerons was formed at Inverness on 1st September 1914 as part of Kitchener's First New Army, K1. The battalion started with a nucleus of 200 officers and men from the 3rd (Special Reserve) Battalion Cameron Highlanders, and the companies were recruited by districts, apart from D Company which was recruited from the Glasgow Stock Exchange. The battalion moved south to Aldershot where it assembled. During the winter 1914-1915 the 5th Camerons trained at Aldershot, Alresford and Bordon.

The 5th Camerons moves to France – May 1915

The 5th Camerons moved to France under Lochiel's command, arriving on 10 May 1915 at Boulogne. The battalion formed part of 26 (Highland) Brigade of the 9th (Scottish) Division. On 30th June 1915 the 5th Camerons took over in the trenches from the 4th Camerons at Locon near Festubert.

Loos – 1915

The first major battle for the 5th Camerons was the attack at Loos, where the British used gas for the first time in the war. On 25th September 1915 the 5th Camerons and 7th Camerons together attacked the German positions on the Hohenzollern Redoubt. The first objective of the 5th Camerons, was a trench nicknamed 'Little Willie'. The 9th (Scottish) Division attack achieved surprise and made good ground, but on the left flank the artillery fire failed to cut the German wire, and the 5th Camerons was left unsupported. When the battalion was relieved after three days fighting, only two officers and 70 men remained unwounded of the 820 who had started the attack.

Corporal James Dalgleish Pollock wins the Victoria Cross, 27th September 1915

As the 5th Camerons held on to the Hohenzollern Redoubt against fierce German counter attacks, Corporal James Dalgleish Pollock was awarded the Victoria Cross. The citation read:

'For most conspicuous bravery near the Hohenzollern redoubt on 27th September 1915. At about 12 noon, when the enemy's bombers in superior numbers were successfully working up the 'Little Willie' trench towards the Hohenzollern redoubt, Corporal Pollock, after obtaining permission, got out of the trench alone, walked along the top edge with the utmost coolness and disregard of danger, and compelled the enemy's bombers to retire by bombing them from above. He was under heavy machine gun fire the whole time, but continued to hold up the progress of the Germans for an hour, when he was at length wounded'. (London Gazette 18th November 1915)

Corporal James Dalgleish Pollock, VC

The Battle of the Somme – 1916

The Battle of the Somme started on 1st July 1916, and the 9th (Scottish) Division was committed to the attack on 14th July. In a week of most severe fighting the 5th Camerons took part in the capture of Longueval, Delville Wood and Waterlot Farm, at a cost of 446 casualties.

The Butte de Warlencourt – 1916

During the summer of 1916, as the 5th Camerons was slowly brought up to strength again with drafts, the battalion held positions on Vimy Ridge. In October the 9th (Scottish) Division returned to the Somme, and the 5th Camerons took part in the attacks on the Butte de Warlencourt, made in the most unpleasant and difficult muddy conditions.

Arras – 1917

The 9th (Scottish) Division moved to Arras in December 1916, and on 9th April 1917 took part in the attack North of the River Scarpe. The flanking battalion, south of the river, was the 6th Camerons. The attack by the 9th (Scottish) Division was an unqualified success, making considerable gains of ground with relatively light casualties. But on 1st May an attack by the 5th Camerons on the Roeux chemical works had the misfortune to be heavily shelled by British artillery who, because of faulty maps, hit the attacking troops rather than the objective. The 5th Camerons lost over 300 casualties.

Passchendaele – 1917

During July and August 1917 the 5th Camerons held positions near Cambrai , and then in September moved to Ypres. On 12th October the battalion attacked at Passchendaele. The assembly area was heavily shelled, and the advance was decimated by enfiladed machine guns. The 5th Camerons lost over 200 casualties.

The German offensive – 1918

When the Germans launched their last major offensive on 21st March 1918, the 5th Camerons was holding positions on the Somme. The sector bore the full brunt of the German attack and, as the 9th (Scottish) Division withdrew to stabilise the line, the 5th Camerons had a loss of 400 casualties.

The final Allied offensive – 1918

In April 1918 the 9th (Scottish) Division moved north to Flanders, and on 19th July it made a successful attack which captured the village of Meteren.

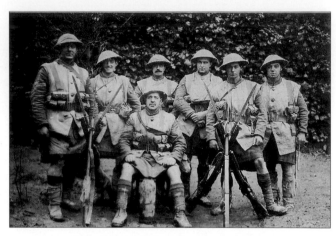

The 5th 'Lochiel's' (Service) Battalion
The Queen's Own Cameron Highlanders in France, 1918

On 28th September the 5th Camerons took part in the attack which finally captured the ridge of Passchendaele. During October 1918 the 9th (Scottish) Division advanced from Ypres to the Scheldt, fighting a series of actions which pushed the line forward 26 miles. After the Armistice the 5th Camerons crossed the Rhine into Germany on 13th December, and the battalion was billeted at Solingen.

A King's Colour was presented to the 5th Camerons by Sir Herbert Plumer at Solingen in February 1919. The battalion was disbanded on 15th November 1919.

6th (SERVICE) BATTALION
THE QUEEN'S OWN CAMERON HIGHLANDERS

Formation of the 6th Camerons – September 1914

When Lieutenant Colonel Donald W Cameron of Lochiel appealed in August 1914 for men to join the Cameron Highlanders, the response was so great that on 8th September 1914 it was decided to form a further battalion, the 6th Camerons, from the surplus men of Lochiel's 5th Battalion. The battalion formed part of Kitchener's Second New Army, K2.

The 6th Camerons included a complete company of Glasgow University students and many volunteers from the Glasgow Stock Exchange. The battalion was accommodated and trained in camps at Rushmoor, Bramshot, Basingstoke and Chisledon.

Move to France – July 1915

The 6th Camerons moved to France, arriving at Boulogne on 10th July 1915. The battalion formed part of 45 Brigade in the 15th (Scottish) Division, together with the 13th Royal Scots, 7th Royal Scots Fusiliers, and 11th Argyll and Sutherland Highlanders. The battalion took over in the line near Loos on 22nd July 1915.

Loos – 1915

The first major battle for the 6th Camerons was the attack at Loos on 25th September 1915 when, for the first time in the war, the British used gas. 45 Brigade started the battle as the reserve brigade of the 15th (Scottish) Division. The 6th Camerons was called forward to defend the left flank of the attack, and advanced against heavy machine gun fire. On the second day the battalion led the 46 Brigade attack on Hill 70. In the face of intense rifle and machine gun fire the 6th Camerons attacked repeatedly, and suffered 387 casualties before Hill 70 was taken.

Lieutenant Colonel Angus F Douglas-Hamilton wins the Victoria Cross, 25th-26th September 1915

The Commanding Officer of the 6th Camerons was Lieutenant Colonel Angus Douglas-Hamilton. Killed at Loos, he was awarded the Victoria Cross posthumously. The citation read:

'For most conspicuous bravery and devotion to duty when commanding his battalion during operations on the 25th and 26th September 1915, on Hill 70. On the 26th, when the battalions on his right and left had retired, he rallied his own battalion again and again, and led his men forward four times. The last time he led all that remained, consisting of about fifty men, in a most gallant manner and was killed at their head. It was mainly due to his bravery, untiring energy, and splendid leadership that the line at this point was enabled to check the enemy's advance'. (London Gazette 18th November 1915)

*Lieutenant Colonel
Angus F Douglas-Hamilton, VC*

The Battle of the Somme – 1916

After the casualties at Loos the 6th Camerons spent the next three months holding the line at Hulluch and in the Hohenzollern sector, as drafts were absorbed and the battalion rebuilt.

The Battle of the Somme started on 1st July 1916, and the 15th (Scottish) Division was committed during the third phase in August. The 6th Camerons carried out a successful attack on the Switch Line on 12th August, and took part in the 45 Brigade attack on Martinpuich on 15th September which cost the battalion 240 casualties.

Arras – 1917

In the attack on the German positions east of Arras, which started on 9th April 1917, the 6th Camerons advanced after the opening attack and successfully exploited the objective. The next day, as the battalion continued the advance to Monchy Le Preux, it came under enfiladed machine gun fire from Rocux, but managed to capture Monchy at a cost of 272 casualties. On 23rd April the 6th Camerons took part in the operations to consolidate the gains of the opening advance, suffering a further 140 casualties at Cavalry Farm near Guemappe.

The Third Battle of Ypres – 1917

On 31st July 1917 the 6th Camerons took part in the attack on the Passchendaele ridge which pushed the German lines back 2000 yards and improved the security of Ypres. The 6th Camerons lost their Commanding Officer, Colonel J C Russell, and 296 casualties in the severe fighting to win its objectives.

The final German offensive – 1918

During the final German offensive in March 1918 the 6th Camerons were in the Arras sector. In the 15th (Scottish) Division's withdrawal the 6th Camerons suffered 287 casualties, but the operation checked the German advance and saved Arras from being overrun.

Amalgamation of 6th and 7th Camerons – 1918

Because of the casualties at Arras, all the battalions in the 15th (Scottish) Division were short of men, and so each brigade was reduced from four battalions to three. The three surplus battalions were used to bring the remainder up to strength. Under this reorganisation the 6th and 7th Camerons were amalgamated at Arras on 10th June 1918.

The Marne – 1918

In July 1918 the 15th (Scottish) Division was moved south to support the French in the Epernay sector on the River Marne. In the attack at Buzancy the 6th Camerons captured the Sucrerie at a cost of 286 casualties.

The final Allied offensive – 1918

In the battalion's last operation of the war the 6th Camerons returned to Loos, to the same ground where it had first gone into battle in 1915. In October, as the Germans withdrew, the 15th (Scottish) Division advanced. The Armistice was announced as the 6th Camerons were on the march at St Anne.

The 6th Camerons was presented with a King's Colour by Sir Richard Butler at Braine-le-Comte on 21st January 1919. The battalion was disbanded on 25th June 1919.

7th (SERVICE) BATTALION
THE QUEEN'S OWN CAMERON HIGHLANDERS

Formation of the 7th Camerons – September 1914

The 7th Camerons was formed at Inverness on 18th September 1914, from the men who answered Lochiel's appeal for volunteers to join the Cameron Highlanders. Like the 5th and 6th Battalions, the 7th Camerons contained a high proportion of young professional men from Glasgow and Inverness who responded to Lochiel's appeal.

The 7th Camerons left Inverness on 30th November 1914 for Aldershot. During the winter of 1914-15 the battalion trained at Liphook, Cirencester and Chiseldon.

Move to France – 1915

The 7th Camerons moved to France, arriving at Boulogne on 9th July, 1915. The battalion formed part of 44 Brigade in the 15th (Scottish) Division, together with the 9th Black Watch, 8th Seaforth, and 10th Gordons. The battalion took over in the line at Houchin on 28th July 1915.

Loos – 1915

The first major battle for the 7th Camerons was the attack at Loos on 25th September 1915, which was preceded by the first British gas attack of the war. The 7th Camerons started as the support battalion of 44 Brigade. When the 8th Seaforth and 9th Black Watch had taken Loos, the 7th Camerons passed through them and attacked the half finished German redoubt on Hill 70. The battalion secured Hill 70, the Commanding Officer Lieutenant Colonel J W Sandilands rallying the survivors of nine battalions to hold it. The 7th Camerons lost 548 casualties in the attack.

During the winter of 1915-1916 the 15th (Scottish) Division was given a chance to recover its strength. The 7th Camerons held the line in the Loos sector and in the Hohenzollern Redoubt, as new drafts arrived and the battalion was reorganised and retrained.

The Battle of the Somme – 1916

The Battle of the Somme started on lst July 1916, and the 15th (Scottish) Division was committed in the third phase. On 17th August the 7th Camerons successfully attacked the Switch Line of the German positions at Contalmaison, but lost 231 casualties.

Arras – 1917

When the attack on the German positions east of Arras started on 9th April 1917, the 7th Camerons took part with 44 Brigade. The brigade advanced 4000 yards and gained all its first objectives. Two days later the 7th Camerons attacked Monchy, suffering heavy casualties from enfilade machine gun fire. With the survivors of several other battalions the 7th Camerons held Monchy against heavy German counter attacks. On 23rd April the battalion took part in the operations to consolidate the gains of the opening attack. The two phases of the battle of Arras cost the battalion 659 casualties, and for a time it was reduced to the effective strength of a company.

The Third Battle of Ypres – 1917

In July 1917 the 7th Camerons moved to Ypres for the attack on the German positions on Passchendaele Ridge overlooking Ypres. They carried out a successful battalion raid on 28th July, and next day took part in the attack by 44 Brigade. The operations gained 2000 yards and did much to improve security of the British lines round Ypres, but cost the 7th Camerons a further 292 casualties.

The final German offensive – 1918

During the winter of 1917-1918 the 7th Camerons held the line in the Arras and Cambrai area, and the battalion was gradually built up again with new drafts. When the German offensive started on 21st March 1918, the 7th Camerons was in the Arras sector. In the 15th (Scottish) Division's withdrawal, the 7th Camerons lost 388 casualties in the operation which managed to check the German advance and save Arras from being overrun.

Amalgamation with 6th Camerons – 1918

Because of the casualties at Ypres and Arras, all the battalions in the division were well below strength, and so each brigade was reduced from four battalions to three, the surplus battalions being used to bring the remainder up to strength. Under this reorganisation the 7th Camerons was amalgamated with the 6th Camerons at Arras on 10th June 1918.

After the war a King's Colour was presented to a representative party of the 7th Camerons by HRH The Duke of York at Inverness on 17th September 1920.

8th (RESERVE) BATTALION
THE QUEEN'S OWN CAMERON HIGHLANDERS

Formation of the 8th Camerons – December 1914

The 8th Camerons was formed on 14th December 1914 at Cameron Barracks Inverness as part of Kitchener's Fourth New Army, K4. The battalion was started with a nucleus of the 3rd (Special Reserve) Battalion from Invergordon, and included a contingent from the Glasgow Stock Exchange who had joined the Camerons in answer to Lochiel's appeal for recruits for the regiment.

Inverness and Tain – 1914-1915

The 8th Camerons formed part of the 101st Brigade in the 34th Division. The battalion moved from Inverness to Tain in May 1915. Due to recruiting difficulties throughout the country the role of the K4 battalions was changed, and in July 1915 the 8th Camerons became a Reserve battalion instead of a Service battalion.

Catterick 1915 and Stirling – 1916

The 8th Camerons moved to Catterick in October 1915, and in April 1916 to Stirling. There on 1st September 1916 the battalion was redesignated the 40th Training Reserve Battalion, but carried on wearing the uniform of the Cameron Highlanders until 1918.

Kent – 1917-1918

In September 1917 the 40th Training Reserve Battalion was moved to Kent and formed part of the coastal defences. Its designation was changed to 286 Infantry Battalion. In October 1917 the 101st Brigade was disbanded, and the 40th Training Reserve Battalion was renamed the 52nd (Graduated) Battalion Gordon Highlanders.

1919-1920

After the Armistice in November 1918, the battalion moved to Germany as part of the Army of Occupation. It returned to Catterick in 1919, and then to Glencorse, where it was disbanded in March 1920.

9th (LABOUR) BATTALION
THE QUEEN'S OWN CAMERON HIGHLANDERS

Formation of the 9th Camerons – August 1916

The 9th Camerons was formed at Blairgowrie in August 1916 for use on labouring tasks, such as unloading stores in the docks and repairing roads. The officers and men were drawn from the category B2. The battalion was not issued with the kilt, and it wore khaki service dress with the Balmoral bonnet of the Cameron Highlanders.

The 9th Camerons move to France – September 1916

The 9th Camerons moved to France in September 1916 and worked in the docks at Le Havre, Calais and other French ports.

The 9th Camerons transferred to the Labour Corps – May 1917

On the formation of the Labour Corps in May 1917 the 9th Camerons was transferred to it as No 7 and No 8 Labour Companies.

After the war a King's Colour was presented to a representative party of the 9th Camerons by HRH The Duke of York at Inverness on 17th September 1920.

11th (SERVICE) BATTALION
THE QUEEN'S OWN CAMERON HIGHLANDERS

Formation of the 11th Camerons – June 1918

The 11th Camerons was formed at Etaples on 9th June 1918, at first as a Labour battalion, the reason for its designation as a battalion of Cameron Highlanders being a mystery. The men, drawn from Category B, were from twenty nine separate labour companies, and were mainly English and Irish. However, when in July 1918 the battalion was moved to 120 Brigade of the 40th Division, there was a major change, and officers and men from Scottish regiments were brought in to replace the original cadre. At the same time the role of the battalion was changed from a Labour to a Service battalion, and the battalion was dressed in the uniform of the Cameron Highlanders, including the kilt.

Service in the line – August-November 1918

The 11th Camerons served in the trenches from August 1918 until the Armistice, under the command of Lieutenant Colonel the Hon O R Vivian, DSO MVO, later Lord Swansea.

The 11th Camerons was disbanded on 1st June 1919. A King's Colour was presented to the battalion by Sir Beavoir de Lisle at Roubaix on 20th January 1919.

CHAPTER IV
THE REGIMENTS – 1919-1939

1. REGULAR ARMY BATTALIONS

1st BATTALION SEAFORTH HIGHLANDERS

1st Seaforth in Scotland – 1919-1922

After World War I a cadre of the 1st Seaforth returned from Egypt to Fort George in June 1919. It moved to Glencorse in July where it joined up with a nucleus of the 3rd (Special Reserve) Battalion whose numbers brought it up to strength. The reformed 1st Seaforth returned to Fort George in November 1919 as the Home service battalion of the regiment. During the coal strike of 1921 the 1st Seaforth was sent to Bridge of Allan and Cowdenbeath for strike duty.

The 1st Seaforth provided the Royal Guard at Ballater in 1919. On 3rd December 1920 HRH The Prince of Wales was appointed Colonel in Chief of the Seaforth Highlanders.

1st Seaforth in Ireland – 1921-1926

In July 1921 the 1st Seaforth left Fort George for Ireland, and after a short time in Dublin moved to Belfast for duties in aid of the civil power. The battalion remained in Northern Ireland until 1926, at a very difficult period of political friction with the newly independent Irish Free State and of civil disorder in Ulster.

1st Battalion Seaforth Highlanders in Northern Ireland in 1922.

1st Seaforth in Aldershot and Dover – 1926-1933

In January 1926 the 1st Seaforth moved to Aldershot, and during the General Strike the battalion provided escorts for food convoys across London. In November 1928 the 1st Seaforth moved to Dover where, on 29th June 1929, the battalion trooped the Regimental Colour before HRH The Prince of Wales, the Colonel in Chief.

1st Seaforth in Palestine – 1933

In December 1933 the 1st Seaforth left Dover at the start of a tour as Foreign service battalion of the regiment. The tour started in Palestine where the battalion was stationed in Jerusalem. By happy chance the 2nd Seaforth was also in Palestine, at the end of its Foreign service tour, and was stationed at Haifa, only 100 miles away. A series of social, ceremonial and sporting events was held to mark this unique occasion before the 2nd Seaforth left for Great Britain four months later.

1st Seaforth in Egypt – 1934-1936

In September 1934 the 1st Seaforth moved to Cairo. The following year there was an international threat that the Italians, who had already attacked Abyssinia, might also invade Egypt, and so the 1st Seaforth was sent for a month to protect the RAF airfield at Mersa Matruh in the Western Desert.

1st Battalion Seaforth Highlanders in Cairo 1936.

1st Seaforth in the Palestine troubles – 1936

When a state of emergency was declared in Palestine during the Arab revolt, the 1st Seaforth was sent back to Palestine. The battalion remained there from May to October 1936. The 1st Seaforth mounted an intensive programme of operations to counter terrorist activities which ranged from widespread sabotage, to cutting of telephone wires and oil pipe lines, ambushes on convoys, and guerilla attacks by organised gangs. The battalion carried out night patrols, village searches and ambushes, picqueted roads by day, and operated a striking force of a company group supported by tanks, armoured cars and guns. The 1st Seaforth returned to Cairo in October 1936.

1st Seaforth in Hong Kong – 1937-1938

In December 1936 the 1st Seaforth left Cairo for Hong Kong, having handed over the Citadel barracks to the 2nd Camerons. War broke out between Japan and China in 1937, and the main task of the battalion was to prepare the defences of Hong Kong against invasion. In September 1937 Hong Kong was devastated by a typhoon which struck it, with winds reaching an estimated 164 mph, and the 1st Seaforth did much useful work in clearing up and restoring the colony to normal.

1st Seaforth in Shanghai – 1938-1940

In March 1938 the 1st Seaforth was sent from Hong Kong to Shanghai. The battalion's task was to protect the British Sector of the International Settlement against the truculent behaviour of the Japanese, and against terrorist attacks.

At the time of the Munich crisis in September 1938 the 1st Seaforth was ordered back to Hong Kong. The battalion embarked on HMS Birmingham at four hours notice. The ship sailed at her full speed of 29 knots, and arrived at Kowloon next day, after a record voyage. The battalion returned to Shanghai the following week and remained there until 1940.

1st Battalion Seaforth Highlanders in Shanghai, 1938.

2nd BATTALION SEAFORTH HIGHLANDERS

2nd Seaforth in India – 1919-1932

After World War I the 2nd Seaforth returned for a short time to Fort George, and then went abroad to India as the Foreign service battalion of the regiment, arriving in Meerut in November 1919.

From Meerut the 2nd Seaforth was sent for a year's duty on the North-West Frontier at Landi Kotal. Having moved to Umbala by train in November 1922, the battalion marched the 500 miles to the North-West Frontier. The march took nearly two months, covering up to 23 miles a day, with the Pipes and Drums and the Military Band playing alternately on the march. The 2nd Seaforth spent over a year on the frontier, until moving to Nowshera in 1924. In 1927 the battalion marched the 250 miles to its next station at Lahore.

Types of dress worn by the 2nd Battalion Seaforth Highlanders in India 1932.

2nd Seaforth on the North-West Frontier 1930-1931

Having moved to Jhansi in 1929, the 2nd Seaforth returned to the North-West Frontier in August 1930 for operations against the Afridi tribesmen. From a base at Miri Khel, west of Peshawar, the battalion helped to build roads and strongpoints to prevent infiltration by the Afridis, and it saw active service against the tribesmen.

2nd Seaforth in Palestine – 1932-1933

In November 1932 the 2nd Seaforth left Jhansi, and moved to Haifa in Palestine for the last part of the Foreign service tour. After a peaceful and uneventful start, Jewish immigration increased, and in late 1933 demonstrations and riots developed as Arab resentment grew.

2nd Battalion Seaforth Highlanders during operations on the North-West Frontier of India, 1930-1931

In December 1933 the 1st Seaforth arrived in Palestine at the start of its Foreign tour. It was the first occasion on which the 1st and 2nd Seaforth had met in peacetime, apart from a very brief encounter as the two battalions were reforming at Fort George in June 1919. With the 1st Seaforth in Jerusalem and the 2nd Seaforth in Haifa, only 100 miles apart, the regiment took full advantage of the opportunity for social and sporting meetings between the two battalions.

2nd Seaforth in Dover – 1934-1937

On return to Great Britain the 2nd Seaforth was stationed at Dover Castle, taking over the barracks from the 1st Seaforth. On 5th July 1935 the 2nd Seaforth received its 8th Stand of Colours from the Colonel in Chief, HRH The Prince of Wales. When the 2nd Seaforth left Dover in 1937, the two battalions of Seaforth Highlanders had served continuously in Dover for nine years.

2nd Seaforth in Glasgow – 1937-1939

The 2nd Seaforth moved to Maryhill Barracks Glasgow in September 1937, and remained there until the outbreak of war in 1939. The battalion furnished the Royal Guard at Ballater in 1938.

1st BATTALION THE QUEEN'S OWN CAMERON HIGHLANDERS

lst Camerons in Scotland – 1919

After World War I the 1st Camerons remained in Germany while demobilisation was carried out. Meanwhile at Invergordon the Foreign Service Details were formed from a nucleus of the 3rd (Special Reserve) Battalion, and these were united with the cadre of the 1st Camerons on its return to Inverness in April 1919. In July 1919 the lst Camerons embarked for India for a tour as the Foreign service battalion of the regiment.

lst Camerons in India – 1919-1925

On arrival in India the 1st Camerons moved first to Rawalpindi, and then from May to October 1920 the battalion was sent up to the Kurram valley on the North-West Frontier to deter Afghan border raiders. In 1922 a detachment supported the police in dealing with riots in Rawalpindi.

In November 1922 the 1st Camerons moved by train from Rawalpindi to Calcutta. On 9th January 1923, the battalion received its 6th Stand of Colours from General Sir Havelock Hudson, GOC in C Eastern Command.

1st Camerons in Burma – 1925-1930

In November 1925 the lst Camerons moved from Calcutta to Burma, where the battalion was stationed at first in Maymyo, with a company detachment at Mandalay. When the battalion moved to Rangoon in 1928, it provided a company detachment to Port Blair in the Andaman Islands. In early 1929 the 1st Camerons moved into the new cantonment at Mingaladon, outside Rangoon. During the labour dispute in the Rangoon docks in 1930 the battalion was called out to disperse rioters and to provide guards and picquets.

A picquet of the 1st Battalion The Queen's Own Cameron Highlanders in the Rangoon riots of 1930.

1st Camerons in India – 1930-1934

In November 1930 the lst Camerons returned to India, and the battalion was stationed at Fyzabad, in the United Provinces, under command of 6th (Lucknow) Brigade. In 1931 the 1st Camerons carried out a Flag March in the Gonda district, a periodic demonstration to dispel rumours of the end of the British Raj. The battalion received a memorable welcome, being the first British troops to visit the area since 1861.

1st Camerons in Sudan – 1934-1936

In December 1934 the lst Camerons moved to the Sudan for the final part of the battalion's tour of Foreign service, and was stationed in Khartoum until March 1936.

1st Camerons in Great Britain – 1936-1939

On the return of the 1st Camerons to Great Britain in 1936, the battalion was stationed at Catterick. In 1937 the 1st Camerons took part in the ceremonial parades in London for the Coronation of HM King George VI, the Colonel in Chief of the Regiment.

The lst Camerons won first place in the Highland Brigade Gathering at Redford Barracks, Edinburgh, the first to be held in Great Britain, in which all six regiments of the Highland Brigade took part.

In October 1938 the battalion moved to Aldershot and was stationed there at the outbreak of World War II in 1939.

1st Battalion The Queen's Own Cameron Highlanders march past HM King George VI, the Colonel in Chief, after Church parade at Aldershot, 1939.

2nd BATTALION THE QUEEN'S OWN CAMERON HIGHLANDERS

2nd Camerons in Great Britain – 1919-1920

After World War I the 2nd Camerons remained at Tiflis in the Caucasus while demobilisation was carried out, and then in May 1919 the cadre of the battalion returned to Inverness. It moved to Dreghorn Camp, Edinburgh where it joined up with a nucleus from the 3rd (Special Reserve) Battalion, and moved to Aldershot as the Home service battalion of the regiment in September 1919.

2nd Camerons in Ireland – 1920-1922

In May 1920 the 2nd Camerons moved to Ireland. The battalion was stationed in Queenstown, with detachments in the small towns round Cork. It was to be a turbulent tour of duty, in a part of Ireland reduced to anarchy by the events of the Sinn Fein rebellion. The battalion's task was to preserve order and protect loyalists, by patrolling the country and searching for illegal weapons.

2nd Camerons in Aldershot – 1922-1923

In February 1922, after the establishment of the Republic of Ireland, the 2nd Camerons moved to Aldershot where the battalion formed part of the 1st Guards Brigade.

2nd Camerons in Germany – 1923-1926

In October 1923 the 2nd Camerons left Aldershot for Germany for service with the British Army of the Rhine. The battalion was stationed at Mullheim, near Cologne, until December 1924, and then for a year in Wiesbaden.

2nd Camerons in Edinburgh – 1926-1930

In November 1926 the 2nd Camerons returned from Germany to Redford Barracks, Edinburgh. The battalion provided the Guard of Honour when the Scottish National War Memorial at Edinburgh Castle was opened by HRH The Prince of Wales on 14th July 1927, in the presence of HM King George V and HM Queen Mary. In February 1928 the 2nd Camerons and the Scots Greys formed the ceremonial procession for the funeral of Field Marshal Earl Haig.

During June 1928 the 2nd Camerons carried out an interesting exercise when the battalion embarked at Edinburgh on the battleship HMS Rodney and the battle cruisers HMS Renown and Repulse, and landed near Fort George. After tactical exercises with the 2nd Battalion The Black Watch, the 2nd Camerons returned to Edinburgh on foot. In Lochaber the battalion paraded before Lochiel at Achnacarry, and visited Erracht, the former home of Lieutenant General Sir Alan Cameron who had raised the 79th in 1793. By the time the battalion reached Edinburgh it had marched 250 miles.

In 1929 the 2nd Camerons provided the ceremonial troops for the Reunion of the Church of Scotland and the United Free Church, for the 600th Anniversary of Edinburgh's Charter granted by King Robert the Bruce, for two levées held by HRH The Duke of York, and for many other public occasions.

2nd Battalion The Queen's Own Cameron Highlanders route marching in Scotland 1928.

2nd Camerons in Aldershot – 1930-1935

In October 1930 the 2nd Camerons returned to Aldershot. A most important sporting success was to win the Army Football Cup in 1933, the trophy being presented by HM King George V, Colonel in Chief of the Regiment.

On 14th July 1933 HRH The Duke of York (later King George VI), Honorary Colonel of the 4th Camerons, presented the 2nd Camerons with the battalion's 3rd Stand of Colours at Aldershot. During August – September1934 the 2nd Camerons carried out public duties in London, mounting guard at St. James's Palace, Buckingham Palace, and the Bank of England.

2nd Camerons in Palestine – 1935-1936

In November 1935 the 2nd Camerons left Aldershot for Palestine at the start of a tour as the Foreign service battalion of the regiment. From April to October 1936 the battalion was engaged in operations in aid of the civil power against the Arab rebels, and tasks included patrols, convoy escorts, riot control duties, cordons and searches, and guards against terrorist attacks on vital installations.

2nd Camerons in Egypt – 1936-1938

In December 1936 the 2nd Camerons moved to Cairo, and in January 1938 to Moascar on the Suez Canal. The battalion carried out mobile desert training and, despite its limited motor transport, this was a useful foretaste of the desert warfare for which it was destined two years later.

2nd Battalion The Queen's Own Cameron Highlanders on anti-terrorist duty in Palestine 1936.

2nd Camerons in India – 1938-1939

In November 1938 the 2nd Camerons moved to India, and the battalion was stationed at Ahmednagar until August 1939.

2. THE DEPOTS

DEPOT SEAFORTH HIGHLANDERS, Fort George

*HRH The Prince of Wales as-Colonel in-Chief, unveils the
Seaforth Highlanders World War I Memorial at Fort George in 1923.*

The Depot of the Seaforth Highlanders remained at Fort George, with the role of training recruits for the regular battalions of the regiment.

DEPOT THE QUEEN'S OWN CAMERON HIGHLANDERS, Cameron Barracks, Inverness

Recruits under instruction on the range at Cameron Barracks in the 1930s.

The Depot of the Cameron Highlanders remained at Cameron Barracks, Inverness, with the role of training recruits for the regular battalions of the regiment.

3. THE TERRITORIAL ARMY BATTALIONS
SEAFORTH HIGHLANDERS TA

The 4th/5th and 6th Battalions Seaforth Highlanders in camp at Fort George in 1930.

4th (ROSS-SHIRE) BATTALION
SEAFORTH HIGHLANDERS, TA – 1920-1921 and 1939

After World War I the 4th Seaforth was reconstituted as the Territorial Army battalion of Ross-shire, with its Headquarters at Dingwall. In 1922, on the reduction in size of the Territorial Army, the battalion was amalgamated with the 5th Battalion to form the 4th/5th Battalion Seaforth Highlanders. In 1939, when the Territorial Army was expanded again, the 4th Battalion was restored once more as a complete battalion.

5th (SUTHERLAND AND CAITHNESS) BATTALION
SEAFORTH HIGHLANDERS, TA – 1920-1921 and 1939

After World War I the 5th Seaforth was reconstituted as the Territorial Army battalion of Sutherland and Caithness, with its Headquarters at Golspie. In 1922, on the reduction in size of the Territorial Army, the battalion was amalgamated with the 4th Battalion to form the 4th/5th Battalion Seaforth Highlanders. In 1939, when the Territorial Army was expanded again, the 5th Battalion was restored once more as a complete battalion.

4th/5th (ROSS, SUTHERLAND AND CAITHNESS) BATTALION
SEAFORTH HIGHLANDERS, TA – 1921-1939

In 1921 the newly reformed Territorial Army was reduced in size, and among the amalgamations ordered the 4th Seaforth and 5th Seaforth were joined to become the 4th/5th Seaforth. The battalion had two Ross-shire companies dressed in the Mackenzie kilt and uniform of the Seaforth Highlanders, and two Sutherland and Caithness companies dressed in the Sutherland kilt and badge of the old Sutherland Rifle Volunteers. The Headquarters was at Golspie, and the battalion had 34 Drill Halls, with 9 Permanent Staff Instructors.

In 1939, when war was imminent, the Territorial Army was doubled, and the 4th and 5th Seaforth became separate battalions again.

6th (MORAYSHIRE) BATTALION SEAFORTH HIGHLANDERS, TA – 1920-1939

After World War I the 6th Seaforth was reconstituted as the Territorial Army battalion of Moray. The Headquarters was at Elgin. On the expansion of the Territorial Army in 1939, the 6th Seaforth was divided into two battalions, and formed the 6th and 7th Seaforth Highlanders.

7th (MORAYSHIRE) BATTALION SEAFORTH HIGHLANDERS, TA – 1939

In 1939, when war was imminent, the Territorial Army was doubled, and the 6th Seaforth split into two battalions, the newly formed battalion becoming the 7th Seaforth. It was recruited from Morayshire.

THE QUEEN'S OWN CAMERON HIGHLANDERS, TA

4th Battalion The Queen's Own Cameron Highlanders TA march along Princes Street during camp at Edinburgh in 1936.

4th BATTALION
THE QUEEN'S OWN CAMERON HIGHLANDERS, TA – 1920-1939

After World War I the 4th Camerons was reconstituted as the Territorial Army battalion of Inverness-shire and Nairnshire, with its Headquarters at Inverness. As the battalion grew, it had 17 Drill Stations to cover its Territorial area.

In 1920 the regiment was honoured by the appointment of HRH The Duke of York and Earl of Inverness as Honorary Colonel of the 4th Camerons. On his succession to the throne as King George VI he became Colonel in Chief of The Queen's Own Cameron Highlanders.

5th BATTALION THE QUEEN'S OWN CAMERON HIGHLANDERS, TA – 1939

In 1939, when war was imminent, the Territorial Army was doubled, and the 4th Camerons split into two battalions. The newly formed battalion was designated the 5th Camerons.

10th (LIVERPOOL SCOTTISH) BATTALION
THE KING'S REGIMENT (LIVERPOOL), TA – 1920-1937

1st Battalion The Liverpool Scottish at camp on the Isle of Man in 1933.

After World War I the Liverpool Scottish was reformed in March 1920. Since before World War I an unofficial affiliation had existed with the Cameron Highlanders, and this was formalised by Army Order No 481 of June 1922 when the Liverpool Scottish became affiliated to The Queen's Own Cameron Highlanders. All enlistments to the Liverpool Scottish were then allocated a Cameron Highlanders regimental number.

1st BATTALION THE LIVERPOOL SCOTTISH,
THE QUEEN'S OWN CAMERON HIGHLANDERS, TA – 1937-1939

In September 1937 the Liverpool Scottish was officially redesignated as The Liverpool Scottish, The Queen's Own Cameron Highlanders, and became an integral part of the Camerons, and its connection with The King's Regiment (Liverpool) ceased. In 1938 the 1st Battalion Liverpool Scottish received new Colours from HM King George VI, Colonel in Chief of The Queen's Own Cameron Highlanders, at Everton Football Club Ground in Liverpool.

2nd BATTALION THE LIVERPOOL SCOTTISH,
THE QUEEN'S OWN CAMERON HIGHLANDERS, TA – 1939

In 1939, when war was imminent, the Territorial Army was doubled, and the 1st Battalion The Liverpool Scottish split into the 1st and 2nd Battalions The Liverpool Scottish, The Queen's Own Cameron Highlanders TA.

THE LOVAT SCOUTS TA

The Lovat Scouts were reconstituted as a Scout regiment in 1922. Headquarters of the regiment was at Inverness, and there were three squadrons:

    A Squadron – Inverness-shire
    B Squadron – The Islands (North and South Uist, Benbecula, Skye)
    C Squadron – Sutherland, Ross-shire Caithness

The role of the regiment was observation and reconnaissance, and the establishment included one pony for every four men, and bicycles for the remainder. In 1936 the role was changed to that of mobile troops for reconnaissance and protection, probably in a minor theatre of war.

The Lovat Scouts in camp at Strathpeffer in 1923

CHAPTER V
THE REGIMENTS IN WORLD WAR II
1. BATTALIONS IN WORLD WAR II

During the Second World War the regiments were again greatly expanded. By contrast to Kitchener's recruiting campaign of 1914, which ignored the Territorial system and led to the formation of a new Third Army, the expansion for World War II was achieved by doubling the Territorial Army.

Because the campaigns of World War II were widely dispersed over Europe, the Middle East, Africa, the Far East and other theatres, the accounts of individual battalions are generally more varied than World War I, and the brief records in this book may give a misleading impression of the relative importance of a battalion's war history. A battalion which happened to serve, for example, in North Africa or North West Europe tended to gain a greater share of the limelight than a battalion which served with equal distinction against the Japanese in the Far East, but which belonged to what was sometimes termed the 'Forgotten Army'. The length of a battalion's narrative is, therefore, no yardstick of the merits of a battalion's fighting record.

BATTALIONS OF THE REGIMENTS – WORLD WAR II

	Seaforth Highlanders	**The Queen's Own Cameron Highlanders**	**Lovat Scouts**
REGULAR ARMY BATTALIONS	1st Seaforth 2nd Seaforth 2nd Seaforth (Re-formed in 1940 after St Valéry)	1st Camerons 2nd Camerons 2nd Camerons (Re-formed in 1942 after Tobruk)	
TERRITORIAL ARMY BATTALIONS	4th Seaforth 5th Seaforth 6th Seaforth 7th Seaforth	4th Camerons 4th Camerons (Re-formed in 1940 after St Valéry. Re-designated 2nd Camerons in 1942) 5th Camerons 1st Liverpool Scottish 2nd Liverpool Scottish	Lovat Scouts
HOME DEFENCE BATTALIONS	8th Seaforth (Re-designated 30th Seaforth, 1941)	6th Camerons (Re-designated 30th Camerons, 1942)	
RESERVE BATTALIONS	9th Seaforth	7th Camerons (Re-designated 5th [Scottish] Parachute Battalion in 1942)	

2. BRIGADES AND DIVISIONS OF WORLD WAR II

5th Battalion The Queen's Own Cameron Highlanders with the 51st Highland Division in North Africa 1942

Regular Army

In the years between the two World Wars, Regular battalions on Home service were grouped into Regular Army brigades and divisions in the United Kingdom. The Regular battalions went to France with these formations in the British Expeditionary Force in 1939.

In early 1940, to strengthen the Territorial Army formations in France, a Regular battalion was exchanged with a Territorial battalion in each Territorial Army brigade. Thus the 2nd Seaforth became part of 152 (Highland) Brigade in the 51st (Highland) Division, while the 6th Seaforth moved to a Regular Army formation, 17 Brigade in the 5th Division.

Battalions serving on Foreign service in India were grouped under the brigades and divisions of the Indian Army.

Territorial Army

The Territorial Army, when it was re-formed in 1920, retained the system of numbering used by the brigades and divisions of the Territorial Force in World War I. The Seaforth and Cameron battalions of the Territorial Army formed 152 (Highland) Brigade in the 51st (Highland) Division.

When the Territorial Army was doubled in 1939 a duplicate Highland division, the 9th (Highland) Division, was formed. The designation perpetuated the number of the 9th (Highland) of World War I, the first division to be formed from Highland battalions in Kitchener's New Army of 1914-15. In the 9th (Highland) Division of 1939 the newly formed 5th Seaforth and 5th Camerons became part of 26th (Highland) Brigade. After the loss of the 51st Highland Division at St Valéry in 1940, the 9th (Highland) Division was re-designated as the 51st (Highland) Division, and 26 (Highland) Brigade became a new 152 (Highland) Brigade.

FORMATIONS IN WHICH BATTALIONS SERVED IN WORLD WAR II

Battalion	Dates	Brigade	Division
REGULAR ARMY			
1st Seaforth	Sep 39 – Aug 40	-	Shanghai
	Aug 40 – Nov 40	-	Hong Kong
	Nov 40 – Feb 41	6 (Indian) Brigade	Malaya
	Feb 41 – Mar 42	-	14th Army
	Mar 42 – Aug 45	1 (Indian) Brigade	23rd (Indian) Division
2nd Seaforth	Sep 39 – Mar 40	17 Brigade	5th Division
	Mar 40 – Jun 40	152 (Highland) Brigade	51st (Highland) Division
2nd Seaforth (Re-formed)	Jul 40 – Aug 45	152 (Highland) Brigade	51st (Highland) Division
1st Camerons	Sep 39 – Aug 45	5 Brigade	2nd Division
2nd Camerons	Sep 39 – Jun 42	11 (Indian) Brigade	4th (Indian) Division
2nd Camerons (Re-formed)	Dec 42 – Nov 43	228 Brigade	Shetland Islands
	Jan 44 – Jul 45	11 (Indian) Brigade	4th (Indian) Division
TERRITORIAL ARMY			
4th Seaforth	Sep 39 – Jun 40	152 (Highland) Brigade	51st (Highland) Division
5th Seaforth	Sep 39 – Jul 40	26 (Highland) Brigade	9th (Highland) Division
	Jul 40 – Aug 45	152 (Highland) Brigade	51st (Highland) Division
6th Seaforth	Sep 39 – Mar 40	152 (Highland) Brigade	51st (Highland) Division
	Mar 40 – Aug 45	17 Brigade	5th Division
7th Seaforth	Sep 39 – Jul 40	26 (Highland) Brigade	9th (Highland) Division
	Jul 40 – Sep 40	152 (Highland) Brigade	51st (Highland) Division
	Oct 40 – Oct 41	216 Brigade	Shetland Islands
	Oct 41 – Aug 45	46 Brigade	15th (Scottish) Division
4th Camerons	Sep 39 – Jun 40	152 (Highland) Brigade	51st (Highland) Division
4th Camerons (Re-formed)	Jul 40 – Feb 42	-	Aruba and Bermuda
	Mar 42 – Nov 42	46 Brigade	15th (Scottish) Division
	Nov 42 – Dec 42	228 Brigade	Shetland Islands
(Re-designated)	Dec 42		
5th Camerons	Sep 39 – Jul 40	26 (Highland) Brigade	9th (Highland) Division
	Jul 40 – Aug 45	152 (Highland) Brigade	51st (Highland) Division
Lovat Scouts	Sep 39 – Mar 40	(mounted troops)	9th (Highland) Division
	Mar 40 – May 40	(mounted troops)	Mounted Cavalry Division
	May 40 – Jun 42	-	Faroe Islands Force
	Jun 42 – Aug 42	157 Brigade	52nd (Lowland) Division
	Aug 42 – Jun 43	227 Brigade	UK
	Jan 44 – May 44	(mountain training)	Canada
	Jul 44 – Aug 45	(mountain recce regiment)	10th (Indian) Division
	Jul 45 – Aug 45	11 (Indian) Brigade	4th (Indian) Division

3. THE REGULAR ARMY BATTALIONS

1st BATTALION SEAFORTH HIGHLANDERS

Pipes and drums of 1st Battalion Seaforth Highlanders before leaving Shanghai, 1940

1st Seaforth in Shanghai and Malaya – 1939-1941

When World War II broke out, the 1st Seaforth was stationed in Shanghai as part of the International Force, and the battalion remained there until the British garrison was withdrawn in August 1940. The 1st Seaforth moved to Malaya, first to Singapore, and then to Penang where its role was to defend against parachute landings. In February 1941 the 1st Seaforth left Malaya for India, and the battalion thus escaped the fate of the other British troops captured when the Japanese invaded Malaya and took Singapore a year later.

1st Seaforth in India – 1941-1942

On arrival in India the 1st Seaforth was stationed at Agra. Despite acute shortages of weapons, vehicles and equipment the battalion trained hard, and when the Japanese invasion of Burma began, the 1st Seaforth was sent to protect the border between Assam and Burma. Although this was intended as a temporary move, the battalion remained there for two and a half years.

1st Seaforth in Assam and Burma – 1942-1944

After the 1st Seaforth had arrived at Kohima in Assam in March 1942, the battalion was mobilised, subsequently joining the 1st (Indian) Infantry Brigade of the 23rd (Indian) Division, which was then operating in the Kohima and Imphal areas. The battalion immediately began long range patrolling into Burma as far as the River Chindwin, and acquired much valuable knowledge of the terrain while the Burma Army was withdrawn to Assam. From a battalion defensive position at Shenam the 1st Seaforth patrolled to Tonhe, operating under most difficult monsoon conditions in the flooded Kabaw valley. The battalion suffered many casualties from malaria, for which no effective preventative medicine had yet been developed. From early 1943 the 1st Seaforth carried out offensive patrolling operations on the Chindwin River, being supplied by mule convoys and air drops. The aim of the operations was to distract the Japanese from the airborne landings of General Wingate's second expedition behind enemy lines in Burma.

1st Seaforth at Imphal – 1944

When the Japanese attack on India started in early 1944 the lst Seaforth was withdrawn from the Chindwin and ordered to concentrate at Kunthaung. In early April the 1st (Indian) Brigade moved at short notice to the hills west of Imphal to outflank the Japanese who were advancing along the Ukrhull road. The 1st Seaforth battalion fought two successful actions when it attacked and captured the Japanese held villages of Kasom and Lammu. The lst Seaforth continued fighting in the jungle until late 1944 when, after two-and-a-half years of active operations, the battalion was withdrawn to India to train for the reconquest of Malaya.

2nd BATTALION SEAFORTH HIGHLANDERS

2nd Seaforth in France – 1939-1940

When war broke out in 1939, the 2nd Seaforth mobilised at Maryhill Barracks, Glasgow, and moved to France with the British Expeditionary Force. The battalion formed part of 17 Infantry Brigade in the 5th Division. In March 1940 the Territorial Army divisions were strengthened by the inclusion of a Regular Army battalion in each brigade, and the 2nd Seaforth moved to become the regular battalion of 152 (Seaforth and Cameron) Brigade in the 51st (Highland) Division, the Territorial battalions in the brigade being the 4th Seaforth and 4th Camerons.

2nd Seaforth at St Valéry-en-Caux – 1940

When the Germans advanced in May 1940 the 51st Highland Division was detached to French command. The 2nd Seaforth held positions in the Maginot Line in the Saar district, from which the battalion fought a withdrawal action. The 51st Highland Division was then switched to hold positions north of Abbeville. On 4th June 1940, the final day of the evacuation of the main part of the British Expeditionary Force at Dunkirk, the 51st Highland Division still held positions at Abbeville. Faced with the German advance in overwhelming strength, the 51st Highland Division withdrew south west down the French coast. At St Valéry-en-Caux the 51st Highland Division was cut off from its French allies and surrounded. The 2nd Seaforth, after a determined resistance, was forced to surrender on 12th June 1940.

2nd Seaforth reformed – July 1940

After the disaster of St Valéry, the 51st Highland Division was reconstituted from the 9th (Scottish) Division, the formation which had come into existence in 1939 when the Territorial Army was doubled. The Seaforth Highlanders re-raised the 2nd Battalion, and it took its place in the reconstituted 152 Highland Infantry Brigade, now composed of the 2nd Seaforth, 5th Seaforth, and 5th Camerons.

2nd Seaforth at El Alamein – 1942

On 14th August 1942 the 2nd Seaforth landed in Egypt with the 51st Highland Division. After six weeks intensive preparation the battalion took part in the attack by the 8th Army at El Alamein, which began on 23rd October 1942. The 2nd Seaforth started the battle in Corps reserve, and on 24th October the battalion was called forward to attack a German strongpoint and to form a bridgehead through the minefield which was holding up the 2nd Armoured Brigade. The battalion suffered 100 casualties in successfully holding this bridgehead for 36 hours. In the final phase of the battle, Operation 'Supercharge', 152 Brigade made the break through the enemy defences to allow the armour to operate beyond the minefields. The 2nd Seaforth had the task of mopping up and exploiting the objective.

The Prime Minister, Mr Winston Churchill, visits 152 Highland Brigade training in Egypt before the battle of El Alamein 1942.

*2nd Battalion Seaforth Highlanders
before the Battle of El Alamein*

2nd Seaforth in Tripoli – 1943

On 20-21st January 1943 the 2nd Seaforth was attached to 154 Highland Brigade for the attack at Corradini known as the 'Battle of the Hills'. On 23rd January 1943 the 51st Highland Division reached Tripoli, and the 2nd Seaforth took part in the Victory Parade on 4th February where the salute was taken by the Prime Minister, Mr Winston Churchill.

2nd Seaforth at Wadi Akarit – 1943

In early April 1943 the advancing 8th Army reached a bottleneck where the Germans held strong positions on the Djebel Roumana ridge, and along the Wadi Akarit which connected it to the sea. When the 51st Highland Division attacked on 6th-7th April, 152 Brigade's objective was the Djebel Roumana. The task of the 2nd Seaforth was to follow the 5th Seaforth and 5th Camerons onto the objective, mop up, and to link up with the brigade attacking the Wadi Akarit positions on the right flank. Although the 2nd Seaforth suffered heavy casualties, the battalion successfully held the ridge against strong enemy counter attacks. The campaign in North Africa cost the 2nd Seaforth 483 casualties.

2nd Seaforth in Sicily – 1943

After the battle of Wadi Akarit the 2nd Seaforth trained in Algeria for the invasion of Sicily. The 51st Highland Division concentrated at Sousse, before embarking in landing craft to sail via Malta for Sicily. 152 Brigade was in reserve during the landings on 10 July 1943, but once the beachhead was established the Brigade advanced. On 13th July 1943 the 5th Seaforth encountered stiff opposition from a German Parachute battalion at Francofonte, and next day the 2nd Seaforth carried out a successful battalion attack which wiped out half the German Parachute force. The 2nd Seaforth had some hard fighting in the Plain of Catania, and in the attack on the Sferro Hills on 31st July-1st August 1943. The campaign in Sicily cost the 2nd Seaforth 194 casualties.

2nd Seaforth in Great Britain – 1943-1944

After the capture of Sicily from the German and Italian forces, the 2nd Seaforth returned to Great Britain in November 1943. The 51st Highland Division was billeted in Hertfordshire, Essex, and Buckinghamshire while it prepared for the landings in Normandy.

2nd Seaforth in Normandy – 1944

The 2nd Seaforth landed in Normandy three days after D Day, coming ashore at Courseulles. The battalion took part in two months of difficult operations to hold the bridgehead over the River Orne against fierce German counter attacks. When the break-out began in August 1944, the 2nd Seaforth attacked and captured the strongly held German positions at Tilly-la-Campagne.

On 2nd September 1944 the 51st Highland Division liberated St Valéry, and on 10th September the 2nd Seaforth took part in the 51st Highland Division attack on German positions holding Le Havre.

2nd Seaforth in Holland – 1944

The 2nd Seaforth advanced through France and Belgium, and the battalion's next operation was the Battle of the Maas, which was intended to clear south west Holland and open up the port of Antwerp. On 23rd October 1944 the 2nd Seaforth attacked successfully across water obstacles at Schijndel. By 5th November the 51st Highland Division had cleared the country south of the River Maas, and on 14th November the 2nd Seaforth attacked across the Nederwert Canal, using assault boats and 'Buffaloes'. On 17th November the 2nd Seaforth crossed the Zig (or Uitwaterings) Canal through a bridgehead established by the 5th Camerons, and took Beringen.

2nd Seaforth in the Ardennes – 1945

In January 1945 the 51st Highland Division was sent to check the last desperate German counter attack of the war, the offensive in the Ardennes. The fighting was in bitter weather and in deep snow. On 11th January the 2nd Seaforth captured Ronchampey and next day occupied Laroche.

2nd Seaforth in the Reichswald – 1945

On 9th February 1945 the 2nd Seaforth crossed the German frontier, and for a week the battalion was engaged in fierce close-quarter fighting through the Reichswald Forest towards the German defences on the Siegfried Line. By 16th February the 2nd Seaforth was through the Reichswald, and attacked towards Goch, forcing a bridgehead over the anti-tank ditch. By early March the 2nd Seaforth was on the west bank of the Rhine. The three weeks hard fighting through the Reichswald and Siegfried Line had cost the battalion 120 casualties.

2nd Seaforth at the Rhine Crossing – 1945

In the operation to cross the Rhine the 51st Highland Division was one of the assault divisions. The 2nd Seaforth was under command of 153 Highland Brigade, and crossed the Rhine in assault boats on the night of 23rd-24th March 1945. On the east bank the battalion exploited from Esserden. Then, having rejoined 152 Brigade, the battalion advanced over the Oudi Issel River using the remains of a bridge destroyed by the enemy.

2nd Seaforth in Germany – 1945-1946

The 2nd Seaforth fought further actions at Adelheide and Ganderkesee, and took part in the capture of Bremervorde, two days before the German Army surrendered on 4th May 1945. The battalion took part in the Victory Parade at Bremerhaven on 12th May 1945.

1st BATTALION
THE QUEEN'S OWN CAMERON HIGHLANDERS

1st Camerons move to France – 1939

1st Battalion The Queen's Own Cameron Highlanders in Aldershot, before moving to France in 1939.

When war broke out in 1939, the 1st Camerons mobilised at Aldershot. The battalion moved to France with the British Expeditionary Force, forming part of the 5th Infantry Brigade in the 2nd Division. Having arrived at Cherbourg on 24th September 1939, the 1st Camerons prepared positions at Aix.

On 5th December 1939 the battalion, commanded by Lieutenant Colonel D N Wimberley, was inspected in the field by HM King George VI, Colonel-in-Chief of the Regiment. The King was particularly impressed by the battalion, which paraded in the kilt, and at his command the regiment was permitted to wear a Royal blue hackle in the Balmoral bonnet. From this important occasion originated the Royal blue hackle worn by the Cameron Highlanders and their successor regiments, the Queen's Own Highlanders and The Highlanders.

1st Camerons at La Bassée – 1940

When the Germans advanced into Belgium in May 1940, the 2nd Division moved forward to the River Dyle, east of Brussels. During the withdrawal of the British Expeditionary Force to the Channel the 1st Camerons fought an effective counter-attack action on the River Escaut. On 25th May 1940 the battalion, in a defensive position on the La Bassée canal, held off an attack by about 300 German tanks, until ordered to withdraw towards Dunkirk.

1st Camerons at Dunkirk – 1940

1st Battalion The Queen's Own Cameron Highlanders preparing defences in France in 1939.

1st Camerons at Dunkirk – 1940

On 31st May 1940, having withdrawn to Dunkirk, the 1st Camerons embarked on the ships which were to evacuate it to Great Britain. The 1st Battalion The Queen's Own Cameron Highlanders, although by then reduced to a strength of seventy nine, was still an effective fighting unit, and it still wore the kilt. It was the last battalion of any Scottish regiment to wear the kilt in action.

1st Camerons in Great Britain – 1940-1942

On its return to Great Britain the 1st Camerons was reformed in Yorkshire. In the hasty programme of reinforcement to bring the Regular battalions up to strength, the 1st Camerons received drafts from the Depot Cameron Highlanders, the West Yorkshire Regiment, the Green Howards, and the Highland Light Infantry. After training in Yorkshire and the South of England, the 1st Camerons embarked for overseas service on 11th April 1942.

1st Camerons in India – 1942-1944

The 1st Camerons sailed round the Cape of Good Hope to India, where the battalion was to spend two years training for Combined Operations and jungle warfare, combined with an internal security role. In March 1944, as the Japanese advanced through Burma and India came under threat, the 2nd Division was ordered to move to Assam, to halt the Japanese advance at Kohima.

1st Camerons at Kohima – 1944

On arrival in Assam, the 1st Camerons started patrolling towards Kohima. On 14th April 1944, by a successful attack on the Japanese position at Zubza, the road was opened for the relief of Kohima. In the critical operations to halt the Japanese advance the 1st Camerons successfully penetrated the Japanese lines and, having achieved surprise, captured the Naga village on 'Point 5120', a hill of particular tactical importance. The battalion then took Aradura Spur, a bastion of the Japanese defences. With Kohima recaptured, the 1st Camerons advanced south, attacking the Japanese at Viswema, until by 22nd June 1944 the road from Kohima to Imphal was reopened. The battle for Kohima cost the 1st Camerons 283 casualties.

1st Camerons at the Irrawaddy and Mandalay – 1944-1945

In November 1944 the 2nd Division advanced out of Assam into Burma. The 1st Camerons crossed the River Chindwin at Kalewa on 23rd-24th December, and despite resolute Japanese opposition established a bridgehead over the River Mu on 3rd-4th January 1945. The battalion then cleared a series of villages and reached Shwebo on 11th January 1945.

On 24th-25th February 1945 the 1st Camerons succeeded in establishing a bridgehead over the Irrawaddy river. From this the 2nd Division was able to advance on Mandalay, the 1st Camerons carrying out battalion attacks at Kyauktalon and on Ava fort on the outskirts of Mandalay. After the occupation of Mandalay on 18th March 1945, the battalion advanced south down the Irrawaddy valley, attacking the Japanese positions at Legyi, north of Mount Popa.

1st Battalion The Queen's Own Cameron Highlanders cross the River Irrawaddy in Burma 1945.

1st Camerons return to India – 1945

In early May 1945 the 1st Camerons returned by air from Burma to India, where the battalion was to prepare for a sea-borne assault on Rangoon. But after the Japanese surrender on 14th August 1945 ('VJ' Day), the battalion remained in India until March 1946.

2nd BATTALION
THE QUEEN'S OWN CAMERON HIGHLANDERS

2nd Camerons in Egypt – 1939-1940

As the Foreign service battalion stationed in India, the 2nd Camerons mobilised in Ahmednagar in July 1939. The battalion moved to Egypt with the 11th (Indian) Infantry Brigade of the 4th (Indian) Division. In Egypt the 2nd Camerons trained for desert warfare and, when Italy entered the war in June 1940, the battalion joined General Richard O'Connor's Western Desert Force. The first task was to prepare defensive positions against threatened invasion by the Italians.

2nd Camerons at Sidi Barrani – 1940

The Italian advance started in September 1940, and the first infantry action in the Western Desert was a raid by the 2nd Camerons on the Italian Camp at Maktila on 22nd-23rd October 1940. The battalion's first major operation came on 9th December 1940, when it took part in the attack on Nibeiwa Camp, and in the capture of Sidi Barrani next day. By speed and surprise General O'Connor's two divisions had destroyed an army five times their own strength, and achieved the first British victory of the war.

2nd Camerons in Eritrea – 1941

With Egypt free from the threat of invasion for the moment, the 4th (Indian) Division was sent to attack the Italian army in Eritrea. The 2nd Camerons sailed down the Red Sea, landing at Port Sudan in January 1941. After advancing through Kassala, the 2nd Camerons spearheaded the 5th (Indian) Brigade attack on the Italian positions at Agordat on 31st January 1941.

2nd Camerons at Keren – 1941

As the Italians fell back towards the Red Sea, they occupied strong mountain top positions dominating the road to Keren, and blew down 200 yards of cliff to block the road where it passed through the Dongolaas gorge. On 3rd February the 2nd Camerons succeeded in securing a hill (later known as 'Cameron Ridge') from which the subsequent attacks were made. After over five weeks of heavy fighting the 4th and 5th Indian Divisions broke through the Italian positions, the assaults by the 2nd Camerons on the 8,000 foot Mount Sanchil and Brig's Peak being among the hardest fighting of the operation. In this most successful attack, which broke through to Keren, the 2nd Camerons lost 209 casualties, 41% of their strength.

2nd Camerons in the Western Desert – 1941-1942

Meanwhile in the Western Desert, Rommel's Afrika Corps had advanced as far as the Egyptian border, and in April 1941 the 4th Indian Division returned from Eritrea to Egypt. In June the 2nd Camerons took part in the Battle of Halfaya Pass, followed by the defensive operations as General Sir Claude Auchinleck prepared to take the offensive with Operation 'Crusader'.

During the fighting to relieve the besieged garrison of Tobruk, the 2nd Camerons took part in the attack on El Gubi on 4th December 1941. When the Germans hit back in January 1942, the 4th (Indian) Division withdrew to Gazala, the 2nd Camerons fighting successful rearguard actions at Maraua, El Faida and Carmusa.

2nd Camerons at Tobruk – June 1942

In May 1942 the Germans attacked the Gazala Line, and the 11th (Indian) Infantry Brigade was ordered to hold a sector of the Tobruk defences. The 2nd Camerons held a three mile stretch of the perimeter. As Rommel's advance pushed the 8th Army back into Egypt, Tobruk was left isolated and surrounded. On 18th-19th June the Germans attacked Tobruk in overwhelming strength, and on 21st June the fortress was forced to surrender. But despite the capitulation, the 2nd Camerons fought on. The following day, having ordered every fit man to try to reach El Alamein, 500 miles away, Lieutenant Colonel C S Duncan agreed to march his battalion out of Tobruk into a prisoner of war camp, not as a defeated battalion, but under its Commanding Officer and headed by the pipers playing.

2nd Camerons re-formed – December 1942

On 20th December 1942 the 2nd Battalion was reconstituted. The new battalion was created by redesignating the 4th Battalion, itself re-formed in 1940 after the capture of the 51st Highland Division at St Valéry. The 4th

Camerons had returned from defending the vital oil installations in the Dutch West Indies, and was now in the Shetland Islands. After redesignation as the new 2nd Camerons, the battalion left the Shetlands and sailed for Egypt in December 1943, where it joined the re-formed 11th (Indian) Infantry Brigade in the 4th (Indian) Division.

2nd Camerons in Italy – 1944

In February 1944 the 2nd Camerons moved to Italy, and it returned to active service at the battle of Cassino, losing 250 casualties in a month of bitter fighting to break through the Gustav Line. After the capture of Cassino, the 2nd Camerons moved north for the attack on the next major German defensive position, the Gothic Line. During August-September 1944 the 2nd Camerons fought a series of actions ending with the liberation of San Marino.

2nd Camerons in Greece – 1944-1945

After the German withdrawal from Greece, the British Government provided a military force to supervise democratic elections, and to control the surrender of weapons by the left wing resistance

2nd Battalion The Queen's Own Cameron Highlanders in Italy 1944.

movements. The 2nd Camerons moved to Greece in November 1944 with the 4th (Indian) Division. When the war ended, the battalion was stationed in the Struma Valley, by coincidence the same area as the 2nd Camerons had ended World War 1.

The Pipes and Drums of the 2nd Battalion The Queen's Own Cameron Highlanders beat Retreat after the capture of San Marino, in September 1944

4. THE REGIMENTAL DEPOTS AND
TRAINING ESTABLISHMENTS IN WORLD WAR II

SEAFORTH HIGHLANDERS INFANTRY TRAINING CENTRE – 1939-1941

On the outbreak of war in 1939 the Seaforth Highlanders Regimental Depot was expanded to become the Seaforth Highlanders Infantry Training Centre (ITC) at Fort George.

THE QUEEN'S OWN CAMERON HIGHLANDERS
INFANTRY TRAINING CENTRE – 1939-1941

On the outbreak of war in 1939 the Queen's Own Cameron Highlanders Depot was expanded to become No 34 Cameron Highlanders ITC at Cameron Barracks.

NO 11 (SEAFORTH AND CAMERON)
INFANTRY TRAINING CENTRE – 1941-1946

The ITCs comprised two main elements. The Recruit companies trained the new recruits, including Militia men called up under the Conscription Act of September 1939; while the Depot companies retrained the recalled reservists and other men, and prepared them for posting to battalions.

In August 1941 the Seaforth ITC and the Cameron ITC were linked at Fort George to form No 11 (Seaforth and Cameron) ITC. In 1942, due to shortage of accommodation, the Seaforth and Cameron Depot companies moved from the ITC at Fort George to Redford Barracks, Edinburgh, where until 1944 they formed part of No 1 Infantry Depot.

After the Depot companies had moved, No 11 (Seaforth and Cameron) ITC remained at Fort George until November 1943, when Fort George was required for troops training for the Normandy landings. No 11 (Seaforth and Cameron) ITC then moved to Pinefield Camp, Elgin and remained there until March 1946, when it moved to Redford Barracks, Edinburgh, to join up with other Highland regimental ITCs to form The Highland ITC.

*No 11 (Seaforth and Cameron) Infantry Training Centre
at Fort George in 1942*

THE HIGHLAND ITC /
HIGHLAND BRIGADE TRAINING CENTRE – 1946-1948

The Highland ITC formed at Redford Barracks, Edinburgh in April 1946 from the ITCs of the Highland Regiments was consisted of one training company per regiment. After training at the Highland ITC, recruits were posted to No 8 Highland Holding Battalion until sent to join battalions of their regiments.

The Highland ITC was subsequently redesignated the Highland Group Training Centre, The Highland Brigade Group Training Centre, and The Highland Brigade Training Centre. It moved to Fort George in April 1948.

NO 95 PRIMARY TRAINING CENTRE – 1944-1946

After the departure of the 3rd Division from the Moray Firth area for the Normandy landings in 1944, No 95

Primary Training Centre was formed at Fort George. Army recruits of all arms were trained there, and then progressed to their regimental ITCs; in the case of Seaforth and Cameron recruits this was No 11 ITC at Pinefield Camp, Elgin.

NO 72 PRIMARY TRAINING CENTRE AND DEPOT SEAFORTH HIGHLANDERS – 1946-1948

On the disbandment of No 8 Holding Battalion in November 1946, No 72 Primary Training Centre and Depot Seaforth Highlanders was formed at Fort George.

NO 79 PRIMARY TRAINING CENTRE AND DEPOT THE QUEEN'S OWN CAMERON HIGHLANDERS – 1946-1948

On the disbandment of No 8 Holding Battalion in November 1946, No 79 Primary Training Centre and Depot The Queen's Own Cameron Highlanders was formed at Cameron Barracks, Inverness.

THE REGIMENTAL DEPOTS – 1941-1946

After the formation of No 11 ITC in 1941, the Regimental Depots were reduced to small Regimental Depot Parties. These remained at Fort George and Cameron Barracks throughout the war, and looked after the interests of their regiments until the Depots were re-established in 1946. The Regimental Military Bands, consisting mainly of boy soldiers and repatriated prisoners of war, were also based at the Depots, and did much valuable work entertaining troops and civilians in the north of Scotland.

From late 1943 to mid-1944, while training and rehearsals for the Normandy landings took place in the Moray Firth area, a combined Naval and Military Headquarters, including Headquarters of the 3rd Division, was based in Cameron Barracks, and troops of the 3rd Division occupied Fort George.

The Pipes and Drums of No 34 (Cameron Highlanders) ITC
welcome No 40 Inverness Company ATS to Cameron Barracks in 1939.

5. THE TERRITORIAL ARMY BATTALIONS

4th (ROSS-SHIRE) BATTALION SEAFORTH HIGHLANDERS TA

4th Seaforth mobilises – 1939

When war broke out on 3rd September 1939, the 4th Seaforth mobilised at Dingwall. The battalion formed part of 152 (Highland) Brigade in the 51st Highland Division. The 4th Seaforth moved to the south of England, where it was visited by HM King George VI at Aldershot on 18th January 1940.

4th Seaforth moves to France – 1940

The 4th Seaforth sailed for France with the British Expeditionary Force on 26th January 1940. The battalion then moved into defensive positions in the Maginot Line in the Saar Valley.

4th Seaforth at St Valéry-en-Caux – 1940

The German advance in May 1940 by-passed the Maginot Line, and the 51st Highland Division was moved back to a new position on the Somme at Abbeville. The 4th Seaforth withdrew from the Saar in contact with the enemy. On 4th June, the last day of the evacuation of the BEF further north at Dunkirk, the 4th Seaforth and the 4th Camerons took part in the desperate counter-attack on the German bridgehead over the Somme at Abbeville. By now the overwhelming strength of the German advance forced the 51st Highland Division to fall back to the coastal town of St Valéry-en-Caux, where it was hoped that the division would be evacuated. There, cut off from the remaining elements of the French Army, the 4th Seaforth with much of the 51st Highland Division was surrounded by the German advance and forced to surrender on 12th June 1940.

5th (SUTHERLAND & CAITHNESS) BATTALION SEAFORTH HIGHLANDERS TA

5th Seaforth in Great Britain – 1939-1942

When war broke out on 3rd September 1939, the 5th Seaforth mobilised at Golspie. The battalion formed part of the 26 (Highland) Brigade in the 9th (Highland) Division, the duplicate division of the 51st formed when the Territorial Army was doubled in 1939. When the 51st Highland Division was reformed after St Valéry, the 5th Seaforth became part of the new 152 (Highland) Infantry Brigade, together with the 2nd Seaforth and 5th Camerons. The battalion trained in the United Kingdom until it sailed for Egypt in June 1942.

5th Seaforth at El Alamein – 1942

On 14th August 1942 the 5th Seaforth landed in Egypt with the 51st Highland Division. After six weeks intensive preparation, the battalion took part in the attack by the 8th Army at El Alamein which began on 23rd October 1942. The first task for the 5th Seaforth was to secure the start line for the Highland Division. The battalion took over in the line on 27th October, and then on 1st-2nd November took part in Operation 'Supercharge', in which 152 Brigade broke through the enemy defences to allow the armour to exploit beyond the minefields. The 5th Seaforth was the right assault battalion of the brigade, with the 5th Camerons on its left. The battalion lost 177 casualties at El Alamein.

5th Seaforth in Tripoli – 1943

On 21st January 1943 the 5th Seaforth made a frontal attack at Corradini, as part of the 'Battle of the hills' in which 154 Brigade outflanked the enemy positions. When the 51st Highland Division reached Tripoli, the 5th Seaforth took part in the Victory Parade on 4th February, where the salute was taken by the Prime Minister, Mr Winston Churchill.

5th Seaforth at Mareth – 1943

In February 1943 the 51st Highland Division reached Mareth, the enemy defensive line sited behind the tank obstacle of the Wadi Zigzau, which had been extended by an artificial anti-tank ditch. The task of the 51st Highland Division was to establish a firm base for an attack by the 50th Division. The 5th Seaforth occupied the tank ditch during the attempts to break through the Mareth line. Eventually the Mareth position was outflanked to the south.

*5th Battalion Seaforth Highlanders
in the anti-tank ditch at Mareth 1943.*

5th Seaforth at Wadi Akarit – 1943

In early 1943 the 8th Army reached the bottleneck where the Germans held a strong position on the Djebel Roumana ridge, and north along the Wadi Akarit which connected it to the sea. When the 51st Highland Division attacked on 6th-7th April 1943, 152 Brigade's objective was the Djebel Roumana. The 5th Seaforth was the right assault battalion, with the 5th Camerons on its left. The battalion took its objective and then withstood a heavy German counter attack. The campaign in North Africa cost the 5th Seaforth 472 casualties.

5th Seaforth in Sicily – 1943

After the battle of Wadi Akarit, the 5th Seaforth trained in Algeria for the invasion of Sicily. The battalion embarked at Sousse and sailed via Malta for Sicily. During the landings on 10th July 1943, 152 Brigade was in reserve until the beachhead was established, when the brigade advanced. On 13th July the 5th Seaforth encountered a German parachute battalion holding a strong position at Francofonte. After repeated attacks by the 5th Seaforth, the position was eventually captured next day by the 2nd Seaforth. The 5th Seaforth had some hard fighting in the Plain of Catania, and in the 152 Brigade attack on 31st July-lst August 1944 to capture the Sferro Hills. The campaign in Sicily cost the 5th Seaforth 132 casualties.

*5th Battalion Seaforth Highlanders
landing at Cape Passero, Sicily, July 1944.*

5th Seaforth in Great Britain – 1943-1944

After the capture of Sicily, the 51st Highland Division returned to Great Britain in November 1943 to prepare for the invasion of Normandy. The 5th Seaforth were billeted in Hertfordshire and Essex.

5th Seaforth in Normandy – 1944

The 5th Seaforth landed at Courseulles in Normandy between 7th-9th June 1944, and moved into the Orne bridgehead near Escoville. The battalion had seven weeks of intensive fighting against strong German counter-attacks until the breakout from Caen. In Operation 'Totalise' on 7th-8th August 1944 the 5th Seaforth, together with the 2nd Seaforth, captured the strongly held village of Tilly-la-Campagne.

On 2nd September 1944 the 51st Highland Division liberated St Valéry-en-Caux, the 5th Seaforth and 5th Camerons being the first Highland battalions to enter the town. The 51st Highland Division then took part in the attack on the German positions holding Le Havre, the 5th Seaforth and the 5th Camerons breaching the minefield for the divisional attack.

5th Seaforth in Belgium and Holland – 1944

In October 1944 the 5th Seaforth advanced rapidly through France, Belgium and Holland. On 4th November the battalion made an assault crossing over the Aftwaterings Canal, and cleared the country as far as the River Maas. On 14th November the battalion made a further assault crossing over the Nederwert Canal, and three days later captured Zelen.

5th Seaforth in the Ardennes – 1945

After the German counter-attack in the Ardennes, a desperate attempt to recapture the Low countries, the 51st Highland Division took part in the counter offensive in January 1945. In deep snow and bitter cold the 5th Seaforth captured Genes and Mierchamps.

5th Seaforth in the Reichswald – 1945

The 51st Highland Division took a prominent part in the operation to breach the Siegfried Line and to defeat the German forces west of the Rhine.

5th Battalion Seaforth Highlanders in action in Holland 1945.

From 9th February the 5th Seaforth had a week of difficult fighting through the Reichswald Forest. Continuing beyond the Reichswald, the battalion captured Asperden and attacked Siebengewald with the 2nd Seaforth on 27th-28th February.

5th Seaforth at the Rhine Crossing – 1945

The 51st Highland Division was one of the assault divisions in the operation to cross the Rhine. The 5th Seaforth crossed on 24th March 1945 and, passing through the 2nd Seaforth in the bridgehead, captured the village of Groin. On 28th March the battalion established a bridgehead over the River Astrang, through which the armour passed for the final advance into Germany.

The 5th Seaforth in Germany – 1945-1946

During the final weeks of the war the 5th Seaforth met only minor opposition, and when the German Army surrendered on 4th May 1945, the battalion had reached Bremervorde. The 5th Seaforth took part in the Victory Parade at Bremerhaven on 12th May 1945. For the rest of the summer the battalion was billeted in the Cuxhaven peninsula, carrying out dock duties, and with responsibility for internal security. During the winter of 1945-1946 the 5th Seaforth guarded the SS concentration camp at Sandbostel, moving to Hanover in February 1946. The 5th Seaforth was disbanded on 3rd September 1946.

6th (MORAYSHIRE) BATTALION SEAFORTH HIGHLANDERS TA

6th Seaforth mobilises – 1939

When war broke out on 3rd September 1939, the 6th Seaforth mobilised at Elgin. In October 1940 the battalion moved south to Aldershot as part of 152 (Highland) Brigade in the 51st Highland Division.

6th Seaforth moves to France – 1940

On 26th January 1940 the 6th Seaforth moved to France with the 51st Highland Division in the British Expeditionary Force. During the period of preparation before the expected German attack, an adjustment was made to the groupings of the British Expeditionary Force to improve the standard of military training. In March 1940 a Regular Army battalion was included in each Territorial Army brigade. As part of this reorganisation the 6th Seaforth was replaced in 152 Brigade by the 2nd Seaforth. The 6th Seaforth took the place of the 2nd Seaforth in 17 Brigade of the 5th Division, and remained with brigade for the remainder of the war. The battalion joined 17 Brigade at Hallouin.

6th Seaforth at Dunkirk – 1940

During the German advance into the Netherlands in May 1940, the 6th Seaforth held positions in Belgium, and then on the Scarpe near Arras. The 6th Seaforth moved to Ypres as the left hand battalion of the British line, but when the Belgian Army surrendered, the battalion had to fall back to Dunkirk. After a long rearguard action, the 6th Seaforth was evacuated from Dunkirk on 1st June 1940.

6th Seaforth in Madagascar – 1942

After Dunkirk the 6th Seaforth was reformed at Turriff, and remained in Great Britain until March 1942. The battalion then embarked with 17 Brigade for overseas service. On 6th May the 6th Seaforth took part in the capture of Madagascar, an operation intended to secure the convoy route round the Cape of Good Hope. The attack cost the battalion 4 officers and 14 soldiers killed. After the landings 17 Brigade, including the 6th Seaforth, attacked and occupied Antisirane.

6th Seaforth in India – 1942

On 10th June 1942, after four weeks in Madagascar, the assault force was relieved by South African troops. The 6th Seaforth re-embarked for Bombay where the battalion was earmarked for the defence of India against the Japanese. On arrival it was sent by rail to Ranchi, where it carried out duties against civil disturbances.

6th Seaforth in Iraq and Iran – 1942-1943

By September 1942 the Germans had advanced towards the Caucusus and the Caspian Sea, and were threatening Iran and Iraq. The 5th Division was ordered to move to north Persia. The 6th Seaforth embarked at Bombay and landed in Iran at Basrah, moving via Shaiba and Baghdad to Kermanshaw. After training at Qum, the 6th Seaforth carried out internal security duties in Teheran during the bread riots of the winter 1942-1943, sharing duties with two Russian battalions. Among several unusual operations was the successful kidnapping of the pro-German General Zahidi, carried out by Captain Fitzroy Maclean of the Cameron Highlanders and a platoon of the 6th Seaforth.

6th Seaforth in Sicily – 1943

In January 1943 the 6th Seaforth moved from Iran to Egypt. When the invasion of Sicily took place on 10th July 1943, the battalion was among the assault troops . The 6th Seaforth took part in the capture of Syracuse and Augusta, in the operations on the Simeto River and the Catania Plain, and in the capture of Catania.

6th Seaforth in Italy – 1943-1944

On 3rd September 1943 the 5th Division crossed the Straits of Messina and landed in Italy. 17 Brigade, including the 6th Seaforth, was the assault brigade, and met little trouble during the landing and the subsequent advance. During October and November there was stiff opposition from German rearguards at Isernia. In November 1943 the 6th Seaforth moved to the Adriatic front near Ortona.

On 2nd January 1944 the 5th Division was transferred from the 8th Army to the 5th Army, and the 6th Seaforth returned to the west of Italy to take part in the operation to cross the Garigliano river, the first attack on the Gustav Line. The assault river crossing, carried out at night, was a difficult and costly operation, confused by mine fields and broken country, but the 5th Division succeeded in establishing its bridgehead.

After the Anzio landings the 5th Division was sent to reinforce the Anzio beachhead in February 1944. The 6th Seaforth took part in the defence of Anzio against strong German counter-attacks, and then in the advance on Rome in June 1944.

6th Seaforth in North West Europe – 1945

After 12 months fighting in Italy, the 6th Seaforth returned to Egypt to rest and refit. In March 1945 the battalion landed at Marseilles and moved north through France to join the Allied advance in Belgium. The battalion's last operation of the war was the advance into Germany through the bridgehead across the River Elbe. The 6th Seaforth finished the war at Lubeck.

The massed Pipes and Drums of the 2nd, 5th, 6th, and 7th Battalions Seaforth Highlanders, and the 1st Seaforth Highlanders of Canada, at the Seaforth Highlanders Gathering held at Cuxhaven in July 1945.

7th (MORAYSHIRE) BATTALION SEAFORTH HIGHLANDERS TA

7th Seaforth in Great Britain – 1939-1944

When war broke out on 3rd September 1939, the 7th Seaforth mobilised at Elgin, and then moved to Forres on 9th September. The newly formed battalion, still less than 300 strong, formed part of 26 (Highland) Brigade in the 9th (Highland) Division, the duplicate division of the 51st formed when the Territorial Army was doubled in 1939. After a short period with 152 (Highland) Brigade when the 51st Highland Division was re-formed after St Valéry, the 7th Seaforth was sent to garrison the Shetland Islands.

In October 1941 the 7th Seaforth moved to Northumberland to join 46 (Highland) Infantry Brigade in the 15th (Scottish) Division, and it was to stay with the brigade for the rest of the war. The 15th (Scottish) Division remained in Great Britain until the Normandy landings in 1944.

7th Seaforth at the River Odon – 1944

The 7th Seaforth sailed for Normandy on 16th June 1944, ten days after the initial landings. The first major operation for the 15th (Scottish) Division was Operation 'Epsom', the attack to seize the crossings over the River Odon, in preparation for the advance south from Caen. The plan included two battalion attacks by 7th Seaforth, at Cheux and Le Valtru. Having crossed the Odon the battalion cleared the area south of the river and attacked further positions on the Eterville ridge. In some of the hardest fighting of the campaign the 7th Seaforth suffered over 300 casualties.

7th Seaforth at Caumont – 1944

In July 1944 the 15th (Scottish) Division was moved to the American sector and took part in Operation 'Bluecoat', the break-out from Caumont. In the successful opening stages the 7th Seaforth captured Quarry Hill, and then became the advance guard until the division met strong opposition at Lassy.

7th Seaforth in the advance to the Rhine – 1944-1945

Having crossed the River Seine south of Rouen, the 7th Seaforth led the 46 Brigade advance, taking the village of Grand Roncherelles by a night attack, and then occupying Les Andelys. The 7th Seaforth continued into Belgium and Holland, receiving enthusiastic welcomes from the liberated populations of Courtrai and Loos. On 21st September the battalion established the bridgehead over the Wilhelmina canal from which the 15th (Scottish) Division cleared the area of Best. In a week of fighting to protect the Nijmegen corridor against German counter-attack, the 7th Seaforth took part in the attack by 46 Brigade which captured the villages of Liesel and Slot. Then, having crossed the Deurne canal, the battalion advanced to the River Maas. On 3rd December 1944, under command of 44 Brigade, the 7th Seaforth took part in the assault on Blerick. During January 1945 the 7th Seaforth fought successive actions at Hasselt, Schloss Moyland, and Schloss Kalbeck, as the division fought its way through the Siegfried Line to reach the Rhine.

7th Seaforth at the Rhine Crossing – 1945

After a period of training in river-crossing techniques, the 7th Seaforth crossed the Rhine north of Xanten on 24th March 1945, and captured Mehr. A strong-counter attack by German paratroops was only defeated by the Commanding Officer Lieutenant Colonel P M Hunt bringing down fire on his own battalion positions in the village.

7th Seaforth in Germany – 1945

In the final advance into Germany the 7th Seaforth crossed the River Elbe on 29th April 1945. The 15th (Scottish) Division carried out its third major assault river-crossing of the campaign, the only division to assault across the Seine, the Rhine and the Elbe. When the German army surrendered on 4th May 1945, the 7th Seaforth was approaching Lubeck. The battalion occupied Keil until its disbandment in January 1946.

*7th Battalion Seaforth Highlanders
cross the Rhine in March 1945.*

4th BATTALION
THE QUEEN'S OWN CAMERON HIGHLANDERS TA

4th Camerons mobilises – 1939

When war broke out on 3rd September 1939, the 4th Camerons mobilised at Inverness. The battalion formed part of 152 (Highland) Brigade in the 51st Highland Division. The 4th Camerons moved to the south of England where the battalion was visited by HM King George VI, Colonel in Chief of the Regiment, at Aldershot on 18th January 1940.

4th Camerons moves to France – 1940

The 4th Camerons left for France with the British Expeditionary Force on 26th January 1940. After arriving at Le Havre, the battalion moved forward to defensive positions in the Maginot Line in the Saar Valley.

4th Camerons at St Valéry-en-Caux – 1940

When the Germans advanced in May 1940, bypassing the Maginot Line, the 51st Highland Division withdrew from the Saar to a new line on the Somme at Abbeville. The 4th Camerons moved by train to Rouen, and then in busses to the new positions. On 4th June 1940, the last day of the evacuation of the BEF further north at Dunkirk, the 4th Camerons together with the 4th Seaforth took part in the counter-attack on the German bridgehead over the Somme. But the overwhelming strength of the German advance had now forced the 51st Highland Division to fall back to the coastal town of St Valéry-en-Caux, where it was hoped that the division would be evacuated. There, cut off from the French Army, and with no ships available, 4th Camerons with much of the 51st Highland Division was forced to surrender on 12th June 1940.

4th Camerons reformed – 1940-1942

In July 1940 the 4th Battalion was reconstituted in Inverness. The new battalion sailed in August 1940 for Aruba in the Dutch West Indies, where its task was to guard the vital oil refineries. The battalion also maintained a strong detachment in Bermuda. The 4th Camerons returned to Great Britain in February 1942, joining 46 Brigade in the 15th (Scottish) Division, until moving in November 1942 to garrison the Shetland Islands.

4th Camerons redesignated as the 2nd Camerons – 1942

After the loss in June 1942 of the 2nd Camerons at the siege of Tobruk, the regiment was determined to re-form its lost Regular Battalion. This was achieved by the redesignation of the 4th Camerons as the 2nd Battalion on 2nd December 1942

5th BATTALION
THE QUEEN'S OWN CAMERON HIGHLANDERS TA

5th Camerons in Great Britain – 1939-1942

When war broke out on 3rd September 1939, the 5th Camerons mobilised at Inverness. The battalion moved to Tain as part of 26 (Highland) Brigade in the 9th (Highland) Division, the duplicate division of the 51st, formed when the Territorial Army was doubled in 1939. When the 51st Highland Division was re-formed after St Valéry, the 5th Camerons formed part of the new 152 (Highland) Infantry Brigade, together with the 2nd and 5th Seaforth. The battalion trained in the United Kingdom until it sailed for Egypt in June 1942.

5th Camerons at El Alamein – 1942

On 11th August 1942 the 5th Camerons landed in Egypt with the 51st Highland Division. After six weeks of intensive preparation, the battalion took part in the attack by the 8th Army at El Alamein which began on 23rd October 1942. In the early stages of the battle the 5th Camerons carried out two separate tasks. Two companies provided covering parties for the Royal Engineers who made vehicle breaches in the enemy minefields; and two companies assaulted under command of 154 Brigade. In Operation 'Supercharge' on 2nd November 1942, 152 Brigade broke through the enemy defences to allow the armour to exploit beyond the minefields. The 5th Camerons was the left battalion of the brigade attack, with the 5th Seaforth on its right.

The 8th Army Commander, Lieutenant General B L Montgomery, meets officers of the 5th Camerons in September 1942, before the battle of El Alamein, with Major General D N Wimberley, GOC 51st Highland Division, and (right) Lieutenant Colonel R D M C Miers, commanding the 5th Camerons.

5th Camerons in Tripoli – 1943

On 16th January 1943, while moving in desert formation as the advanced guard of the division, the 5th Camerons was heavily shelled at Buerat. After the 51st Highland Division reached Tripoli, the 5th Camerons took part in the Victory Parade where the salute was taken by the Prime Minister, Mr Winston Churchill.

5th Camerons at Mareth – 1943

In February 1943 the 51st Highland Division reached Mareth, an enemy defensive line sited behind the tank obstacles of the Wadi Zigzau which had been extended by an artificial anti-tank ditch. The task of the 51st Highland Division was to establish a firm base for an attack by the 50th Division. The divisional plan was for the 5th Camerons to advance through the 5th Seaforth, which held a section of the anti-tank ditch, and then to attack the enemy positions which were interfering with the advance. Heavy shell fire cost the 5th Camerons 121 casualties, but the Mareth position was eventually outflanked to the south.

5th Camerons at Wadi Akarit – 1943

In early 1943 the 8th Army reached the bottleneck where the Germans held a strong position on the Djebel Roumana ridge, and along the Wadi Akarit, which connected it to the sea. In the attack by the 51st Highland Division on 6th-7th April 1943, 152 Brigade's objective was the Djebel Roumana. The 5th Camerons was the left assault battalion, with the 5th Seaforth on its right. The battalion took its objective and then withstood the heavy German counter-attacks. The campaign in North Africa cost the 5th Camerons 565 casualties.

5th Camerons in Sicily – 1943

After the battle of Wadi Akarit, the 5th Camerons trained in Algeria for the invasion of Sicily. The battalion embarked at Sousse, and sailed via Malta for Sicily. During the landings on 10th July 1943, 152 Brigade was in reserve. After the beachhead was established, the brigade advanced with the 5th Camerons as the advance guard, the battalion clearing several enemy positions. On 13th July the 5th Seaforth was held up by a German parachute battalion holding a strong position at Francofonte. While the 2nd Seaforth assaulted the main position, the 5th Camerons carried out a successful flanking attack. In its last battle of the Sicily campaign, the 5th Camerons was the leading battalion of the attack by 152 Brigade on the Sferro Hills. The battalion took its objective against determined opposition, and was reinforced during the attack by two companies of the 2nd Seaforth. The campaign in Sicily cost the 5th Camerons 68 casualties.

5th Camerons in Great Britain – 1943-1944

After the capture of Sicily, the 51st Highland Division returned to Great Britain in November 1943 to prepare for the invasion of Normandy. The 5th Camerons was billeted in Hertford.

5th Camerons in Normandy – 1944

The 5th Camerons landed at Courseulles in Normandy on 'D + 1', 7th June 1944, and moved into the Orne bridgehead. The battalion had seven weeks of intensive fighting against strong German counter-attacks until the break out from Caen. In Operation 'Totalise' on 7th-8th August the 5th Camerons advanced down the axis of the Falaise road to capture the village of Lorquichon and to occupy Poussy.

On 2nd September 1944 the 51st Highland Division liberated St Valéry-en-Caux, the 5th Camerons and 5th Seaforth being the first Highland battalions to enter the town. The 51st Highland Division then took part in the attack on the German positions holding Le Havre, the 5th Camerons and 5th Seaforth breaching the minefield for the divisional attack.

Pipers of the 5th Battalion The Queen's Own Cameron Highlanders play at St Valéry after its recapture by the 51st Highland Division in September 1944.

5th Camerons in Belgium and Holland – 1944

In October 1944 the 5th Camerons advanced rapidly through France, Belgium and Holland. The battalion met tough opposition when it attacked the German positions at Schijndel and Vught. On 4th November the 5th Camerons carried out an assault crossing over the Aftwaterings canal and cleared the country as far as the River Maas. This was followed by a further assault crossing over the Nederwert Canal on 14th November. An outstandingly successful action was the crossing of the Zig Canal on 17th November 1944, when the 5th Camerons managed to cross a collapsed bridge and hold a bridgehead against a strong counter-attack, until the 2nd Seaforth could pass through.

5th Battalion The Queen's Own Cameron Highlanders at Schijndel 1944.

5th Camerons in the Ardennes – 1945

When the Germans counter-attacked in the Ardennes, in a desperate attempt to recapture the Low countries, the 51st Highland Division took part in the counter offensive in January 1945. In deep snow and bitter cold, the 5th Camerons carried out a series of attacks on the villages of the Ardennes.

5th Camerons in the Reichswald – 1945

The 51st Highland Division took a prominent part in the operations to breach the Siegfried Line and to defeat the German forces west of the Rhine. The 5th Camerons entered the Reichswald forest on 9th February 1945, and in a week of most difficult close-quarter action the battalion fought its way through the forest. The 5th Camerons then continued beyond Reichswald to attack Hervost and advance to Asperden.

5th Camerons at the Rhine Crossing – 1945

The 51st Highland Division was one of the assault divisions in the operation to cross the Rhine. The 5th Camerons crossed on 24th March 1945 and, passing through the 2nd Seaforth in the bridgehead, attacked and captured Mittleburg after a hard fight. On 27th March 1945 the 5th Camerons went on to capture Isselburg.

5th Camerons in Germany – 1945-1946

The final advance into Germany started on 7th April 1945 and included an attack at Adelheide. The last action of the war for the 5th Camerons was at Glinde. The 5th Camerons took part in the Victory Parade at Bremerhaven on 12th May 1945.

For the rest of the summer the battalion was billeted at Cuxhaven, moving to Westertimke for the winter, where duties included guarding the prisoner-of-war camps. 152 Brigade moved to Hanover in 1946 with the role of maintaining law and order. In October 1946 the 5th Camerons was disbanded in Inverness.

1st BATTALION THE LIVERPOOL SCOTTISH, THE QUEEN'S OWN CAMERON HIGHLANDERS TA

1st Liverpool Scottish in Great Britain – 1939-1945

When war broke out in 1939 the 1st Liverpool Scottish was mobilised at Liverpool. The battalion formed part of 165 (Liverpool) Infantry Brigade in the 55th (West Lancashire) Division.

The 1st Battalion Liverpool Scottish remained in Great Britain during the war, and was of indispensable value to The Queen's Own Cameron Highlanders as a supplier of large numbers of reinforcements for battalions on active service overseas. Its role at home was defence against invasion.

No 4 Independent Company, Liverpool Scottish in Norway – 1940

When the Germans invaded Norway in 1940, the 1st Battalion Liverpool Scottish provided a contingent for an Independent Company of volunteers which served in Norway. After the fall of Norway most of the volunteers served with the Commandos.

1st Liverpool Scottish in Gibraltar – 1945-1947

At the end of the war, when the 55th Division was disbanded, the 1st Liverpool Scottish moved to Gibraltar. The battalion remained there until disbanded in February 1947.

2nd BATTALION THE LIVERPOOL SCOTTISH, THE QUEEN'S OWN CAMERON HIGHLANDERS TA

When war broke out in 1939 the 2nd Battalion Liverpool Scottish was mobilised in Liverpool. It formed part of 165 (Liverpool) Infantry Brigade in the 55th (West Lancashire) Division. In the early days of the war the 2nd Liverpool Scottish was responsible for the security of the Merseyside Docks, and then from late 1939 it was given coastal defence and anti-invasion roles.

In September 1942 the 2nd Liverpool Scottish was transferred to the 218th Independent Brigade guarding vulnerable points in Yorkshire. On 1st November 1942 the battalion was converted into the 89th Anti-Tank Regiment RA. It was eventually disbanded in 1946.

THE LOVAT SCOUTS TA

The Lovat Scouts mobilise – 1939

When war broke out in September 1939 the role of the Lovat Scouts was intended to be 'mounted scouts, to provide mobile troops for reconnaissance and protection'. The regiment mobilised at Beauly with its ponies, and started mounted training. The regiment formed part of the 9th (Highland) Division. In March 1940 the Lovat Scouts joined the Mounted Cavalry Division in Nottinghamshire.

The Lovat Scouts in the Faroe Islands – 1940-1942

In May 1940 the Lovat Scouts sailed for the Faroe Islands, a Danish possession of strategic importance in the north Atlantic. The regiment had tried hard to persuade the War Office to allow it to return to its most effective role of front line observers with the British Expeditionary Force in France. The task of protecting the Faroes against German occupation was in fact close to the regiment's role of providing mobile troops for reconnaissance and protection, 'probably in a minor theatre of war'. The Lovat Scouts concentrated the regiment's resources on protecting Thorshavn and the deep water anchorage of Skallefjord, while two squadrons garrisoned the outlying islands.

The Lovat Scouts in Great Britain and Canada – 1942-1943

In June 1942 the Lovat Scouts returned to Scotland, being stationed first at Nairn and then moving to Caithness in September 1942. The Lovat Scouts reorganised as an infantry battalion, forming part of 157 Brigade in the 52nd (Lowland) Division. The regiment provided the Royal Guard for the Royal family's summer visits to Balmoral in 1942 and 1943.

In 1943 the regiment was selected for training as a Mountain Recce Regiment, and was earmarked for the Italian campaign. Special training started in 1943 in the Cairngorms, and continued at the School of Mountain Warfare in North Wales, before the Lovat Scouts moved to Canada in January 1944 for ski and mountain warfare training in the Rocky Mountains.

The Lovat Scouts training in Caithness, 1942

The Lovat Scouts training for mountain warfare in Canada in 1944

The Lovat Scouts in Italy – 1944-1945

The Lovat Scouts sailed for Italy in July 1944, landing at Naples, and joining the 10th (Indian) Division as mountain recce troops near Arezzo. During the Allies' advance north to the Gothic Line the regiment carried out intensive patrolling, including many long range operations behind the enemy lines. The powers of observation of the Scouts, and their skill at operating in the mountainous terrain of the Appenines, proved of incalculable value to the 8th Army. In January 1945 the Lovat Scouts carried out a refresher course in ski-mountaineering in preparation for snow warfare in north Italy, but in the event the regiment seldom used skis. When the ceasefire in Italy was announced, the Lovat Scouts were holding positions south of Bologna.

The Lovat Scouts in Austria and Greece – 1945-1946

Having escorted a large batch of German prisoners south to Taranto, the Lovat Scouts moved north to Klagenfurt in Austria. The regiment's tasks were to intercept German soldiers escaping through the hills, to arrest Nazi and SS officials, and to search for weapons.

In July 1945 the Lovat Scouts moved to Salonika in northern Greece to join the 11th (Indian) Brigade of the 4th (Indian) Division, part of the British military force which supervised the democratic elections and controlled the surrender of weapons by left wing resistance movements. The regiment was disbanded in October 1946.

6. HOME DEFENCE BATTALIONS

THE NATIONAL DEFENCE COMPANIES – 1939

When war broke out in 1939, a number of National Defence Companies were formed of ex-soldiers enlisted for home service, and many older men, including former World War I soldiers were encouraged to join. Because recruiting was slow, these companies were given regimental identities, and became Home Defence battalions. The battalions were allotted tasks defending vital installations in and around their regimental areas, thus relieving Territorial Army battalions of routine guards and garrison duties, and freeing them for intensive war training.

8th (HOME DEFENCE) BATTALION SEAFORTH HIGHLANDERS – 1939-1941

The 8th Seaforth originated as a National Defence Company formed in November 1939. Having been redesignated as the 8th Seaforth, the battalion undertook guards and duties all over the north of Scotland, with its headquarters at Golspie.

30th (HOME DEFENCE) BATTALION SEAFORTH HIGHLANDERS – 1941-1943

In December 1941 the 8th Seaforth was redesignated the 30th (Home Defence) Battalion Seaforth Highlanders, but its role of Home Defence duties in the north of Scotland remained unchanged..

6th (HOME DEFENCE) BATTALION
THE QUEEN'S OWN CAMERON HIGHLANDERS – 1939-1942

The 6th Camerons originated as a National Defence Company formed in November 1939. Having been redesignated as the 6th (Home Defence) Battalion The Queen's Own Cameron Highlanders, the battalion undertook guards and duties all over the north of Scotland, with its headquarters in the Rose Street Drill Hall, Inverness.

30th (HOME DEFENCE) BATTALION
THE QUEEN'S OWN CAMERON HIGHLANDERS – 1942-1943

In April 1942 the 6th Camerons became the 30th (Home Defence) Battalion The Queen's Own Cameron Highlanders, but its role of Home Defence duties remained unchanged. The battalion was reduced to two independent Cameron Defence Companies in February 1943, and these were disbanded in 1946.

7. RESERVE AND HOLDING BATTALIONS

9th BATTALION SEAFORTH HIGHLANDERS – 1940-1943

The 9th Seaforth was formed in September 1940 at Market Harborough, and then moved to Easter Ross. The battalion was at first intended to be a Field Force battalion.

In November 1942 the battalion became the 9th Reserve Battalion Seaforth Highlanders, and subsequently the 9th Holding battalion Seaforth Highlanders. It was stationed at Lairg, Wick, Watten, Overstrand, Scarborough, Hoddam Castle, and Strathpeffer.

50th HOLDING BATTALION
THE QUEEN'S OWN CAMERON HIGHLANDERS – 1940

In May 1940 the 50th Holding Battalion The Queen's Own Cameron Highlanders was formed at Loughborough from a cadre drawn from No 34 (Cameron Highlanders) Infantry Training Centre. It was intended to receive intakes from civilian life and, after training, to post them to battalions. In October 1940 the 50th Holding Battalion was renamed the 7th Camerons.

7th BATTALION
THE QUEEN'S OWN CAMERON HIGHLANDERS – 1940-1942

On the redesignation of the 50th Holding Battalion as the 7th Camerons, the battalion moved to Wick in a coastal defence role in October 1940. In October 1941 the 7th Camerons moved to Ayr, and in November the battalion joined the 15th (Scottish) Division at Alnwick in Northumberland. In spring 1942 it moved to Harwich and then Colchester.

In August 1942 the 7th Camerons was given a new role when it was converted into a parachute battalion. Re-designated the 5th (Scottish) Parachute Battalion, The Parachute Regiment, the battalion distinguished itself in action in North Africa, Italy, the south of France, and Greece. The regimental origins were maintained by the Pipes and Drums which continued to wear the kilt of 79th tartan.

NO 11 (SEAFORTH AND CAMERON) HOLDING BATTALION – 1944-1946

When the campaign in North West Europe started in 1944, the regimental Depot Companies of No 1 Infantry Depot in Edinburgh became so large that Holding Battalions were formed. The Seaforth and Cameron Depot Companies became No 11 (Seaforth and Cameron) Holding Battalion, which formed at Forres in November 1944, moved to Strathpeffer in January 1945, and to Stobs in November 1945. In early 1946 the 11th (Seaforth and Cameron) Holding Battalion amalgamated with those of other Highland regiments to form No 8 Highland Holding Battalion at Stewarton.

NO 8 HIGHLAND HOLDING BATTALION – 1946

No 8 Highland Holding Battalion, having formed at Stewarton, moved to Cameron Barracks, Inverness in July 1946. It remained there until disbanded in November 1946.

CHAPTER VI
THE REGIMENTS SINCE WORLD WAR II
1. THE REGULAR ARMY BATTALIONS
1st BATTALION SEAFORTH HIGHLANDERS

1st Battalion Seaforth Highlanders march through Dingwall
after the Regiment received the Freedom of the Royal Burgh in 1954.

1st Seaforth in Malaya – 1945

At the end of the war the 1st Seaforth was in India, training for the reconquest of Malaya. After the Japanese surrender on 14th August 1945 the operation went ahead as planned, and the 1st Seaforth landed unopposed at Port Dickson in September 1945.

1st Seaforth in Java – 1946

In 1946 the 1st Seaforth moved to Java to preserve law and order in the Dutch colony under the difficult circumstances which followed the Japanese surrender. The 78th Highlanders had taken part in the capture of the island from the Dutch in 1811. Soon after the battalion arrived in 1946 there were violent riots, as Indonesian nationalists mounted their campaign to achieve independence from the Dutch.

1st Seaforth in Malaya 1946-1951

In October 1946 the 1st Seaforth moved to Ipoh in Malaya, and then to Singapore. In early 1948 the communists launched their guerilla war aimed at taking over the Federation of Malaya, and the 1st Seaforth began three years of jungle operations. The 1st Seaforth operated at first in Johore and later in east and central Pahang, and the battalion's operations accounted for nearly 100 terrorists.

1st Seaforth in Edinburgh – 1951-1952

The 1st Seaforth left Malaya in 1951 and returned to Redford Barracks, Edinburgh. In 1951 the battalion provided the Royal Guard at Ballater, and provided Guards of Honour and ceremonial contingents for the Proclamation of HM Queen Elizabeth and the funeral of HM King George VI.

1st Seaforth in Germany – 1952-1954

In April 1952 the 1st Seaforth left Edinburgh for Buxtehude in West Germany, where the battalion formed part of 31 Lorried Infantry Brigade in the 7th Armoured Division of the British Army of the Rhine. In June 1953 the 1st Seaforth sent a detachment to London to take part in the Coronation parade of HM Queen Elizabeth.

1st Seaforth in Elgin – 1954

The 1st Seaforth returned briefly to Scotland in May 1954, spending six weeks at Pinefield Camp, Elgin before embarking for the Middle East. It was the first time that the 1st Seaforth had returned to Elgin since the Earl of Seaforth paraded his regiment for inspection at Elgin in 1778. On 15th May 1954 the Seaforth Highlanders received the Freedom of the Royal Burgh of Dingwall, and the parade included detachments from the 1st Seaforth, the Depot Seaforth, the 11th Seaforth TA, the Seaforth Cadets, and the Regimental Association.

1st Seaforth in Egypt – 1954-1955

In 1954 the 1st Seaforth sailed for Egypt to join the Middle East Land Forces in the Canal Zone. The British Army was in the process of moving its Middle East base from Egypt to Cyprus, and the battalion's task was to protect British lives and property from the attacks of Egyptian terrorists.

1st Seaforth in Aden – 1955

In June 1955 the battalion was due to leave Egypt for Gibraltar when it was sent at short notice to Aden, to support the Aden Protectorate Levies in operations against dissident tribesmen. The 1st Seaforth spent five months in the Western Aden Protectorate, before rejoining the Advance party which had moved direct from Egypt to Gibraltar.

1st Battalion Seaforth Highlanders in Aden, 1955. Pipers rally the tribesmen at Mafidh.

1st Seaforth in Gibraltar – 1955-1957

The 1st Seaforth was complete in Gibraltar by November 1955, and spent two years as the garrison battalion. The battalion stood by for duty during the Suez landings, but was not required to embark.

1st Seaforth in Germany – 1957-1961

In October 1957 the 1st Seaforth returned to West Germany where it was stationed in Munster, forming part of 6 Brigade in the 2nd Division of the British Army of the Rhine. The 1st Seaforth received its 9th Stand of Colours at Munster from Field Marshal Sir Gerald Templer, Chief of the Imperial General Staff, on 14th August 1958.

On 25th November 1960 the 1st Seaforth held its farewell parade at Munster, before the amalgamation of Seaforth and Camerons. The salute was taken by the Colonel of the Regiment, General Sir James Cassels.

General Sir James Cassels, Colonel of the Regiment, inspects the 1st Battalion Seaforth Highlanders at the final parade in Munster on 25th November 1960.

*1st Battalion Seaforth Highlanders arrive at Redford Barracks, Edinburgh
before amalgamation with 1st Battalion The Queen's Own Cameron Highlanders, 1961.*

Amalgamation – 7th February 1961

In January 1961 the 1st Seaforth left Munster for Redford Barracks, Edinburgh where on 7th February 1961 the Seaforth Highlanders were amalgamated with The Queen's Own Cameron Highlanders to form the:

**QUEEN'S OWN HIGHLANDERS
(SEAFORTH AND CAMERONS)**

2nd BATTALION SEAFORTH HIGHLANDERS

2nd Seaforth in Germany and Great Britain – 1945-1948

After the end of the war the 2nd Seaforth remained in Germany for a year, being responsible for law and order in Neustadt near Hanover. In 1946 the battalion returned to Great Britain, and was stationed at Knook Camp near Warminster, and then at Bicester.

2nd Seaforth amalgamated with 1st Seaforth – 1948

As part of the post war reductions of the infantry, the 2nd battalions of the infantry regiments were removed from the Order of Battle. In May 1948 the 2nd Seaforth, the former 78th Highlanders raised in 1793, was reduced to cadre strength and amalgamated with the 1st Seaforth.

1st BATTALION
THE QUEEN'S OWN CAMERON HIGHLANDERS

HM The Queen inspects 1st Battalion The Queen's Own Cameron Highlanders at Balmoral,
at the presentation of new Colours in 1955.

1st Camerons in Japan – 1946-1947

In March 1946 the lst Camerons left India for Japan, where the battalion formed part of the British Occupational Force in Japan. The 1st Camerons was stationed at Hiro on Shikoku Island, where the battalion's tasks included dismantling military installations and suppressing black market activities.

1st Camerons in Malaya – 1947-1948

In February 1947 the 1st Camerons left Japan for Malaya. The battalion was stationed at Ipoh, with companies detached in other parts of Perak. The role of the 1st Camerons was internal security, in co-operation with the police force. The battalion moved to Johore Bahru in January 1948, before returning to Great Britain in April 1948 at cadre strength.

1st Camerons in Great Britain – 1948-1949

In April 1948 the lst Camerons returned to Great Britain, the battalion's arrival in Edinburgh coinciding with the disbandment of the 2nd Battalion at Inverness. The 1st Battalion was quickly rebuilt to strength with Regular soldiers from both battalions, its composition being roughly two thirds Regular soldiers and one third National Servicemen. In October 1948 the lst Camerons moved to Bulford as the nucleus of an operational brigade, ready for service overseas at short notice.

lst Camerons in Tripoli – 1949-1951

In February 1949 the 1st Camerons sailed for Tripoli where the battalion joined the 1st Guards Brigade. During the Malayan campaign and the Korean War, the battalion was required to send drafts to other Scottish regiments engaged in hostilities.

1st Camerons in Egypt – 1951-1952

There had been increasing pressure from the Egyptian government for Great Britain to withdraw its troops from Egypt, and in November 1951 the 1st Camerons moved at short notice to reinforce the Suez Canal Zone garrison. The battalion was based at Tel-el-Kebir, the Ordnance Depot holding the strategic reserve of stores and equipment for the Middle East, and its task was to protect the base against Egyptian sabotage, theft and sniping. The battalion was regularly involved in countering terrorist activity.

1st Battalion The Queen's Own Cameron Highlanders Mortar Platoon training in Egypt, 1951.

1st Camerons in Edinburgh – 1952

In April 1952 the 1st Camerons left Port Said and returned to Edinburgh. During the battalion's short stay there, the 1st Camerons provided the Guard of Honour and Royal Guards at the Palace of Holyrood for HM The Queen's first visit to the Scottish capital after her accession.

1st Camerons in Austria – 1952-1953

In August 1952 the 1st Camerons left Edinburgh for Spittal in Austria, where the battalion formed part of British Troops Austria, the occupation force for the British zone of Austria. In June 1953 the 1st Camerons sent a detachment to London to take part in the Coronation parade of HM Queen Elizabeth.

1st Camerons in Germany – 1953-1955

The 1st Camerons left Austria in November 1953 for Luneburg in West Germany, where the battalion formed part of the 31st Lorried Infantry Brigade in the 7th Armoured Division of the British Army of the Rhine. On 24th June 1954 HRH Prince Philip, Duke of Edinburgh paid his first visit to the 1st Battalion having been appointed Colonel-in-Chief of the Regiment in 1953 .

1st Camerons in Elgin – 1955

In February 1955 the 1st Camerons left Luneburg for Elgin, where the battalion prepared for service in the Far East. On 30th May 1955 HM The Queen presented the 1st Camerons with its 7th Stand of Colours at Balmoral Castle.

1st Camerons in Korea – 1955-1956

After the end of the Korean war in 1953, a United Nations force remained in South Korea to maintain the security of the country. The 1st Camerons arrived in Korea in July 1955, and joined the 1st Commonwealth Division. The battalion was stationed south of the Imjin river, near the 38th Parallel, and its operational role was to occupy prepared defensive positions nearby, if hostilities broke out again. Its duties included the task of patrolling the De-Militarised Zone. When the Commonwealth Division was disbanded, the 1st Camerons came under operational control of the 21st US Infantry Regiment.

1st Camerons in Aden – 1956-1958

During the months before leaving Korea in August 1956, the 1st Camerons trained for jungle warfare, the battalion being due to move to Malaya for counter-insurgency operations. But this move was overtaken by the international crisis in Egypt, where President Nasser had nationalised the Suez Canal, and British and French troops landed at Suez. The 1st Camerons had embarked at Inchon for Singapore, but the

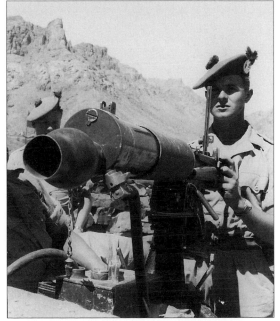

1st Battalion The Queen's Own Cameron Highlanders. Medium machine gun section in Aden, 1956.

battalion was re-routed to Aden, where the repercussions of Arab Nationalism were threatening the internal security of the Colony and the Protectorate. The main roles of the 1st Camerons in Aden were internal security in Aden Colony, and to operate with the Aden Protectorate Levies in preventing incursions by tribesmen from across the border of Yemen. The battalion was based in Aden Colony, with companies detached to Dhala, Mukeiras and Beihan in the Protectorate, and guarding the BP oil refinery at Little Aden. In 1957, while serving in Aden, the 1st Camerons won the Duke of Edinburgh's Trophy for marksmanship and physical fitness.

1st Camerons in Dover – 1958-1960

In March 1958 the 1st Camerons returned to Great Britain, and the battalion was stationed at Dover, forming part of 19 Infantry Brigade in the 3rd Division. The battalion was the last infantry battalion to occupy Dover Castle, before its use as barrack accommodation was discontinued. The battalion trained for its role in the Strategic Reserve, being ready to move at short notice by air to any part of the world.

1st Camerons in Edinburgh – 1960-1961

In early 1960 the 1st Camerons returned to Redford Barracks, Edinburgh. The year included many ceremonial events, including the laying up of the battalion's 6th Stand of Colours in Glasgow Cathedral, Guards of Honour for the General Assembly of the Church of Scotland, and the Royal Guard at Ballater.

Orders of dress worn by 1st Battalion The Queen's Own Cameron Highlanders in Dover, 1957.

On 25th November 1960 the 1st Battalion held its farewell parade at Edinburgh before the amalgamation of Seaforth and Camerons. The salute was taken by Major General Douglas Wimberley, Colonel of the Regiment.

Amalgamation – 7th February 1961

On 7th February 1961, at Redford Barracks, Edinburgh, The Queen's Own Cameron Highlanders were amalgamated with the Seaforth Highlanders to form the:

QUEEN'S OWN HIGHLANDERS
(SEAFORTH AND CAMERSONS)

Major General D N Wimberley, Colonel of the Regiment, takes the salute at
the final parade of 1st Battalion The Queen's Own Cameron Highlanders on 25th November 1960,
before amalgamation in 1961.

2nd BATTALION
THE QUEEN'S OWN CAMERON HIGHLANDERS

2nd Camerons in Austria, Italy and Trieste – 1945-1947

In July 1945 the 2nd Camerons left Greece, having been relieved by the Lovat Scouts, and moved to Austria, where the battalion was stationed around Klagenfurt. The battalion returned to Italy in September 1945, and was stationed at Verona, Bassano, and Gradisca, moving to Trieste in May 1946.

2nd Camerons in Great Britain – 1947-1948

In September 1947 the 2nd Camerons returned to Great Britain, where it was stationed at Didcot.

2nd Camerons disbanded – 1948

As part of the post war reductions of the infantry, the 2nd battalions of the infantry regiments were removed from the Order of Battle. On 30th June 1948 the 2nd Camerons, after just over 50 years distinguished existence, returned to Inverness where the battalion was disbanded.

1st BATTALION QUEEN'S OWN HIGHLANDERS (SEAFORTH AND CAMERONS)

1st Queen's Own Highlanders formed in Edinburgh – 1961

The amalgamation of the Seaforth Highlanders and The Queen's Own Cameron Highlanders took place on 7th February 1961, in a simple ceremony at Redford Barracks, Edinburgh when the two regular battalions were formed into a single new battalion. The officers and sergeants of the 1st Seaforth and the 1st Camerons assembled in the officers mess, where the two stands of Colours were combined to symbolise the union, and a toast was drunk to the new regiment. That morning, at Edinburgh Castle, the last guard mounted by the 1st Camerons was relieved by the first guard mounted by the 1st Queen's Own Highlanders.

Lieutenant Colonel Niall Baird, first Commanding Officer, gives the toast to 1st Battalion Queen's Own Highlanders on its formation at Edinburgh 1961

The first guard found by 1st Battalion Queen's Own Highlanders mounts at Edinburgh Castle on Amalgamation Day, 7th February 1961.

In March 1961 a detachment of the new 1st Battalion toured the regimental area, with the Colours, Pipes and Drums, and Regimental Band. The detachment took part in two important ceremonies when the Regiment received the Freedom of Inverness on 4th March 1961, and the Freedom of Dingwall on 11th March 1961. The detachment also marched through Kingussie, Fort William, Nairn, Grantown-on-Spey, Forres, Elgin, Dornoch, Wick and Thurso.

On 24th March 1961 HRH Prince Philip, Duke of Edinburgh, Colonel in Chief of the Queen's Own Highlanders, visited the 1st Battalion for the first time at Redford Barracks, Edinburgh.

1st Queen's Own Highlanders in the Far East – 1961-1964

On 8th April 1961 the 1st Queen's Own Highlanders sailed for the Far East. On arrival in Singapore the battalion was stationed in Selarang Barracks, and was the British battalion of 99 Gurkha Infantry Brigade, in the 17th Gurkha Division.

On 6th February 1962 the battalion trooped the Regimental Colours of the 1st Seaforth and 1st Camerons in Singapore.

1st Queen's Own Highlanders in the Brunei rebellion – 1962-1963

The operational role of 1st Battalion Queen's Own Highlanders was to maintain the internal security of Singapore, but the battalion also carried out training in the British dependencies in North Borneo, supporting the civil authorities in preventing piracy, and acting as a deterrent to Indonesian interference with the North Borneo Territories. On 8th December 1962 armed rebellion broke out in the Sultanate of Brunei, where a rebel force led by Azahari attacked the Sultan's palace, and also police stations and installations throughout Brunei. The rebels took hostages and seized the Shell oilfield at Seria.

Detachment of 1st Battalion Queen's Own Highlanders marches through Inverness, March 1961.

Battalion Headquarters and A Company of the 1st Queen's Own Highlanders moved at very short notice from Singapore to Brunei by air, while the destroyer HMS Cavalier sailed at full speed carrying B Company. 60 men of A Company landed by five Twin Pioneer aircraft at Seria and seized Panaga Police Station. Simultaneously the remainder of A Company landed by Beverley aircraft at Anduki Airfield, captured the control tower, and seized the Bailey bridge over the Sungei Bera. Next morning the battalion advanced through Seria, A Company clearing a strong rebel force from the Sultan's summer palace, and B Company releasing 46 European hostages from the rebel held Police Station. Finally B Company 1st/2nd Gurkhas cleared Kuala Belait. The battalion returned to Singapore in February 1963 on the Commando ship HMS Albion, after its first active service since the amalgamation of the regiment.

Queen's Own Highlanders deplaning from a Twin Pioneer at Seria, 1962.

1st Battalion Queen's Own Highlanders clearing houses in Seria, during the Brunei rebellion, 1962

1st Queen's Own Highlanders in Brunei and North Borneo – 1963

The 1st Battalion returned to Borneo in May 1963, when its duties included long range patrolling of the Indonesian border, and the training of local tribesmen as Border Scouts.

1st Queen's Own Highlanders in Edinburgh – 1964

Presentation of Colours to 1st Battalion Queen's Own Highlanders at Holyrood 1964.
The Colonel-in-Chief, HRH Prince Philip, Duke of Edinburgh inspects the Battalion,
accompanied by the Commanding Officer, Lieutenant Colonel W G McHardy.

In March 1964 the 1st Queen's Own Highlanders returned to Edinburgh and was billeted at Milton Bridge camp. On 21st May 1964 the battalion received its first Stand of Colours from HRH Prince Philip, Duke of Edinburgh, Colonel in Chief of the Regiment, at the Palace of Holyrood in Edinburgh.

1st Queen's Own Highlanders in Germany – 1964-1966

In June 1964 the 1st Queen's Own Highlanders moved to Mercer Barracks in Osnabrück, West Germany. The battalion formed part of 12 Infantry Brigade, in the 2nd Division, in the British Army of the Rhine. It was equipped with Armoured Personnel Carriers (APCs), the wheeled one ton Humber APC, until these were replaced in late 1965 by tracked Armoured Fighting Vehicles, the AFV 432.

In 1965 and 1966 the 1st Battalion won the Army Championship at the Regular Army Skill at Arms Meeting at Bisley.

The old Colours of the 1st Seaforth and 1st Camerons were then marched off parade at Holyrood in 1964.

1st Queen's Own Highlanders in Berlin – 1966-1968

The 1st Queen's Own Highlanders moved from Osnabrück to Berlin in August 1966, where the battalion formed part of the Berlin Infantry Brigade in the four power occupation force comprising British, US, Russian and French troops.

In 1967 the battalion again won the Army Championship at the Regular Army Skill-at-Arms Meeting at Bisley.

1st Battalion Queen's Own Highlanders on guard at Spandau Prison, Berlin, 1966.

1st Battalion Queen's Own Highlanders at Edinburgh Castle, December 1970.

1st Queen's Own Highlanders in Edinburgh -1968-1971

In September 1968 the 1st Queen's Own Highlanders returned to Redford Barracks, Edinburgh. Its three year tour in Great Britain included a period of nine months in the Gulf, where the battalion served in the Trucial States.

1st Queen's Own Highlanders in Sharjah – 1969-1970

From May 1969 to February 1970, under Great Britain's treaty obligations to protect the Trucial States and maintain stability in the oil-producing countries of the Middle East, the 1st Queen's Own Highlanders spent a nine month tour at Sharjah in the Trucial States. The battalion was based at the RAF airfield in Sharjah, and trained in desert and mountain operations throughout the Trucial States and Oman.

**1st Queen's Own Highlanders in Edinburgh –
1970-1971**

On its return to Great Britain in 1970, the 1st Queen's
Own Highlanders provided the ceremonial and
administrative duties for the Commonwealth Games
held in Edinburgh, including Royal Guards of Honour
for HM The Queen and HRH Prince Philip, Duke of
Edinburgh.

**1st Queen's Own Highlanders in Germany – 1971-
1976**

PIn April 1971 the 1st Queen's Own Highlanders moved
to Belfast Barracks, Osnabrück, in West Germany. The
battalion formed part of 12 Mechanised Brigade, in the
2nd Division, in the British Army of the Rhine. The
battalion was equipped once again with AFV 432
Armoured Personnel Carriers.

In 1971 the 1st Queen's Own Highlanders represented
Great Britain in the CENTO Small Arms Competition
(NISHAN VII) and won first place, the only British
battalion ever to win this competition.

**1st Queen's Own Highlanders in Northern Ireland –
1971-1972**

In November 1971 the 1st Queen's Own Highlanders
began its first tour of duty in Ulster since the troubles in
Northern Ireland started again in 1969. The battalion
was deployed in East Belfast, with Battalion Tactical

*An APC of 1st Battalion Queen's Own Highlanders in
Germany 1976.*

Headquarters, B Company and D Company in Ballymacarret, and A, Support, and Headquarters Companies as the
brigade and battalion reserve at Sydenham Royal Naval Aircraft Yard. The battalion returned to Osnabrück in
March 1972.

1st Queen's Own Highlanders in Northern Ireland – 1972

In July 1972, as part of Operation 'Motorman' (the re-establishing of government control over the so called 'no
go' areas of Belfast), the 1st Battalion Queen's Own Highlanders was flown to Northern Ireland at less than a
week's notice, and remained there until November 1972. The battalion was deployed with Tactical Headquarters
and A Company at Dungannon, B Company with the Life Guards in Belfast, D Company with the 1st Gordons in
Armagh and Lurgan, and Support Company with the 1st Welsh Guards in Belfast.

1st Queen's Own Highlanders in Northern Ireland – 1973-1974

In December 1973 the 1st Queen's Own Highlanders moved to Belfast for the battalion's third tour of duty in
Northern Ireland. The battalion's area of responsibility was the Lower Falls, with Battalion Tactical Headquarters
in the Hastings Street Mill, A Company in the Reservation, B and D Companies in the Albert Street Mill, and
Support Company at Broadway. The battalion returned to Osnabrück in April 1974.

1st Queen's Own Highlanders in Germany – 1974-1976

Having returned from Northern Ireland, the 1st Queen's Own Highlanders trooped the Regimental Colour, in
Osnabrück on 21st July 1974 before the Colonel of the Regiment, General Sir Peter Hunt.

In November 1974 the 1st Queen's Own Highlanders battle group carried out mechanised training and field firing
at Suffield in Canada, with two armoured squadrons and a battery of field artillery under command.

In 1975 the battalion won the Army Championship at the Regular Army Skill-at-Arms Meeting at Bisley.

On 26th April 1976 detachments of the 1st Battalion Queen's Own Highlanders and the 2nd Battalion 51st
Highland Volunteers TAVR represented the regiment when it was granted the Freedom of Tain.

1st Battalion Queen's Own Highlanders Troop the Colour in Osnabrück, 1974.

1st Queen's Own Highlanders in Edinburgh – 1976-1980

In June 1976 the 1st Queen's Own Highlanders returned to Great Britain, and the battalion was stationed at Ritchie Camp, Kirknewton, near Edinburgh. The 1st Battalion celebrated its return to Scotland by trooping the Regimental Colour in the Northern Meeting Park at Inverness on 21st July 1976, before Lieutenant General Sir Chandos Blair, Colonel of the Regiment.

During nearly four years based at Kirknewton, the battalion spent six months in Belize, and carried out two tours, each of four months, in Northern Ireland.

1st Battalion Queen's Own Highlanders Troop the Colour at Inverness, in 1976

1st Queen's Own Highlanders in Belize – 1976-1977

In August 1976 the 1st Queen's Own Highlanders flew to the colony of Belize (formerly British Honduras) in Central America. The battalion formed part of the British force based in Belize, to defend the colony against invasion by Guatemala. The battalion was deployed throughout the country, with Battalion Headquarters and one company at Belize Airport, and with company groups in Cayo and Toledo Districts. The battalion was supported by an armoured recce squadron of the Life Guards, a light battery of 3rd Regiment Royal Horse Artillery, and by RAF Puma helicopters and Harriers.

B Company group 1st Battalion Queen's Own Highlanders, commanded by Major J J G Mackenzie, in Belize 1976.

1st Queen's Own Highlanders in Edinburgh – 1977-1978

In February 1977 the 1st Queen's Own Highlanders returned to Edinburgh. The battalion provided the Royal Guard at Ballater during the summer of 1977. On 15th October 1977 the Regiment received the Freedom of the District of Sutherland at Golspie, with a detachment of the 1st Queen's Own Highlanders on parade. During the firemen's strike in November-December 1977, the battalion undertook fire-fighting duties in Edinburgh, and tackled 257 fires.

1st Queen's Own Highlanders in Northern Ireland – 1978

From April to August 1978 the 1st Queen's Own Highlanders carried out a tour of duty in North Armagh. Battalion HQ, Support and HQ Companies were based at Armagh, A Company at Cookstown, B Company at Dungannon, and D Company at Middletown.

1st Queen's Own Highlanders in Edinburgh 1978-1979

The Earl of Seaforth's Highland Regiment was originally passed as fit for service at Elgin on 15th May 1778. On the bicentenary of this date the 1st Battalion Queen's Own Highlanders was on operational duty in Northern Ireland. The Bicentenary celebrations were therefore delayed until after the battalion had returned to Edinburgh. The Bicentenary was celebrated at Elgin where, on 14th October 1978, the Regiment was granted the Freedom of Moray District. On parade at Elgin with the 1st Queen's Own Highlanders were detachments of the 51st Highland Volunteers, the Cameron Highlanders of Ottawa, the Cameron Highlanders of Canada, and the Seaforth Highlanders of Canada.

The 1st Queen's Own Highlanders spent a short period training in Gibraltar in late 1978.

1st Queen's Own Highlanders in Northern Ireland – 1979

From July to October 1979 the 1st Battalion Queen's Own Highlanders carried out its most testing tour of duty in Northern Ireland when it was responsible for the difficult border country

The Colour party with the Regimental Colour of 1st Battalion Queen's Own Highlanders marches through Elgin after the Regiment had received the Freedom of Moray in 1978.

On patrol in South Armagh 1979.

of South Armagh. Battalion HQ and Support Company were based at the Bessbrook linen mill, A Company at Forkhill, B Company at Newtonhamilton, and D Company at Crossmaglen. The battalion had the great misfortune to lose its Commanding Officer, Lieutenant Colonel D N A Blair, and his signaller, killed in an IRA bomb attack at Warren Point, when 16 other British soldiers died. Three other soldiers of the battalion also died during the tour of duty. But despite these losses the battalion achieved outstanding success in its anti-terrorist operations.

The Prime Minister, Mrs Margaret Thatcher, visits D Company 1st Battalion Queen's Own Highlanders at Crossmaglen in 1979. She is met by Major N J Ridley, the company commander.

1st Queen's Own Highlanders in Hong Kong -- 1980-1981

In March 1980 the 1st Queen's Own Highlanders moved to Hong Kong where the battalion was stationed at Stanley Fort. The main operational role was to prevent illegal immigration from China. During its tour in Hong Kong the battalion arrested over 9000 immigrants, by using foot patrols, ambushes, boats, helicopters and ponies. Companies also trained in Brunei and New Zealand.

1st Queen's Own Highlanders at Tidworth – 1981

In December 1981 the 1st Queen's Own Highlanders left Hong Kong and returned to Great Britain. The battalion formed part of 1 Infantry Brigade in the United Kingdom Mobile Force (Land).

A patrol of the 1st Battalion Queen's Own Highlanders using a night viewing device to locate illegal immigrants in Hong Kong 1981.

1st Queen's Own Highlanders in the Falklands – 1982

When Argentina invaded the Falkland Islands in April 1982, the 1st Battalion Queen's Own Highlanders was twice placed on stand-by to take part in the recapture of the Islands. The battalion flew to Ascension Island, and then embarked on the troopship MV Norland. In the event it reached the Falklands shortly after the end of hostilities. The battalion relieved two brigades, and deployed with Battalion Headquarters and Headquarters Company in Port Stanley, A Company at Goose Green, B Company (less a platoon in South Georgia) at North Arm and then Roy Cove, D Company at Fox Bay, Support Company at Port Stanley then North Arm.

The battalion had the role of clearing up Port Stanley and the settlements where fighting had taken place, and of restoring normal life to the civil community. It returned Tidworth in December 1982. In recognition of the battalion's outstanding service to the civil community in the Falklands, it was awarded the Wilkinson Sword of Peace.

1st Battalion Queen's Own Highlanders dismantle Argentinian bunkers in Port Stanley, the Falkland Islands, 1982.

HRH Prince Philip, Duke of Edinburgh, Colonel-in-Chief, inspects the 1st Battalion Queen's Own Highlanders
before presenting new Colours at Tidworth, 1983

1st Queen's Own Highlanders at Tidworth – 1982-1983

On 23rd July 1983 the 1st Battalion Queen's Own Highlanders was presented with its Second Stand of Colours at Tidworth by HRH Prince Philip, Duke of Edinburgh, Colonel-in-Chief of the regiment. The Wilkinson Sword of Peace was also presented at the start of the parade.

On 6th August 1983 a guard of the 1st Battalion represented the regiment when it received the Freedom of Nairn.

1st Queen's Own Highlanders in Northern Ireland – 1983-1985

In November 1983 the 1st Queen's Own Highlanders moved to Northern Ireland for a residential tour. The battalion was based at Alexander Barracks, Aldergrove, beside Belfast airport. The battalion's main operational task was to maintain one company detached as a reinforcement to 4th Battalion Ulster Defence Regiment in County Fermanagh, on a roulement system. During the battalion's tour its companies also operated throughout the province.

1st Queen's Own Highlanders at Fort George – 1985-1988

In November 1985 the 1st Battalion returned to the regimental area when it moved to Fort George. During 1983-1985 the Fort had been extensively modernised, and the 1st Queen's Own Highlanders was to be the first battalion to enjoy the new facilities. On 5th July 1986 a guard of the 1st Battalion paraded at Wick when the Regiment received the Freedom of Caithness District. The battalion later carried out a month's field training in Kenya.

1st Battalion Queen's Own Highlanders at Fort George, 1986

1st Queen's Own Highlanders in Belize – 1987

In April 1987 the 1st Queen's Own Highlanders returned to Belize for a six month tour. The battalion was permanently deployed as two battle groups, each of two companies with armoured recce and artillery support. Battle Group North occupied Airport Camp and Holdfast Camp in Cayo District, while Battle Group South occupied Rideau and Salamanca Camps in Toledo District. The battalion moved back to Fort George in October 1987.

1st Queen's Own Highlanders in Germany – 1988-1993

In March 1988 the 1st Queen's Own Highlanders moved from Fort George to Münster in Germany. The battalion at first formed part of 6 Armoured Brigade in the 3rd Armoured Division, and was then regrouped in January 1989 to 33 Armoured Brigade. It was equipped with AFV 432 Armoured Personnel Carriers. In 1989 the battalion carried out battle group training at Suffield, in Canada.

During the five year period in Münster the 1st Queen's Own Highlanders completed two tours of duty in Northern Ireland in 1990 and 1992-1993, and took part in the Gulf War in 1991.

1st Battalion Queen's Own Highlanders in Germany, 1989

In August 1990, on return from the tour in Belfast, the 1st Queen's Own Highlanders provided the guard when the Regiment received the Freedom of the Orkney Islands, at Kirkwall on 22nd August, and the Freedom of Badenoch and Strathspey District at Grantown on Spey, on 24th August.

The 1st Battalion celebrated the 30th anniversary of the formation of the Regiment by trooping the Regimental Colour in Münster before the Colonel of the Regiment, Major General John Hopkinson The battalion then received a visit to from HRH Prince Philip, Duke of Edinburgh, Colonel-in-Chief of the Regiment.

1st Queen's Own Highlanders in Northern Ireland – 1990

The 1st Queen's Own Highlanders carried out its 7th tour of duty in Northern Ireland from February to July 1990. It was grouped under 39 Infantry Brigade as the Belfast Roulement Battalion, with responsibility for north and west Belfast. Battalion Headquarters and A Company were based at North Howard Street Mill, B Company at Girdwood Park, D Company at Fort Whiterock.

1st Queen's Own Highlanders in the Gulf War – 1991

The 1st Battalion Queen's Own Highlanders took part in Operation 'Granby', the military action to recover Kuwait from the occupying forces of Iraq. The battalion deployed piecemeal, Battalion Headquarters providing command for the Armoured Delivery Group, the reinforcements of vehicles and crews, including three armoured squadrons and three armoured infantry companies, which were ready to replace casualties if they occurred. A (Atbara) Company Group provided the guard force for HQ 1 Armoured Division in the field, and B (Alamein) Company Group the guard for Headquarters British Forces Middle East in Riyadh. The battalion also provided reinforcements for units of the 7th and 4th Armoured Brigades, including 1st Battalion Royal Scots and 3rd Battalion Royal Regiment of Fusiliers. The Regimental Band deployed as medical orderlies in October 1990 under command of 1st Armoured Division Field Ambulance.

The ground campaign began on G Day, 24th February 1991, and lasted for 100 hours. The 1st Armoured Division entered Iraq through the breach in the frontier obstacles cleared by US engineers. When the cease fire was declared at 0800 hours on 28th February, the battalion regrouped about 20 miles north-west of Kuwait City. The battalion suffered the sad loss of three soldiers serving as reinforcements with 3rd Battalion Royal Regiment of Fusiliers, who were killed when their Warrior APC was hit by a missile fired from a US aircraft. The battalion returned to Münster in late March 1991.

Operations in aid of the civil power, Belfast 1990.

A Milan anti-tank guided missile team in the Gulf 1991.

1ST QUEEN'S OWN HIGHLANDERS BATTLE HONOUR
For its part in the Gulf War the 1st Battalion Queen's Own Highlanders was awarded the Battle Honour:

GULF 1991

1st Battalion Queen's Own Highlanders marks the cease fire in the Gulf, 1991

1st Queen's Own Highlanders in Northern Ireland – 1992-1993

The 1st Queen's Own Highlanders carried out its 8th and final tour of duty in Northern Ireland from November 1992-May 1993. It formed part of 39 Infantry Brigade, and was responsible for West Belfast. Battalion Headquarters and A Company were based in North Howard Street Mill, B Company at New Barnsley RUC Station, and D Company at Fort Whiterock.

1st Battalion Queen's Own Highlanders final tour of duty in Belfast 1993

The Bicentenaries of the 78th and 79th Highlanders

Guard of the 1st Battalion Queen's Own Highlanders marches through Dingwall
in the Bicentenary year of the raising of the 78th Highlanders (Ross-shire Buffs)

A guard of the 1st Queen's Own Highlanders represented the Regiment at the Bicentenary celebrations of the 78th Highlanders (Ross-shire Buffs) and the 79th Cameron Highlanders which took place in the regimental area in September 1993. The guard from the battalion was on parade when the Regiment was granted the Freedom of Lochaber District at Fort William on 3rd September 1993.

The Pipes and Drums of 1st Battalion Queen's Own Highlanders at Erracht
in the Bicentenary year of the raising of the 79th Cameron Highlanders.

1st Battalion Queen's Own Highlanders marches past the Colonel-in-Chief at the Farewell Review, 1994

1st Queen's Own Highlanders in Edinburgh – 1993-1994

The 1st Queen's Own Highlanders left Münster in November 1993, and moved to Dreghorn Barracks Edinburgh. There in July 1994 the farewell events of the Queen's Own Highlanders were held, preceded on 22nd July by a service of thanksgiving in St Giles Cathedral. On 23rd July HRH Prince Philip, Duke of Edinburgh, reviewed the Regiment at Dreghorn Barracks as Colonel-in-Chief. On parade for the Review were the 1st Battalion Queen's Own Highlanders, detachments of 2nd Battalion 51st Highland Volunteers TA, V Company The Liverpool Scottish TA, the Queen's Own Highlanders Cadets, the Regimental Associations and their Pipe Band. In the afternoon a Farewell Gathering was held on the playing field at Dreghorn Barracks.

The final ceremonial event of the Queen's Own Highlanders was the granting of the Freedom of the Western Isles to the Regiment on 2nd September 1994. The 1st Battalion provided a guard for the ceremony which took place at Stornoway.

Amalgamation – 17th September 1994

On 17th September 1994, at Dreghorn Barracks, Edinburgh, the Queen's Own Highlanders (Seaforth and Camerons) were amalgamated with The Gordon Highlanders to form:

THE HIGHLANDERS
(SEAFORTH, GORDONS and CAMERONS)

*The massed Pipes and Drums of the Regiment and the Regimental Associations beat Retreat for the last time
at the Farewell Gathering 1994.*

1st BATTALION THE HIGHLANDERS
(SEAFORTH, GORDONS AND CAMERONS)

The pre-amalgamation ceremony – 1994

On 14th September 1994 the two regular battalions carried out a pre-amalgamation goodwill ceremony at the bridge over the River Spey at Craigellachie, the boundary between the two regimental districts.

1st Battalion The Highlanders, the formation parade at Edinburgh on 17th September 1994

1st Battalion The Highlanders formed in Edinburgh – 1994

The amalgamation of the Queen's Own Highlanders (Seaforth and Camerons) and The Gordon Highlanders took place on 17th September 1994 at Dreghorn Barracks, Edinburgh.

The officers and men of the 1st Gordons moved from nearby Redford Barracks shortly before the amalgamation, and the companies of the new battalion were formed. The first Colonel of the Highlanders, General Sir Jeremy Mackenzie, reviewed the formation parade. Then, at a Drumhead service, the Colours were regrouped, with the two Queen's Colours and the two Regimental Colours in pairs. Finally the new battalion marched past the Colonel of the Regiment and off parade.

1st Highlanders in Northern Ireland – 1994-1997

Immediately after amalgamation the 1st Highlanders started training for the battalion's first operational service in Northern Ireland. From December 1994 the 1st Highlanders became the Province Reserve Battalion, and then in April 1995 the battalion moved to Ebrington Barracks, Londonderry for a two year residential tour.

1st Highlanders in Catterick – 1997

In April 1997 the 1st Highlanders moved to Catterick Garrison, where it formed part of 19 Mechanised Brigade.

2. DEPOTS AND REGIMENTAL HEADQUARTERS

DEPOTS

Fort George in the late 1940s

Primary Training Centres and Depots – 1946-1948

In 1946 each infantry regiment was allowed to establish its own Primary Training Centre (PTC) and Depot, at which all Regular and National Service recruits were trained for six weeks. Recruits for Highland regiments were then sent to the Highland Infantry Training Centre (HITC) at Redford Barracks, Edinburgh for further training and drafting.

72 PTC and Depot Seaforth Highlanders was established at Fort George, and 79 PTC and Depot The Queen's own Cameron Highlanders at Cameron Barracks, Inverness.

The Regimental Depots – 1948-1951

In April 1948 the PTCs were disbanded. The Depot Seaforth at Fort George, and the Depot Camerons at Cameron Barracks continued as holding units for officers and soldiers awaiting posting or release from the army. The Depots also had roles as regimental headquarters, and to assist training of the Territorial Army and Army Cadet Force.

The training establishments at Fort George – 1948-1957

On the disbandment of the PTCs in 1948, the Highland Infantry Training Centre moved from Edinburgh to Fort George where it became the Highland Group Training Centre (HGTC) , and trained recruits for all regiments of the Highland Brigade.

From 1948 this training became the responsibility of an infantry battalion. The intention was that each Highland battalion should undertake this in turn, but because of the shortage of battalions to meet cold war commitments, the only battalion to fill this role was the lst Battalion Highland Light Infantry, from 1948 to 1950.

In 1950 this arrangement was superseded when the Highland Brigade Training Centre (HBTC) was set up to train all recruits for the Highland regiments. In 1951 regimental depots again took over the six weeks primary training for recruits,and the HBTC became the Highland Brigade Depot (HBD), combined with the Depot Seaforth under one commanding officer, with the role of carrying out four weeks of continuation training for recruits. From 1952 the regimental depots once more became responsible for all recruit training, and the role of the HBD was limited to specialist and leadership training, until it was disbanded in 1957.

The Regimental Depots – 1951-1960

In 1951 the establishments of the regimental depots were increased, so that each regiment became responsible for training its own Regular and National Service recruits. Seaforth recruits trained at Fort George, and Cameron recruits at Cameron Barracks. After six weeks training at the regimental depots, recruits moved to Fort George for four weeks continuation training at the Highland Brigade Depot. From 1952 the regimental depots carried out all their own recruit training.

As part of reductions in the size of the infantry, the regimental depots were closed in 1960-1961.

The Highland Brigade Depots – 1960-1968

On the closure of the regimental depots, brigade depots were set up once again to carry out training of recruits and junior soldiers and musicians. The site chosen for the Highland Brigade Depot was Bridge of Don Barracks, Aberdeen. As the barracks had to be extended and modernised to provide adequate accommodation, a temporary arrangement was made in late 1960 in which two combined Highland regimental depots were set up. At Fort George was The Depot Seaforth, Gordons, and Camerons, (redesignated The Depot Queen's Own Highlanders and Gordons on the amalgamation of Seaforth and Camerons in February 1961); and at Stirling Castle was The Depot Black Watch and Argyll and Sutherland Highlanders. These two depots were combined to form The Highland Brigade Depot at Fort George in January 1964, and then moved to the completed Bridge of Don Barracks in May 1964.

Scottish Infantry Depots – 1968-1993

On 1st July 1968, the regiments of the Highland and Lowland Brigades were combined to form the Scottish Division. The Highland Brigade Depot at Aberdeen became the Scottish Infantry Depot (Bridge of Don) for training junior soldiers, and the Lowland Brigade Depot at Penicuik became the Scottish Infantry Depot (Glencorse) for training adult recruits.

In a further reduction in training establishments in 1986, the two depots combined to form the Scottish Division Depot (Glencorse). In the reorganisation of army training under 'Options for Change' this was superseded by the Army Training Regiment (Glencorse) which carried out training of recruits for the Scottish and King's Divisions.

REGIMENTAL HEADQUARTERS

The Depots as Regimental Headquarters – 1881-1960

From their establishment in 1881, the infantry regimental depots had the role of acting as regimental headquarters (RHQ) to their regiments. Regimental business included acting as staff for the Colonel of the Regiment, recruiting of officers and soldiers, public relations, running the regimental associations and benevolent funds, producing the regimental journal, maintaining historical records, and looking after the funds and the collections of regimental property and historic items. From 1881 to 1961 RHQ of the Seaforth Highlanders was incorporated in the Depot Seaforth at Fort George, and RHQ of the Cameron Highlanders in the Depot Camerons at Cameron Barracks.

Regimental Headquarters Queen's Own Highlanders – 1960-1994

When the infantry regimental depots were superseded in 1960, and recruit training became the responsibility of the Highland Brigade Depot, each regiment was allowed to set up its own RHQ, with a small establishment of retired officers and civilian clerical staff, to carry on the regimental business formerly undertaken by the depots.

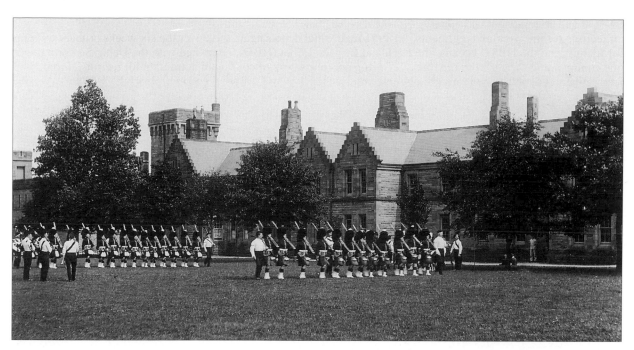

The Regimental Headquarters at Cameron Barracks, Inverness before World War I.

Regimental Headquarters Queen's Own Highlanders was formed in 1960, shortly before the amalgamation of the Seaforth and Camerons. It was set up at Cameron Barracks in the former Depot Headquarters building.

On the amalgamation of Seaforth and Camerons in 1961, the two regiments decided to form the Queen's Own Highlanders Regimental Trust, run by RHQ, and controlling all regimental funds and property under one set of trustees.

RHQ also provided office facilities and clerical support for the regimental associations. The benevolent funds, and the activities of the regimental associations, remained under the management and control of the Seaforth, Cameron, and Queen's Own Highlanders Regimental Associations.

Regimental Headquarters The Highlanders – 1994

On the formation of The Highlanders in 1994, RHQ Queen's Own Highlanders became RHQ of the new regiment, at Cameron Barracks, Inverness. An out-station was also maintained at the former RHQ Gordons at Aberdeen.

The Regimental Museums

On its formation in 1961 the trustees of the Queen's Own Highlanders Regimental Trust became the owners of the regimental museum collections of the Seaforth and the Cameron Highlanders. These collections originated in the medals, pictures and trophies acquired by officers of the regular battalions during the 19th century , and used to furnish and decorate their mess rooms. As the collections grew, they became too large to take overseas, and so an increasing proportion had to be left for safe keeping at the regimental depots. In 1936 the Depot Camerons set up their collection as a Regimental Museum at Cameron Barracks. The Depot Seaforth set up its Regimental Museum at Fort George shortly after World War II.

In 1964, when the Highland Brigade Depot vacated Fort George and moved to Aberdeen, the Queen's Own Highlanders were allowed the use of the empty building formerly used as the Depot Seaforth officers mess, to set up the Seaforth and Cameron museum collections as a combined Regimental Museum of the Queen's Own Highlanders at Fort George. It was officially opened to the public in 1966, and the displays completed the following year.

The museum building was fully modernised as part of the programme of work to refurbish Fort George during 1983-1985. The Regimental Museum today is a fully registered museum with the Museums and Galleries Commission, and is among the most popular regimental museums in Great Britain.

*The Pipes and Drums of 1st Battalion Queen's Own Highlanders beat Retreat
at a Regimental Association gathering at the Regimental Museum at Fort George.*

3. THE TERRITORIAL ARMY

SEAFORTH HIGHLANDERS

11th BATTALION SEAFORTH HIGHLANDERS TA – 1947-1967

When the Territorial Army was re-formed in 1947, the 11th Battalion Seaforth Highlanders was raised. The battalion was recruited from the area covered by the three original Seaforth Territorial battalions, the 4th (Ross-shire), 5th (Sutherland and Caithness), and 6th (Morayshire). The 11th Seaforth formed part of 152 (Highland) Infantry Brigade in the 51st (Highland) Division.

The organisation of the 11th Seaforth was:

Battalion Headquarters	Dingwall
A Company	Ross and Cromarty
B Company	Morayshire
C Company	Caithness
D Company	Sutherland
S Company	Morayshire

In the reorganisation of the Territorial Army in 1961, the troop of Lovat Scouts recruited from Alness and Tain was transferred to the 11th Seaforth.

In 1953 a detachment of the 11th Seaforth took part in the Coronation procession of HM Queen Elizabeth. On 14th July 1966 the 11th Seaforth received its First Stand of Colours at Fort George from the Colonel of the Regiment, General Sir James Cassels.

On the amalgamation of the Seaforth Highlanders and The Queen's Own Cameron Highlanders in 1961 the 11th Seaforth remained as one of the three TA battalions in the new regiment. The 11th Seaforth retained its designation, and continued to wear the uniform of the Seaforth Highlanders.

On 31st March 1967 the battalion was disbanded as part of the reduction and reorganisation of the Territorial Army. Under the new organisation it formed:

     B (Seaforth) Company, 51st Highland Volunteers (T&AVR II)
     B (Seaforth) Company, 3rd Queen's Own Highlanders (T&AVR III)
     C (Seaforth) Company, 3rd Queen's Own Highlanders (T&AVR III).

General Sir James Cassels, Chief of the Imperial General Staff, presents Colours to 11th Battalion Seaforth Highlanders at Fort George in 1966.

THE QUEEN'S OWN CAMERON HIGHLANDERS

4th/5th BATTALION THE QUEEN'S OWN CAMERON HIGHLANDERS TA – 1947-1967

The Pipes and Drums of the
4th/5th Battalion The Queen's Own Cameron Highlanders in 1955.

When the Territorial Army was re-formed in 1947, the 4th/5th Battalion The Queen's Own Cameron Highlanders was raised, the designation commemorating the two Cameron Territorial battalions which had fought in World War II. The 4th/5th Camerons formed part of 152 (Highland) Infantry Brigade in the 51st (Highland) Division.

The organisation of the 4th/5th Camerons was:

Battalion Headquarters	Inverness
A Company	Badenoch
B Company	Lochaber and Skye [Skye was later transferred to C (Islands) Company]
C Company	Uist and Skye
D Company	Nairn
Support Company	Inverness
Headquarters Company	Inverness

In the reorganisation of the Territorial Army in 1961, the Lovat Scouts recruited from Newtonmore and Kingussie were transferred to the 4th/5th Camerons.

In 1953 a detachment of the 4th/5th Camerons took part in the Coronation procession of HM Queen Elizabeth.

On the amalgamation of The Queen's Own Cameron Highlanders and the Seaforth Highlanders in 1961, the 4th/5th Camerons remained as one of the three TA battalions in the new regiment. The 4th/5th Camerons retained its designation, and continued to wear the uniform of The Queen's Own Cameron Highlanders.

On 31st March 1967 the 4th/5th Camerons was disbanded as part of the reduction and reorganisation of the Territorial Army. Under the new organisation it formed:

> C (Cameron) Company, 51st Highland Volunteers (T&AVR II)
> D (Cameron) Company, 3rd Queen's Own Highlanders (T&AVR III)

THE LIVERPOOL SCOTTISH, THE QUEEN'S OWN CAMERON HIGHLANDERS

1st BATTALION THE LIVERPOOL SCOTTISH TA – 1947-1967

When the Territorial Army was re-formed in 1947, the 1st Battalion Liverpool Scottish was raised again. The Headquarters of the battalion was the Fraser Street Drill Hall in Liverpool. The battalion became a motor battalion in 23rd Armoured Brigade, but in 1956 it reverted to an infantry role and became part of 125 Brigade in the 42nd (South Lancashire) Division.

In 1953 a detachment of the 1st Liverpool Scottish took part in the Coronation procession of HM Queen Elizabeth. The battalion won the Territorial Army Shield in the Duke of Edinburgh's Trophy Competition in 1957 and 1960.

On the amalgamation of The Queen's Own Cameron Highlanders and the Seaforth Highlanders in 1961, the 1st Liverpool Scottish remained as one of the three TA battalions in the new regiment. The 1st Liverpool Scottish retained its designation and continued to wear the uniform of the Liverpool Scottish.

Pipers and drummers of V Company,
The Liverpool Scottish.

On 31st March 1967 the 1st Liverpool Scottish was disbanded as part of the reduction and reorganisation of the Territorial Army. At the same time the Fraser Street Drill Hall was closed, and Headquarters of the Liverpool Scottish moved to Forbes House, a new drill hall at Score Lane, Liverpool.

Under the new organisation the Liverpool Scottish formed:

> V (Liverpool Scottish) Company, 51st Highland Volunteers (T&AVR II)
> R (King's/Liverpool Scottish) Battery, West Lancashire Regiment RA, TA.

THE LOVAT SCOUTS

C (LOVAT SCOUTS) SQUADRON SCOTTISH HORSE, RAC, TA – 1947-1949

When the Territorial Army was re-formed in 1947, one squadron of Lovat Scouts was raised. Its headquarters were at Cameron Barracks, Inverness, and it was designated as C Squadron of the Scottish Horse, a tank regiment in the Royal Armoured Corps. The Lovat Scouts wore the blue diced bonnet previously worn by the regiment.

677 MOUNTAIN REGIMENT (LOVAT SCOUTS) RA,TA – 1949-1950

In 1949 the Lovat Scouts changed role to become mountain artillery, and were redesignated as 677 Mountain Regiment (Lovat Scouts) RA, TA. The regiment comprised one battery recruited from Uist and mounted on pack ponies, and one battery equipped with jeeps from Inverness-shire, Ross-shire, and Sutherland.

540 LIGHT ANTI-AIRCRAFT REGIMENT (LOVAT SCOUTS) RA, TA – 1950

In 1950 the regiment changed to a light anti-aircraft role, and regiment was redesignated as 540 Light Anti-Aircraft Regiment (Lovat Scouts) RA, TA with its headquarters at Inverness. The regiment comprised three light anti-aircraft batteries armed with Bofors guns in Inverness, Stornoway, and Elgin; and 850 Mountain Battery armed with 4.2 inch mortars, recruited from Inverness-shire, the Western Isles, and Ross-shire.

532 LIGHT ANTI AIRCRAFT REGIMENT (LOVAT SCOUTS) RA, TA – 1950-1954

In May 1950 540 LAA Regiment was amalgamated with parts of 532 LAA Regiment to form 532 Light Anti-Aircraft Regiment (Lovat Scouts) RA, TA. The regiment retained its headquarters at Inverness, and was made up of light anti-aircraft batteries in Inverness, Elgin, and Falkirk; and 850 Mountain Battery as before. In 1953 the mountain battery was disbanded, leaving the regiment with its light anti-aircraft role.

The Mountain Battery of the Lovat Scouts training in 1952.

540 LIGHT ANTI-AIRCRAFT REGIMENT (LOVAT SCOUTS) RA, TA – 1954-1967

In 1954 the former territorial area of the regiment was restored. On the disbandment of coastal artillery regiments in 1956, the regiment absorbed 412 Coast Artillery Regiment TA. The organisation of the regiment was:

Regimental Headquarters	Inverness
Inverness Battery	Inverness, Newtonmore, Kingussie, Wick, Thurso
Ross Battery	Stornoway, Tain, Alness
Moray Battery	Elgin, Forres, Nairn

The 1961 reorganisation of the Territorial Army brought extensive changes to the regiment. The troop at Alness and Tain was transferred to the 11th Seaforth, and the troop at Newtonmore and Kingussie to the 4th/5th Camerons. To replace them 861 (Independent) LAA Battery (Orkney and Zetland) RA, TA was transferred to the regiment, and the new organisation became:

Regimental Headquarters	Inverness
Ross Battery	Stornoway, Wick, Thurso
Moray Battery	Elgin, Lossiemouth
Orkney and Zetland Battery	Kirkwall, Lerwick

On 31st March 1967 the regiment was disbanded as part of the reduction and reorganisation of the Territorial Army. Under the new organisation it formed:

A (Lovat Scouts) Company 3rd Queen's Own Highlanders (T&AVR III)
Orkney and Zetland Battery (Lovat Scouts) RA, (T&AVR III)

ORKNEY AND ZETLAND BATTERY (LOVAT SCOUTS) (T&AVR III) – 1967-1969

On 1st April 1967, as part of the reorganisation of the Territorial Army, the Orkney and Zetland Battery (Lovat Scouts) remained as part of the Territorial and Army Volunteer Reserve III. Under a further reduction of the Territorial Army in 1969, the battery became No 1 (Lovat Scouts) Company of the 51st Highland Volunteers, and was converted to infantry. The company retained the distinctive blue bonnet of the Lovat Scouts.

QUEEN'S OWN HIGHLANDERS

3rd BATTALION QUEEN'S OWN HIGHLANDERS (T&AVR III) – 1967-1969

On 1st April 1967, as part of the reorganisation of the Territorial Army, the 3rd Battalion Queen's Own Highlanders was formed. The battalion had a Home Defence role as part of the Territorial and Army Volunteer Reserve III.

The organisation of the 3rd Queen's Own Highlanders was:

Battalion Headquarters	Inverness
A (Lovat Scouts) Company	Inverness
B (Seaforth) Company	Ross and Cromarty
C (Seaforth) Company	Morayshire
D (Cameron) Company	Fort William, Skye, Uist

Each company continued to wear the uniform of its antecedent TA battalion.

Under a further reorganisation of the Territorial Army the 3rd Queen's Own Highlanders was reduced to cadre strength in December 1968, and the battalion was finally disbanded on 31st March 1969.

51st HIGHLAND VOLUNTEERS

51st HIGHLAND VOLUNTEERS (T&AVR II) – 1967-1971

On 1st April 1967 the 51st Highland Volunteers were formed. They were at first organised as a single composite battalion, with companies from the Highland battalions disbanded in 1967. The role of the 51st Highland Volunteers was to provide a reserve for the Regular Army in NATO, as part of the Territorial and Army Volunteer Reserve II.

The original organisation of the 51st Highland Volunteers was:

Battalion Headquarters	Perth
A (Black Watch) Company	Perth, Dundee
B (Seaforth) Company	Wick, Brora
C (Cameron) Company	Inverness
D (Gordon) Company	Aberdeen, Keith
E (Argyll & Sutherland) Company	Stirling
London Scottish Company	London
V (Liverpool Scottish) Company	Liverpool

Each company continued to wear the uniform of its antecedent TA battalion, and all members of the 51st Highland Volunteers wore the Highland Brigade bonnet badge.

On the reduction of the T&AVR III at the end of 1968, C Company 51st Highland Volunteers was expanded to include Elgin and Dingwall, and two new companies were formed from the 3rd Queen's Own Highlanders and O and Z Battery Lovat Scouts The new companies were:

No 1 (Lovat Scouts) Company	Kirkwall, Lerwick
No 2 (Queen's Own Highlanders) Company	Stornoway, Fort William

On 1st April 1971 the Territorial and Army Volunteer Reserve was expanded, and the 51st Highland Volunteers divided into two battalions, with their headquarters at Perth and Elgin. Each battalion included companies tasked with Home Defence and companies committed to NATO.

1st BATTALION 51st HIGHLAND VOLUNTEERS
T&AVR – 1971`-1985   TA – 1985-1992

V (Liverpool Scottish) Company give three cheers for H M Queen Elizabeth, The Queen Mother,
after the presentation of Colours to 1st Battalion 51st Highland Volunteers at Perth in 1986.

The 1st Battalion 51st Highland Volunteers was made up from the companies drawn from the south of Highland District and from England. The original organisation of the battalion was:

       Battalion Headquarters (Perth)
       A (Black Watch) Company
       B (Argyll and Sutherland) Company
       London Scottish Company
       V (Liverpool Scottish) Company
       HQ Company

V (Liverpool Scottish) Company remained in the 1st 51st Highland Volunteers throughout the battalion's existence. The battalion received Colours from HM Queen Elizabeth the Queen Mother at Perth on 4th July 1986.

In 1992, as part of the reorganisation of the Territorial Army, the 1st Battalion 51st Highland Volunteers was redesignated the 3rd (Volunteer) Battalion the Black Watch. Under this reorganisation V (Liverpool Scottish) Company was transferred in September 1992 to a new composite battalion, 5th/8th Battalion The King's Regiment, and the London Scottish Company to The London Regiment.

2nd BATTALION 51st HIGHLAND VOLUNTEERS
T&AVR – 1971-1985   TA – 1985-1994

HRH Prince Philip, Duke of Edinburgh, presents Colours to 2nd Battalion 51st Highland Volunteers at Elgin in 1986.

On its formation on 1st April 1971 the 2nd Battalion 51st Highland Volunteers was made up of the companies drawn from the north of Highland District. The original organisation was:

Battalion Headquarters	Elgin
A (Lovat Scouts) Company	Kirkwall, Lerwick
B (Queen's Own Highlanders) Company	Wick, Brora, Thurso
C (Queen's Own Highlanders) Company	Inverness, Dingwall, Fort William
D (Gordons) Company	Aberdeen, Laurencekirk
E (Queen's Own Highlanders) Company	Stornoway, Portree
G (Gordons) Company	Aberdeen, Peterhead
HQ Company	Elgin

The 2nd 51st Highland Volunteers wore the Highland Brigade bonnet badge throughout its existence, while companies wore the uniform of their parent regiments. In 1972 the Lovat Scouts in the battalion adopted a parade uniform of the kilt of Hunting Fraser tartan, a dress hitherto worn only by the pipers and drummers of the Lovat Scouts.

On the formation of the 3rd Battalion 51st Highland Volunteers in 1975, B and G Companies were transferred to the new 3rd Battalion. E Company merged into C (Queen's Own Highlanders) Company, and the Portree detachment was disbanded.

In 1981 the organisation of the three battalions of the 51st Highland Volunteers was rationalised to improve command and communications. The new organisation of the 2nd Battalion was:

Battalion Headquarters	Elgin
A (Queen's Own Highlanders and Lovat Scouts) Company	Wick, Thurso, Brora, Kirkwall
B (Gordons) Company	Peterhead, Keith
C (Queen's Own Highlanders) Company	Inverness, Stornoway, Fort William, Dingwall
D (Gordons and Lovat Scouts) Company	Aberdeen, Laurencekirk, Lerwick
HQ Company	Elgin

Further detachments were opened at Nairn, Turriff, and Inverurie.

In 1985 the Territorial and Army Volunteer Reserve was reorganised, given a more active operational role, and reverted to the old name of the Territorial Army. To cover the defence of United Kingdom each battalion raised Home Service Force (HSF) companies. Two companies were added to 2nd 51st Highland Volunteers.

Y (HSF) Company	Elgin, Inverness, Stornoway, Wick, Kirkwall, Fort William
X (HSF) Company	Aberdeen, Laurencekirk, Peterhead, Lerwick

On 26th June 1986 the 2nd Battalion 51st Highland Volunteers received Colours from HRH Prince Philip, Duke of Edinburgh, at the Cooper Park, Elgin.

In 1992, as part of reductions to the Territorial Army, the HSF companies were disbanded. On the amalgamation of the Queen's Own Highlanders with the Gordon Highlanders in 1994, the 2nd Battalion Highland Volunteers was redesignated as 3rd (Volunteer) Battalion The Highlanders (Seaforth, Gordons and Camerons).

3rd BATTALION 51st HIGHLAND VOLUNTEERS
T&AVR – 1975-1985   TA – 1985-1992

On 1st April 1975 the 3rd Battalion 51st Highland Volunteers was formed. Originally limited to a Home Defence role, its companies were recruited from areas around sites of strategic importance. The 3rd Battalion was formed by transferring existing companies from the 1st and 2nd Battalions 51st Highland Volunteers. The organisation of the battalion was:

Battalion Headquarters	Peterhead
B (Queen's Own Highlanders) Company	Wick
C (Argyll and Sutherland) Company	Grangemouth
D (Argyll and Sutherland) Company	Dumbarton
HQ (Gordons) Company	Peterhead

In 1980 the structure of the battalion was changed, and Battalion Headquarters moved to Stirling. B(Queen's Own Highlanders) Company and HQ (Gordons) Company reverted to the 2nd Battalion 51st Highland Volunteers.

Under the reorganisation of the Territorial Army in 1992 the 3rd Battalion 51st Highland Volunteers was redesignated as 3rd (Volunteer).Battalion The Argyll and Sutherland Highlanders

THE HIGHLANDERS
(SEAFORTH, GORDONS AND CAMERONS)

3rd (VOLUNTEER) BATTALION THE HIGHLANDERS – 1994

In September 1994, on the amalgamation of the Queen's Own Highlanders and the Gordon Highlanders to form The Highlanders, the 2nd Battalion 51st Highland Volunteers was redesignated as 3rd (Volunteer) Battalion The Highlanders (Seaforth, Gordons and Camerons). The battalion wore the same uniform as the regular battalion of the regiment.

The organisation of the battalion was:

Battalion Headquarters	Elgin
Support Group	Wick, Thurso, Kirkwall
B Company	Peterhead, Keith
C Company	Inverness, Dingwall, Fort William, Stornoway
D Company	Aberdeen, Laurencekirk, Lerwick

V (LIVERPOOL SCOTTISH) COMPANY
5th/8th (VOLUNTEER) BATTALION THE KING'S REGIMENT – 1992

Under the reduction and reorganisation of the TA in 1992, V (Liverpool Scottish) Company was transferred from 1st Battalion 51st Highland Volunteers to 5th/8th Battalion The King's Regiment. The company continued to wear the uniform of the Liverpool Scottish, but reverted to the 1908 pattern of bonnet badge instead of the Highland Brigade badge worn since 1967 by the 51st Highland Volunteers.

The Headquarters of The Liverpool Scottish remained at Forbes House, Score Lane, Liverpool. The command arrangement did not affect the affiliation between The Liverpool Scottish and the Queen's Own Highlanders, originating in the 1920 affiliation with the Cameron Highlanders. In 1994, on the amalgamation between the Queen's Own Highlanders and the Gordon Highlanders, The Liverpool Scottish affiliation passed to The Highlanders.

4. THE REGIMENTAL CADETS

ARMY CADET FORCE

THE QUEEN'S OWN HIGHLANDERS CADETS

Although the Army Cadet Force dates back to 1860, there were no cadets in the regimental area until 1942, when the War Office expanded the Army Cadet Force. Cadet battalions badged as Seaforth Highlanders were raised from Ross-shire, Sutherland, and Moray; and a Cadet battalion badged as Cameron Highlanders from Inverness-shire and Nairnshire.

On the amalgamation of the Seaforth and Camerons in 1961, all cadet battalions in the Queen's Own Highlanders regimental area were combined to form the Northern Counties Army Cadet Force. Each battalion retained the uniform of its original TA battalion. In 1967 the cadets were reorganised to form the North Highland Cadets, a single battalion with six county companies. The companies were recruited from:

        1 (Caithness) Company
        2 (Inverness and Nairn) Company
        3 (Western Isles) Company
        4 (Moray) Company
        5 (Ross) Company
        6 (Sutherland) Company

In 1975 the battalion was redesignated the 1st Cadet Battalion, Queen's Own Highlanders (Seaforth and Camerons) ACF, and all companies adopted the uniform of the Queen's Own Highlanders. In 1982 the designation was shortened to the Queen's Own Highlanders Battalion ACF.

On the amalgamation in 1994 of the Queen's Own Highlanders with The Gordon Highlanders, it was decided that no immediate change of uniform or designation would be made to the two cadet battalions of The Highlanders.

THE LIVERPOOL SCOTTISH CADETS

The Liverpool Scottish Cadets were formed between the wars. The two companies have always had a close association with the parent battalion, and latterly with V (Liverpool Scottish) Company.

Cadets of the Western Isles Company,
Queen's Own Highlanders Cadet Battalion at camp in 1991.

COMBINED CADET FORCES

GORDONSTOUN SCHOOL CCF

Originally a company of the 1st Moray Cadet Battalion (Seaforth Highlanders), the Gordonstoun School Cadet Force became an independent CCF in 1961. The cadets in its Army Section wore the uniform of the Seaforth Highlanders. From 1961, until the CCF was discontinued in 1975, the Gordonstoun School CCF was affiliated to the Queen's Own Highlanders.

FORT AUGUSTUS ABBEY SCHOOL CCF

The Fort Augustus Abbey School CCF was started in 1963 and was affiliated to the Queen's Own Highlanders. The cadets in its Army Section wore the uniform of The Queen's Own Cameron Highlanders. The CCF was disbanded when the school closed in 1993.

THE EDINBURGH ACADEMY CCF

The Edinburgh Academy CCF was started as an Officer Training Corps in 1908. When selecting a uniform for the OTC Mr R J MacKenzie, the Rector of the school at the time, requested permission of the Commanding Officer of the 2nd Battalion Seaforth Highlanders, stationed at the time in Edinburgh Castle, for the OTC to wear the regimental Mackenzie tartan, and this was agreed. The Army Section of the CCF still wear the tartan today. In 1983 the Edinburgh Academy CCF was formally affiliated to the Queen's Own Highlanders, and adopted the bonnet badge of the regiment

The Pipes and Drums of the Edinburgh Academy CCF in 1994.

CHAPTER VII
ALLIED AND AFFILIATED REGIMENTS
1. ALLIED REGIMENTS OF CANADA

The Canadian regiments allied to the Queen's Own Highlanders are listed in their order of precedence in the Canadian Army Militia.

THE CAMERON HIGHLANDERS OF OTTAWA

The origins of the regiment

The Cameron Highlanders of Ottawa trace their origin to the Militia companies raised in 1861 for garrison duty during the American Civil War. In 1866 nine independent companies were formed into the 43rd Carleton Battalion of Infantry, nicknamed the 'Carleton Blazers'. Disbanded in 1875, a successor regiment was formed in 1881 designated the 43rd Ottawa and Carleton Battalion of Rifles, with the motto of the city of Ottawa, 'Advance'. During the South African War the regiment provided a company of The Royal Canadian Regiment. After the Duke of Cornwall (later HM King George V) had inspected the regiment in 1901, it was redesignated the 43rd Regiment, Duke of Cornwall's Own Rifles.

The Regiment in World War I

During World War I the regiment provided men for the 2nd Battalion Canadian Expeditionary Force (CEF), and formed the 38th and 207th Battalions CEF. The 38th Battalion CEF served in Bermuda during 1915-1916, and from 1916 onwards in France and Flanders with 12 (Canadian) Infantry Brigade in the 4th (Canadian) Division. The battalion was awarded 16 Battle Honours. The 207th Battalion CEF provided reinforcements for battalions in the field.

Captain Thain Wendell MacDowell
VC, DSO

Captain Thain W MacDowell wins the Victoria Cross – 9th April 1917

While serving with the 38th Battalion CEF, Captain Thain Wendell MacDowell was awarded the Victoria Cross for his gallantry during the fighting on Vimy Ridge from 9-13 April 1917. The citation read:

'For most conspicuous bravery and indomitable resolution in the face of heavy machine gun and shell fire. By his initiative and courage this officer, with the assistance of two runners was enabled, in the face of great difficulties, to capture two machine guns, besides two officers and seventy-five men. Although wounded in the hand, he continued to hold the position gained, in spite of heavy shell fire, until eventually relieved by his battalion. By his bravery and prompt action he undoubtedly succeeded in rounding up a very strong enemy machine gun post.'
(London Gazette 8 June 1917)

Private C J P Nunney DCM, MM wins the Victoria Cross on 1-2 September 1918

While serving with the 38th Battalion CEF, Private Claude Joseph Patrick Nunney was awarded the Victoria Cross posthumously for his conspicuous bravery during the fighting at Drocourt-Quéant on 1-2 September 1918. The citation read:

'For most conspicuous bravery during the operations against the Drocourt-Quéant line on 1 and 2 September 1918. On 1 September, when his battalion was in the vicinity of Vis-en-Artois, preparatory to the advance, the enemy laid down a heavy barrage and counter-attacked. Private

Private Claude Joseph Patrick Nunney
VC, DCM, MM

Nunney, who was at this time at company headquarters, immediately on his own initiative proceeded through the barrage to the company outpost lines, going from post to post and encouraging the men by his own fearless example. The enemy were repulsed and a critical situation was saved. During the attack on 2 September his dash continually placed him in advance of his companions, and his fearless example undoubtedly helped greatly to carry the company forward to its objectives. He displayed throughout the highest degree of valour, until severely wounded'. (London Gazette 14 December 1918)

Private Nunney had already been awarded the DCM and MM earlier during the war, but died of wounds received in the action when he won the Victoria Cross.

The Ottawa Highlanders

After World War I the regiment was reorganised as the Ottawa Regiment (The Duke of Cornwall's Own), perpetuating the 38th and 207th Battalions CEF. In 1922 it was redesignated The Ottawa Highlanders, and in 1923 was allied to The Queen's Own Cameron Highlanders.

The Cameron Highlanders of Ottawa

In 1933 the Ottawa Highlanders were redesignated The Cameron Highlanders of Ottawa. In 1936 the regiment was presented with new Colours at Ottawa by Lord Tweedsmuir, Governor General of Canada.

The Cameron Highlanders of Ottawa (MG)

In 1936 the Cameron Highlanders of Ottawa amalgamated with B Company, 4th Battalion Canadian Machine Gun Corps, and the designation was altered to include the abbreviation 'MG'.

1st Battalion Cameron Highlanders of Ottawa (MG) – 1939-1945

During War II the Camerons of Ottawa formed three battalions. The 1st Battalion mobilised on 2nd September 1939, and served in Iceland in 1940-1941. It landed in Normandy on 'D' Day, 6th June 1944, with the 3rd (Canadian) Infantry Division, and subsequently fought at Carpiquet, Buron, Authie, and Caen. It took part in the closing of the Falaise Gap, the pursuit across the Seine, the capture of Boulogne and Calais, and the clearing of the Scheldt estuary. Having crossed the Rhine it attacked Emerich, crossed the rivers Ems and Leda, and ended the war at Emden. It was awarded 20 Battle Honours. The 1st Battalion was demobilised in Ottawa in 1945.

2nd (Reserve) Battalion Cameron Highlanders of Ottawa – 1940-1946

The 2nd (Reserve) Battalion was formed in Canada in 1940, and served in Ottawa. When the 1st Battalion was demobilised in 1945, the 2nd Battalion absorbed many of its officers and men. In 1946 the 2nd Battalion was reorganised as an infantry regiment in the Reserve Force, and became The Cameron Highlanders of Ottawa.

3rd Battalion Cameron Highlanders of Ottawa – 1945-1946

The 3rd Battalion was formed in Holland in 1945 for service with the Canadian occupation forces in Germany. It was disbanded in 1946.

The Cameron Highlanders of Ottawa – since 1946

After World War II the Cameron Highlanders of Ottawa became an infantry regiment in the Canadian Army Reserve Force, which was redesignated the Canadian Army Militia in 1957. The headquarters of the regiment are The Drill Hall, Cartier Square, Ottawa.

In 1967 HRH Prince Philip, Duke of Edinburgh, was appointed Colonel in Chief of the Cameron Highlanders of Ottawa. The same year the Regiment received new Colours from HM Queen Elizabeth at Ottawa. In 1969 the regiment was granted the Freedom of the City of Ottawa.

On the amalgamation in 1961 of the Seaforth Highlanders and The Queen's Own Cameron Highlanders, the alliance with the Cameron Highlanders was renewed with the Queen's Own Highlanders. On the amalgamation of the Queen's Own Highlanders and The Gordon Highlanders in 1994, the alliance was renewed with The Highlanders.

THE QUEEN'S OWN CAMERON HIGHLANDERS OF CANADA

The 79th Cameron Highlanders of Canada in 1910

The raising of the 79th Cameron Highlanders of Canada

The regiment was authorised on 1st February 1910, and raised in Winnipeg, Manitoba as The 79th Cameron Highlanders of Canada, a Militia regiment. It was allied to The Queen's Own Cameron Highlanders in 1911, and wore the same uniform, with variations in its badges. The alliance with the Camerons was cemented when the 79th Cameron Highlanders of Canada sent a contingent to the Coronation of HM King George V in 1911, and the contingent was attached to the 1st Camerons in Aldershot. The 79th Cameron Highlanders of Canada received their first stand of Colours in Winnipeg in 1910, presented by Mrs D C Cameron, wife of the Lieutenant Governor of Manitoba.

The 79th Cameron Highlanders of Canada in World War I

The 79th Cameron Highlanders of Canada was one of four regiments which each provided a company to form a composite Highland battalion, the 16th Battalion 'The Canadian Scottish', in the First Contingent of the Canadian Expeditionary Force (CEF) which left Canada in October 1914 and arrived in France in February 1915. A further company went to form the 27th Battalion CEF.

The regiment subsequently formed the 43rd Battalion (Cameron Highlanders of Canada) CEF which served in France with 9 (Canadian) Brigade in the 3rd (Canadian) Division. It was awarded 18 Battle Honours. In 1916 the regiment also raised the 174th and 179th Battalions CEF which served as reinforcement units in Great Britain.

Lieutenant Robert Shankland DCM wins the Victoria Cross, 26th October 1917

On 26th October 1917, during the fighting in the capture of Bellevue Spur, on Passchendaele ridge near Ypres, Lieutenant Robert Shankland of the 43rd Battalion CEF was awarded the Victoria Cross. The citation read:

'For most conspicuous bravery and resource in action under critical and adverse conditions. Having gained a position he rallied the remnant of his own platoon and men of other companies, disposed them to command the ground in front, and inflicted heavy casualties upon the retreating enemy. Later he dispersed a counter-attack, thus enabling supporting troops to come up unmolested. He then personally communicated to Headquarters an accurate and valuable report as to the position on the brigade frontage, and, after doing so, rejoined his command and carried on until relieved. His courage and splendid example inspired all ranks, and, coupled with his great gallantry and skill,, undoubtedly saved a very critical situation'.
(London Gazette 18 December 1917)

Lieutenant Robert Shankland, VC, DCM

The Queen's Own Cameron Highlanders of Canada after World War I

After the war the 79th Cameron Highlanders of Canada were reorganised as a Militia regiment, perpetuating the 43rd, 174th and 179th Battalions CEF. In 1920 the regiment became The Cameron Highlanders of Canada, with 2nd and 3rd Reserve Battalions. In recognition of its fine war service, the regiment was redesignated The Queen's Own Cameron Highlanders of Canada in 1923, .

The Queen's Own Cameron Highlanders of Canada in World War II

When World War II broke out, the Camerons of Canada mobilised in September 1939. The 2nd (Reserve) Battalion was formed in Canada in 1940. In December 1940 the 1st Battalion Cameron Highlanders of Canada moved to Great Britain. On 19th August 1942 the battalion took part in the Dieppe Raid, suffering 346 casualties. The battalion, rebuilt to fighting strength, landed in Normandy in July 1944 with 6 (Canadian) Brigade in the 3rd (Canadian) Division. The battalion fought in the closing of the Falaise Gap, the pursuit across the Seine, the battles of the Scheldt and the Rhineland, and the clearing of northern Holland. The Camerons of Canada ended the war at Oldenburg, and the battalion was awarded 19 Battle Honours. The 1st Battalion was disbanded in Winnipeg in 1945.

2nd (Reserve) Battalion The Queen's Own Cameron Highlanders of Canada – 1940-1946

The 2nd (Reserve) Battalion was formed in Winnipeg in 1940, and served in Canada as a reinforcement unit. When the 1st Battalion was disbanded in 1945, the 2nd Battalion was redesignated as The Queen's Own Cameron Highlanders of Canada, and continuity was thus preserved.

The Queen's Own Cameron Highlanders of Canada – since 1946

After World War II the Camerons of Canada became an infantry regiment in the Canadian Army Reserve Force, which in 1957 was redesignated the Canadian Army Militia. In 1955 the Headquarters of the regiment were moved from 202 Main Street Winnipeg to the Minto Armouries.

On 18th November 1961 the Camerons of Canada received new Colours at Winnipeg from The Hon Errick F Willis QC, Lieutenant Governor of Manitoba. In 1967 HRH Prince Philip, Duke of Edinburgh, was appointed Colonel in Chief of The Queen's Own Cameron Highlanders of Canada. In May 1970 the regiment was granted the Freedom of the City of Winnipeg.

On the amalgamation in 1961 of the Seaforth Highlanders and The Queen's Own Cameron Highlanders, the alliance with the Cameron Highlanders was renewed with the Queen's Own Highlanders. On the amalgamation of the Queen's Own Highlanders and The Gordon Highlanders in 1994, the alliance was renewed with The Highlanders.

THE SEAFORTH HIGHLANDERS OF CANADA

The Seaforth Highlanders of Canada on parade at Seaforth Armoury, Vancouver in 1978.

The raising of the 72nd Seaforth Highlanders of Canada

The regiment was authorised on 24th November 1910, and raised in Vancouver, British Columbia, in 1911 as the 72nd Highlanders of Canada, a Militia regiment. On its alliance to the Seaforth Highlanders in 1911, it was redesignated the 72nd Seaforth Highlanders of Canada. The regiment wore the same uniform as the Seaforth Highlanders, with a cougar as the collar badge. The regiment received its first Stand of Colours from HRH The Duke of Connaught in 1912.

The 72nd Seaforth Highlanders of Canada in World War I

The Seaforth of Canada was one of four regiments which each provided a large contingent to form a composite Highland battalion, the 16th Battalion 'The Canadian Scottish', in the First Contingent of the Canadian Expeditionary Force (CEF), which left Canada in October 1914 and arrived in France in February 1915.

The regiment formed the 72nd Battalion CEF, which went to France in 1916 with 12 (Canadian) Brigade of the 4th (Canadian) Division. The regiment also formed the 231st Battalion CEF which served as a reinforcement battalion. The 72nd Seaforth Highlanders of Canada were awarded 16 Battle Honours in World War I, representing the actions of both the 72nd Battalion CEF, and the 16th 'Canadian Scottish' Battalion CEF. The 72nd Battalion CEF received Colours from Lieutenant General Sir Arthur Currie, Chief of the General Staff, on 1st April 1919.

The Seaforth Highlanders of Canada between the Wars

The 72nd Regiment, Seaforth Highlanders of Canada was reorganised in 1920 as the Seaforth Highlanders of Canada, its 1st Battalion perpetuating the 72nd Battalion CEF, and the 2nd (Reserve) Battalion perpetuating the 231st Battalion CEF. In 1925 HRH The Prince of Wales was appointed Colonel-in-Chief of the Regiment. The Seaforth Armoury in Vancouver was opened as the headquarters of the regiment in 1936.

The Seaforth of Canada in World War II

When World War II broke out the Seaforth of Canada mobilised in Vancouver and moved to Great Britain in December 1939 with 2 (Canadian) Brigade of the 1st (Canadian) Division. The 2nd (Reserve) Battalion was formed in Canada in 1940. After training in Great Britain the 1st Battalion landed in Sicily on 10th July 1943, and took part in the campaigns in Sicily and Italy. Its actions included the battles of the River Moro and Ortona, and the fighting to breach the Hitler and Gothic Lines.

In March 1945 the battalion left Italy with the 1st Canadian Corps and moved to North West Europe. It fought at the River Ijssel, and ended the war in Amsterdam. The Seaforth of Canada earned 23 Battle Honours in Sicily and Italy, and 2 in North West Europe.

Private Ernest A Smith wins the Victoria Cross on 21st October 1944

During the fighting in the Po Valley in October 1944, Private Ernest A 'Smokey' Smith was awarded the Victoria Cross when having sited his Piat (projector infantry anti-tank), he was approached by a Mark V Panther tank which wounded his comrade with machine gun fire. The citation read:

Private Ernest Smith VC

'At a range of 30 feet, and having to expose himself to the full view of the enemy, Private Smith fired the Piat and hit the tank putting it out of action. Ten German infantry immediately jumped off the back of the tank and charged him with schmeissers and grenades. Without hesitation Private Smith moved out onto the road and at point blank range with his tommy gun killed four Germans and drove the remainder back. Almost immediately another tank opened fire and more enemy infantry closed in on Smith's position. Obtaining some abandoned tommy gun magazines from a ditch, he steadfastly held his position, protecting his comrade and fighting the enemy with his tommy gun until they finally gave up and withdrew in disorder'. (London Gazette 20th December 1944)

The Seaforth Highlanders of Canada since 1946

After World War II the Seaforth Highlanders of Canada became an infantry regiment in the Canadian Army Reserve Force, which was redesignated the Canadian Army Militia in 1957. The headquarters of the regiment are The Seaforth Armoury, Vancouver.

On 3rd June 1962 the regiment received new Colours from HRH Prince Philip, Duke of Edinburgh at Vancouver, and in 1967 Prince Philip was appointed Colonel-in-Chief of the Seaforth Highlanders of Canada. The regiment was granted the Freedom of the City of Vancouver in 1978.

On the amalgamation in 1961 of the Seaforth Highlanders and The Queen's Own Cameron Highlanders, the alliance with the Seaforth Highlanders was renewed with the Queen's Own Highlanders. On the amalgamation of the Queen's Own Highlanders and The Gordon Highlanders in 1994, the alliance was renewed with The Highlanders.

FORMER ALLIANCE

THE PICTOU HIGHLANDERS

The origins of the regiment

The Pictou Highlanders traced their origin to a battalion raised by the Commanding Officer of the 78th Highlanders (Ross-shire Buffs) from expatriate Highlanders living in Pictou County, in Canada, at the time when the 78th was stationed in Halifax during 1869-1871. The battalion was authorised in 1871 and designated the 78th Colchester and Hants, or Highlanders Battalion of Infantry. In 1910 the battalion was reorganised and became The Pictou Regiment 'Highlanders'.

The Pictou Highlanders in World War I

During World War I the regiment formed 17th Battalion Canadian Expeditionary Force (CEF) which served in Great Britain as a Training battalion, while the majority of its officers and men served in France. It also formed the 246th Battalion CEF, which served as a reinforcement battalion.

The Pictou Highlanders after World War I

The regiment was reformed in 1920 as The Pictou Highlanders, and perpetuated the 17th and 246th Battalions CEF. Its headquarters were at Glasgow, Nova Scotia. The regiment was allied to the Seaforth Highlanders, and wore the Seaforth uniform apart from the bonnet badge.

The Pictou Highlanders in World War II

During World War II the Pictou Highlanders carried out coastal defence duty in Newfoundland, and provided companies for garrison duty in Bermuda and the Bahamas. A 2nd (Reserve) Battalion was formed in Canada.

The Pictou Highlanders after World War II

The regiment was re-formed in 1946 as a regiment of the Canadian Army Reserve Force and designated The Pictou Highlanders (Motor). In 1954 the regiment was amalgamated with the North Nova Scotia Highlanders to form the 1st Battalion Nova Scotia Highlanders, and the alliance with the Seaforth Highlanders ended.

2. ALLIED REGIMENTS OF
THE AUSTRALIAN MILITARY FORCES

10th/27th BATTALION
THE ROYAL SOUTH AUSTRALIA REGIMENT

Officers and NCOs of the Mount Gambier Company, South Australian Scottish in 1900.

The origins of the regiment

The Royal South Australia Regiment traces its descent from the Militia and Volunteer units formed in the 19th Century. A contingent fought in the South African War. The South Australian Scottish Regiment descends through the 74th (Boothby Battalion) which was formed in 1911, and which fought in France and Flanders, Gallipoli, and Egypt during World War I.

After World War I the regiment was reformed as the 2nd Battalion 27th Infantry (Boothby Regiment). In 1921 it amalgamated with the 5th Battalion 27th Infantry to form the 27th Battalion South Australian Infantry. The regiment adopted the Mackenzie kilt in 1938 when it became the 27th Battalion (South Australian Scottish Regiment).

27th Battalion (South Australian Scottish Regiment) in World War II

During World War II the 27th Battalion (South Australian Scottish Regiment) formed two battalions. The 1/27th Battalion fought against the Japanese in New Guinea and the 2/27th Battalion fought in the Middle East and the South West Pacific.

27th Battalion (South Australian Scottish Regiment) – 1948-1960

On the reintroduction of voluntary military training with the Citizen Military Forces in 1948, the 27th Battalion (The South Australian Scottish Regiment) was reformed. The alliance with the Seaforth Highlanders was officially authorised in 1952.

The Royal South Australian Regiment – 1960

Under the reorganisation of 1960, the 27th Battalion (The South Australian Scottish Regiment) was amalgamated with the 10th Battalion (Adelaide Rifles) and the 43rd Battalion (Bushmen's Rifles) to form The Royal South Australia Regiment. In 1965 a second battalion was formed which bore the old designation the 27th Battalion Royal South Australia Regiment, but it was disbanded again in 1975. Under a further reorganisation in 1984 the 27th Battalion was re-formed, and it was linked with the 10th Battalion in 1987 to form the 10th/27th Battalion Royal South Australia Regiment. The headquarters of the regiment are in Adelaide, South Australia.

After the amalgamation of Seaforth Highlanders and The Queen's Own Cameron Highlanders in 1961, the alliance with the Seaforth Highlanders was renewed with the Queen's Own Highlanders. On the amalgamation of the Queen's Own Highlanders and The Gordon Highlanders in 1994, the alliance was renewed with The Highlanders.

16th BATTALION
THE ROYAL WESTERN AUSTRALIA REGIMENT

16th Battalion (The Cameron Highlanders of Western Australia) in 1938

The origins of the regiment

The Cameron Highlanders of Western Australia form part of the Royal Western Australia Regiment, which traces its descent from the local forces raised to keep order during the gold rush of 1899. In 1901 a number of detachments were formed into the 5th (Goldfields) Battalion Western Australian Infantry. A contingent served in the South African War. In World War I the battalion formed the 2/2nd Battalion Pioneer Regiment, and served in France and Flanders, Gallipoli, and Egypt.

16th Battalion (The Cameron Highlanders of Western Australia) – 1936

After World War I the regiment was re-formed as the 16th Battalion (The Goldfields Regiment). In 1936 it was brought up to strength and re-formed as a Scottish battalion. The choice of the 79th tartan and the designation The Cameron Highlanders of Western Australia commemorated an earlier Highland regiment in Western Australia which existed from 1904-1911, and which wore the 79th tartan. The alliance with The Queen's Own Cameron Highlanders was officially authorised in February 1938, and the regiment adopted the uniform and badge of the Cameron Highlanders. The headquarters of the regiment was at Perth, Western Australia.

16th Battalion (The Cameron Highlanders of Western Australia) in World War II

During World War II the 16th Battalion (The Cameron Highlanders of Western Australia) formed two battalions. The 1/16th Battalion fought against the Japanese in New Britain from 1944-1945. The 2/16th Battalion served in the Western Desert, Syria and New Guinea. The regiment was disbanded in 1946.

16th Battalion (The Cameron Highlanders of Western Australia) – 1948-1960

On the reintroduction of voluntary military training in the Citizen Military Forces in 1948, the 16th Battalion (The Cameron Highlanders of Western Australia) was reformed, and was linked with 28th Battalion (The Swan Regiment) to form the 16/28th Infantry Battalion (The Cameron Highlanders of Western Australia). The link ceased in 1952.

16th Battalion The Royal Western Australia Regiment – 1960

On the formation in 1960 of The Royal Western Australia Regiment, the 16th Battalion (The Cameron Highlanders of Western Australia) amalgamated with other regiments to form the 16th Battalion The Royal Western Australian Regiment. In the new regiment The Cameron Highlanders of Western Australia formed B (Cameron) Company, which continued to wear the kilt of 79th tartan. The 16th Battalion Royal Western Australia Regiment received new Colours in 1962 from HRH Prince Philip, Duke of Edinburgh, at Perth.

After the amalgamation of Seaforth Highlanders and The Queen's Own Cameron Highlanders in 1961, the alliance with the Cameron Highlanders was renewed with the Queen's Own Highlanders. On the amalgamation of the Queen's Own Highlanders and The Gordon Highlanders in 1994, the alliance was renewed with The Highlanders.

Since 1988 the 16th Battalion The Royal Western Australia Regiment has its Depot at Cameron Lines, Irwin Barracks, Karrakatta, Perth, Western Australia.

FORMER ALLIANCES WITH THE AUSTRALIAN INFANTRY

37th, 39th, 52nd BATTALIONS

The three battalions, all drawn from Victoria, were allied to The Queen's Own Cameron Highlanders for periods before and during World War II. The recurrent changes in the organisation of the Australian Military Forces tend to obscure the continuity of the alliances, which were much valued by both the Cameron Highlanders and the battalions of Australian Infantry.

37th Battalion – 1930

An alliance was authorised between The Queen's Own Cameron Highlanders and the 37th Battalion Australian Infantry (The Henty Regiment) in November 1930. The battalion was recruited from Henty, Victoria, and had its headquarters at East Malvern.

37th/52nd Battalion – 1930-1936

In 1930 the 37th Battalion was linked with the 52nd Battalion Australian Infantry (The Gippsland Regiment), also recruited from Victoria. In 1932 the alliance with the Cameron Highlanders was extended to the 37th/52nd Battalion, which wore the badge and buttons of The Queen's Own Cameron Highlanders.

37th/39th Battalion and 52nd Battalion – 1937-1939

In 1936 the 37th and 52nd Battalions were split, and each retained its alliance with the Cameron Highlanders. The 37th Battalion was then linked with the 39th Battalion to become the 37th/39th Battalion (The Henty Regiment, and in 1938 the alliance with the Cameron Highlanders was extended to it. In 1939 the 37th and 39th Battalions separated again, when the 39th Battalion was linked with the 24th Battalion until 1941.

37th/52nd Battalion in World War II

In World War II the 37th Battalion served in Australia until 1942, when it was linked again with the 52nd Battalion. The 37th/52nd Battalion served in action against the Japanese in New Guinea from 1943, until it returned to Australia for disbandment in 1946.

39th Battalion in World War II

In World War II the 39th/24th Battalion served in Australia until 1941, when the battalions were split again. The 39th Battalion served in action against the Japanese in New Guinea from early 1942. In March 1943 the battalion was disbanded in Queensland.

61st BATTALION (THE QUEENSLAND CAMERON HIGHLANDERS)

The 61st Battalion (The Queensland Cameron Highlanders) was raised in Brisbane in 1938 and an alliance with The Queen's Own Cameron Highlanders was authorised in 1939. The battalion wore the kilt of 79th tartan.

61st Battalion (The Queensland Cameron Highlanders) in World War II

The 61st Battalion served in New Guinea from August 1942 where it fought with distinction in the defeat of the Japanese at Milne's Bay, and in the later operations in New Guinea. When the battalion was disbanded in 1946 it passed its stock of kilts of 79th tartan to The Scots College, Warwick, Queensland, so that its Highland tradition would be perpetuated.

ALLIED CADET FORCES

THE SCOTS COLLEGE, WARWICK, QUEENSLAND

When the 61st Battalion (The Queensland Cameron Highlanders) was disbanded in 1946, the battalion handed its kilts of 79th tartan to The Scots College, Warwick, Queensland. The members of the Cadet Force have worn the kilt of 79th tartan ever since. The Scots College was originally founded in 1919, and was subsequently linked with the Presbyterian Girls College (PGC). In 1992 a regimental alliance was established between 17 RCU, the Cadet Force of the Scots College (PGC) of Warwick, Queensland, and the Queen's Own Highlanders. This alliance was renewed with The Highlanders.

THE SCOTS COLLEGE, SWANBOURNE, WESTERN AUSTRALIA

The Cadet Force of the Scots College, Swanbourne, Perth, Western Australia has had close links with the Cameron Highlanders of Western Australia since the alliance with the regiment was established in 1938. A regimental alliance was established in 1998 between the Cadet Force of the Scots College, Swanbourne and The Highlanders.

3. ALLIED REGIMENTS OF NEW ZEALAND

4th BATTALION (OTAGO AND SOUTHLAND) THE ROYAL NEW ZEALAND INFANTRY REGIMENT

The origins of the regiment

The regiment traces its descent from the Dunedin and Invercargill Militia battalions established in 1860, and to the companies of Otago Rifle Volunteers raised from 1862 onwards. In 1898 they were formed into the 1st Otago Rifle Battalion, which provided contingents to fight in the South African War. Under the Defence Act of 1909 four infantry regiments were established in the Provinces of Otago and Southland, each comprising a territorial battalion and cadets.

The Otago Regiment in World War I

In 1914 each regiment in Otago and Southland provided a company to form the Otago Regiment of the New Zealand Expeditionary Force. The Otago Regiment served with the Australian and New Zealand Army Corps at Gallipoli and in Egypt. Having been expanded to three battalions in 1916, it served in France and Flanders.

Sergeant Donald F Brown VC

Sergeant Donald F Brown wins the Victoria Cross – 15th September 1916

Sergeant Donald Forrester Brown of the Otago Regiment, serving with the 2nd Infantry Battalion New Zealand Forces, was awarded the Victoria Cross during the attack on High Wood on 14th June 1917. The citation read:

'For most conspicuous bravery and determination in attack when the company to which he belonged suffered very heavy casualties in officers and men from machine-gun fire. At great personal risk this NCO advanced with a comrade and succeeded in reaching a point within thirty yards of the enemy guns. Four of the gun crew were killed and the gun captured. The advance of the company continued till it was again held up by machine-gun fire. Again Sergeant Brown and his comrade with great gallantry rushed the gun and killed the crew. After this second position had been won, the company came under very heavy shell fire, and the utter contempt for danger and coolness under fire of this NCO did much to keep up the spirit of his men. On a subsequent occasion in attack, Sergeant Brown showed most conspicuous gallantry. He attacked single handed a machine-gun which was holding up the attack, killed the crew and captured the gun. Later, whilst sniping the retreating enemy, this very gallant soldier was killed'. (London Gazette 14 June 1917)

Sergeant Richard Travis wins the Victoria Cross – 27th September 1918

Sergeant Richard Travis, DCM, MM of the 2nd Battalion The Otago Regiment, was awarded the Victoria Cross at Hébuterne on 27th September 1918. The citation read:

'For most conspicuous bravery and devotion to duty. During surprise operations it was necessary to destroy an impassable wire block. Sergeant Travis, regardless of all personal danger, volunteered for this duty. Before zero hour, in broad daylight, and in close proximity to enemy posts, he crawled out and successfully destroyed the block with bombs, thus enabling the attacking parties to pass through. A few minutes later a bombing party on the right of the attack was held up by two enemy machine-guns, and the success of the operation was in danger. Perceiving this, Sergeant Travis with great gallantry and utter disregard for danger, rushed the position, and killed the crew and captured the guns. An enemy officer and three men immediately rushed at him from a bend in the trench and attempted to retake the guns. These four he killed single-handed, thus allowing the bombing party, on which much depended, to advance. The success of the operation was almost entirely due to the heroic work of this gallant NCO, and to the vigour with which he made and used opportunities for inflicting casualties on the enemy. He was killed twenty-four hours later when, under a most intense bombardment prior to an enemy counter-attack, he was going from post to post encouraging the men'. (London Gazette 29 September 1918)

The regiment after World War I

After World War I the Otago Regiment was re-formed with two battalions. In 1923 these were redesignated as the 1st Battalion The Otago Regiment and 1st Battalion The Southland Regiment.

The regiment in World War II

During World War II the territorial identities of battalions were discontinued. Officers and men of the Otago and Southland battalions fought in Greece, Crete, North Africa and Italy with the 20th, 23rd, and 26th Battalions of the 2nd New Zealand Division; and in the Pacific with 30th and 37th Battalions of the 3rd New Zealand Division.

The Otago and Southland Regiment – 1948-1962

The regiment was re-formed after World War II as 1st Battalion The Otago Regiment and lst Battalion The Southland Regiment. An alliance between The Queen's Own Cameron Highlanders and lst Battalion The Southland Regiment was authorised on 9th March 1948.

In October 1948 the Otago Regiment and the Southland Regiment were amalgamated to form the 1st Battalion The Otago and Southland Regiment, and the alliance was renewed with The Queen's Own Cameron Highlanders. On the amalgamation of the Seaforth Highlanders and the Cameron Highlanders in 1961, the alliance was renewed with the Queen's Own Highlanders (Seaforth and Camerons).

4th Battalion (Otago and Southland) The Royal New Zealand Infantry Regiment – 1962

In 1962, under the reorganisation of the New Zealand territorial regiments, the regiment became the 4th Battalion (Otago and Southland) The Royal New Zealand Infantry Regiment. The regiment received new Colours from the Governor General of New Zealand on 15th February 1975.

On the amalgamation of the Queen's Own Highlanders with The Gordon Highlanders in 1994, the alliance was renewed with The Highlanders.

7th BATTALION (WELLINGTON (CITY OF WELLINGTON'S OWN) AND HAWKES BAY) THE ROYAL NEW ZEALAND INFANTRY REGIMENT

The origins of the regiment

The Wellington Regiment traces its descent from the Wellington Veteran Volunteer Corps, formed in 1867 by British settlers, many of whom had served in the 65th Foot. In 1898 it became the Wellington Rifle Volunteer Battalion, and included the Wellington Highland Rifles Company which wore the uniform of the Seaforth Highlanders. In 1911 it was redesignated the 5th (Wellington) Regiment.

The Hawkes Bay Regiment traces its descent from the Napier Rifle Volunteers, formed in the Hawkes Bay area in 1863. The volunteer companies were grouped to form regiments which were later designated the 9th (Ruahine) and 17th (Hawkes Bay) Regiments of Infantry. The 9th and 17th Regiments provided contingents for service in the South African War.

The regiments in World War I

In 1914 the 5th (Wellington) Regiment joined the expedition which occupied German Samoa. In 1915 it returned to New Zealand and formed the New Zealand Rifle Brigade. It served in Egypt, Gallipoli, and then in

The Wellington Highland Rifles Company in 1911

France and Flanders. The 9th and 17th Regiments provided company groups for service with New Zealand Infantry battalions in World War I.

The regiment after World War I

After the New Zealand Rifle Brigade was disbanded in 1919, the re-formed Wellington Regiment inherited its traditions. In 1938 the regiment was granted the Freedom of the City of Wellington, and redesignated The Wellington Regiment (City of Wellington's Own).

The 9th (Hawkes Bay) and 17th (Ruahine) Regiments amalgamated in the 1920s to form the Hawkes Bay Regiment.

The regiment in World War II

During World War II the territorial identities of the battalions were discontinued. Members of the Wellington Regiment served with the 19th, 22nd, and 25th Battalions of New Zealand Infantry in Greece, Crete, North Africa and Italy, and the Wellington Regiment also formed three battalions for home defence against the Japanese invasion threat. Members of the Hawkes Bay Regiment served with the 19th, 22nd, 25th, and 28th (Maori) Battalions in Greece, Crete, North Africa and Italy, and with the 36th Battalion in the Pacific.

The regiment after World War II

The Wellington Regiment and The Hawkes Bay Regiment were re-formed after the war. In 1950 an alliance was authorised between the Wellington Regiment and the Seaforth Highlanders, the proposal stemming from the friendship established by the 2nd and 5th Battalions Seaforth Highlanders with the 2nd New Zealand Division in North Africa during 1942-1943.

On the amalgamation of the Seaforth Highlanders and the Cameron Highlanders in 1961, the alliance was renewed with the Queen's Own Highlanders (Seaforth and Camerons).

7th Battalion (Wellington (City of Wellington's Own) and Hawkes Bay)
The Royal New Zealand Infantry Regiment – 1964

In 1964, under the reorganisation of the New Zealand territorial regiments, The Wellington Regiment (City of Wellington's Own) and The Hawkes Bay Regiment were amalgamated to form the 7th Battalion (Wellington (City of Wellington's Own) and Hawkes Bay) The Royal New Zealand Infantry Regiment. The alliance with the Queen's Own Highlanders was renewed. On the amalgamation of the Queen's Own Highlanders with The Gordon Highlanders in 1994, the alliance was renewed with The Highlanders.

The regiment received new Colours from the Governor General of New Zealand on 23rd February 1979.

4. AFFILIATED REGIMENT

7th DUKE OF EDINBURGH'S OWN GURKHA RIFLES

*General Sir Peter Hunt, Colonel of the Queen's Own Highlanders
presents a regimental pipe banner to the 7th Gurkhas in Hong Kong, 1968.*

The 7th Gurkhas were formed in Burma in 1902. During World War II the 2nd Battalion 7th Gurkha Rifles had a particularly close association with the 2nd Camerons when the two battalions fought alongside in the 4th Indian Division, taking part in the campaigns in the Western Desert and Italy.

After World War II the 7th Gurkha Rifles were affiliated to the Cameronians (Scottish Rifles). On the disbandment of the Cameronians in 1968, a new affiliation was approved with the Queen's Own Highlanders (Seaforth and Camerons). In 1980 the 1st/7th Gurkha Rifles and lst Battalion Queen's Own Highlanders served together in Hong Kong.

Under the defence cuts of 1994 the 7th Gurkha Rifles became part of The Royal Gurkha Rifles, and the affiliation ceased.

CHAPTER VIII

1. DESIGNATIONS

The designations of the antecedent regiments of the Queen's Own Highlanders varied over the years. The following show the official designations as published in the Army List.

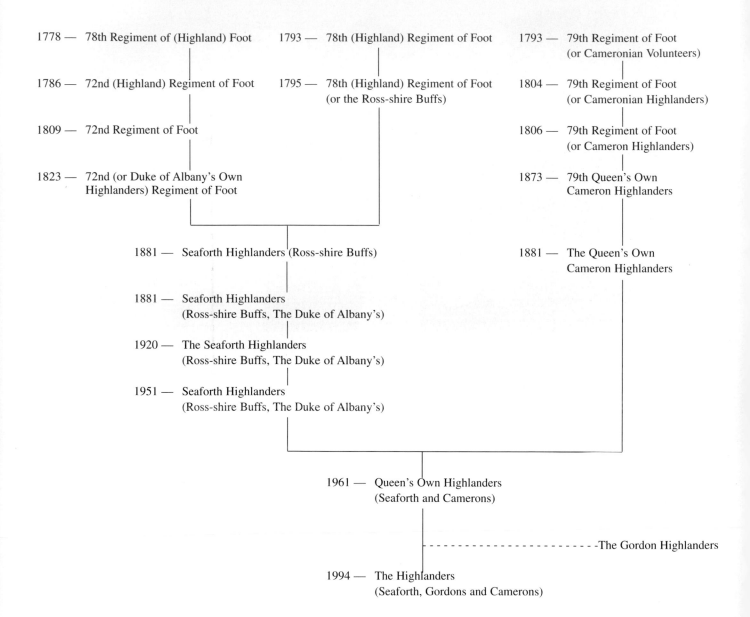

1778 — 78th Regiment of (Highland) Foot

1786 — 72nd (Highland) Regiment of Foot

1809 — 72nd Regiment of Foot

1823 — 72nd (or Duke of Albany's Own Highlanders) Regiment of Foot

1793 — 78th (Highland) Regiment of Foot

1795 — 78th (Highland) Regiment of Foot (or the Ross-shire Buffs)

1793 — 79th Regiment of Foot (or Cameronian Volunteers)

1804 — 79th Regiment of Foot (or Cameronian Highlanders)

1806 — 79th Regiment of Foot (or Cameron Highlanders)

1873 — 79th Queen's Own Cameron Highlanders

1881 — Seaforth Highlanders (Ross-shire Buffs)

1881 — Seaforth Highlanders (Ross-shire Buffs, The Duke of Albany's)

1920 — The Seaforth Highlanders (Ross-shire Buffs, The Duke of Albany's)

1951 — Seaforth Highlanders (Ross-shire Buffs, The Duke of Albany's)

1881 — The Queen's Own Cameron Highlanders

1961 — Queen's Own Highlanders (Seaforth and Camerons)

- -The Gordon Highlanders

1994 — The Highlanders (Seaforth, Gordons and Camerons)

2. THE REGIMENT AND THE ROYAL FAMILY

HRH Prince Frederick Augustus, Duke of York and Albany(1763-1827)

The 72nd Duke of Albany's Own Highlanders took their title, granted in 1823, from Field Marshal HRH Prince Frederick Augustus, Duke of York and Albany, the Commander in Chief. The second son of King George II, his Cypher 'F' with Ducal Coronet was one of the devices borne on the Regimental Colour of the Queen's Own Highlanders.

HM Queen Victoria (1819-1901)

The 79th Cameron Highlanders were granted the title 'The Queen's Own Cameron Highlanders' by HM Queen Victoria on 10th July 1873 as a personal favour by the Queen. The Cypher of HM Queen Victoria was granted as an additional badge to The Queen's Own Cameron Highlanders by HM King George V in 1921, and was borne on the Regimental Colour of the Queen's Own Highlanders.

HM King Edward VII (1841-1910)

In September 1866 HRH Prince Edward, Prince of Wales reviewed the Sutherland Rifle Volunteers at Dunrobin, and was appointed their Honorary Colonel. He continued to hold the appointment on his succession as HM King Edward VII, relinquishing it in 1908 on the formation of the Territorial Army, when the Sutherland Rifle Volunteers became the 5th (Territorial) Battalion Seaforth Highlanders.

HRH Prince Leopold, Duke of Albany (1853-1884) (right)

On 4th March 1882 HRH Prince Leopold, fourth son of Queen Victoria, was appointed Honorary Colonel of the 3rd Militia Battalion Seaforth Highlanders. After his death in 1884, at HM Queen Victoria's request, Prince Leopold's Cypher 'L' with Ducal Coronet was added to the bonnet badge worn by officers of the Seaforth Highlanders.

HRH Prince Albert, Duke of Clarence and Avondale (1864-1892) (left)

On 19th July 1890 HRH Prince Albert, Duke of Clarence and Avondale, eldest son of HRH The Prince of Wales (later King Edward VII), was appointed Honorary Colonel of the 1st Volunteer Battalion The Queen's Own Cameron Highlanders. He died in 1892, while holding the appointment.

HM King George V (1865-1936) (right)

On 12th November 1902 HRH Prince George, Prince of Wales was appointed Colonel-in-Chief of The Queen's Own Cameron Highlanders. On his succession to the throne as HM King George V in 1910, he remained Colonel-in-Chief of The Queen's Own Cameron Highlanders, until his death in 1936.

HRH Prince Leopold, Duke of Albany and Saxe-Coburg-Gotha (1884-1953) (left)

On 19th July 1905 HRH Prince Leopold, Duke of Albany, grandson of Queen Victoria, was appointed Colonel-in-Chief of the Seaforth Highlanders. His appointment ceased in 1914 when he elected to remain in Germany after the outbreak of war.

HM King Edward VIII (1894-1972)   (right)

On 3rd December 1920 HRH Prince Edward, Prince of Wales was appointed Colonel-in-Chief of the Seaforth Highlanders. On his succession to the throne in 1936 as HM King Edward VIII, he remained Colonel-in-Chief until his abdication in the same year.

HM King George VI (1895-1952)   (left)

On 1st July 1920 HRH Prince Albert, Duke of York, Earl of Inverness, was appointed Honorary Colonel of the 4th (Territorial) Battalion The Queen's Own Cameron Highlanders. On his succession to the throne on 10th December 1936 as HM King George VI, he became Colonel-in-Chief of The Queen's Own Cameron Highlanders, and held the appointment until his death in 1952.

HRH Prince Philip, Duke of Edinburgh   (right)

On 2nd June 1953 HRH Prince Philip, Duke of Edinburgh, was appointed Colonel-in-Chief of The Queen's Own Cameron Highlanders. On the amalgamation of the Seaforth Highlanders and The Queen's Own Cameron Highlanders on 7 February 1961, he was appointed Colonel-in-Chief of the Queen's Own Highlanders (Seaforth and Camerons). On the amalgamation of the Queen's Own Highlanders with The Gordon Highlanders on 17th September 1994, he was appointed Colonel-in-Chief of The Highlanders (Seaforth, Gordons and Camerons). His Cypher was borne on the Colours of the Queen's Own Highlanders.

HRH Prince Charles, Prince of Wales

HRH Prince Charles, Prince of Wales held the appointment of Colonel-in-Chief of The Gordon Highlanders until the amalgamation of the Queen's Own Highlanders and The Gordon Highlanders on 17th September 1994. On the formation of The Highlanders (Seaforth, Gordons and Camerons) he became Deputy Colonel-in-Chief of The Highlanders.

3. COLONELS OF THE REGIMENT

(Note: Colonels are shown with the final ranks, orders and decorations which they held)

1788 78th Regiment of (Highland) Foot
1786 72nd (Highland) Regiment of Foot
1809 72nd Regiment of Foot
1823 72nd (or Duke of Albany's Own Highlanders) Regiment of Foot

1777-1781 Col Kenneth Mackenzie, Earl of Seaforth
1782-1783 Col Thomas F Mackenzie Humberston
1783-1794 Lt Gen James Murray
1794-1798 Lt Gen Sir Adam Williamson, KB
1798-1815 Gen James Stuart
1815-1817 Gen Rowland Hill, Viscount Hill, GCB, GCH, KC
1817-1823 Gen Sir George Murray, GCB, GCH
1823-1836 Lt Gen Sir John Hope, GCH
1836-1847 Lt Gen Sir Colin Campbell, KCB
1847-1851 Lt Gen Sir Neil Douglas KCB, KCH
1851-1870 Gen Sir John Aitchison, GCB
1870   Gen Charles G J Arbuthnot
1870-1881 Gen Charles Gascoyne
1881-1893 Gen Sir Edward Selby Smyth, KCMG

1793 78th (Highland) Regiment
1795 78th (Highland) Regiment of Foot (or Ross-shire Buffs)

1793-1796 Lt Gen Francis Humberston Mackenzie, Lord Seaforth
1796-1809 Lt Gen Alexander Mackenzie-Fraser
1809-1812 Lt Gen Sir James H Craig, KB, KH
1812-1822 Lt Gen Sir Samuel Auchmuty, GCB
1822-1834 Lt Gen Sir Edward Barnes, GCB
1834-1837 Lt Gen Sir Lionel Smith, GCB, GCH
1837-1851 Gen Paul Anderson. CB, KC
1851-1853 Lt Gen Sir Neil Douglas, KCB, KCH
1853-1860 Gen Sir William Chalmers, CB, KCH
1860-1863 Lt Gen Roderick MacNeil of Barra
1863-1885 FM Sir Patrick Grant, GCB, GCMG

1793 79th (Highland) Regiment of Foot (or Cameronian Volunteers)
1804 79th Regiment of Foot (or Cameronian Highlanders)
1806 79th Regiment of Foot (or Cameron Highlanders)
1873 79th Queen's Own Cameron Highlanders

1793-1828 Lt Gen Sir Alan Cameron of Erracht, KCB
1828-1841 Gen Sir Ronald C Ferguson of Raith and Novar, GCB
1841-1842 Lt Gen Hon John Ramsay of Kelly
1842-1849 Gen Sir James MacDonell, GCB, KCH
1849-1854 Lt Gen James Hay, CB
1854-1862 Gen Sir William H Sewell, KCB
1862-1868 Gen Hon Sir Hugh Arbuthnott, KCB
1868-1870 Lt Gen John F Glencairn Campbell, CB
1870-1876 Gen Henry Cooper
1870-1879 Gen Sir Alfred H Horsford, GCB
1879-1887 Gen Sir John Douglas of Glenfinart, GCB

1881-1961 Seaforth Highlanders (Ross-shire Buffs, The Duke of Albany's)

1863-1885 FM Sir Patrick Grant GCB, GCMG, (2nd Battalion to 1885)
1881-1893 Gen Sir Edward Selby Smyth, KCMG, (1st Battalion to 1885)
1893-1897 Gen Sir William Parke, KCB
1897-1907 Gen Sir Archibald Alison Bt, GCB
1907-1911 Lt Gen Mostyn de la Poer Beresford
1911-1914 Gen Sir George D Barker, GCB
1914-1924 Maj Gen Robert H Murray, CB, CMG
1924-1931 Maj Gen Sir Colin Mackenzie, KCB
1931-1939 Maj Gen Sir Archibald B Ritchie, KBE, CB, CMG
1939-1947 Lt Gen Sir William M Thomson, KCMG, CB, MC
1947-1957 Maj Gen Sir John E Laurie Bt, CBE, DSO
1957-1961 FM Sir A James H Cassels, GCB, KBE, DSO

1881-1961 The Queen's Own Cameron Highlanders

1881-1887 Gen Sir John Douglas of Glenfinart,GCB
1887-1904 Gen Sir Richard C H Taylor, GCB
1904-1914 Gen Sir Ian S M Hamilton, GCB, GCMG, DSO, TD
1914-1929 Lt Gen Sir J Spencer Ewart, KCB
1929-1943 Maj Gen Neville J G Cameron, CB, CMG
1943-1951 Maj Gen Sir James S Drew, KBE, CB, DSO, MC
1951-1961 Maj Gen Douglas N Wimberley, CB, DSO, MC,

1961-1994 Queen's Own Highlanders (Seaforth and Camerons)

1961-1966 FM Sir A James H Cassels, GCB, KBE, DSO
1966-1975 Gen Sir Peter M Hunt, GCB, DSO, OBE
1975-1983 Lt Gen Sir Chandos Blair, KCVO, OBE, MC
1983-1994 Maj Gen John C O R Hopkinson, CB

1994 The Highlanders (Seaforth, Gordons and Camerons)

1994   Gen Sir Jeremy J G Mackenzie, KCB, OBE

COLONELS OF THE QUEEN'S OWN HIGHLANDERS

Field Marshal Sir A James H Cassels, GCB, KBE, DSO
Colonel of the Queen's Own Highlanders 1961-1966

General Sir Peter M Hunt, GCB, KBE, DSO
Colonel of the Queen's Own Highlanders 1966-1975
(from the painting by Howard Barron)

Lieutenant General Sir Chandos Blair, KCVO, OBE, MC
Colonel of the Queen's Own Highlanders 1975-1983

Major General John C O R Hopkinson CB
Colonel of the Queen's Own Highlanders 1983-1994

4. BATTLE HONOURS

BATTLE HONOURS – 1778-1881

72nd HIGHLANDERS		*78th HIGHLANDERS (ROSS-SHIRE BUFFS)*		*79th CAMERON HIGHLANDERS*	
Carnatic	(1782-96)	Assaye (+ ELEPHANT)	(1803)	Egmont op Zee	(1799)
Hindoostan	(1782-96)	Maida (2nd/78th)	(1806)	Egypt (+ SPHINX)	(1801)
Mysore	(1782-96)	Java	(1811)	Corunna	(1809)
Cape of Good Hope 1806		Koosh-ab	(1857)	Busaco	(1810)
South Africa 1835		Persia	(1857)	Fuentes d'Onor	(1811)
Sevastopol	(1855)	Lucknow	(1858)	Salamanca	(1812)
Central India	(1858)	Afghanistan 1879-80		Pyrenees	(1813)
Peiwar Kotal	(1878)			Nivelle	(1813)
Charasiah	(1879)			Nive	(1813)
Kabul 1879				Toulouse	(1814)
Kandahar 1880				Peninsula	(1809-14)
Afghanistan 1878-80				Waterloo	(1815)
				Alma	(1854)
				Sevastopol	(1855)
				Lucknow	(1858)

BATTLE HONOURS – 1881-1914

1st BATTALION SEAFORTH HIGHLANDERS		*2nd BATTALION SEAFORTH HIGHLANDERS*		*1st BATTALION THE QUEEN'S OWN CAMERON HIGHLANDERS*	
Tel-el-Kebir	(1882)	Chitral	(1895)	Tel-el-Kebir	(1882)
Egypt 1882		Paardeberg	(1899)	Egypt 1882	
Atbara	(1898)	South Africa 1899-1902		Nile 1884-85	
Khartoum	(1898)			Atbara	(1898)
				Khartoum	(1898)
				South Africa 1900-02	

CAMPAIGN AND THEATRE HONOURS AWARDED TO MILITIA AND VOLUNTEER UNITS WHICH SENT CONTINGENTS TO SERVE OVERSEAS DURING THE SOUTH AFRICAN WAR

3rd (Militia) Battalion Seaforth Highlanders	Mediterranean	1900-01
1st (Ross Highland) Volunteer Battalion Seaforth Highlanders	South Africa	1900-02
1st Sutherland (Sutherland Highland) Rifle Volunteers	South Africa	1900-02
3rd (Morayshire) Volunteer Battalion Seaforth Highlanders	South Africa	1900-02
1st (Inverness Highland) Volunteer Battalion The Queen's Own Cameron Highlanders	South Africa	1900-02
The Lovat Scouts (Imperial Yeomanry)	South Africa	1900-02
8th (Scottish) Volunteer Battalion The King's Liverpool Regiment	South Africa	1902

BATTLE HONOURS - WORLD WAR I

After World War I the Army Council appointed the Battles Nomenclature Committee to define the time and place of each action of the war. In 1920 the committee published its report 'The Official Names of the Battles and other Engagements fought by the Military Forces of the British Empire during the Great War 1914-1919'. Regimental committees then worked out the Battle Honours to which their regiments were entitled. To qualify for a Battle Honour a battalion had to have had its Headquarters and at least 50% of its strength within the boundaries of the battle within the dates specified in the report.

The complete list of Battle Honours was published in Army Orders in 1925. The lists were published in the regimental journals Cabar Feidh (July 1924) and The 79th News (July 1925). Ten Battle Honours were then selected to be borne on the King's Colour. These are shown in CAPITAL Letters in the lists below. The same ten Battle Honours were allowed to be borne on the colours of each regular and territorial battalion of the regiment which had existed before 1920. The Queen's Own Highlanders bear on their Colours the combined list of Battle Honours awarded to the Seaforth and the Cameron Highlanders.

WORLD WAR I BATTLE HONOURS SEAFORTH HIGHLANDERS

BATTLE HONOUR	BATTALIONS WHICH QUALIFIED						
Le Cateau	2nd						
Retreat from Mons	2nd						
MARNE, 1914	2nd						
Aisne, 1914	2nd						
La Bassée, 1914	1st						
Armentières, 1914	2nd						
Festubert, 1914	1st						
Givenchy, 1914	1st						
Neuve Chapelle	1st	4th					
YPRES, 191	2nd						
St Julien	2nd						
Frezenberg	2nd						
Bellewarde	2nd						
Aubers	1st	4th					
Festubert, 191	1st	4th	5th	6th			
LOOS	1st	4th			7th	8th	9th
SOMME, 1916	2nd	4th	5th	6th	7th	8th	9th
Albert, 1916	2nd						
Bazentin		4th	5th	6th	7th		9th
Delville Wood					7th		9th
Pozières		4th				8th	
Flers-Courcelette						8th	
Le Transloy	2nd				7th	8th	9th
Ancre Heights						8th	
Ancre, 1916		4th	5th	6th			
ARRAS, 1917	2nd	4th	5th	6th	7th	8th	9th
VIMY, 1917		4th	5th	6th			
Scarpe, 1917	2nd	4th	5th	6th	7th	8th	9th
Arleux					7th		9th
YPRES, 1917	2nd	4th	5th	6th	7th	8th	9th
Pilckem		4th	5th	6th		8th	
Menin Road		4th	5th	6th	7th		9th
Polygon Wood	2nd						
Broodseinde	2nd						
Poelcappelle					7th		9th

	1st	2nd	4th	5th	6th	7th	8th	9th	
Passchendaele						7th		9th	
CAMBRAI, 1917			4th	5th	6th				
SOMME, 1918		2nd	4th	5th	6th	7th	8th	9th	
St Quentin			4th	5th	6th	7th		9th	
Bapaume, 1918			4th	5th	6th	7th		9th	
ARRAS, 1918		2nd	4th	5th	6th		8th		
Lys		2nd	4th	5th	6th	7th		9th	
Estaires		2nd	4th	5th	6th				
Messines, 1918						7th		9th	
Hazebrouck		2nd	4th	5th	6th				
Bailleul						7th		9th	
Kemmel						7th		9th	
Béthune		2nd	4th	5th	6th				
MARNE, 1918							8th		
Soissonais-Ourcq							8th		
Tardenois			4th	5th	6th				
Scarpe, 1918		2nd	4th	5th	6th				
Drocourt-Quéant		2nd							
Hindenburg Line		2nd	4th	5th	6th				
CAMBRAI, 1918		2nd	4th	5th	6th				
YPRES, 1918						7th		9th	
Courtrai						7th		9th	
Selle		2nd	4th	5th	6th				
VALENCIENNES		2nd	4th	5th	6th				
France & Flanders, 1914	1st	2nd	4th						
France & Flanders, 191	1st	2nd	4th	5th	6th	7th	8th	9th	
France & Flanders, 1916		2nd	4th	5th	6th	7th	8th	9th	
France & Flanders, 1917		2nd	4th	5th	6th	7th	8th	9th	
France & Flanders, 1918		2nd	4th	5th	6th	7th	8th	9th	
Macedonia, 1917									1 Gar Bn
Macedonia, 1918									1 Gar Bn
Megiddo	1st								
Sharon	1st								
PALESTINE, 1918	1st								
Tigris, 1916	1st								
Kut el Amara, 1917	1st								
BAGHDAD	1st								
Mesopotamia, 191	1st								
Mesopotamia, 1916	1st								
Mesopotamia, 1917	1st								
Mesopotamia, 1918	1st								

WORLD WAR I BATTLE HONOURS
THE QUEEN'S OWN CAMERON HIGHLANDERS

BATTLE HONOUR	BATTALIONS WHICH QUALIFIED				
Retreat from Mons	1st				
MARNE, 1914	1st				
AISNE, 1914	1st				
YPRES, 1914	1st				
Langemarck, 1914	1st				
Gheluvelt	1st				
Nonne Bosschen	1st				
Givenchy, 1914	1st				
NEUVE CHAPELLE			4th		
Hill 60		2nd			
YPRES, 191		2nd			
Gravenstafel		2nd			
St Julien		2nd			
Frezenberg		2nd			
Bellewarde		2nd			
Aubers	1st		4th		
Festubert, 191			4th		
LOOS	1st		4th	5th	6th 7th
SOMME, 1916	1st			5th	6th 7th
Albert, 1916	1st			5th	
DELVILLE WOOD				5th	
Pozières	1st				6th 7th
Morval	1st				
Le Transloy				5th	6th 7th
Ancre Heights					6th 7th
ARRAS, 1917				5th	6th 7th
Scarpe, 1917				5th	6th 7th
Arleux					6th
YPRES, 1917	1st			5th	6th 7th
Pilckem					6th 7th
Menin Road				5th	
Polygon Wood				5th	
Poelcappelle				5th	
Passchendaele	1st			5th	
SOMME, 1918				5th	6th 7th
St Quentin				5th	
Bapaume, 1918				5th	
ARRAS, 1918	1st				6th 7th
Lys	1st			5th	
Estaires	1st				
Messines, 1918				5th	
Kemmel				5th	
Béthune	1st			5th	
MARNE, 1918					6th
Soissonais-Ourcq					6th
Drocourt-Quéant	1st				
Hindenburg Line	1st				

Epéhy	1st					
St Quentin Canal	1st					
YPRES, 1918				5th		
Courtrai	1st					
SAMBRE	1st					
France & Flanders, 1914	1st					
France & Flanders, 1915	1st	2nd	4th	5th	6th	7th
France & Flanders, 1916	1st			5th	6th	7th
France & Flanders, 1917	1st			5th	6th	7th
France & Flanders, 1918	1st			5th	6th	
Struma		2nd				
MACEDONIA, 1915		2nd				
MACEDONIA, 1916		2nd				
MACEDONIA, 1917		2nd				
MACEDONIA, 1918		2nd				

WORLD WAR I BATTLE HONOURS - THE LOVAT SCOUTS

FRANCE & FLANDERS, 1916
FRANCE & FLANDERS, 1917-
FRANCE & FLANDERS, 1918
GALLIPOLI, 1915
EGYPT, 1915
EGYPT, 1916
MACEDONIA, 1916
MACEDONIA, 1917
MACEDONIA, 1918

WORLD WAR I BATTLE HONOURS - THE LIVERPOOL SCOTTISH

BELLEWAARDE
SOMME, 1916
Ginchy
Morval
YPRES, 1917
PILCKEM
MENIN ROAD
PASSCHENDAELE
CAMBRAI, 1917
LYS
ESTAIRES
FRANCE & FLANDERS, 1914
FRANCE & FLANDERS, 1915
FRANCE & FLANDERS, 1916
FRANCE & FLANDERS, 1917
FRANCE & FLANDERS, 1918

BATTLE HONOURS – WORLD WAR II AND LATER

After World War II the Army Council appointed the Battles Nomenclature Committee to define the time and place of each action of the war. Regimental committees then worked out the Battle Honours to which their regiments were entitled.

The complete list of Battle Honours was notified to regiments in 1957, and published in the regimental journals Cabar Feidh and The 79th News in May 1957. Ten Battle Honours were selected to be borne on the Queen's Colour. These are shown in CAPITAL letters in the lists below. The Colours of the Queen's Own Highlanders bear the combined Battle Honours awarded to the Seaforth and the Cameron Highlanders.

WORLD WAR II BATTLE HONOURS SEAFORTH HIGHLANDERS

BATTLE HONOUR   BATTALIONS WHICH QUALIFIED

Battle Honour				
Ypres-Comines Canal				6th
Somme, 1940		4th		
Withdrawal to Seine	2nd	4th		
ST VALERY-EN-CAUX	2nd	4th		
Odon				7th
Cheux				7th
CAEN				7th
Troarn	2nd		5th	
Mont Pincon				7th
Quarry Hill				7th
Falaise	2nd		5th	
Falaise Road	2nd			
Dives Crossing	2nd		5th	
Lisieux			5th	
Nederrijn				7th
Best				7th
Le Havre	2nd		5th	
Lower Maas	2nd		5th	7th
Meijel				7th
Venlo Pocket	2nd		5th	7th
Ourthe	2nd		5th	
RHINELAND	2nd		5th	7th
Reichswald	2nd		5th	
Goch	2nd		5th	
Moyland				7th
Rhine	2nd		5th	7th
Uelzen				7th
Artlenberg				7th
North West Europe, 1940	2nd	4th	6th	
North West Europe, 1944	2nd		5th	7th
North West Europe, 1945	2nd		5th 6th	7th
EL ALAMEIN	2nd		5th	
Advance on Tripoli	2nd		5th	
Mareth	2nd		5th	
Wadi Zigzaou			5th	
AKARIT	2nd		5th	
Djebel Roumana	2nd		5th	
North Africa, 1942	2nd		5th	

North Africa, 1943	2nd	5th	
Landing in Sicily	2nd	5th	6th
Augusta			6th
Francofonte	2nd	5th	
Adrano	2nd	5th	
Sferro Hills	2nd	5th	
SICILY, 1943	2nd	5th	6th
Garigliano Crossing			6th
ANZIO			6th
Italy, 1943			6th
Italy, 1944			6th
MADAGASCAR			6th
Middle East, 1942			6th
IMPHAL	1st		
Shenan Pass	1st		
Litan	1st		
Tengnoupal	1st		
BURMA, 1942	1st		
BURMA, 1943	1st		
BURMA, 1944	1st		

WORLD WAR II BATTLE HONOURS
THE QUEEN'S OWN CAMERON HIGHLANDERS

BATTLE HONOUR	BATTALIONS WHICH QUALIFIED		
Defence of Escaut	1st		
ST OMER-LA BASSEE	1st		
Somme, 1940		4th	
St Valéry-en-Caux		4th	
Falaise			5th
Falaise Road			5th
La Vie Crossing			5th
Le Havre			5th
Lower Maas			5th
Venlo Pocket			5th
Rhineland			5th
REICHSWALD			5th
Goch			5th
RHINE			5th
North-West Europe. 1940	1st	4th	
North-West Europe, 1944			5th
North-West Europe, 1945			5th
Agordat		2nd	
KEREN		2nd	
Abyssinia, 1941		2nd	
SIDI BARRANI		2nd	
Tobruk, 1941		2nd	
Gubi II		2nd	

Carmusa	2nd	
Gazala	2nd	
Tobruk, 1942	2nd	
EL ALAMEIN		5th
Mareth		5th
Wadi Zigzaou		5th
AKARIT		5th
Djebel Roumana		5th
North Africa, 1940	2nd	
North Africa, 1941	2nd	
North Africa, 1942	2nd	5th
North Africa, 1943		5th
Francofonte		5th
Adrano		5th
Sferro Hills		5th
Sicily, 1943		5th
Cassino I	2nd	
Poggio del Grillo	2nd	
GOTHIC LINE	2nd	
Tavoleto	2nd	
Coriano	2nd	
Pian di Castello	2nd	
Monte Reggiano	2nd	
Rimini Line	2nd	
San Marino	2nd	
Italy, 1944	2nd	
KOHIMA	1st	
Relief of Kohima	1st	
Naga Village	1st	
Aradura	1st	
Shwebo	1st	
MANDALAY	1st	
Ava	1st	
Irrawaddy	1st	
Mt Popa	1st	
Burma, 1944	1st	
Burma, 1945	1st	

BATTLE HONOURS SINCE WORLD WAR II

Since the end of World War II the regiment has earned the following Battle Honour:

GULF 1991   1st Battalion Queen's Own Highlanders

5. *THE COLOURS*

The Colours of the regiment are its most treasured and respected possession. They bear the Battle Honours awarded to the regiment, and the various badges and devices which have been granted to mark particular associations or honours.

When the 72nd, 78th and 79th Highlanders were raised in the 18th Century, the Colours were intended to be a conspicuous rallying point in battle, and their size was 6' x 6' 6", almost double the size of those carried today, and the pikes were 9' 10" long. The Colours today are 3' 9" x 3' and the pikes, including the Royal Crest, are 8' 7½"

Until 1857 the Colours were provided by the Colonel of the Regiment at his own expense, but since then they have been issued at public expense.

The Colours of 1st Battalion Queen's Own Highlanders Seaforth and Camerons

(Note – The Battle Honour 'GULF 1991' was added to the Regimental Colour in 1991.)

The Queen's Colour

The Queen's Colour (termed the 'King's Colour' if the sovereign is a King) is the Union Flag. When Battle Honours were awarded after World Wars I and II, each regiment was allowed to select ten of its Battle Honours to the borne on the King's/Queen's Colour. The Queen's Colour of the Queen's Own Highlanders bears the Battle Honours borne on the Queen's Colours of the Seaforth Highlanders and the Cameron Highlanders.

The Regimental Colour

The Regimental Colour is made in the Facing colour of the regiment. The design for the Regimental Colour of the Queen's Own Highlanders was Buff with a Royal Blue fringe. In the centre, on a crimson background, is the regimental badge surrounded by the name of the regiment, and this is encircled by a wreath of thistles, roses and shamrocks, with the regimental motto *'Cuidich n' Righ'* at the foot.

The Regimental Colour also bears:

> The Cypher of HM Queen Victoria within the Garter, granted to The Queen's Own Cameron Highlanders by HM King George V in 1921.

> The Cypher and Coronet of HRH Prince Philip, Duke of Edinburgh, Colonel-in-Chief of the Queen's Own Highlanders from 1961 to 1994.

The Cypher and Coronet of HRH Prince Frederick Augustus, Duke of York and Albany, from whom the 72nd Duke of Albany's Own Highlanders derived their title in 1823.

The Sphinx superscribed 'EGYPT', the Battle Honour awarded to the 79th Cameron Highlanders for the regiment's service in the campaign in Egypt in 1801.

An Elephant superscribed 'ASSAYE', the Battle Honour awarded to the 78th Highlanders (Ross-shire Buffs) for the regiment's service at the Battle of Assaye in 1803.

The Battle Honour Honours awarded to the antecedent regiments before World War I.

The Battle Honour 'Gulf 1991' awarded to the Queen's Own Highlanders.

The last recorded occasion on which the Colours of the regiment were carried in action was during the campaign in Afghanistan 1878-1880, when the 72nd Duke of Albany's Own Highlanders carried their Colours at the battle of Charasiah on 6th October 1879.

The Colours of 1st Battalion Queen's Own Highlanders
at Grantown on Spey, 1990

THE COLOURS OF THE REGIMENT

1st Battalion SEAFORTH HIGHLANDERS (and its predecessors)

Stand	Year presented	Presentation	Present location (in 1998)
		78th (later 72nd) Highlanders	
1st	1778	Provided by the Earl of Seaforth. Taken into service in Edinburgh.	(Not known)
		72nd Highlanders	
2nd	1787	Provided by Maj Gen James Murray, Colonel of the Regiment. Taken into service in India.	(Not known)
3rd	1800	Provided by Lt Gen James Stuart, Colonel of the Regiment. Presented at Perth by Lt Col Hugh Fraser of Knockie.	(Not known)
		72nd Duke of Albany's Own Highlanders	
4th	1825	Provided by Lt Gen Sir John Hope, Colonel of the Regiment. Presented by Lady Hope at Bruntsfield Links, Edinburgh, 1st August 1842.	S U S Museum, Edinburgh Castle.
5th	1842	Provided by Lt Gen Sir Colin Campbell, Colonel of the Regiment. Presented by FM the Duke of Wellington at Windsor Castle, 26th January 1842.	Garrison Church, Fort George.
6th	1857	Presented by HRH the Duke of Cambridge at Shorncliffe, 24th August 1857.	Windsor Castle
		1st Battalion Seaforth Highlanders	
7th	1884	Presented by HM Queen Victoria at Osborne, 16th August 1884.	S N War Memorial, Edinburgh Castle.
8th	1911	Presented by HM King George V at Delhi, 11th December 1911.	St Giles's Church, Elgin.
9th	1958	Presented by FM Sir Gerald Templer, Chief of the Imperial General Staff, at Münster, West Germany, 14th August 1958. Carried by 1st Battalion Queen's Own Highlanders from 1961 to 1964.	Garrison Church Fort George.
		2nd/72nd Highlanders	
1st	1805	Provided by Lt Gen James Stuart. Carried until 1815.	King's Colour - (Not known) Regimental Colour - S U S Museum, Edinburgh Castle.

2nd Battalion SEAFORTH HIGHLANDERS (and its predecessors)

78th Highlanders

1st	1793	Provided by Col Francis H Mackenzie of Seaforth. Taken into service at Fort George.	Garrison Church Fort George.
2nd	C 1801	Provided by Maj Gen A Mackenzie-Fraser. Taken into service in India.	(Not known)
3rd	1818	Provided by Maj Gen Sir Samuel Auchmuty. Taken into service in Ireland.	(Not known)
4th	1839	Provided by Lt Gen Paul Anderson Taken into service in Scotland.	S U S Museum Edinburgh Castle.
5th	1854	Provided by the estate of the late Lt Gen Paul Anderson. Taken into service in India.	S U S M Edinburgh Castle.
6th	1868	Presented at Montreal by Lady Windham, wife of Lt Gen Sir Charles Windham, Commander of the Forces in British North America, 30th May 1868.	Balmoral Castle.

2nd Battalion Seaforth Highlanders

7th	1899	Presented by HM Queen Victoria at Balmoral Castle on 29th September 1899	Garrison Church Fort George.
8th	1935	Presented by HRH The Prince of Wales, Colonel-in-Chief, at Dover on 5th July 1935.	Garrison Church Fort George.

2/78th Highlanders

1st	1794	Provided by Col Francis H Mackenzie of Seaforth Carried until 1797.	Garrison Church Fort George.
2nd	1804	Provided by Col A Mackenzie-Fraser. Carried from 1804-1816	S U S Museum Edinburgh Castle.

The ASSAYE Colour of the 78th Highlanders

1st	1803	Granted by the Government of India to the 78th Highlanders to commemorate the service of the 78th at the battle of Assaye.	(Not known)
2nd	1889	Replica purchased by the officers of 2nd Battalion Seaforth Highlanders.	Garrison Church Fort George.

1st Battalion THE QUEEN'S OWN CAMERON HIGHLANDERS (and its predecessors)

79th Cameron Highlanders

1st	1794	Provided by Major Alan Cameron of Erracht. Taken into service at Stirling in January 1794.	(Remnants) Regimental Museum Fort George.
2nd	1815	Provided by Maj Gen Alan Cameron of Erracht. Taken into service in Paris in 1815.	Regimental Museum Fort George.
3rd	1828	Provided by Lt Gen Sir Ronald Ferguson. Presented by Lady Douglas, wife of Colonel Sir Neil Douglas at Montreal, 18th June 1828.	Regimental Museum Fort George.
4th	1854	Provided by the Colonel of the Regiment. Taken into service at Portsmouth, 21st April 1854.	Balmoral Castle.
5th	1873	Presented by HM Queen Victoria at Parkhurst, 17th April 1873.	S N War Memorial Edinburgh Castle.

(Note: The green Regimental Colour was subsequently replaced by a Royal Blue Colour when the 79th became a Royal regiment as The Queen's Own Cameron Highlanders in 1873)
Green Regimental Colour in the Regimental Museum Fort George.

6th	1923	Presented by Gen Sir Havelock Hudson in Calcutta 9th January 1923.	Glasgow Cathedral
7th	1955	Presented by HM Queen Elizabeth at Balmoral, 30th May 1955. Carried by 1st Battalion Queen's Own Highlanders 1961-1964.	Garrison Church Fort George.

2nd Battalion THE QUEEN'S OWN CAMERON HIGHLANDERS (and its predecessors)

2nd/79th Cameron Highlanders

1st	1804	Provided by Col Alan Cameron of Erracht. Taken into service at Stirling. (Carried by the 1st Battalion at the battle of Waterloo)	Regimental Museum Fort George.

2nd Battalion The Queen's Own Cameron Highlanders

2nd	1898	Presented by HM Queen Victoria at Balmoral, 29th October 1898	S N War Memorial Edinburgh Castle.
3rd	1933	Presented by HRH the Duke of York at Aldershot, 14th July 1933.	Inverness Town Hall

1st Battalion
QUEEN'S OWN HIGHLANDERS (SEAFORTH AND CAMERONS)

1st Battalion Queen's Own Highlanders (Seaforth and Camerons)

1st	1964	Presented by HRH Prince Philip, Duke of Edinburgh, Colonel-in-Chief, at Holyrood, Edinburgh, 21st May 1964.	Garrison Church Fort George.
2nd	1983	Presented by HRH Prince Philip, Duke of Edinburgh, Colonel-in-Chief, at Tidworth, 23rd July 1983. Carried by 1st Battalion The Highlanders, 1994-1999.	Still in use (1998)

SEAFORTH HIGHLANDERS –
Militia, Territorial, and Service battalions

3rd (Militia) Battalion Seaforth Highlanders

-	1885	Presented by HRH the Duchess of Albany at Ballater on 30th September 1885.Fort George.	Garrison Church

4th (Territorial) Battalion Seaforth Highlanders

-	1909	Presented by HM King Edward VII at Windsor, on 19th June 1909. Carried by 4th/5th Battalion from 1920, and from 1947-1966 by 11th Battalion.	St Clement's Church Dingwall.

6th (Territorial) Battalion Seaforth Highlanders

-	1909	Gifted by Sir George Cooper and presented by the Duke of Richmond and Gordon at Elgin on 18th September 1909.	St Giles's Church Elgin

11th (Territorial) Battalion Seaforth Highlanders

-	1966	Presented by Gen Sir James Cassels, Chief of the Imperial General Staff, at Fort George on 14th July 1966. Carried by 2nd Bn 51st Highland Volunteers until 1986.	Fort George

7th (Service) Battalion Seaforth Highlanders

-	1919	King's Colour presented by Gen Sir Henry Plumer at Solingen, Germany on 19th February 1919.	Garrison Church Fort George.

8th (Service) Battalion Seaforth Highlanders

-	1919	King's Colour presented by Lt Gen Sir Richard Butler at Nivelles, Belgium on 10th February 1919.	Garrison Church Fort George.

9th (Service) Battalion Seaforth Highlanders (Pioneers)

-	1919	King's Colour presented by Brig Gen A H Marindin at Malmedy, Belgium on 10th June 1919.	Garrison Church Fort George.

10th (Service) Battalion Seaforth Highlanders

-	1919	King's Colour issued after the war, but not formally presented. Fort George.	Garrison Church

THE QUEEN'S OWN CAMERON HIGHLANDERS –
Militia, Territorial, and Service battalions

Inverness, Moray, Nairn, Banff Militia

1st   1803   Taken into service at Inverness.   Regimental Museum
Fort George.

3rd (Militia) Battalion The Queen's Own Cameron Highlanders

2nd   1909   Presented by Colonel The Mackintosh of Mackintosh   The Old High Church
at Fort George, 28th June 1909.   Inverness.

4th (Territorial) Battalion The Queen's Own Cameron Highlanders

1909   Gifted by Maj Gen J Spencer Ewart.   Fort George
Presented by HM King Edward VII at Windsor,
19th June 1909. Carried by 4th/5th Battalion 1947-1967, and
by 2nd Battalion 51st Highland Volunteers until 1985.

5th (Service) Battalion The Queen's Own Cameron Highlanders

1919   King's Colour presented by Gen Sir Henry Plumer   Destroyed when
at Solingen, Germany 19th February 1919.   Fort William Town
Hall was burnt down.

6th (Service) Battalion The Queen's Own Cameron Highlanders

1919   King's Colour presented by Lt Gen Sir Richard Butler   The Old High Church
at Braine-le-Compte, 21st January 1919.   Inverness.

7th (Service) Battalion The Queen's Own Cameron Highlanders

1919   King's Colour presented by HRH the Duke of York   The Old High Church
at Cameron Barracks, Inverness, 17th September 1920.   Inverness.

9th (Service) Battalion The Queen's Own Cameron Highlanders

1919   King's Colour presented by HRH the Duke of York   S N War Memorial
at Cameron Barracks, Inverness, 17th September 1920.   Edinburgh Castle.

11th (Service) Battalion The Queen's Own Cameron Highlanders

1919   King's Colour presented by Lt Gen Sir Beauvoir de Lisle   S N War Memorial
at Roubaix, 20th January 1919.   Edinburgh Castle.

THE LIVERPOOL SCOTTISH

1st/10th (Scottish) Battalion The King's (Liverpool) Regiment

1st   1909   Gifted by Lord Strathcona. Presented by   Liverpool Cathedral.
                HM King Edward VII at Knowsley, 5th July 1909

1st Battalion The Liverpool Scottish, The Queen's Own Cameron Highlanders TA

2nd   1938   Presented by HM King George VI   Still in use (1998) by
                at Everton Football Ground, 19th May 1938.   5/8 Kings TA.

2nd/10th (Scottish) Battalion The King's (Liverpool) Regiment

-      1919   King's Colour issued in 1919, but not formally presented.   S N War Memorial
                                                                           Edinburgh Castle.

2nd Battalion 51st HIGHLAND VOLUNTEERS TA

2nd Battalion 51st Highland Volunteers TA

-      1986   Presented by HRH Prince Philip Duke of Edinburgh,   Still in use (1998)
                Elgin, 26th June 1986.
                Carried by 3rd Battalion The Highlanders from 1994.

6. THE VICTORIA CROSS

The Victoria Cross is the highest award for gallantry for members of the armed services of Great Britain and the British Commonwealth. It takes precedence over all other decorations. Instituted by Royal Warrant on 29th January 1856, the medals are made from the bronze of Russian cannon captured at Sevastopol.

The Victoria Cross has been awarded to members of the regiment and its allied regiments on 30 occasions. They are listed in chronological order.

1.	**Lieut Andrew C Bogle**	78th Highlanders	29 July 1857	Oonao (Indian Mutiny)
2.	**Lieut Joseph P H Crowe**	78th Highlanders	12 August 1857	Boorbia (Indian Mutiny)
3.	**Lieut & Adjt Herbert T MacPherson**	78th Highlanders	25 September 1857	Lucknow (Indian Mutiny)
4.	**Surgeon Joseph Jee**	78th Highlanders	25/26 September 1857	Lucknow (Indian Mutiny)
5.	**Asst Surgeon Valentine M McMaster**	78th Highlanders	25 September 1857	Lucknow (Indian Mutiny)
6.	**C/Sgt Stewart McPherson**	78th Highlanders	26 September 1857	Lucknow (Indian Mutiny)
7.	**Pte Henry Ward**	78th Highlanders	25/26 September 1857	Lucknow (Indian Mutiny)
8.	**Pte James Hollowell**	78th Highlanders	26 September 1857	Lucknow (Indian Mutiny)
9.	**Lieut Aylmer S Cameron**	72nd Highlanders	30 March 1858	Kotah (Indian Mutiny)
10.	**L/Cpl George Sellar**	72nd Highlanders	14 December 1879	Kabul (Afghanistan)
11.	**Sgt John Mackenzie, DCM**	Seaforth	6 June 1900	Doompassi (Ashanti)
12.	**Sgt Donald D Farmer**	1st Camerons	13 December 1900	Nooitgedacht (South Africa)
13.	**Pte Ross Tollerton**	1st Camerons	14 September 1914	Aisne (World War I)
14.	**Lt Col Angus F Douglas-Hamilton**	6th Camerons	25/26 September 1915	Loos (World War I)
15.	**Cpl James D Pollock**	5th Camerons	27 September 1915	Loos (World War I)
16.	**Cpl Sidney Ware**	1st Seaforth	6 April 1916	Mesopotamia (World War I)
17.	**Dmr Walter Ritchie**	2nd Seaforth	1 July 1916	Somme (World War I)
18.	**L/Sgt Thomas Steele**	1st Seaforth	22 February 1917	Mesopotamia (World War I)
19.	**Lieut Donald Mackintosh**	2nd Seaforth	11 April 1917	Arras (World War I)
20.	**Sgt Alexander Edwards**	6th Seaforth	31 July-1 August 1917	Ypres (World War I)
21.	**L/Cpl Robert McBeath**	5th Seaforth	20 November 1917	Cambrai (World War I)
22.	**Sgt John M Meikle, MM**	4th Seaforth	20 July 1918	Marfaux (World War I)

LIVERPOOL SCOTTISH

23.	**Capt Noel G Chavasse, MC**	1st Liverpool Scottish	9 August 1916	Somme (World War I)
24.	**Capt Noel G Chavasse, VC, MC**	1st Liverpool Scottish	31 July-2 August 1917	Ypres (World War I)

ALLIED REGIMENTS

25.	**Sgt Donald F Brown**	2nd Inf Bn NZF	15 September 1916	Somme (World War I)
26.	**Capt Thain W McDowell**	38th Bn CEF	9-13 April 1917	Vimy Ridge (World War I)
27.	**Lieut Robert Shankland, DCM**	43rd Bn CEF	26 October 1917	Ypres (World War I)
28.	**Sgt Richard C Travis, DCM, MM**	Otago Regt NZF	24 July 1918	Hébuterne (World War I)
29.	**Pte Claud J P Nunney, DCM, MM**	38th Bn CEF	1-2 September 1918	Drocourt Quéant (World War I)
30.	**Pte Ernest A Smith**	Seaforth of Canada	22 October 1944	Italy (World War II)

7. CAMPAIGN MEDALS

CAMPAIGN MEDALS BEFORE 1881

MEDAL	CLASPS	REGIMENTS WHICH QUALIFIED	
Military General Service Medal – 1793-1814	_Egypt_ _Maida_ _Corunna_ _Talavera_ _Busaco_ _Fuentes d'Onor_ _Java_ _Salamanca_ _Pyrenees_ _Nivelle_ _Nive_ _Toulouse_	2/78th (1806) 78th (1811)	79th (1801) 79th (1809) Det 79th (1809) 79th (1810) 79th (1811) 79th (1812) 79th (1813) 79th (1813) 79th (1813) 79th (1814)
Army of India Medal – 1799-1826	_Assaye_ _Argaum_ _Gawilghur_	78th (1803) 78th (1803) 78th (1803)	
Waterloo Medal – 1815			79th (1815)
South Africa Medal – 1834-1853	72nd (1835)		
Crimean War Medal – 1854-1856	_Alma_ _Balaclava_ _Sevastopol_	72nd (1855)	79th (1854) 79th (1854) 79th (1854-55)
Turkish Crimea Medal – 1855	72nd (1855)		79th (1855)
India General Service Medal – 1854-1895	_Persia_ _North West Frontier_	78th (1856-57)	79th (1863, 1868)
Indian Mutiny Medal – 1857-1858	_Defence of Lucknow_ _Lucknow_ _Central India_	72nd (1858)	78th (1857) 78th (1857-58) 79th (1858)
Ashantee War Medal – 1873-1874	_Coomassie_		Draft 79th (1874)
2nd Afghan War Medal – 1878-1880	— _Peiwar Kotal_ _Charasiah_ _Kabul_ _Kandahar_	72nd (1878) 72nd (1879) 72nd (1879) 72nd (1880)	78th (1879-80)
Kabul to Kandahar Star – 1880	72nd (1880)		

CAMPAIGN MEDALS – 1881-1914 – REGULAR BATTALIONS

MEDAL	CLASPS	REGULAR BATTALIONS WHICH QUALIFIED		
Egypt Medal – **1882-1889**	*Tel-el-Kebir* *Nile 1884-1885*	1 Seaforth (1882)	2 Seaforth (two coys 1882)	1 Camerons (1882) 1 Camerons (1884-85)
Khedive's Egypt Star – **1882-1891**		1 Seaforth (1882)	2 Seaforth (two coys 1882)	1 Camerons (1882)
India General Service **Medal – 1854-1895**	*Hazara 1888* *Hazara 1891*		2 Seaforth (1888) 2 Seaforth (1891)	
India General Service **Medal – 1895-1902**	*Relief of Chitral*		2 Seaforth (1895)	
Queen's Sudan Medal – **1896-1898**		1 Seaforth (1898)		1 Camerons (1898)
Khedive's Sudan Medal – **1896-1908**	*Atbara* *Khartoum*	1 Seaforth (1898) 1 Seaforth (1898)		1 Camerons (1898) 1 Camerons (1898)
Queen's South Africa **Medal – 1899-1902**	*Cape Colony* *Paardeberg* *Orange Free State* *Driefontein* *Transvaal* *Johannesburg* *Diamond Hill* *Wittebergen* *South Africa 1901* * *South Africa 1902* *		2 Seaforth (1899-1902) 2 Seaforth (1900) 2 Seaforth (1900-1902) 2 Seaforth (1900) 2 Seaforth (1900-1902) 2 Seaforth (1900) 2 Seaforth (1901) 2 Seaforth (1902)	1 Camerons (1900-02) 1 Camerons (1900-02) 1 Camerons (1900-02) 1 Camerons(1900) 1 Camerons (1900) 1 Camerons (1900) 1 Camerons (1901) 1 Camerons (1902)
King's South Africa **Medal – 1901-1902**	*South Africa 1901* * *South Africa 1902* *		2 Seaforth (1901) 2 Seaforth (1902)	1 Camerons (1901) 1 Camerons (1902)
India General Service **Medal – 1908-1935**	N W Frontier 1908	1st Seaforth (1908)		

* Note – The **'*South Africa 1901*'** and **'*South Africa 1902*'** clasps could be added to either the Queen's South Africa Medal or the King's South Africa Medal, depending on individual entitlement.

CAMPAIGN MEDALS SINCE 1914 – REGULAR BATTALIONS

MEDAL	CLASPS	REGULAR BATTALIONS WHICH QUALIFIED				
1914 Star		1 Seaforth	2 Seaforth	1 Camerons		
1914-15 Star					2 Camerons	
British War Medal – **1914-1918**		1 Seaforth	2 Seaforth	1 Camerons	2 Camerons	
Victory Medal – **1914-1919**		1 Seaforth	2 Seaforth	1 Camerons	2 Camerons	
India General Service Medal 1908-1935	*N W Frontier –* *1930-31*		2 Seaforth (1930-31)			
General Service Medal –1918-62	*Palestine*	1 Seaforth (1936)			2 Camerons (1936)	
1939-1945 Star		1 Seaforth	2 Seaforth	1 Camerons	2 Camerons	
Africa Star			2 Seaforth		2 Camerons	
Burma Star		1 Seaforth		1 Camerons		
Italy Star			2 Seaforth		2 Camerons	
France & Germany Star			2 Seaforth			
War Medal		1 Seaforth	2 Seaforth	1 Camerons	2 Camerons	
Defence Medal		1 Seaforth	2 Seaforth	1 Camerons	2 Camerons	
General Service Medal –1918-62	*S E Asia –* *1945-46* *Malaya* *Arabian* *Peninsula* *Brunei*	1 Seaforth (1945-46) 1 Seaforth (1948-51)		1 Camerons (1956-58)		1 QO HLDRS (1962-63)
General Service Medal –1962	*Borneo* *Northern Ireland*					1 QO HLDRS (1962-63) 1 QO HLDRS (1969-94) 1 HLDRS (1994 –)
Gulf War Medal	*Gulf 1991*					1 QO HLDRS (1991)

CAMPAIGN MEDALS BEFORE 1914 – MILITIA AND VOLUNTEERS

MEDAL	BATTALIONS, COMPANIES, DETACHMENTS WHICH QUALIFIED	
Queen's South Africa† Medal – 1899-1902	Seaforth Vol Coys	Cameron Vol Coy Lovat Scouts
King's South Africa† Medal – 1901-1902	Seaforth Vol Coys	Cameron Vol Coy Lovat Scouts Liverpool Scottish Det
Queen's Mediterranean Medal – 1899-1902	3rd (Militia) Seaforth (1900-01)	

† (Note. The Volunteer companies and detachments were used to reinforce Regular battalions in South Africa, and individual entitlements to clasps vary widely.)

CAMPAIGN MEDALS SINCE 1914 – TERRITORIAL AND SERVICE BATTALIONS

MEDAL	TERRITORIAL AND SERVICE BATTALIONS WHICH QUALIFIED			
1914 Star	1/4 Seaforth		1/10 Liverpool Scottish	
1914-15 Star	1/5 Seaforth 1/6 Seaforth 7 Seaforth 8 Seaforth 9 Seaforth	1/4 Camerons 5 Camerons 6 Camerons 7 Camerons		1/1 Lovat Scouts 1/2 Lovat Scouts
British War Medal – 1914-1918	1/4 Seaforth 1/5 Seaforth 1/6 Seaforth 7 Seaforth 8 Seaforth 9 Seaforth 1 Gar Bn Seaforth	1/4 Camerons 5 Camerons 6 Camerons 7 Camerons 9 Camerons 11 Camerons	1/10 Liverpool Scottish 2/10 Liverpool Scottish	1/1 Lovat Scouts 1/2 Lovat Scouts 10 Camerons

Victory Medal – 1914-1919	1/4 Seaforth 1/5 Seaforth 1/6 Seaforth 7 Seaforth 8 Seaforth 9 Seaforth 1 Gar Bn Seaforth	1/4 Camerons 5 Camerons 6 Camerons 7 Camerons 9 Camerons 11 Camerons	1/10Liverpool Scottish 2/10 Liverpool Scottish	1/1 Lovat Scouts 1/2 Lovat Scouts 10 Camerons
Territorial War Medal for Service Overseas		2/10 Liverpool Scottish		
1939-1945 Star	4 Seaforth 5 Seaforth 6 Seaforth 7 Seaforth	4 Camerons 5 Camerons		Lovat Scouts
Africa Star	5 Seaforth	5 Camerons		
Italy Star	5 Seaforth 6 Seaforth	5 Camerons		Lovat Scouts
France & Germany Star	5 Seaforth 6 Seaforth 7 Seaforth	5 Camerons		
War Medal	4 Seaforth 5 Seaforth 6 Seaforth 7 Seaforth 8 Seaforth 9 Seaforth	4 Camerons 5 Camerons 6 Camerons 7 Camerons 1 Liverpool Scottish 2 Liverpool Scottish		Lovat Scouts
Defence Medal	4 Seaforth 5 Seaforth 6 Seaforth 7 Seaforth 8 Seaforth 9 Seaforth	4 Camerons 5 Camerons 6 Camerons 7 Camerons 1 Liverpool Scottish 2 Liverpool Scottish		Lovat Scouts

8. DRESS OF THE QUEEN'S OWN HIGHLANDERS

1st Battalion Queen's Own Highlanders on parade in Osnabruck, 1976.

The Highland regiments, more than any other part of the British Army, have managed to preserve a distinctive form of dress. To anyone unfamiliar with the Scottish regiments the variety of uniform, badges, tartans, and accoutrements is often bewildering. Yet the dress of a regiment, and the occasions when it is worn, is methodically laid down in Regimental Standing Orders, and these are only varied on the authority of the Colonel of the Regiment.

The dress of the Queen's Own Highlanders was a rich inheritance, being a combination of that worn by the Seaforth Highlanders and The Queen's Own Cameron Highlanders before the amalgamation of 1961. The notes in this book put on record the dress worn by the Queen's Own Highlanders, and give some of the background to how the various items evolved.

On the further amalgamation of the Queen's Own Highlanders with the Gordon Highlanders in 1994, a new dress was evolved for The Highlanders, which once again sought to retain in the new regiment the many historic features worn by its antecedents.

TARTANS

The dress worn by the army has always been closely controlled by the War Office Clothing Board, and in recent times by the Army Dress Committee. The principle has always been that variations are not permitted without good reason and economical justification. The history and design of military tartan is therefore well established and relatively easy to follow; there is none of the conjecture surrounding the history of civilian clan and family tartans.

The Queen's Own Highlanders used two principal tartans: the 78th or Mackenzie of Seaforth, and the 79th or Cameron of Erracht. Both have been worn continuously, and without significant variation in sett, since 1793.

The 78th, or Mackenzie of Seaforth Tartan

Although there is no documentary record of the origin of the 78th tartan, it is generally accepted that the tartan was designed for the 78th Highlanders when they were raised by Colonel Francis Humberston Mackenzie in 1793.

There is no evidence that it was used by earlier Mackenzie regiments, for example the 72nd Highlanders when they were raised in 1778.

When the Highland regiments were raised in the 18th century, the normal dress was the kilt of the Government tartan, originally made for the Highland Independent Companies which became the Black Watch. But as further Highland regiments were raised, their Colonels sought to establish regimental identities by introducing distinctive regimental tartans. The easiest way to do this was to introduce variations into the Government tartan.

The 78th Highlanders simply added red and white stripes to the Government tartan, and it is possible that the idea came from the colours of the red and white hose worn by the Highland regiments. The result has been known for over two hundred years as the 78th or Mackenzie of Seaforth tartan. This well known and distinctive tartan was used by many of the Fencible, Militia and Volunteer regiments raised in Ross-shire, and was widely termed the 'Ross-shire Military Tartan'. The civilian Mackenzie tartan is derived from it.

The 78th or Mackenzie of Seaforth tartan was worn as the kilt by all ranks of the Queen's Own Highlanders, except for pipers, drummers, and military bandsmen who wore it as trews. Since 1994 it has been worn as trews by all ranks of The Highlanders.

The 79th, or Cameron of Erracht Tartan

The 79th tartan is unique in being the only regimental tartan dating from the 18th century which is not derived from the Government or Black Watch tartan. It is said to have been designed for the 79th by Mrs Marjory Cameron of Erracht, mother of Major Alan Cameron of Erracht who raised the regiment. She was born a MacLean of Drimnin, and there have been theories that she devised the 79th tartan by combining two or more clan tartans, such as the Cameron, MacLean or MacDonald. But it is now accepted that no rigid system of clan tartans as such existed in 1793, and that they did not evolve until the early 19th century. It is therefore more likely that she used a design that was popular at the time in Lochaber. The tartan includes the 'Clan Donald motif', a feature in common use by weavers in the west Highlands from earliest times, and not confined to any clan or district. Thus it is arguable that the 79th tartan is, in fact, older than the various clan tartans from which it is sometimes assumed to have been derived.

There are also three recognised Cameron tartans in civilian use, but none has any similarity to the 79th tartan. The Clan Cameron tartan, which is predominantly red, was first illustrated in 1842; the 'Hunting' Cameron, predominantly green and less conspicuous, was introduced in 1956 as being more suitable for sporting wear on the hill; the Cameron of Lochiel tartan, the personal tartan of the Chief and his family, is known to date back at least to 1810.

The 79th or Cameron of Erracht tartan has been in continuous use by the regiment since 1793, and remains solely a regimental tartan. It was worn by the Queen's Own Highlanders as the tartan patch in the Balmoral bonnet, as the kilt and plaid by pipers, drummers and military bandsmen, and as trews by the remainder of the regiment. Since 1994 The Highlanders have worn it as the tartan patch in the Balmoral bonnet, and as the kilt and plaid worn by pipers and drummers.

OTHER TARTANS FORMERLY USED BY THE REGIMENTS

The Government or Black Watch Tartan

It is believed that when the Earl of Seaforth raised the 78th (later 72nd) Highlanders in 1778, he dressed his regiment in the Government or Black Watch tartan. The earliest reference to it is in the account books of the tartan manufacturers which mention supplies of 'black, blue and green tartan for the 72nd'. In 1809 the 72nd was one of the five Highland regiments which was deprived of the Highland dress and status, and thus ceased to wear the Government tartan.

The Royal Stuart Tartan – Prince Charles Edward sett

When the 72nd was restored to the status of a Highland regiment in 1823 as the 72nd (or Duke of Albany's Own) Highlanders, it was authorised to resume the Highland dress. In deference to the Commander-in-Chief of the Forces HRH Prince Frederick Augustus, Duke of York and Albany, from whom came the regiment's new designation, the 72nd adopted the Royal Stuart tartan.

The design of the 72nd's uniform owed much to the public interest in Highland dress aroused by King George IV's visit to Scotland the previous year. The regiment wore trews of Royal Stuart tartan in the Prince Charles Edward sett, except for the pipers who wore it as the kilt. According to tradition the tartan had been worn by Prince Charlie when he occupied the Palace of Holyrood after his Jacobite army captured Edinburgh in 1745. It is identical to the normal Royal Stuart, except that the red background stripes are reduced in width.

The 72nd Highlanders wore the Prince Charles Edward sett from 1824 until, under the Army Reforms of 1881, they were amalgamated with the 78th Highlanders to become the Seaforth Highlanders, and became a kilted regiment again. Both the 72nd and 78th had originated as Mackenzie regiments, and so it was natural that the Seaforth Highlanders should wear the kilt of Mackenzie tartan.

The Royal Stuart tartan of the 72nd was commemorated in the ribbons carried on the drones of the pipes by pipers of the Queen's Own Highlanders.

The Royal Stuart Tartan

In the early days of the Highland regiments the Royal Stuart tartan, being predominantly red and therefore somewhat flamboyant, was sometimes used as the 'musick tartan' for the military bands which were raised and maintained by the officers at their own expense. The 'band of musick' of the 78th Highlanders wore the Royal Stuart tartan shortly after the regiment was raised in 1793. Latterly the tartan has become associated with the Royal family, and now it is only worn by Scottish regiments which have received Royal authority to do so.

In 1943 HM King George VI honoured The Queen's Own Cameron Highlanders in this way when, as Colonel-in-Chief, he ordered that the pipers should be dressed in the Royal Stuart tartan, to mark the 150th anniversary of the raising of the 79th Cameron Highlanders. On the amalgamation of the Cameron Highlanders and the Seaforth Highlanders in 1961, the pipers of the Queen's Own Highlanders reverted to the 79th or Cameron of Erracht tartan.

TARTANS OF THE MILITIA REGIMENTS

The Militia regiments, from their formation in the Napoleonic wars until the mid 19th century, wore normal Line infantry uniform, and so had no particular associated tartans. After the introduction of voluntary service in 1852, the Militia regiments started to adopt Highland dress, depending on the interest of the officers who commanded them.

The Ross-shire Militia. From the time of its redesignation in 1860 as the Highland Rifle Militia, the Ross-shire Militia wore the Mackenzie tartan.

The Inverness Militia. From its revival by Lord Lovat in 1855 and redesignation as The Highland Light Infantry Militia, the Inverness Militia wore the Hunting Fraser tartan. In 1881, when the regiment became the 3rd (Militia) Battalion The Queen's Own Cameron Highlanders, it changed to the dress and tartan of the Cameron Highlanders.

TARTANS OF THE RIFLE VOLUNTEERS

In the early years of the Rifle Volunteers the companies enjoyed a marked degree of autonomy, some favoured tartan and Highland dress, while others preferred simple, inexpensive uniform. Much depended on what the volunteers were prepared to spend on their dress. On the consolidation of the companies into battalions, their dress eventually became standardised.

Ross-shire Rifle Volunteers. From 1873 the battalion adopted the Mackenzie tartan of the 78th Highlanders, as the accepted military tartan of Ross-shire .

Sutherland Rifle Volunteers. From 1867 most companies adopted the kilt of Government tartan, but it was worn pleated in the style of the 93rd Sutherland Highlanders to show the green, instead of the blue pleats of the Black Watch kilt. The Sutherland kilt remained in use after 1881, despite the fact that the Sutherland Rifle Volunteers became a Volunteer battalion of the Seaforth Highlanders.

Moray Rifle Volunteers. Apart from the Carr Bridge Company which wore the kilt of Grant tartan, the Moray Rifle Volunteers did not adopt the Highland dress until after they had become a Volunteer battalion of the Seaforth Highlanders in 1881. They adopted trews of the Mackenzie tartan in 1886.

Inverness-shire Rifle Volunteers. The original companies wore a remarkable variety of dress, their tartans including Cameron of Erracht, Government, Celtic, Macpherson, Fraser, Mackintosh, and MacDonald of the Isles. The dress was standardised in 1880, when all companies adopted the kilt of Government tartan. Having become part of the Cameron Highlanders in 1881, the battalion changed to the dress and tartan of the Cameron Highlanders in 1893.

TARTANS OF THE TERRITORIAL BATTALIONS

Since the formation of the Territorial Force in 1908, the dress of the Territorial battalions has generally conformed with that of the Regular battalions. There are two historic exceptions among the Seaforth and Cameron Territorial battalions.

The Sutherland Tartan. When the Sutherland Rifle Volunteers became the 5th (Sutherland and Caithness) Battalion Seaforth Highlanders in 1908, the battalion did not adopt the tartan or dress of the Seaforth Highlanders, but continued to wear the Sutherland tartan, and to maintain its distinctive badges and accoutrements. The Sutherland tartan remained in use until the battalion was finally disbanded after World War II.

The Forbes Tartan. When the Liverpool Scottish were raised in 1900, the regiment adopted the kilt of Forbes tartan as a compliment to their first Commanding Officer Colonel Christopher Forbes Bell. The Liverpool Scottish continued to wear the kilt of Forbes tartan as a battalion of The Queen's Own Cameron Highlanders, and as a company of the 51st Highland Volunteers. Since 1992 V (Liverpool Scottish) Company has continued to wear the kilt of Forbes tartan as a company of 5th/8th Battalion The King's Regiment.

FACINGS

The term 'facings', used from the 17th century onwards, comes from the material used to 'face' or line a soldier's coat. For comfort and convenience the cuffs, lapels, and skirts of the red coats of the British infantry regiments could be worn turned back, thus showing the facings of the coats. Each regiment its own colour of facings, which were a valuable means of identification, particularly in the smoke and confusion of battle. The facing colour was also used as the background colour for the drums, for the silk of the Regimental Colour, and as a stripe in the centre of the sergeants' red sashes. The drummers, with their important role of passing orders on the battlefield by drum beat, wore coats of 'reversed colours' so that they could be easily identified; their coats being of the regimental facing colour and faced with red.

The facings of the 72nd Highlanders when they were raised in 1778 were yellow. The 78th Highlanders, raised in 1793, had buff facings, from which they derived their nickname 'the Ross-shire Buffs', which became their secondary title. When the 72nd and 78th Highlanders were amalgamated in 1881, the facings of the newly formed Seaforth Highlanders were yellow, following the general rule that all Scottish regiments, with the exception of Royal regiments, were to have yellow facings. However in 1899 the Seaforth Highlanders were allowed to revert to the pre-1881 buff facings of the 78th.

The facings of the 79th Cameron Highlanders from their raising in 1793 were green. However, when the regiment was redesignated the 79th Queen's Own Cameron Highlanders in 1873, the facings were altered to the Royal blue of a Royal regiment.

On the amalgamation of the Seaforth and the Camerons in 1961, the new regiment was allowed to perpetuate both tartans and both facings of the old regiments. The facings of the Queen's Own Highlanders were therefore Royal blue and buff. These unique facings were seen in the Regimental Colour of buff silk fringed with Royal blue, in the Royal blue background of the drums, on the pipe banners which were buff on the obverse and Royal blue on the reverse, on the officers mess jackets with their blue collars and cuffs and buff lapels, and in the blue and buff bugle cords of the drummers.

On the amalgamation of the Queen's Own Highlanders and the Gordon Highlanders in 1994, the facings selected for the Highlanders were yellow, the original facings of the 72nd and of the Gordons. The Royal blue and buff of the Queen's Own Highlanders remained prominent, being retained for the facings of the mess jackets and on the pipe banners of the regiment.

BADGES AND INSIGNIA

Badges of the Queen's Own Highlanders

Left hand column:-

Sporran badge

Buttons-

   Cairngorm, Large, Small

Officer's waist belt clasp

Officer's cross belt plate

Centre column:-

Officer's and Senior NCO's bonnet badge

Rank and file bonnet badge

Officer's kilt pin

Highland Brigade bonnet badge (1961-1970)

Right hand column:-

Collar badges

Shoulder title

Soldier's waist belt plate

Bandsman's plaid brooch

The Badge of the Queen's Own Highlanders

The badge of the Queen's Own Highlanders is officially described as:

> **'A stag's head caboshed, between the attires the Thistle ensigned with the Crown, with the motto *Cuidich 'n Righ'*.**

The 'Thistle ensigned with the Imperial Crown' was the Badge of Scotland, as sanctioned by Queen Anne in 1707. The regiment has used it since 1873, when HM Queen Victoria granted it to the 79th Cameron Highlanders and commanded that the regiment should in future be styled the 79th Queen's Own Cameron Highlanders.

The stag's head 'caboshed' (a heraldic term meaning cut off to show no part of the neck) comes from the Arms of the Mackenzies of Seaforth. There are two possible explanations of how the Arms and the Gaelic motto *Cuidich 'n Righ* originated. Tradition has it that in the 13th century King Alexander III of Scotland was unhorsed while hunting deer in the Forest of Mar, and was attacked by an angry stag. His life was saved by Colin, the feudal lord of Kintail who, with a shout of *Cuidich 'n Righ* -'Help the King', struck the stag such a blow behind the antlers with his sword that it severed the head and upper jaw from the body. An alternative, although possibly less romantic explanation is that the annual reddendo, or feudal tribute, which the Mackenzies of Seaforth were required to render to their sovereign, was a stag. From this derived the stag's head Coat of Arms used by the chiefs, the motto *Cuidich 'n Righ* translated as 'Tribute to the King', and the Gaelic patronym of the Mackenzie chiefs, *Cabar Feidh* – 'the Deer's Antlers'.

Both the 72nd and the 78th Highlanders were raised by the Mackenzies of Seaforth, and both regiments used the 'stag's head caboshed' on their badges and accoutrements. In the 72nd the stag's head was used with the motto '*Cabar Feidh*', while the 78th used the stag's head with the motto '*Cuidich 'n Righ*'. The 78th Highlanders used the motto '*Cuidich 'n Righ*' on their Colours and appointments from the earliest years of the regiment, using the old spelling of '*Rhi*'. This was altered to '*Righ*' by a War Office Order issued at the request of the 78th in April 1869.

The Thistle and Crown, the Badge of Scotland used by the Cameron Highlanders, combined with the stag's head caboshed and Gaelic motto of the Seaforth Highlanders, made up the uniquely distinctive badge of the Queen's Own Highlanders. On the further amalgamation of the Queen's Own Highlanders with the Gordon Highlanders in 1994, it became the badge of The Highlanders.

Bonnet Badges

As part of the administrative reforms of the early 1960s, the infantry regiments of the Line were grouped into brigades, and wore brigade cap badges. From their formation in 1961 the Queen's Own Highlanders, in common with all the Highland regiments, wore the Highland Brigade badge. A regimental exception was the special pipers badge worn by the pipers of the Queen's Own Highlanders from 1961 to 1970.

When regimental cap badges were reintroduced in 1970, the Queen's Own Highlanders used two patterns of bonnet badge. Officers, warrant officers, and sergeants wore a three-piece silver or silver-plated badge, consisting of the Thistle and Crown, a three dimensional stag's head, and the scroll bearing the motto '*Cuidich 'n Righ*'. Rank and file wore a flat, two-piece badge made of anodised metal. The regimental badge was worn in the glengarry, the Balmoral bonnet, and in the feather bonnet worn by drummers and bandsmen. A woven version of the badge, in black thread on a green background, was worn on the front of the tropical hat while serving in the Far East in 1980-81.

On the amalgamation of the Queen's Own Highlanders and the Gordon Highlanders in 1994, the Queen's Own Highlanders badge became the bonnet badge of The Highlanders. All ranks of The Highlanders were issued at public expense with a white metal three piece badge, of the pattern previously worn by officers, warrant officers and sergeants of the Queen's Own Highlanders.

Collar badge

The collar badge used by all ranks of the Queen's Own Highlanders, when wearing the green No 1 dress or white No 3 dress tunic, was the 'Elephant superscribed Assaye', the badge and Battle Honour commemorating the service of the 78th Highlanders (Ross-shire Buffs) at the battle of Assaye in 1803. The same design of badge, in silver or white metal, was worn by all ranks; except for the Pipe Major, who wore the brass Elephant collar badge used by the Seaforth Highlanders before 1961.

Cross belt plate

The plate worn by officers on the white buff cross belt (or shoulder belt) with green No 1 dress or white tropical No 3 dress, was of turned brass with the regimental badge in silver mounted on it. It was also worn by the Regimental Sergeant Major and the Bandmaster.

Shoulder titles

The shoulder titles of the Queen's Own Highlanders were made of brass, with the letters 'QO HIGHLANDERS'. In combat uniform a cloth shoulder title with the same lettering was worn, the letters woven in black thread on olive green cloth. The shoulder titles worn by officers had the badge of rank woven in white thread above the regimental title.

Officers waist belt clasp

Officers of the Queen's Own Highlanders wore the waist belt clasp of the Cameron Highlanders, with the figure of St Andrew and his Cross surrounded by a wreath of thistles, mounted on an oval brass background. The same clasp was used with both the white buff belt on parade, and the embroidered dirk belt worn by field officers in mess dress. On the amalgamation of the Queen's Own Highlanders and the Gordon Highlanders in 1994, it became the officers waist belt clasp of The Highlanders.

Soldiers waist belt plate

The soldiers waist belt plate of the Queen's Own Highlanders was similar to that worn by the Cameron Highlanders. On the brass oblong plate was the bonnet badge of the Cameron Highlanders, with the figure of St Andrew and his cross as used in the badge of the Order of the Thistle. On the waist belt badge, however, the word 'CAMERON' on the scroll was replaced by 'WATERLOO'. On the amalgamation of the Queen's Own Highlanders and the Gordon Highlanders in 1994, it became the soldiers waist belt plate of The Highlanders.

Sporran badges

The white metal sporran badge worn by the Queen's Own Highlanders in the leather sporran, and in the hair sporran worn by soldiers, comprised the Thistle and Crown of the regimental badge.

The hair sporran worn by officers, Regimental Sergeant Major, Bandmaster, and Drum Major had a brass cantle engraved with thistles, from the officers' hair sporran of the Seaforth Highlanders, embellished with the regimental badge and the Cypher of HRH Prince Philip, Duke of Edinburgh, Colonel-in-Chief of the Queen's Own Highlanders.

Buttons

The buttons of the Queen's Own Highlanders have the regimental badge of the Thistle and Crown and the stag's head, but the scroll and motto are omitted. The reason for this is that, at the time of the amalgamation of Seaforth and Camerons, the process of producing buttons had to start early enough for them to be ready for the new regiment to wear on amalgamation day, 7th February 1961. The original design proposed for the badge did not include the scroll and motto, and the decision to add the scroll was taken after the die for the buttons had been made. On the amalgamation of the Queen's Own Highlanders and the Gordon Highlanders in 1994, the buttons became the pattern used by The Highlanders.

Pipers' and bandsmen's badges and insignia of the Queen's Own Highlanders

Left hand column:-
Rank and file bonnet badge
Brass shoulder title
Collar badges
Plaid brooch
*   (pipers and bandsmen)*

Centre column:-
Pipers' sword belt fittings -
*   Duke of Albany's star (72nd)*
*   Sword belt buckle (79th)*
*   Sword belt badge (79th)*
*   Sword belt slide (79th)*
*   Sword belt tip (79th)*

Right hand column:-
Pipers' bonnet badge (1961-1970)
Sporran badge
Buttons
Pipers' waist belt plate (1973-1994)

Pipers' bonnet badge (1961-1970)

During the years 1961 to 1970, when the Queen's Own Highlanders wore the Highland Brigade bonnet badge, the pipers wore a bonnet badge of regimental design. It comprised the Crown, St Andrew's Cross, belt and buckle of the regimental badge of the Cameron Highlanders, with the stag's head of the Seaforth Highlanders. The lettering on the belt was 'SEAFORTH AND CAMERONS'. The badge was discontinued after the reintroduction of regimental bonnet badges in 1970.

Pipers' buttons

The pipers wore the normal brass regimental buttons until 1987, when a new design of square button, in white metal with the regimental badge of the Queen's Own Highlanders, was introduced for pipers. It was based on the old patterns worn until amalgamation by pipers of the Seaforth and the Cameron Highlanders.

Pipers' and bandsmen's plaid brooch

The plaid brooch worn by pipers and bandsmen was designed for the Queen's Own Highlanders. The white metal ornaments on a brass circle included two devices from the Regimental Colour: the Cypher of HRH Prince Frederick, Duke of York and Albany, from whom the 72nd Duke of Albany's Own Highlanders took their title from 1823 to 1881; and the Sphinx awarded to the 79th Cameron Highlanders for service in Egypt in 1801. In the centre was a bar with the word ALAMEIN, the Battle Honour awarded to both Seaforth and Camerons for their distinguished service at the battle of El Alamein in 1942. The oak leaves came from the plant badge of Clan Cameron, which featured in the accoutrements of the Cameron Highlanders.

Pipers' waist belt plate

From 1961 to 1973 the pipers of the Queen's Own Highlanders wore the pipers' waist belt clasp of the Cameron Highlanders, an elegant white metal oval design with St Andrew and his cross. This was superseded in 1973 by an oblong white metal belt plate with the regimental badge of the Queen's Own Highlanders.

Pipers' sword belt fittings

The white metal ornaments on the black sword belts worn by the pipers of the Queen's Own Highlanders were of Seaforth and Cameron origins. At the top was the Duke of Albany's star of the 72nd Highlanders. Below the buckle was a small badge of the Cameron Highlanders. The buckle, slide, and tip came from the pipers' sword belts worn by the 79th Cameron Highlanders from the 1840s.

Pipe Major's and Drum Major's plaid brooches

The Pipe Major of the Queen's Own Highlanders wore an officer's plaid brooch of the Seaforth Highlanders, with the Thistle and Crown replacing the Duke of Albany's Cypher. The Drum Major wore a staff plaid brooch of The Queen's Own Cameron Highlanders.

Pipe Major's waist belt plate

The Pipe Major of the Queen's Own Highlanders wore an oblong waist belt plate, with the regimental badge on a thistle design.

Pipe Major's arm badge

The Pipe Major of the Queen's Own Highlanders normally wore an embroidered regimental badge on his right sleeve, above the badge of rank.

Pipe Major's plaid brooch, Queen's Own Highlanders.

Pipers', drummers' and bandsmen's arm badges

Pipers, drummers and bandsmen of the Queen's Own Highlanders wore the standard Army embroidered proficiency badges depicting bagpipes, drum, and lyre.

Kilt pin

The Seaforth Highlanders pattern of silver kilt pin was worn by officers, Regimental Sergeant Major, Pipe Major, Drum Major and Bandmaster of the Queen's Own Highlanders.

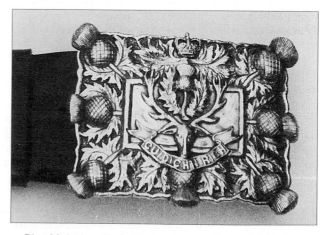

Pipe Major's waist belt plate, Queen's Own Highlanders.

KILT, TREWS, AND PLAIDS

Orders of dress, 1st Battalion Queen's Own Highlanders, 1976

The kilt

When the 72nd, 78th and 79th Highlanders were raised in the late 18th century, the standard dress for Highland soldiers was the belted plaid (Gaelic – *breacan an fhéilidh*), a single piece of tartan combining kilt and plaid. By about 1800 the Highland regiments had adopted the more practical little kilt or philibeg (Gaelic – *feile-beag*), similar to the kilt as worn today, although more roughly stitched together.

The 72nd Highlanders were originally raised as a kilted regiment, but in 1809, together with the 73rd, 74th, 75th, and 91st Highlanders, they were removed from the Highland establishment. They did not become kilted again until, after amalgamation with the 78th Highlanders in 1881, they became the 1st Battalion Seaforth Highlanders. The 78th Highlanders (Ross-shire Buffs) and the 79th Cameron Highlanders were both raised as kilted regiments and retained the kilt throughout their history.

On the amalgamation of the Seaforth and the Cameron Highlanders in 1961, the Queen's Own Highlanders remained a kilted regiment. Officers and men, except for pipers, drummers and bandsmen, wore the kilt of the 78th or Mackenzie of Seaforth tartan; while pipers, drummers and bandsmen wore the kilt of 79th or Cameron of Erracht tartan.

Trews

Trews (Gaelic – *triubhas*) were originally tight fitting breeks, made of tartan and cut on the cross. 'Trews', in the military usage of the Scottish regiments, are simply tartan trousers cut square, with a seam up the inside of the leg. They have been used in the Highland regiments for undress uniform since the 1830s, but have never been rated as more than a convenient and comfortable form of barrack dress. They are not a substitute for the principal dress of a Highland regiment, which is the kilt.

The Queen's Own Highlanders wore tartan trews for barrack duties, and in the evening after retreat. Officers and soldiers wore trews of 79th or Cameron of Erracht tartan, except for pipers, drummers, and bandsmen who wore trews of 78th or Mackenzie of Seaforth tartan: thus reversing the tartans worn as the kilt.

Belted plaid and fly plaid

The subject of plaids is confusing, because the term 'belted plaid' has two meanings. In its old sense it meant the *breacan an fhéilidh*, the double width plaid and kilt which the Highland regiments discontinued in about 1800. In its later sense 'belted plaid' refers to the piece of tartan which officers and soldiers continued to wear, fixed at the left shoulder.

The officers' belted plaid was fixed at the left shoulder with a plaid brooch, and was buckled round the waist with a strip of tartan, under the skirts of the coatee or doublet. It was worn in different orders of dress by both the Seaforth and the Cameron Highlanders. It was worn in the Queen's Own Highlanders by the Bandmaster, who wore an officer's belted plaid of 79th or Cameron of Erracht tartan.

The soldiers belted plaid, known as the fly plaid ('fly' may possibly come from the Gaelic – *feile*), was also fixed at the left shoulder by a loop of tape. Since full dress was discontinued in 1914, the fly plaid has only been worn by drummers. The drummers of the Queen's Own Highlanders wore the fly plaid of 79th or Cameron of Erracht tartan, and it is worn by the drummers of The Highlanders.

Full plaid (or scarf, shoulder plaid, big plaid)

From the 1820s officers of Highland regiments started to wear a scarf or full plaid in some orders of dress. It was fixed at the left shoulder with a plaid brooch, and ran across the chest under the right arm. It remained an item of full dress uniform until the 20th century.

From the mid-19th century the full plaid also became part of the full dress for pipers and bandsmen. It could be folded with the tartan on the cross. Latterly it was worn pleated square and with the pleats sewn in for regularity and convenience. The full plaid of 79th or Cameron of Erracht tartan was worn by pipers and bandsmen of the Queen's Own Highlanders. Since 1994 it has been worn by pipers of the Highlanders.

TUNICS, JERSEYS AND SHIRTS

The orders of dress for the Army are laid down in Army Clothing Regulations, but regiments produce their own detailed Regimental Standing Orders to take into account the dress of the particular regiment. The Queen's Own Highlanders based their regulations for different orders of dress on whichever tunic, shirt or jersey was worn.

No 1 dress tunic (green)

Until 1914 the full dress tunic of the Highland regiments was the scarlet doublet, except for pipers who wore green. After World War II a new ceremonial uniform was introduced termed 'Number 1 dress'. For Highland regiments this included a coatee of 'piper' green, with regimental buttons, collar badges, and facings on the tails of the coatee. Officers wore badges of rank on gilt shoulder cords.

*1st Battalion Queen's Own Highlanders in No 1 Dress
for the Farewell Parade of the regiment in 1994.*

No 6 dress (tropical shirt)

In tropical climates the standard army issue shirt, which varies according to the pattern in use at the time, can be worn with the kilt, shorts, or slacks as No 6 dress. The lst Battalion Queen's Own Highlanders normally produced local dress regulations to define the details of dress and the occasions when it was worn.

No 7 dress (red mess jacket)

Captain N F M Lamb   *Captain N G Smith*   *Sergeant R Towns*   *Colour Sergeant G Brown*
No 7A dress, 1976   *No 7 B Dress*   *No 7 A Dress*   *No 7 B Dress*

From the establishment of the Standing Army in 1660, the colour of the coats worn by British regiments of foot was red. Before full dress was discontinued in 1914, Highland regiments wore the red doublet and feather bonnet. The traditional red still survives in the mess dress jackets worn by officers, warrant officers and sergeants.

The mess dress jacket evolved from the red shell jacket, which was introduced in about 1830 for wear with undress uniform. It had a high collar, and was buttoned up to the neck. From the 1850s it became the custom, when dining in mess, to wear the jacket unbuttoned, to make a more comfortable uniform for wear when off duty. The jacket was worn with a white shirt and bow tie, with the collar turned down, and with a waistcoat of tartan or of the regimental facing colour.

Officers of the Queen's Own Highlanders wore a scarlet mess jacket with buff lapels, blue collar and cuffs, white piping, and gold braid shoulder cords. Miniature medals are worn with mess dress. The original waistcoat worn from 1961 was of 79th or Cameron of Erracht tartan, with three Cairngorm buttons as worn by the Seaforth Highlanders. But in the1990s the regiment reverted to the dark blue mess dress waistcoat of the Cameron Highlanders, with gold piping and five gilt buttons with St Andrew in silver.

The warrant officers and sergeants pattern of mess jacket was similar, but the lapels, collar and cuffs were buff, and it had no white piping. The waistcoat was of the 79th or Cameron of Erracht tartan, with three brass regimental buttons. Warrant officers and sergeants of the Pipes and Drums and the Regimental Band wore a waistcoat of Mackenzie tartan. The mess jacket and waistcoat are worn with the kilt or trews.

No 8 dress (white tropical mess jacket)

In tropical climates the red mess jacket is replaced by a white tropical mess jacket.

Sgt J Peddie in No 8 Dress
in 1969

No 9 dress (fatigue or working dress)

Private S Griffiths in No 9 dress, 1980.

Pioneer Sgt K Hunter in No 9 dress, 1980.

No 9 dress varies according to local conditions and may include khaki flannel shirt, overalls, denims, or protective clothing used when working on vehicles. The special clothing worn by cooks and butchers comes under this order of dress.

Other orders of dress

A number of other types of dress are used which are not covered by the numbered orders of dress. Examples are:

Full dress. Although full dress is officially obsolete, the drummers of the Queen's Own Highlanders wore the red doublet on regimental occasions. The red doublets were maintained at regimental expense, and had regimental buttons, blue collar and cuffs, buff epaulettes, and were worn with drummers' lace on the sleeves and wings on the shoulders.

Mess orderlies' dress. The officers mess steward wore a green tail coat with buff and blue striped waistcoat on formal occasions. Orderlies in the officers and sergeant's messes were normally dressed in a green coatee, modified to wear with a cummerbund and trews. The style varied from time to time.

HEAD DRESS

The feather bonnet

The feather bonnet has been worn by the Highland regiments since the 18th century, although its size and style have evolved from simple beginnings. The hat worn throughout the Highlands was the flat blue bonnet, a shapeless woollen cap, with strings or ribbons woven in and out for tightening it round the head. The earliest records of Highland military dress show the Black Watch, on their formation into a regiment in 1739, wearing this form of bonnet.

The blue bonnet was unimpressive compared with the headdress of the line regiments and the continental armies, and beside the tall mitre caps of the grenadier company. It therefore became the custom to 'cock' the bonnet by setting it up with stiffening material, to make the wearer appear taller. A further improvement was the addition of a diced headband, in imitation of the ribbons originally used for tightening the blue cap.

In the late 18th century the cocked bonnet was heightened still further by the addition of pieces of bearskin, and later with ostrich feathers, until the Highland regiments had evolved their unique feathered bonnet for wear in dress uniform. The feather bonnet was worn cocked to the right, and on the left side was a coloured hackle with a regimental button on a black silk cockade, the distinguishing mark of the Hanoverian Army. Off duty, when the bonnet was worn as the undress cap, it was worn without the feathers, being termed the 'hummel' bonnet; from the word for a stag with no antlers.

After the Napoleonic wars the feather bonnet developed into a much larger form, and later in the 19th century it developed into a wire cage, covered with blue cloth, over which the feathers were fixed. Regiments had their own styles, and both Seaforth and the Cameron Highlanders wore the feather bonnet with five 'foxtails' of ostrich feathers, and with red, white and green dicing. The feather bonnet was worn by all ranks in the Highland regiments until full dress was discontinued in 1914. After World War I it was only worn in the Seaforth and the Cameron Highlanders by drummers and bandsmen, or on occasions such as the Aldershot Tattoo.

During the 20th Century, the enormous spread of pipe bands, beyond the Scottish regiments where they originated, has resulted in the feather bonnet becoming a Scottish national headdress, rather than just the headdress of the Highland soldier. The feather bonnet was worn by drummers and bandsmen of the Queen's Own Highlanders, and is now worn by drummers of The Highlanders.

The glengarry

The 'glengarry' takes its name from the style of bonnet devised by Colonel Alasdair Ranaldson MacDonell of Glengarry for his 'tail' of clansmen, who attended the visit to Edinburgh of King George IV in 1822. The normal Highland headgear at the time was the practical, but unimpressive, flat blue bonnet. To make his retainers look more distinctive, Glengarry dressed them in cocked bonnets.

The glengarry was first introduced to the British army in 1840 by Lieutenant Colonel the Hon Lauderdale Maule, Commanding Officer of the 79th Cameron Highlanders. The Highland regiments at the time wore the hummel bonnet, the blue woollen hat which had to be set up for use on parade by the addition of ostrich feathers. The hummel bonnet, when worn off parade in undress uniform, was an unshapely horror, incompatible with military smartness and style. Colonel Maule's answer was to introduce the glengarry as the undress bonnet of the 79th. Higher in the crown than the present day glengarry, it could be tailored and shaped into a smart upright shape, and could also be carried flat in the haversack. Colonel Maule's idea soon caught on, and the glengarry replaced the hummel bonnet for undress use in the Highland regiments. By the 1870s it was in universal use, even by English and Welsh line regiments.

Regiments developed their own individual styles by the addition of a wide variety of dicing, rosettes and ribbons. The Queen's Own Highlanders wore the plain blue glengarry with black ribbons, as worn by the Cameron Highlanders since 1840, with the black silk rosette from the diced pattern of glengarry worn by the Seaforth Highlanders.

Piper 79th Cameron Highlanders in 1852,
wearing two golden eagles' feathers in the glengarry

The regimental badge and the Royal blue hackle were worn with the glengarry, and pipers wore a golden eagle's feather in ceremonial dress.

On the amalgamation of the Queen's Own Highlanders with the Gordon Highlanders in 1994, the blue glengarry became the bonnet of The Highlanders

The balmoral bonnet (or 'Tam o' Shanter')

The term 'balmoral' bonnet originally referred in the mid-19th century to the blue Highland bonnet when worn flat, instead of the upright glengarry. The term 'Tam o' Shanter', abbreviated to 'TOS', seems to have been a War Office term for the older name balmoral. The two names refer to the same item of headdress. When the Highland regiments went to war in 1914 they wore the glengarry, but it was found to be so impractical for trench warfare, that they generally took to wearing a balaclava or a cap-comforter instead. In early 1915 a flat Highland bonnet was introduced to replace the glengarry. At first, there was no consistent pattern, and bonnets came in a wide variety of styles, with or without ribbons and toories, and ranging in colours from khaki to dark green or blue. By 1916 the standard headgear was a khaki bonnet with toorie. The balmoral was generally worn with a regimental badge and sometimes with a tartan patch.

After World War I the balmoral remained the bonnet worn for training and operations by the Scottish regiments. Since World War II the size of the balmoral bonnet has diminished, and the 'pork pie' to which it is now reduced bears little resemblance to the wide-brimmed, practical bonnet of the trenches in World War I.

The Queen's Own Highlanders wore the khaki balmoral bonnet with a square of 79th or Cameron of Erracht tartan, the regimental badge, and the Royal blue hackle. The badge and hackle could be removed on training or operations, when camouflage or security required. The Queen's Own Highlanders balmoral is worn by The Highlanders.

Hackles

The hackle worn in the feather bonnet was originally an aid to identification in battle. The Grenadier company, on the right of the line, could be identified by their plain white hackles. The Light Infantry company on the left of the line, or deployed as skirmishers, had green hackles, derived from the green camouflaged uniforms worn by the Light Infantry in the North America wars. The Battalion companies in the centre of the line wore hackles of red and white. In 1860-63 the light companies were abolished, and all companies were ordered to wear the white hackle.

There were regimental variations of these rules. Although a War Office letter of 1822 specifically ordered that the red vulture's feather was only to be worn by the 42nd Highlanders, the pipers of the 72nd wore a red hackle from 1823 until they took to wearing the glengarry in 1855. Pipers of the 78th the wore the feather bonnet with a green hackle until 1871, when they changed to the glengarry.

When tropical helmets were introduced for wear in hot climates in the 1870s, a small white hackle was normally worn with them. In the Seaforth Highlanders the pipers carried on the tradition of the 78th by wearing green hackles in their tropical helmets until World War II. Bandsmen of the Seaforth Highlanders, and drummers of the 1st Battalion, carried on the tradition of the 72nd and wore red hackles until 1951.

The Royal blue hackle

After the British Expeditionary Force had gone to France in 1939, the War Office ordered that 'the active service dress of Highland regiments would be the universal battle dress'. This order, which in effect brought an end to the wearing of the kilt by Highland soldiers in battle, caused much resentment in the Highland regiments. A similar order in 1914 had been successfully rescinded the same year, after a storm of Highland protest.

The Commanding Officer of the 1st Battalion The Queen's Own Cameron Highlanders, Lieutenant Colonel Douglas Wimberley (later Major General, and Colonel of the Regiment), appealed against the order in the strongest terms. A vigorous exponent of *esprit de corps*, he was convinced that a regiment should be distinctively dressed. Knowing that War Office decisions take time to alter, he had patches of 79th tartan sewn on the sleeves of the battledress jackets. He also considered that the hackle, as worn in the tropical helmet, would make the balmoral bonnet more distinctive.

On 5th December 1939 HM King George VI visited the British Expeditionary Force in the field, and the 1st Camerons paraded for their Colonel-in-Chief on the Belgian border. The battalion was still dressed in service dress and the kilt, and the King was noticably impressed. Seizing his opportunity, the Colonel Wimberley suggested to His Majesty that if the regiment was not to be allowed to retain the kilt, it should at least be allowed to wear a hackle behind the badge in the balmoral bonnet. The King approved of the idea, and also to the suggestion that the appropriate colour for a Royal regiment was Royal blue. 800 Royal blue hackles were quickly made, and were first worn at Arras on 11th February 1940. The 1st Camerons remained dressed in the kilt throughout the withdrawal to Dunkirk, the last battalion to wear the kilt in action.

After the 1st Camerons had withdrawn to Great Britain, the regiment had to await official War Office approval before the Royal blue hackle could be issued. Changes to dress regulations are of low priority in war time, and the hackle could only be worn by individual officers during the war. It was authorised in 1951 for use by the Cameron Highlanders with the balmoral bonnet, and in 1952 with the blue No 1 dress bonnet.

The Queen's Own Highlanders wore the Royal blue hackle in the glengarry and the balmoral bonnet. It was a proud reminder of the last battalion to wear the kilt in action against the enemy. The Royal blue hackle is worn by The Highlanders in the glengarry and the balmoral bonnet.

Golden eagle's feather

The golden eagle's feather was introduced for wear by the pipers of the 79th Cameron Highlanders by Lieutenant Colonel the Hon Lauderdale Maule in about 1841. The feather comes from the right wing of the golden eagle. The pipers of the Queen's Own Highlanders wore the eagle's feather in the glengarry in ceremonial dress.

Contemporary paintings from the 1850s sometimes show the pipers wearing two eagle feathers. On some occasions it was the practice in the Queen's Own Highlanders for the Pipe Major, when playing in mess, to follow the original custom of wearing two eagle feathers in his glengarry.

BELTS

The cross belt (or sword belt, shoulder belt)

In the early days of the regiment the sword was carried in a variety of ways. Field officers on horse back used a sabre, carried on a waist belt with slings. Flank company officers carried the broadsword on a shoulder belt with slings. Battalion company officers, sergeants, pipers, drummers and bandsmen carried the broadsword in a buff cross belt with a sword frog at the end.

All three patterns of belt survived in the No 1 dress of the Queen's Own Highlanders. Officers, the Regimental Sergeant Major and the Bandmaster wore the white buff cross belt (or shoulder belt) with the broadsword on two slings. The Drum Major carried the broadsword from a staff waist belt with two slings. Pipers wore the black cross belt with a sword frog, although they have not carried swords since 1872.

The Sam Browne belt

The 'Sam Browne' belt takes its name from its inventor General Sir Sam Browne, VC (1824-1901). An officer of the Indian cavalry, he won the Victoria Cross in 1858 during the Indian Mutiny campaign for his gallantry in charging and capturing a nine pounder rebel cannon, accompanied only by his orderly. In taking the cannon he lost his left arm, severed at the shoulder by a rebel gunner. On his recovery he found that, although he could still handle his sword and revolver effectively with only one arm, but that it was difficult to draw his sword, which was carried suspended from sword slings. In about 1860 he devised a leather belt with shoulder brace, sword frog, and holster, to carry sword and revolver more conveniently.

The belt soon became widely popular for use on active service. Officers had them made to their own specifications by saddlers, and there were many variations in style, with pouches, holsters, braces, whistles, and buckles arranged to suit individual taste. The officers of the 72nd and 78th first wore the Sam Browne belt with khaki drill jackets in the Afghanistan campaign of 1878-80. The officers of the 1st Camerons had Sam Browne belts made by the saddler in Gibraltar in 1882, before leaving for the Egyptian campaign. A standard pattern of Sam Browne belt was authorised for officers in Army Dress Regulations of 1900.

The Sam Browne belt is not well suited for carrying the Highland broadsword because of the size of the basket hilt, and so the basket hilt of the sword was often replaced by a small cross hilt. The Seaforth Highlanders generally preferred a pattern of Sam Browne with a slightly wider cross strap and heavier sword frog, because it was better suited to the broadsword. The same pattern is worn by the Household Cavalry.

Officers of the Queen's Own Highlanders used the Household Cavalry pattern of Sam Browne and sword frog when in No. 2 Service Dress, with the broadsword carried in a leather scabbard, and this pattern was adopted by The Highlanders.

White waist belt

A white waist belt, with regimental pattern waist belt plate, was worn with No 1 or No 2 dress, when on parade and on various other occasions.

Green waist belt

A green plastic waist belt, with regimental waist belt plate, was used by soldiers for daily wear in barracks with No 2 service dress jacket.

Tartan waist belt

Tartan waist belts, made under regimental arrangements, were worn with shorts or slacks in some orders of dress, both at home and in tropical stations. The tartan corresponded to the kilt, so that pipers, drummers and bandsmen wore belts of 79th or Cameron of Erracht tartan, while the remainder of the regiment wore belts of Mackenzie of Seaforth tartan.

Black waist belt

The black waist belt was originally part of the distinctive uniform worn by the regimental bandsmen, being intended to contrast with the white jacket which came into general use for bands in about 1830. From the early 1840s pipers too wore black waist belts with their distinctive green doublets. The pipers and bandsmen of the Queen's Own Highlanders wore the black waist belt. Pipers used their own pattern of waist belt plate, and bandsmen wore the normal regimental waist belt plate.

SASHES

Officers sash

The sash worn by officers was originally a mark of identification before uniform developed. In the 18th century the officers sash was large enough to be used as a sling for carrying a wounded officer off the battlefield, and a rather doubtful tradition asserts that its crimson colour was intended to minimise the discolouration caused by blood stains. The sash is used in No 1 dress by officers in Highland regiments, being worn over the left shoulder in the old tradition. The officers sash was also worn by the Regimental Sergeant Major and Bandmaster.

Sergeants sash

When the regiments were raised sergeants wore a crimson sash with a central stripe of the facing colour of the regiment: yellow for the 72nd, buff for the 78th, and green for the 79th. However the colours tended to run in wet weather, and this was discontinued in 1845. In 1856 the War Office ordered that sergeants should wear a worsted red sash over the right shoulder.

In the Queen's Own Highlanders the Pipe Major wore an officer's crimson sash. The Pipe Major and Pipe Sergeant followed the tradition of the Highland regiments by wearing the sash over the left shoulder, so that it crossed diagonally under the black sword belt.

Garters

Since the 18th century the Highland regiments have worn red garters. Originally worn round the top of the hose, with no turn-over, the garters were tied with a knot on the outside of the leg. After the Napoleonic Wars, as Highland dress became more ornamental, the garters were tied in elaborate garter knots, with loops and bows, and sometimes even including rosettes. During the war with Russia in 1854-1856, Highland regiments serving in the mud and snow of the Crimea adopted simpler patterns of garters. They were worn under the turnover of the hose, with only the ends showing as 'garter flashes'.

The Queen's Own Highlanders wore the red garter flashes of the pattern used by the Cameron Highlanders, except for the pipers who wore the Mackenzie garter flashes worn by pipers of the Seaforth Highlanders. The Mackenzie flashes are worn by pipers of The Highlanders.

Highland shoes

From the 18th century until World War I the Highland regiments wore black leather shoes. (The remainder of the infantry also wore shoes until 1823, when they were superseded by half boots.) Highland soldiers' shoes had ornamental brass buckles, and were worn alternately on left and right feet to keep the wear even. From the 1860s the buckles were discontinued, and the shoes were worn with spats on parade and active service . Although shoes remained the normal issue to Highland regiments, they often proved unsatisfactory for wear on active service in India and Africa, when boots were issued instead.

The Highland regiments went to France in World War I wearing shoes and khaki spats, but they proved most unsuitable for the muddy conditions of trench warfare in Flanders, and were soon replaced by ankle boots and short puttees.

The old style of buckled shoe, which survived as the pumps worn in levée dress, has vanished, but buckled shoes are still worn by officers and sergeants in mess dress, and by pipers when wearing long hose.

The present pattern of Highland shoe or brogue (from the Gaelic *bròg*), issued to all Scottish regiments, dates from after World War II.

Spats

The term 'spat' comes from the 'spatterdashes' or gaiters which the infantry of the line wore from the 17th Century until half boots were introduced in 1823. They were intended to protect the soldiers hose from mud spatters, and to prevent stones getting into the shoes. Highland regiments also took to wearing grey canvas half-gaiters during the campaigns of the early 19th century, to protect the diced hose and to keep stones out of the low cut shoes. At the same time the hose could be reduced to the more economical hose tops. After the Napoleonic wars spats came into general use, evolving from the practical canvas half gaiter into the white pipe-clayed spat, with whalebone stiffening, which is still in ceremonial use today.

From the 1890s Highland regiments wore khaki spats in the field. The Seaforth and the Cameron Highlanders fought in Sudan and South Africa in khaki spats, but finding that they were unsuitable for the muddy conditions in Flanders in 1914, changed to wearing boots and puttees.

The Queen's Own Highlanders wore the Seaforth Highlanders pattern of spat, with eight white buttons and rounded at the toe, with a whitened leather strap under the shoe. The Cameron Highlanders wore a black strap under the shoe.

Puttees

The army in India took to wearing puttees (from the Hindustani word for 'bandages') in the 1870s. During the Afghanistan campaign of 1878-80 field officers of the 72nd Highlanders wore long puttees of Prince Charles Edward Stuart tartan with their tartan riding breeches.

When the Highland regiments went to France in 1914 they wore diced hose tops, shoes and khaki spats But these proved impractical for the mud of Flanders, and they were replaced by khaki hose tops, boots and puttees. The 1st Battalion The Queen's Own Cameron Highlanders wore this form of legdress in 1940 when it withdrew to Dunkirk, the last battalion to fight in the kilt.

After battledress trousers superseded the kilt, they were worn with boots and blancoed webbing gaiters. During the 1960s the gaiters were given up, and the more comfortable puttees reintroduced for wear with the kilt or combat dress trousers. In the Queen's Own Highlanders officers wore Fox's Pale puttees, and soldiers wore dark khaki puttees.

CROMAG

A Highland chief carries a *cromag* (Gaelic for a shepherd's crook) as patriarchal 'shepherd' of his people. Officers of the Queen's Own Highlanders, having the same symbolic responsibility for their men, were permitted to carry a *cromag*, thumb stick or ash plant when on the range, or training out of barracks.

The custom started during the South African war of 1899-1902 when officers discarded the swords and Sam Browne belts which made them conspicuous targets for Boer sharpshooters, and took to carrying a cromag or walking stick instead.

COLD STEEL

The broadsword

In the early days of the regiment, the basket-hilted broadsword (often incorrectly termed the 'claymore') was carried by officers, sergeants, pipers, drummers and bandsmen. After the Napoleonic wars the use of the broadsword decreased, and it was withdrawn from sergeants in 1852, drummers in 1872, and pipers in the late 1870s; although the pipers of the 72nd carried them in the Afghanistan campaign of 1878-80.

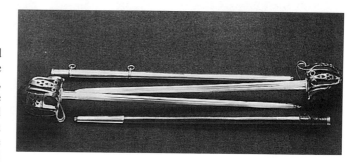

Broadswords with plated and leather scabbards

Field (i.e. mounted) officers of both the Seaforth and the Cameron Highlanders carried a different type of sword. Seaforth field officers used the broadsword with a half-basket hilt, while Cameron field officers carried a light cavalry sabre.

When the Seaforth Highlanders and the Cameron Highlanders went to war in 1914, officers took their broadswords, but they were soon discarded as unsuitable for the 20th century battlefield. Since World War I the broadsword has remained part of the ceremonial uniform of officers, and also of the Regimental Sergeant Major, Bandmaster, and Drum Major.

In No 2 dress, the normal parade dress worn by the Queen's Own Highlanders, officers carried the broadsword, with the leather scabbard held in the sword frog attached to the Sam Browne belt. In ceremonial No 1 dress officers carried the broadsword, with the plated scabbard on sword slings attached to the white buff cross belt or shoulder belt. The Drum Major carried the sword slung from the waist belt.

Officers' dirks

Although the dirk is a weapon of great antiquity, used in the Highlands from at least the 15th Century, its use as a military weapon in the Highland regiments has never been significant. It was carried by officers of the 72nd, 78th, and 79th Highlanders when the regiments were raised in the late 18th century, but its use was mainly ceremonial. By the mid-19th century the officer's dirk had evolved into a magnificent ornamental weapon, with cast gilt mountings, carved black wooden handle surmounted by a large Cairngorm, a small knife and fork in the black leather scabbard, and the blade etched with Battle Honours and regimental insignia.

9. PIPE BANNERS

Obverse side   *Reverse side*

An officers pipe banner, Queen's Own Highlanders

The long and interesting history of pipe banners goes back to the days of the clans, when the clan piper carried a pipe banner bearing the arms of the chief. The pipers of the 72nd, 78th, and 79th Highlanders carried pipe banners from at least the 1840s. The patterns varied frequently, and Pipe Majors normally carried a more elaborate banner than the other pipers. The Regimental Museum has a large collection in which most forms are included, and the notes below cover only the main trends in regimental design.

The custom of including personal arms on the reverse of banners has been allowed in the regiment from time to time, but there has been no consistent use of them. This was possibly because pipe banners are subject to the laws of heraldry, and many officers were not interested in registering arms.

Pipe banners of the 72nd Duke of Albany's Own Highlanders

The earliest known pipe banners of the 72nd Highlanders date from the 1840s, when the pipers carried yellow silk fish-tailed banners, with the stag's head badge embroidered on each side. During the 1850s the shape was changed to rectangular. From the 1870s officers commanding companies were allowed to have banners with their personal arms on the reverse. After the amalgamation of the 72nd and 78th in 1881 the 1st Battalion Seaforth Highlanders continued to use the rectangular form of banner until World War I. From 1918 to 1939 the 1st Seaforth reintroduced buff, fish-tailed banners, with the regimental badge and 'CABAR FEIDH' on the obverse, and the personal arms of the owner surrounded by Battle Honours on the reverse.

Pipe banners of the 78th Highlanders (Ross-shire Buffs)

The earliest known pipe banners of the 78th Highlanders date from the 1840s, and were buff silk, fish-tailed banners, embroidered with the Union flag, the Assaye Elephant, battle honours and thistles. From the 1850s the banners had the stag's head with scroll and motto, and officers were permitted to have their arms on the reverse. While serving in India in the 1880s the 2nd Battalion Seaforth Highlanders had a new set of buff, fish-tailed banners made, with the stag's head, thistles, and 'Ross-shire Buffs' embroidered, but without personal arms. These remained in use until World War II.

Pipe banners of the Seaforth Highlanders

The 1st and 2nd Battalions of the Seaforth Highlanders continued to use their own styles of pipe banners until their amalgamation in 1948, when a new design was introduced. The banners were buff, fish-tailed, with the regimental badge and the numerals 72 and 78 beneath it. Only a small number of these banners were made

Pipe banners of the 79th Cameron Highlanders

The earliest known pipe banners of the 79th Cameron Highlanders date from 1841, and were green silk, fish-tailed banners. Both sides were identical, bore the Union flag in the top corner, and were embroidered with a wreath of thistles and the numeral LXXIX. After the 79th became a Royal regiment in 1873, the green banners were replaced by blue banners of similar design. The design was never altered significantly, and was used by the 1st Battalion The Queen's Own Cameron Highlanders until 1961. The banners did not bear personal arms.

Pipe banners of the 2nd Battalion The Queen's Own Cameron Highlanders

When the 2nd Camerons was raised in 1897 the pipers carried officers' personal pipe banners, which remained the property of the owner. They were of blue silk, fish-tailed, and embroidered with a wreath of thistles round a red circular design, similar to the centre of the regimental Colour. At the top on the obverse side was the Union flag, and officers were permitted to have their personal crests, monogram, or company letter embroidered on the reverse.

Pipe banners of the Queen's Own Highlanders

On the amalgamation of the Seaforth Highlanders and the Cameron Highlanders in 1961, a new design of pipe banner was introduced for the Queen's Own Highlanders. The banners were buff on the obverse and blue on the reverse, with the regimental badge embroidered on both sides, and a blue and buff fringe. Officers who commanded companies were permitted to have their own banners made, and to have their personal crests or a monogram embroidered in the top corner of the reverse. Officers who commanded a battalion or Depot added the Union flag to the top corner of the obverse side.

Pipe banners of The Highlanders

On the amalgamation of the Queen's Own Highlanders with the Gordon Highlanders in 1994, the Queen's Own Highlanders pipe banners became the pattern used by The Highlanders.

10. MUSIC IN THE REGIMENT

The drummers of the 1st Battalion Seaforth Highlanders with fifes still in use in 1885

THE PIPES AND DRUMS

The drummers

When regiments were raised in the 18th century, their establishments normally allowed two drummers to each company. The drummers held a prominent position in a regiment In battle they had the key role of passing orders by drum beat or bugle call, and were the equivalent of the signals platoon of today. Off they battlefield they provided the drum beatings and fife tunes which regulated the soldier's day in garrison or in the field.

The daily routine included four main events: Reveille, the Troop or assembly, Retreat, and Tattoo. These were marked by the drummers with drum beat and fife, or by bugle call. The Scottish regiments all used the same Fife and Drum Duty known as the 'Scotch Duty', a set of fife tunes and drum beatings dating back to the 16th century. Regimental routine also included fife and drum beatings and bugle calls for all the minor events of the day, such as meals, sending for orderly NCOs, and preparations for guards and parades.

The Drum Major and drummers came under the Adjutant for training and discipline. For their special responsibilities in war and peace, the drummers earned a higher rate of pay than a private soldier. Until 1831, to allow them to be recognised easily in battle, the drummers were distinctively dressed in 'reverse facings', their coats being of the regimental facing colour faced with red. Thus the drummers of the 72nd wore yellow coats faced with red, the 78th buff, and the 79th green; and their coats were trimmed with regimental braid.

The pipers before 1854

When the Highland regiments were raised, many of them were allowed in their Letters of Service to recruit two pipers to the Grenadier company. They were the equivalent of the two fifers allowed in the Line regiments. Like the clans before them, the Highland regiments treated the music of the Great Highland Bagpipe as a normal part of regimental life in war and peace. The pipers were expected to play on the march, to rouse the spirits of men in battle, and to provide music off duty.

It became the normal practice to maintain at least one piper per company, and to recruit a recognised player as Pipe Major with the rank of sergeant. Because the appointment of piper was not recognised by War Office authority, the pipers' duties were largely a matter of regimental custom. In some cases this included playing the Duty Calls of daily routine, but the pipes were not normally accompanied by the drum.

The pipers, being unofficial, wore the same uniform as the rest of the regiment, but there were exceptions. When the 78th Highlanders were raised the pipers wore buff coats similar to those of the drummers, with green hackles in their feathered bonnets. After the 72nd became a Highland regiment again in 1823, its pipers wore the kilt of Prince Charles Edward Stuart tartan, with a red hackle in the feathered bonnet, while the rest of the 72nd wore trews. From 1841 the pipers of the 79th were dressed in distinctive green doublets, glengarries with eagle feathers, and specially made dirks, belts and accoutrements.

Until the mid 19th century the pipers were recognised as an indispensable part of life in the Highland regiments, but to the War Office their status was unofficial, and the expense of maintaining their pipes and their uniform was a matter for the regiments themselves.

Pipers authorised in 1854

In early 1854, anticipating war with Russia, the War Office authorised regiments to recruit up to war establishment of 1,000 rank and file. As part of this increase each Highland regiment was permitted an increment of a Pipe Major and five pipers, thus providing a piper for each of the six service companies in the field. The increase applied to the eight regiments recognised as Highland at the time, which were the 42nd, 71st, 72nd, 74th, 78th, 79th, 92nd, and 93rd Highlanders.

Once the appointment of pipers had been authorised their duties, like those of the drummers, became part of daily routine, and could be written into standing orders. The British army which landed in the Crimea in September 1854 included a Highland Brigade comprising the 42nd Royal Highlanders, the 79th Cameron Highlanders, and the 93rd Sutherland Highlanders. Highland Brigade orders included specific duties for the pipers of the three Highland regiments.

The Pipes and Drums of 1st Battalion Queen's Own Highlanders at Edinburgh in 1969

The evolution of the Pipes and Drums

With the pipers on the establishment at last, the fifes fell into disuse in the Highland regiments. But the drummers still had the duty of beating Reveille, the Troop, Retreat, and Tattoo, the four main events of the soldier's day, and it quickly became the custom for pipers to accompany the drummers instead of the fifes. Pipers had played on the march for many years, and there was no difficulty in combining the quickstep marches of the pipes with drum beatings for use on parade.

For their part the pipers were equally adaptable, and even took over some of the techniques of the fifes. For example since the 18th century the drums and fifes had customarily played marches in 3/4, 3/8, or 9/8 time at Retreat, and the pipes now carried on the tradition by playing 3/4 marches at Retreat. Probably the earliest 3/4 retreat march for the pipes is 'The Green Hills of Tyrol', an air from the opera 'William Tell' which was adapted by the Pipe Major of the 93rd who heard the Sardinian band play it in the Crimea. The playing of 3/4 marches at Retreat is still the custom to this day.

Within a few years the pipes were very much in the ascendancy over drums, and the Pipe Duty had replaced the old Fife and Drum Duty in the daily life of the Highland regiments. Possibly the last of the battalion to retain the fife was the 1st Battalion Seaforth Highlanders in which the drummers continued to use fifes until 1886.

By the 1870s the custom of pipers and drummers playing together as a band was firmly establishe in all Highland regiments. But there was inevitable uncertainty about the correct order in which pipers, drummers, and bandsmen should form up on parade. In 1871 the matter was resolved by HM Queen Victoria who ordered that 'The pipers must always lead'. That remeins the correct precedence in Scottish regiments to this day.

The Pipes and Drums today.

Until World War II the pipers and drummers remained on the strength of their own companies within the battalion, although parading together as a band. The pipers were managed by a committee under the Pipe President, and their pipes and uniform funded by the Pipe Fund.

On parade the Pipes and Drums are commanded by the Drum Major, a custom dating back to pre-1854 days when the Drum Major commanded both drummers and regimental band on parade. The training of pipers is the responsibility of the Pipe Major, who has to qualify for his Pipe Major's certificate at the Army School of Piping at Edinburgh Castle.

Since World War II the Pipes and Drums have remained prominent as ever in the Scottish regiments, although the increment of pipers for Highland battalions was discontinued in the 1970s. Today the pipers and drummers form an infantry platoon for operational duty, and in the 1st Battalion Queen's Own Highlanders they fought as machine gunners in the Gulf War of 1991.

The drummers of 1st Battalion Queen's Own Highlanders
keep up their skills in the Gulf, 1991.

THE PIPE DUTY TUNES OF THE QUEEN'S OWN HIGHLANDERS

The tunes laid down for the Pipe Duty of the Queen's Own Highlanders were selected from those used until 1961 by the Seaforth Highlanders and The Queen's Own Cameron Highlanders. The music and the histories of the tunes, and notes on the procedure for their use, were published in 'The Piper's Day -The Regimental Duty Tunes of the Queen's Own Highlanders'.

REGIMENTAL MARCHES

1.	Regimental march past in quick time	Pibroch of Donuil Dubh
2.	Regimental march	Cabar Feidh
3.	Regimental march	The march of the Cameron men
4.	Regimental slow march	The garb of old Gaul
5.	Regimental charge	The standard on the Braes of Mar

DAILY ROUTINE

6.	Reveille	Johnnie Cope
7.	Long reveille, 2nd tune	Up in the morning early
8.	Breakfast pipes	Brose and butter
9.	Marching off a guard	MacDonald's awa to the war
10.	Dinner pipes	Over the water to Charlie
11.	Tea pipes	Jenny's bawbee
12.	Retreat	Dark lowers the night
13.	First post	72nd Highlanders
14.	Staff parade	Highland laddie
15.	Last post	Lochaber no more
16.	Lights out	Sleep dearie, sleep

PARADE MUSIC

17.	Half hour to parade	Up and waur them all Wullie
18.	Quarter hour to parade	Bundle and go
19.	Assembly	All the blue bonnets are over the border
20.	Fall in	Lads with the kilt
21.	Officers fall in	Mackenzie Highlanders
22.	Marching the Colours on or off parade	Scotland for ever
23.	General salute	The point of war
24.	Royal salute	St Andrew's cross
25.	Inspection tunes	I love the Highlands
26.		Isle of heather
27.		Mist covered mountains
28.		My home
29.	March past in slow time	The Skye Gathering
30.	March past in quick time	Pibroch of Donuil Dubh
31.	Advance in review order	Scotland for ever
32.	Dispersal from parade	25th November 1960

TROOPING THE COLOUR

33.	Keepers of the ground march on	72nd Highlanders
34.	Guards march on	The Inverness Gathering
35.	Warrant Officers and NCOs to the front	The march of the Cameron men
36.	Officers fall in	Mackenzie Highlanders
37.	Officers, WOs and NCOs take post	The Skye Gathering
38.	General salute	The point of war
39.	Slow troop	Loch Duich
40.	Quick troop	Cabar Feidh
41.	Escort moving for the Colours	Scotland for ever
42.	Trooping the Colour along the ranks	St Andrew's cross
43.	March past in slow time	The Skye Gathering
44.	March past in quick time	79th Highlanders
45.		Pibroch of Donuil Dubh
46.	Advance in review order	Scotland for ever
47.	Dispersal from parade	The Highland Brigade at Tel-el-Kebir
48.		27125th November 1960

RETREAT

49.	March on	The march of the Cameron Men
50.	After the drummers call	The point of war
51.	Retreat march	Dark lowers the night
52.	March off	Cabar Feidh

TATTOO

53.	First post	72nd Highlanders
54.	End of final set	The march of the Cameron men

ENTERING AND LEAVING BARRACKS

55.	Entering barracks	Cabar Feidh
56.		79th Highlanders
57.	Leaving barracks	We will take the good old way
58.	Leaving a station	The 79th's Farewell to Gibraltar
59.		Bundle and go
60.	Playing-out a draft	Happy we've been a' thegither
61.	Playing-in a draft	Oh but ye've been lang a-coming

COMPANY MARCHES

62.	A Company	The Dornoch links
63.	B Company	The Highland Brigade at Tel-el-Kebir
64.	C Company	The brown-haired maiden
65.	D Company	The bugle horn
66.	S Company	The 51st Highland Division at Wadi Akarit
67.	HQ Company	Over the Chindwin

REGIMENTAL CUSTOMS

68.	New Year gate ceremony		Happy we've been a' thegither
69.			A good new year to one and all
70.	Chairing-out after 22 years service		Happy we've been a' thegither
71.			A man's a man for all that
72.	Weddings		I hae a wife of my ain
73.	Funerals - march to the burial ground		Flowers of the forest
74.			We will return home to Kintail
75.	Funerals - salute at the graveside		Lochaber no more

PIPERS PLAYING IN MESS

76.	Officers mess first pipes		The red coat
77.	Officers mess second pipes		Bannocks of barley meal
78.	Sergeants mess first pipes		Cuidich 'n righ
79.	Sergeants mess second pipes		Corn rigs
80.	The Cabar Feidh mess set-	March	Cabar Feidh
81.		Strathspey	Cabar Feidh
82.		Reel	Cabar Feidh
83.	The Cameron mess set-	March	Donald Cameron
84.		Strathspey	Maggy Cameron
85.		Reel	Sandy Cameron
86.	Mess foursome reel	Strathspeys	The Marquis of Huntly's Highland fling
87.			Balmoral Castle
88.		Reels	The high road to Linton
89.			Jock Wilson's ball
90.	Final tune of second set		Pibroch of Donuil Dubh
91.	The 78th's walk round		The Liverpool hornpipe

CEOL MOR

92.	Piobaireachd	Salute to the Queen's Own Highlanders

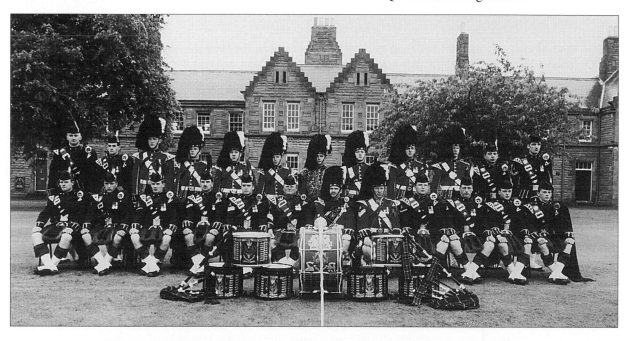

The Pipes and Drums of 1st Battalion Queen's Own Highlanders at Inverness in 1993

THE REGIMENTAL BAND

The military bands of the Army originated in the 18th century as groups of musicians employed privately by the officers to provide entertainment for the regiment off duty. The 'band of musick' normally consisted of up to ten musicians playing oboes, horns, clarinets and bassoons, and capable of playing stringed instruments as well. The Hanoverian monarchy of Great Britain brought military and musical links with Germany, and many of the British army bands were made up of German musicians.

The need for music on parade led to the War Office granting the regimental bands recognition in 1803, and one soldier from each of the ten companies was allowed to be employed as a bandsman. At the same time the bands were ordered to practise regularly with the drums on the march and on parade. On the battlefield the bandsmen acted as stretcher bearers.

The Regimental Band of the 79th Cameron Highlanders in India, 1868, under the bandmaster Herr Ernest Fromm

From the time of their unofficial origins the military bands were distinctively dressed, sometimes with a marked degree of flamboyance. In 1805 the band of the 78th Highlanders, for example, wore the kilt of Royal Stuart or 'music tartan'. From 1830 to 1873 all military bands wore white coats and black belts, as well as the kilt or trews of the regiment.

Until the mid 19th century the musical instruction for a regimental band depended on the regiment finding a competent bandmaster and many regiments, including the 72nd and 79th, employed German civilians. But the standard of music tended to be inconsistent, and the grand reviews held by the Allied armies in the early days of the Crimean war highlighted the need for professional instruction. The result was the formation in 1856 of the Military Music Class. The Royal Military School of Music, Kneller Hall, as it became, has been responsible for training Bandmasters and miltary bandsmen since then, and regimental bands always provided an enviably high standard of music thereafter.

The Regimental Band of the Queen's Own Highlanders was a popular and valuable part of the regiment, which provided a wide range of music, including ceremonial music on parade, music during dinner in the officers and sergeants messes, Scottish dance music, clarsach playing, and the latest in 'pop' music and electronic sound. The Regimental Band carried out its traditional wartime role in 1990-1991 when it deployed to the Gulf as medical staff with 1st Armoured Division Field Ambulance.

In 1994 the infantry regimental bands were removed under the government defence cuts, and replaced by central bands. The successor to the band of the Queen's Own Highlanders was The Highland Band, based in Edinburgh, and responsible for providing occasional military band music for each regiment.

THE REGIMENTAL BAND MUSIC OF THE QUEEN'S OWN HIGHLANDERS

REGIMENTAL MARCH

1.   Queen's Own Highlanders.
(An arrangement of the march of the Seaforth Highlanders 'Scotland for ever', and the march of The Queen's Own Cameron Highlanders 'The march of the Cameron men')

PARADE MUSIC

2.	General salute	Scotland for ever
3.	Royal salute	The National Anthem
4.	March past in slow time	The garb of old Gaul
5.	March past in quick time	Queen's Own Highlanders
6.	Advance in review order	Highland laddie

TROOPING THE COLOUR

7.	Slow troop	Logie of Buchan
8.	Escort moving for the Colour	British grenadiers
9.	Trooping the Colour along the ranks	The grenadiers' march

ARRIVALS AND DEPARTURES

10.	Entering barracks	Queen's Own Highlanders
11.	Draft leaving barracks	The girl I left behind me
12.	Draft leaving a railway station	Auld lang syne

CHURCH PARADE

13.	Fall in	Christchurch bells
14.		The old 100th psalm
15.		Now thank we all our God

PLAYING IN MESS

16.	Going in to dinner	The roast beef of old England
17.	Royal toast	The national anthem
18.	After dinner	Regimental marches of the guests
19.		March of the Cameron men (sung to the clarsach)
20.		Rule Britannia
21.		Garb of old Gaul

The Regimental Band of the Queen's Own Highlanders, 1994

THE REGIMENTAL TOAST

The Gaelic toast of the Queen's Own Highlanders has been used from the earliest days of the Earl of Seaforth's Highland Regiment. 'Cabar Feidh' is the Gaelic patronym for the Chief of Clan Mackenzie, and both the 72nd and the 78th Highlanders were raised by the Chief.

The toast was used in the Queen's Own Highlanders on occasions such as the regimental ceremony to welcome the New Year. A shortened form of the toast was given by the Pipe Major after he had played the pibroch at a mess dinner.

Tir nam Beann, nan Gleann, 's nan Gaisgeach;	Land of hills, glens and heroes;
Far am faighear an t-eun fionn,	Where the ptarmigan thrives
'S far am faigh am fiadh fasgadh.	And where the red deer finds shelter.
Cho fada 's chìtear ceo mu bheann	As long as mist hangs over the mountains
'S a ruitheas uisge le gleann,	And water runs in the glens,
Mairidh cuimhne air éuchd nan treun.	The deeds of the brave will be remembered.
Slàinte agus buaidh gu bràth	Health and success for ever
Le Gillean Chabar Féidh !	To the lads of Cabar Féidh !

CABAR FEIDH GU BRATH !   *CABAR FEIDH GU BRATH !*
                                                                ('The deer's horns for ever')

The Regimental Band of the 72nd Duke of Albany's Own Highlanders, Dublin 1868

11. REFERENCES

PUBLISHED REGIMENTAL HISTORIES

There is an extensive range of published material concerning the history of the regiments. The publications given here are a selective list of books, most of which should be available in specialist military library collections. A much more comprehensive range, including a number of privately published personal accounts of the regiment in peace and war, is available in the library of the Regimental Museum.

Title	Author/Compiler	Printer/Publisher	Date
QUEEN'S OWN HIGHLANDERS (SEAFORTH AND CAMERONS)			
Queen's Own Highlanders - A Short History	Regimental Headquarters	Highland Printers, Inverness	1961
Queen's Own Highlanders 1961-1971	Regimental Headquarters	A Learmonth & Son	1971
Queen's Own Highlanders - A Short History (2nd Edition)	Regimental Headquarters	John Eccles, Inverness	1973
An Introduction to the Queen's Own Highlanders	Regimental Headquarters	Pilgrim Press Ltd	1975
Queen's Own Highlanders - Bicentenary booklet	Regimental Headquarters	Jon Eccles, Inverness	1978
Cuidich 'n Righ - A History of the Queen's Own Highlanders	Lt Col Angus Fairrie	Sunprint, Perth	1983

SEAFORTH HIGHLANDERS

Title	Author/Compiler	Printer/Publisher	Date
Historical Records of the 72nd Regiment	Richard Cannon	Parker, Furnival & Parker	1848
Historical Records of the 72nd Highlanders printed for private circulation)	(MS records of the regiment	Wm Blackwood & Sons	1886
Historical Records of the 78th Highlanders	James McVeigh	J Maxwell & Sons,	1887
Rules and Records of the Officers Mess, 72nd Regiment	(Printed for private circulation)	Wm Blackwood & Sons	1896
History and Services of the 78th Highlanders Volumes I and II	Maj Hugh Davidson	W & A K Johnston	1901
The Seaforth Highlanders in South Africa 1899-1902	Edited by Maj Hugh Davidson	W & A K Johnston	1904
History of 3rd Volunteer Bn Seaforth Highlanders 1860-1906	AJCC and AMS	Northern Scot, Elgin	1906
With the Seaforth Highlanders in the Sudan Campaign	Maj Gen Granville Egerton	Eden Fisher & Co	1909
Betting Book, Officers Mess 78th Highlanders, 1822-1908	(Printed for private circulation)	St Catherine Press Ltd	1909
A Short History of the Seaforth Highlanders	Col George Mackintosh and Capt William M Thomson	St Catherine Press Ltd	1909
War Diary of the 5th Bn Seaforth Highlanders	Capt D Sutherland	John Lane	1920
Seaforth Highlanders of Canada	Bernard McEvoy and Capt A H Findlay	Cowan and Brookhouse	1920
6th Seaforth Highlanders, Campaign Reminiscences	Capt R T Peel and Capt A H Macdonald	W R Walker & Co	1923
Pipers and Pipe Music in a Highland Regiment	Maj Ian H Mackay Scobie	Ross-shire Printing & Publishing Co Ltd	1924
A History of the 4th Bn Seaforth Highlanders	Lt Col M M Haldane	H T & G Witherby	1927
10th Bn Seaforth Highlanders in the Great War	Lt Col C L Addison-Smith	J Bain & Sons	1927
A Short History of the Seaforth Highlanders	Col C S Nairne	Ross-shire Printing & Publishing Co Ltd	1928
Sans Peur - 5th Bn Seaforth Highlanders in World War II	Capt Alastair Borthwick	Eneas MacKay	1946
Seaforth Highlanders	Col John M Sym	Gale and Polden	1962
The Seaforth Highlanders of Canada 1919-1965	R H Roy	Evergreen Press, Vancouver	1969
Battalion - 5th Battalion Seaforth Highlanders 1942-1945 (Reprint of 'Sans Peur' originally published 1947)	Capt Alastair Borthwick	Bâton Wicks	1994

12. SOURCES OF INFORMATION

THE QUEEN'S OWN HIGHLANDERS REGIMENTAL MUSEUM COLLECTION

The Regimental Museum Collection

The principal source of information about the regiment is the Regimental Museum, which comprises the museum collections and archives of:-

> Queen's Own Highlanders (Seaforth and Camerons)
> Seaforth Highlanders
> The Queen's Own Cameron Highlanders
> The Lovat Scouts

The Museum does not hold the personal service records of officers and soldiers, as these are government documents and held in the Records offices.

Address for correspondence:

The Museum is administered by Regimental Headquarters of the Highlanders, at Cameron Barracks, Inverness, and so correspondence and requests for advice may directed to the following address:-

> Queen's Own Highlanders Regimental Museum Collection
> c/o Regimental Headquarters The Highlanders,
> Cameron Barracks,
> Inverness IV2 3XD   Telephone and Fax: 01463 224380

The Regimental Museum Library and Archives

The Museum includes records and archives of the Queen's Own Highlanders and the antecedent regiments, including all known published histories, most of the battalion war diaries from World War I and II, medal rolls, and a wide range of books covering campaigns, battles, uniforms, arms, and relevant military subjects. The Museum Collection includes a large number of documents, photographs and other material which have been presented by members of the regiment and their families.

The Museum welcomes researchers, and will be glad to send details of opening times and facilities available. The Museum does not normally undertake to carry out work on behalf of researchers.

If the Museum cannot answer an enquiry, it will do its best to recommend an alternative source of information, if known.

The Regimental Museum at Fort George

The Regimental Museum is situated at Fort George, Ardersier, Inverness, about twelve miles north east of the town of Inverness. The Museum is housed in the building which was originally the Lieutenant Governor's quarter at Fort George.

The Museum works closely with Historic Scotland, the government agency which looks after Fort George on behalf of the Ministry of Defence. Historic Scotland is responsible for public admission to Fort George, and provides amenities such as guide books and historical displays about the Fort, car parking, restaurant, lavatories etc.

The Museum will be glad to supply a leaflet giving details of opening times, arrangements for admission, and facilities available for visitors.

OTHER SOURCES OF INFORMATION

Other principal sources of information about the regiment and those who have served in it are listed below. Enquirers are advised to apply in writing to the addresses shown, in order to establish what research facilities and assistance are available.

RECORDS OFFICES

The Public Record Office
Ruskin Avenue
Kew
Surrey TW9 7DU

(The PRO does not undertake to carry out research, but visitors can obtain readers tickets to allow them to do their own work. The PRO can supply a list of professional researchers who will carry out work for a fee. Original military records over 70 years old are held, including World War I records.)

The Army Records Office
Bourne Avenue
Hayes
Middlesex UB3 7DX

(The Army Records Office holds military records under 70 years old. Information may be available to enquirers, and a charge is normally made for supplying information. The Records were damaged by enemy bombing in World War II, and so information is not always available.)

The Commonwealth
War-Graves Commission
Marlow Road
Maidenhead
Berkshire SL6 7DX

(The Commission maintains military cemeteries of both World Wars and some minor campaigns. Records are on computer, and casualties are listed both by name, and place of burial or memorial.)

NATIONAL MILITARY MUSEUMS

The main military museums in Great Britain have excellent libraries where researchers may read the published books of reference about the regiment. The principal national military museums include:

The Scottish
United Services Museum
The Castle
Edinburgh EH1 2NG

(Comprehensive collection of published reference books about the armed services, including all Scottish regiments. Researchers are admitted by appointment.)

National Army Museum
Royal Hospital Road
Chelsea
London SW3 4HT

(Museum covers the British Army from its formation in the 17th century. Researchers may obtain a reader's ticket. Library includes comprehensive collection of regimental and military histories.)

The Imperial War Museum
Lambeth Road
London SE1 6HZ

(Museum covers World War I and II. The Museum has extensive campaign records, including regimental histories).

The Regimental Museum at Fort George, Inverness